大学本科翻译研究型系列读本

丛书主编　张柏然

翻译资源与工具读本

Resources and Instruments:A Reader for Translators

主　编　刘华文
副主编　叶君武　刘性峰

南京大学出版社

图书在版编目(CIP)数据

翻译资源与工具读本 / 刘华文主编. — 南京:南
京大学出版社,2014.9
(大学本科翻译研究型系列读本 / 张柏然主编)
ISBN 978 - 7 - 305 - 13976 - 5

Ⅰ. ①翻… Ⅱ. ①刘… Ⅲ. ①翻译－工具书－高等学
校－教学参考资料 Ⅳ. ①H059 - 6

中国版本图书馆 CIP 数据核字(2014)第 217675 号

出版发行　南京大学出版社
社　　址　南京市汉口路 22 号　　　　邮　编　210093
出 版 人　金鑫荣
丛 书 名　大学本科翻译研究型系列读本
丛书主编　张柏然
书　　名　翻译资源与工具读本
主　　编　刘华文
责任编辑　严　艳　裴维维　　　　编辑热线　025 - 83592123
照　　排　南京南琳图文制作有限公司
印　　刷　盐城市华光印刷厂
开　　本　787×1092 1/16　印张 16.75　字数 407 千
版　　次　2014 年 9 月第 1 版　2014 年 9 月第 1 次印刷
ISBN 978 - 7 - 305 - 13976 - 5
定　　价　39.00 元

网址:http://www.njupco.com
官方微博:http://weibo.com/njupco
官方微信号:njupress
销售咨询热线:(025) 83594756

大学本科翻译研究型系列读本
大学翻译学研究型系列教材

总　序

张柏然

　　到了该为翻译学研究型系列教材说几句话的时候了。两年前的炎炎夏日,南京大学出版社责成笔者总揽主编分别针对高等院校翻译学本科生和研究生学习与研究需求的研究型系列读本和导引。俗话说,独木难撑大厦。于是,笔者便千里相邀"招旧部",网罗昔日在南大攻读翻译学博士学位的"十八罗汉"各主其事。寒来暑往,光阴荏苒,转眼两年过去了。期间,大家意气奋发,不辞辛劳,借助网络"上天",躲进书馆"入地",上下求索,查阅浩瀚的文献经典,进而调动自己的学术积累,披沙拣金,辨正证伪,博采众长,字斟句酌,终于成就了这一本本呈现在读者面前的教材。

　　众所周知,教材乃教学之本和知识之源,亦即体现课程教学理念、教学内容、教学要求,甚至教学模式的知识载体,在教学过程中起着引导教学方向、保证教学质量的作用。改革开放以来,我国各类高校组编、出版的翻译教材逐年递增。我们在中国国家图书馆网站上检索主题名含有"翻译"字段的图书,检索结果显示,1980至2009年间,我国引进、出版相关著作1800余种,其中,翻译教材占有很大的比重。近些年来,翻译教材更是突飞猛进。根据有关学者的不完全统计,目前,我国正式出版的翻译教材共有1000多种。* 这一变化结束了我国相当长一段时间内翻译教材"一枝独秀"的境地,迎来了"百花齐放"的局面,由此也反映了我国高校翻译教学改革的深化。

　　但是,毋庸讳言,虽然教材的品种繁多,但是真正合手称便的、富有特色的教材仍属凤毛麟角。教材数量增多并不足以表明教学理念的深刻转变。其中大多都具有包打翻译学天下的纯体系冲动,并没有打破我国既往翻译教材编写从某一理论预设出发的本质主义思维模式和几大板块的框架结构。从教材建设看,我国翻译理论教材在概念陈设、模式架构、内容安排上存在着比较严重的雷同化现象。这表明,教材建设需要从根本上加以改进,而如何改则取决于我们有什么样的教学理念。

　　有鉴于此,我们组编了"大学翻译学研究型系列教材"和"大学本科翻译研究型系列读本"这两套系列教材。前者系研究生用书,它包括《中国翻译理论研究导引》、《当代西方翻译理论研究导引》、《当代西方文论与翻译研究导引》、《翻译学方法论研究导引》、《语言学与翻译研究导引》、《文学翻译研究导引》、《汉语典籍英译研究导引》、《英汉口译理论研究导引》、《语料库翻译学研究导引》和《术语翻译研究导引》等10册;后者则以本科生为主要读者对象,它包括《翻译概论读本》、《文化翻译读本》、《文学翻译读本》、《商务英语翻译读本》、《法律英语翻译读本》、《传媒英语翻译读本》、《科技英语翻译读本》、《英汉口译读本》、《英汉比较与翻译读本》和《翻译资源与工具读本》等10册。这两套教材力图综合中西译论、相关学科(如哲学、美学、文学、语

---

　　* 转引自曾剑平、林敏华:《论翻译教材的问题及编写体系》,《中国科技翻译》,2011年11月。

言学、社会学、文化学、心理学、语料库翻译学等)的吸融性研究以及方法论的多层次研究,结合目前高校翻译教学和研究实践的现状进行创造性整合,编写突出问题型结构和理路的读本和导引,以满足翻译学科本科生和研究生教学与研究的需求。这是深化中国翻译学研究型教材编写与研究的一个重要课题,至今尚未引起翻译理论研究界和教材编写界的足够重视。摆在我们面前的这一课题,基本上还是一片多少有些生荒的地带。因此,我们对这一课题的研究,也就多少带有拓荒性质。这样,不仅大量纷繁的文献经典需要我们去发掘、辨别与整理,中西翻译美学思想发展演变的特点与规律需要我们去探讨,而且研究的对象、范畴和方法等问题,都需要我们进行独立的思考与确定。研究这一课题的困难也就可以想见了。然而,这一课题本身的价值和意义却又变为克服困难的巨大动力,策励着我们不揣浅陋,迎难而上,试图在翻译学研究型教材编写这块土地上,作一些力所能及的垦殖。

这两套研究型系列教材的编纂目的和编纂特色主要体现为:不以知识传授为主要目的,而是培养学生发问、好奇、探索、兴趣,即学习的主动性,逐步实现思维方式和学习方式的转变,引导学生及早进入科学研究阶段;不追求知识的完整性、系统性,突破讲授通史、通论知识的教学模式,引入探究学术问题的教学模式;引进国外教材编写理念,填补国内大学翻译学研究型教材的欠缺;所选论著具有权威性、文献性、可读性与引导性。具体而言,和传统的通史通论教材不同,这两套系列教材是以问题结构章节,这个"问题"既可以是这门课(专业方向)的主要问题,也可以是这门课某个章节的主要问题。在每个章节的安排上,则是先由"导论"说明本章的核心问题,指明获得相关知识的途径;接着,通过选文的导言,直接指向"选文"——涉及的知识面很广的范文,这样对学生的论文写作更有示范性;"选文"之后安排"延伸阅读",以拓展和深化知识;最后,通过"研究实践"或"问题与思考",提供实践方案,进行专业训练,希冀用"问题"牵引学生主动学习。这样的结构方式,突出了教材本身的问题型结构和理路,旨在建构以探索和研究为基础的教与学的人才培养模式,让年轻学子有机会接触最新成就、前沿学术和科学方法;强调通识教育、人文教育与科学教育交融,知识传授与能力培养并重,注重培养学生掌握方法,未来能够应对千变万化的翻译教学与研究的发展和需要。

笔者虽说长期从事翻译教学与研究,但对编写教材尤其是研究型教材还是个新手。这两套翻译学研究型教材之所以能够顺利出版,全有赖各册主编的精诚合作和鼎力相助,全有仗一群尽责敬业的编写和校核人员。特别值得一提的是,在这两套系列教材的最后编辑工作中,南京大学出版社外语编辑室主任董颖和责任编辑裴维维两位女士全力以赴,认真校核,一丝不苟,对保证教材的质量起了尤为重要的作用。在此谨向他(她)们致以衷心的感谢!

总而言之,编写大学翻译学研究型教材还是一项尝试性的研究工程。诚如上面所述,我们在进行这项"多少带有拓荒性质"的尝试时,犹如蹒跚学步的孩童,在这过程中留下些许尴尬,亦属在所难免。作为教材的编撰者,我们衷心希望能听到来自各方的意见和建议,以便日后再版修订,进而发展出更好更多翻译学研究型教材来。

是之为序。

二〇一二年三月二十七日
撰于沪上滴水湖畔临港别屋

前　言

　　我们正处于一个信息化迅速发展的时代,计算机技术、互联网以及语料库技术冲击着传统的翻译理念和翻译方式。无论是翻译的实践者还是翻译的研究者都共同面对如何有效地使用信息化手段从而更好地从事翻译实践和翻译研究的课题,尤其是翻译者更应该适时有效地运用各种语言资源与翻译工具来提高自己的翻译效率和质量。具体地讲,信息时代的翻译资源和工具包括:机器翻译系统、互联网上的语言翻译资源、CD-ROM 上的语言翻译资源、计算机辅助术语管理系统、双语对应语料库、翻译记忆软件和本土化软件工具、机助翻译系统。眼下这部教材的编纂就是旨在在这些方面向学习者介绍翻译与信息资源和工具的关系,使他们对信息时代下的翻译实践有一个较为全面的认识,帮助教材使用者掌握一定的信息资源和工具,提高翻译实践的质量,开拓翻译的研究空间。

　　本教材共分为八章。第一章旨在帮助学习者认识如何建立有效掌控的个人计算环境,培养其使用专业软件处理与语言和翻译相关的复杂任务的技能,帮助他们熟悉自然语言处理和语料库语言学的基本原理,并学会使用这些领域里的专门知识和技术工具从事语言和翻译专业的实践与研究,帮助他们了解机器翻译和计算机辅助翻译的原理和机制,对主要的机译和机助翻译系统拥有初步的认识。第二章围绕在翻译中可使用的电子工具,介绍了网络工具、桌面词典、在线翻译、机器辅助翻译等电子工具的形态,并且试图回答如何充分利用电子工具提高翻译质量以及电子工具对翻译研究范式有何影响等诸如此类的问题。第三章主要介绍电子词典作为工具在翻译中的地位和应用。随着智能手机、平板电脑等设备的普及和不断升级,翻译工作者可资使用的电子工具愈来愈多,与传统的翻译工具相比携带更为便捷、存储量也更为庞大,在有效的使用状态下可以大幅度提高翻译速度和翻译质量。第四章转向了翻译的网络资源。不断发展的网络信息技术为翻译提供了无限量的可用资源,诸如在线词典、搜索引擎、翻译软件、双语文献资源、在线机器翻译、翻译网站等都可以被翻译者利用起来,无论是对翻译实践、翻译教学还是翻译研究都极具利用价值。第五章集中探讨了在信息环境下资源的储存形态同翻译的关系,介绍了三种翻译记忆系统,即翻译记忆模型、翻译记忆检索、翻译记忆编辑环境。第六章针对基于语料库的翻译实践和研究展开了翻译资源及其工具利用方式的讨论。以语料库语言学为先导的语料库技术和翻译的结合对包括句法词法分析、编纂词典和参考书籍、外语教学、机器翻译及文本校对等在内的领域都有着积极的意义。第七章介绍了人工智能、机器翻译理论的起源和发展、国内外研究现状，并就其存在的问题及发展方向作了分析；此外还提出了机器翻译系统的设计框架，包括电子词典的设计方法、电子词典的存储结构、语料库的建立、规则库的建立、语义的消歧系统及跨语本体映射与匹配技术等。第八章以将翻译看成一种跨文化、跨学科的活动为出发点，探讨了如何综合开发和利用翻译资源和工具的课题，揭示了将机器翻译系统、互联网语言翻译资源、计算机辅助术语管理系统、双语平行语料库、翻译记忆软件和本土化软件工具、机助翻译系统等整合为统一的翻译资源环境的意义和方式。

　　本教材的每一章都包括"导论"、"选文"、"延伸阅读"和"问题与思考"四个部分。导论部分对一章的内容做大致的介绍，后面的延伸阅读为使用者提供进一步认识该章内容的阅读书目或文章，而在每一章最后附上的问题与思考则可以帮助使用者考察对每一章所涉及内容的把握程度。

　　本教材是我跟南京工程学院的叶君武和刘性峰两位老师共同编纂的，对他们的热情协作我深表谢意。

刘华文

上海交通大学

2014 年 9 月 30 日

目　录

第一章　绪论：翻译与信息环境

导　论

在今天这样一个多语言网络的信息化时代，传统的手工翻译已经难以满足日益增长的翻译需求，如何有效地使用现代化手段来突破人们之间的语言障碍，成为翻译界共同面临和应对的问题。译者很有必要在自己的翻译工作中使用各种语言资源与翻译工具来提高自己的翻译效率和质量。信息时代的翻译工具有：机器翻译系统、互联网上的语言翻译资源、CD-ROM上的语言翻译资源、计算机辅助术语管理系统、双语对应语料库、翻译记忆软件和本土化软件工具、机助翻译系统。本章旨在帮助学习者认识如何建立有效掌控的个人计算环境，培养其使用专业软件处理与语言和翻译相关的复杂任务的技能，帮助他们熟悉自然语言处理和语料库语言学的基本原理，并学会使用这些领域里的专门知识和技术工具从事语言和翻译专业的实践与研究，促使他们通晓机器翻译和计算机辅助翻译的原理和机制，对主要的机译和机助翻译系统具有专业化的认识，使他们熟悉计算机术语管理的原理，并掌握、创建和使用作为一种翻译工具的机读术语库的技巧。在信息化时代，计算机科学和信息通信技术发展迅速，语言与翻译领域的新技术、新产品层出不穷，译者如掌握了这些新技术和新资源，就可以大大地提高翻译的效率，满足信息时代对翻译的迫切需要。鉴于目前语料库语言学的蓬勃发展态势，本章将初步介绍在信息环境下如何思考翻译与信息技术、翻译与工具之间的关系，帮助学习者认识信息环境的概念，思考信息环境与翻译的关系，认识这两者之间发展的历史以及现状。

选　文

选文一　Technology and Translation（A Pedagogical Overview）

José Ramón Biau Gil　Anthony Pym

导　言

本文研究了几十年来翻译工作转变的几个新维度，指出这主要归因于翻译技术的进步和全球化的进程。随着所需翻译的信息大幅度增加,翻译记忆工具的可用性进一步增强,译者的工作流程及他们与客户的关系都发生了变化。本文概述了以上这些发展和变化、翻译记忆的原理、翻译工作中信息对象的"非线性"属性、本地化工具的使用和机器翻译的角色等内容。

本文指出,虽然翻译技术会增加译文的前后一致性,但也会造成翻译成本和学习费用的增加,使劳动力市场进一步分化等,而解决这些问题的关键在于更好地掌握翻译技术。

Technology extends human capacities. The monkey uses a stick to get a banana, and that stick is technology, in this case a simple tool. More general technologies are collections of tools. Some of them affect our communications, and thus translation.

The use of books rather than scrolls, for example, made it easier to retrieve and cross-reference texts. Concordances were written for complex texts like the Bible, and translations thus had to render the whole text, not just isolated phrases so that the references would work. Similarly, the move from parchment to paper, which was generally cheaper and more transportable, meant that more written copies were made, revised and distributed. And since written culture was more easily re-written, translations were commonly re-translated. Not by chance, the use of paper coincided with the translation schools in Baghdad in the ninth century and Toledo in the thirteenth. Or again, the use of print technology from the fifteenth century supported the ideal of the definitive text, hence the definitive translation, and thus notions of equivalence as a relation between stable, fixed texts.

What might we say now that our key technologies are electronic? Texts on the web are constantly being updated, as is our software. We are sometimes called on to render no more than the updates or adaptations. Our translations might thus be expected to move away from the ideal of equivalence between fixed texts, becoming more like one set of revisions among many. In the fields of electronic technologies, translators are less commonly employed to translate whole texts, as one did for the books with concordances. Translation, like general text production, becomes more like work with databases, glossaries, and a set of electronic tools, rather than on complete definitive source texts.

Here we shall be looking at a series of electronic tools that extend human capacities in certain ways. These tools fundamentally affect (a) communication (the ways translators communicate with clients, authors, and other translators), (b) memory (how much information we can retrieve, and how fast), and (c) texts (how texts now become temporary arrangements of content). Of all the tools, the ones specifically designed to assist translators are undoubtedly those concerning memory. But we shall see that electronic technologies affect all aspects of the translator's work.

1 Translator-client Communications

In our digital age, electronic formats concern not just our texts, but also our communications with clients and other translators. Thanks to the Internet, professionals from all over the world can be in regular contact by e-mail or various forms of instant messaging. Work can be sent and received electronically, across national and cultural borders. This has several consequences.

First, in theory, you can work for clients anywhere in the world. The market for translations need not be your city or your country. A source text received at 5 p.m. in Tarragona can be sent to a translator in New Zealand, who will return the translation before 9 a.m. the following morning, Tarragona time. Time zones can thus be used creatively, and work can thus come from companies that are very far away. All you have to do is list your name, language combinations and areas of specialization on one of the many websites that aim to put translators and clients in touch with each other. One would expect this process to lead to a situation where the fees paid for translations will become virtually the same all over the world, in keeping with theories of a global market. This, however, is very far from happening. Translation is still a service that depends on a high degree of trust between the translator and the client. Little constant high-paid work will come from unseen clients; the fees paid in different countries still vary widely; the best contacts are probably still the ones made face-to-face and by word of mouth.

A second consequence of electronic communications is the increased security risk. Translators quite often work on material that is not in the public domain, and this is indeed one of the reasons why relations of trust are so important. When sending and receiving files, you will have to learn various forms of zipping, secure FTP, or other company-specific forms of encoding, with all their corresponding passwords.

A third consequence is that electronic communications make it relatively easy to distribute very large translation jobs between various intermediaries. The client may want to market their product in 15 European languages. They hire a marketing company, which hires a language-service provider, which hires a series of brokers for each language, who give the work to a series of translation companies, who pass the texts on to translators, often freelancers. In this kind of system, the client may be paying as much as four times what the actual translators are receiving per translated page. But each link in the chain is revising, coordinating and producing the various translation products, adding value as they go. This means the text the translator produces is commonly not the same text as the one actually used, and there can thus be little question of copyright over the translator's work. It also means that translators are sometimes very far removed from the end client and the overall context of the texts they work on. Translators in projects like software localization quite often see no more than lists of phrases, along with glossaries that are to be respected. The resulting work can be quite isolating and dehumanizing.

Electronic communications have also been used to enhance communication between translators, especially through Internet forums for professional translators. These are usually classified by topics and/or language pairs. Some may be open, in others participation is restricted to registered members. The traffic (number of e-mails) in each group varies from a few e-mails a month to hundreds a day. In these forums translators are very willing to exchange advice, give tips, and generally discuss their work. Simply by reading the posted messages, students and novice translators can learn about translation and see the kind of support that professionals give each other. Discussion lists for professionals usually have their own communication guidelines, and so new participants see a specific way of interacting among professionals. For example, when asking about terminology, professional translators usually send a short message in which they give the term, some context, suggested translations and the consulted sources. This model gives valuable hints about terminology mining and teamwork skills. Or again, by reading messages about a specific computer tool, novice translators often discover that the program is in constant evolution and has functions they would have otherwise overlooked. These forums thus build a valuable bridge between students and the professional world. They also put paid to the stereotype of the professional translator somehow isolated behind a wall of dusty dictionaries.

2 Translation Memories

Translation memories (TMs) are programs that create databases of source-text and target-text segments in such a way that the paired segments can be re-used. These tools are invaluable aids for the translation of any text that has a high degree of repeated terms and phrases, as is the case with user manuals, computer products and versions of the same document (website updates). In some sectors, the use of translation memories tools has speeded up the translation process and cheapened costs, and this has led to greater demands for translation services. The memories do not put translators out of work; they ideally do the boring routine parts of translation for us.

Translation memory tools re-use previous translations by dividing the source text (made up of one or several files in electronic format) into segments, which translators translate one-by-one in the traditional way. These segments (usually sentences or even phrases) are then sent to a built-in database. When there is a new source segment equal or similar to one already translated, the memory retrieves the previous translation from the database.

An example of the Trados Workbench translation memory suite can be seen in Figure 1. Here we are translating the segment "Restart your notebook" (highlighted in gray); the memory has proposed "Apague su ordenador portatil" as a translation, based on the translation of a previous segment (in fact the one translated just three segments earlier). But "apague" means "turn off," and here we need "restart." This is where translators either type a new target sentence or modify the result from the memory database. In this case, we would accept the suggested phrase but change "apague" to "reinicie" (restart). We do not have to rewrite the rest of the phrase.

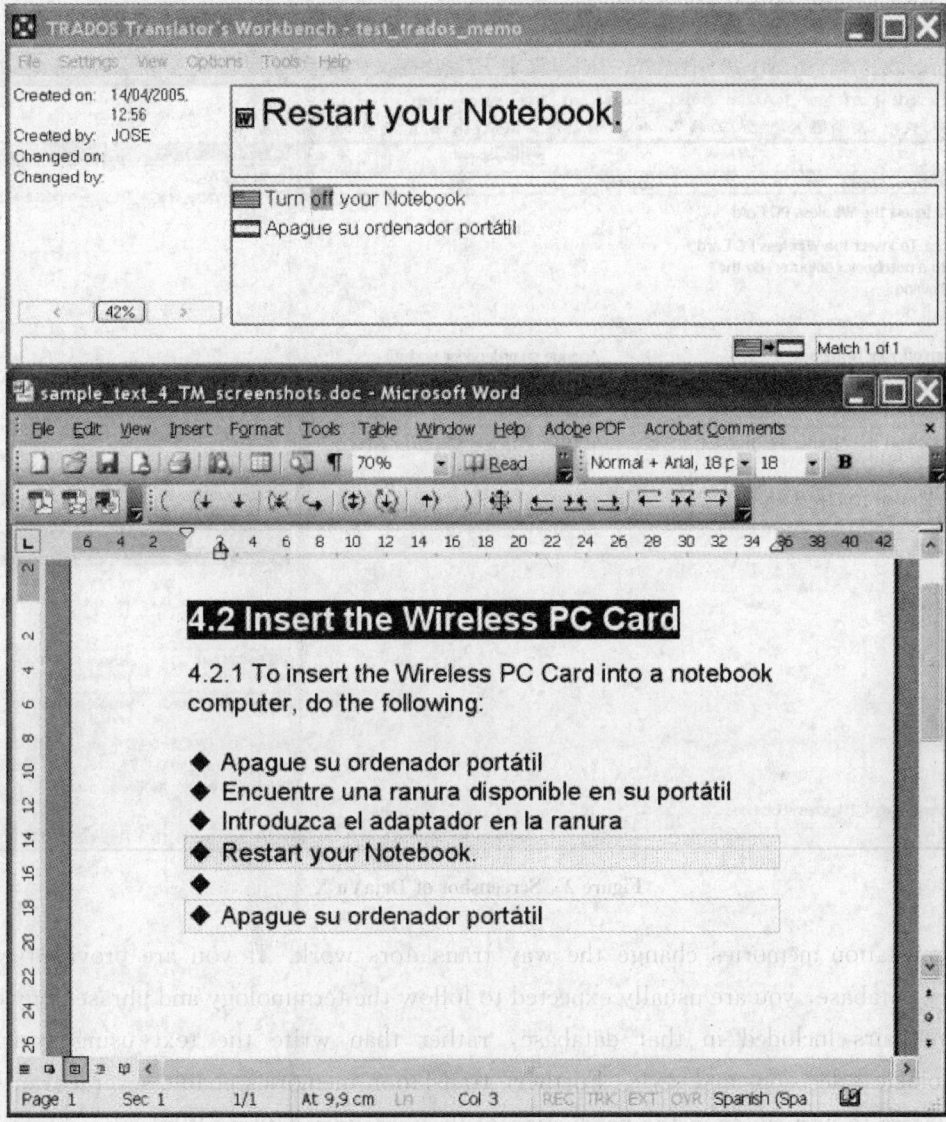

Figure 1 Screenshot of Trados and MS Word

At the top of the screenshot we see that Trados Workbench has highlighted the differences between each segment and reminds us about the language combination with a flag system. With Trados, we can translate Word documents using the Word itself, but files with other formats need to be translated using specific built-in translation environments.

The platform used by most other translation memory suites (DejaVu, SDLX, Star Transit) is quite different. Figure 2 shows the user interface of DejaVu X. Here we have the source text in the left column and the translation in the right one. The suggestions made by the translation memory are in the bottom right corner of the screen. In this system we do not see the document layout, since all the formatting is represented by the bracketed numbers. Formatting is thus protected. This means that translators cannot alter it by mistake. It also means they cannot edit it consciously.

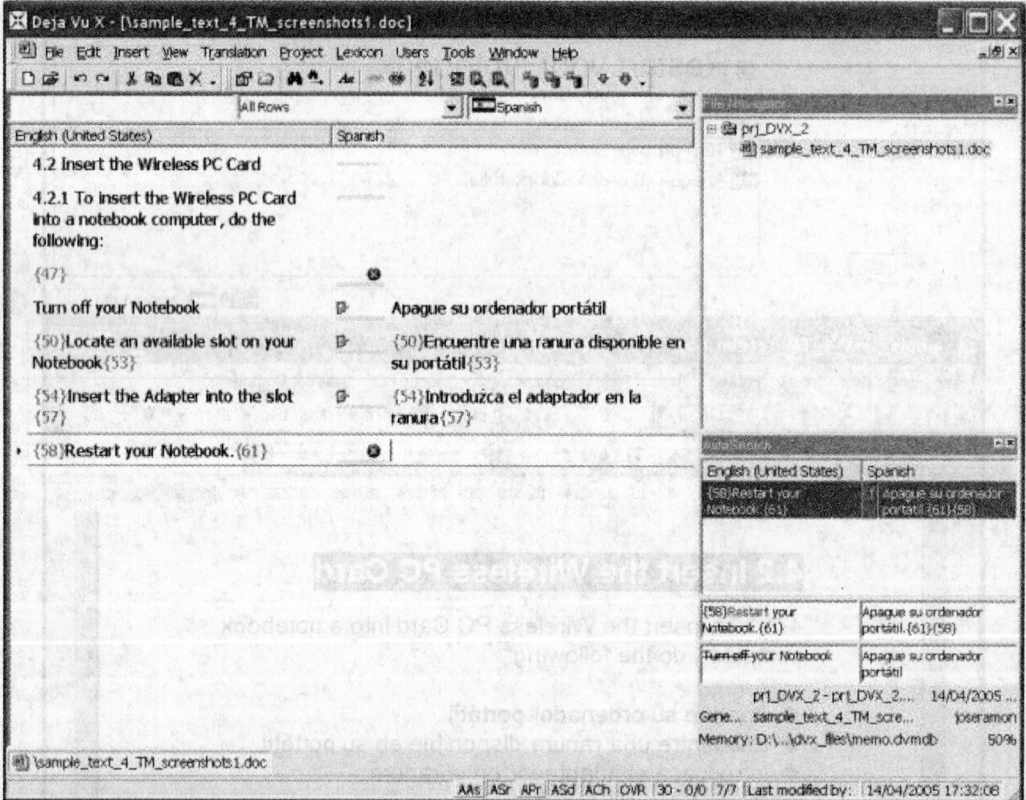

Figure 2　Screenshot of DejaVu X

Translation memories change the way translators work. If you are provided with a memory database, you are usually expected to follow the terminology and phraseology of the segment pairs included in that database, rather than write the text using your own terminological decisions and style. Further, translation memories enable several translators and revisers to participate in the production of the same translation. While this is needed to meet industry deadlines, it may lead to a translation with no cohesive style, made up of a set of sentences put together. The result can read like a "sentence salad" (cf. Bedard, 2000).

The possibility of re-using previous translations means that clients ask translators to work with TM systems and then reduce the translator's fees. The more exact and fuzzy matches there are (equal and similar segments already translated and included in the database), the less they pay. This encourages translators to work fast and often uncritically with the previously translated segments, with a corresponding decline in quality. When higher-quality work is required, special emphasis must be put on revising the outputs of translation-memory tools.

An associated complication of translation memory software is the ownership of the databases. If you sell your translation, should you also sell the database of matching segments that you have created while doing the translation? Should you sell that for an added fee? Then again, if you have used the work of previous translators by importing a database (or receiving one from your client), can we say that the translation is really all yours to sell? These are ethical questions that escape the parameters of traditional copyright agreements. The possible legal frameworks vary from country to country (cf. Megale, 2004). In practice, however, translators receive and deliver databases without paying or charging fees, thus according effective ownership to the clients or language-service providers they work with. At the same time, most translators are used to keeping copies of the databases, or integrating them into their own. To our knowledge, no law has yet been used against them.

This practice, though, will almost certainly die out with the use of the online memories. This system is highly appreciated by clients, since their texts and memory databases remain on a secure server rather than being copied and scattered to translators' personal computers all over the world. Moreover, the owner of the database server (the client or language vendor, never the freelance translator) is the only owner of the memory, as there are no other copies. This means that when these technologies become widespread, translators will not have access to their own previous translations, and project managers will be the only masters of the reference materials translators have access to.

The industrial applications of translation memory tools are based on the idea that translation is a word-replacement activity. On the other hand, translation theories since the 1980s have tended to see translators as communicators whose duties go beyond the replacement of source-text words; translators are employed to provide meaningful communication. Translation memories make this difficult. Indeed, they move translators back to the linguistic equivalence paradigms of the 1960s. Worse, now that texts commonly comprise not only written words but also images, videos and layout (think of any website), translation requires a division of labor. Thanks to our tools, translators are commonly only expected to deal with written words; they are invited to forget about the other elements configuring the text. This division of labor may not always create satisfying long-term employment.

3 Texts Without Ends

The way translators work is also being affected by the nature of the texts we work on. We are all familiar with texts that have automated cross-references (links) to other documents, which enable the reader to jump from one text to another. The most common examples are the links in websites. The use of these links means that there is now no clear beginning or end to texts, and that readings are no longer expected to be linear. Indeed, we now talk about "users" rather than "readers." While this is nothing fundamentally new (concordancing is an ancient activity), digital support has radically extended the role of this kind of text.

A major extension can be seen in content management systems. These are computer programs designed to manage databases comprising "information chunks" (generically known as "content"), usually no longer than a couple of paragraphs, which are combined and updated to create several customized texts according to the user's needs. The information chunks are regularly updated and re-labeled. This means that there is no final text, but a constant flow of updated, rearranged, re-sized and user-adapted provisional texts based on a large database of content in constant change. Think, for example, of a company that produces a series of improved versions of their products, be it software programs or cars, or adapts the products to a series of particular markets. They are not going to rewrite all their user manuals from scratch with each new version. They will logically re-use their existing texts, putting them together and modifying them on each occasion.

XML (extensible Markup Language) is a technology standard used to exchange content. It is a way of tagging information so that it can be retrieved later. Take the following example of an XML text:

```
<item>
<title>Pride and Prejudice</title> was written by <author>Jane
Austen</author> in <year>1813</year>.
</item>
```

```
<item>
<title>Alice in Wonderl and</title> was written by
<author>Lewis Carroll</author> in <year>1866</year>.
</item>
```

By tagging texts as we see above, we can later retrieve information that talks only about authors, for instance, to create a coursebook on literature (in which case we would get both information items). We can also retrieve information based on dates, to create a chronology of publications between 1800 and 1850 (in which case the second item would not appear). With the use of XML in this way, the text production process is anything but linear.

Translating this kind of information cannot be linear either. The updated texts are not translated from scratch, but pre-translated with a translation-memory tool. The translator's duty is to translate only the segments that have been modified, since the non-modified sentences have been retrieved from the memory database. On other occasions, the translator may receive a series of small chunks to translate, usually in a non-problematic format like RTF. These will look like phrases and paragraphs that have no connection with anything. They all have their number or code; they must all respect the established glossaries; they give the translator no indication of how they should fit together. In such cases, translators are obliged to "fly blind," rendering phrases without having any idea of the communicative context.

The development of these work practices has changed the very words used to describe what translators do. Once upon a time, translators worked on source texts, perhaps with the aid of a dictionary. Then, when the importance of contexts and clients was recognized, we talked about "translation projects," involving a lot of background information about specific communicative situations, including specialized glossaries and detailed instructions. In the days of content management, however, it is more exact to refer to "translation programs," on the model of the "maintenance programs" that keep things working day after day, year after year. In the world of content management, translators may be employed on programs that have cycles, rather than on texts that have ends.

4 Localization, Its Terms and Its Tools

These changes have also brought about a series of new terms for the language industry itself. Most prominently, from the 1980s the need to translate and adapt software to new markets led to common use of the term "localization" rather than "translation." This term has been defined by LISA (the Localization Industry Standards Association) as follows:

> Localization involves taking a product and making it linguistically and culturally appropriate to the target locale (country/region and language) where it will be used and sold. (cit. Esselink, 2000: 3)

The word "localization" is associated with "locale," a term to define a specific target market. Locales are often smaller than countries or languages. Localizing a word processor developed in the United States so that it can be sold in the Spanish market involves translating into Spanish the menus, the dialogue boxes and other user-visible messages, translating the online Help files, the publicity and the printed reference material, and adapting any cultural references along the way. But it also involves implementing the word processor with a spellchecker for the variety of Spanish used in the target locale, adapting the "insert date" option so that the text inserted appears as Day/Month/Year, and not Month/Day/Year, including pre-set page settings that match Spanish standards for paper and envelopes, and changing functions so that letter combinations make sense to a Spanish user (the hotkey combination "Alt + E" opens the Edit menu in the English version of Microsoft Word, but the same menu opens with "Alt + M" in the Spanish version, referring to the Spanish word Modificar). All that can be called "localization." It involves more than just translation.

The complexities of localization can be reduced by foreseeing the difficulties and preparing for them in the first version of the product. When this is done, companies save time and money, and may offer better-quality products. This process is called "internationalization":

> Internationalization is the process of generalizing a product so that it can handle multiple languages and cultural conventions without the need for re-design. (LISA definition, cit. Esselink, 2000: 2)

Internationalizing a computer product means designing to handle demands such as the accented characters that will be needed in the localized versions. For example, by designing "Cancel" buttons that are actually much longer than the English word "Cancel," they allow for longer translations in other languages (Annular in Spanish), so that there is no need to resize the button to display the Spanish translation.

The term "globalization" is sometimes used instead of "internationalization," notably by Microsoft. For LISA, however, "globalization" involves a specific reference to the way companies are organized:

> Globalization addresses the business issues associated with taking a product global. In the globalization of high-tech products this involves integrating localization throughout a company, after proper internationalization and product design, as well as marketing, sales, and support in the world market. (LISA definition, cit. Esselink, 2000: 4)

We might thus say that globalization is a mode of organization that uses internationalization in order to prepare for localization.

So, is translation part of localization, or vice versa?

The answer really depends on whom you ask. Software developers argue that translation is only one of the many modifications a program has to go through in order to be localized. Translation scholars, on the other hand, might argue that localization is only a fancy name for the act of adapting a text for a specific target readership, which is something translators have been doing for millennia.

Another answer might be found in the electronic tools that have been developed especially for localization. Apart from text editors, spellcheckers, translation memories and terminology management systems, which are common in translation programs, professional localization tools include functions to resize dialogue boxes, assign and check hotkeys to menus, edit and check programming code, manage non-textual resources (such as icons or sound files), calculate the complexity of a project, and replace programming code to make the program work on another platform. The result might still be a translation, but the work process clearly goes beyond traditional translating.

Software localization requires those specific tools. Without them, we would have something like Figure 3, which shows the programming code for a dialogue box. Translating in this format is extremely dangerous and time-consuming, since you can easily delete or modify code (instructions for the computer) by mistake. Before working in this way, you would need to learn to discriminate natural-language strings from code. Moreover, there are no spellcheckers or advanced text-editing tools available.

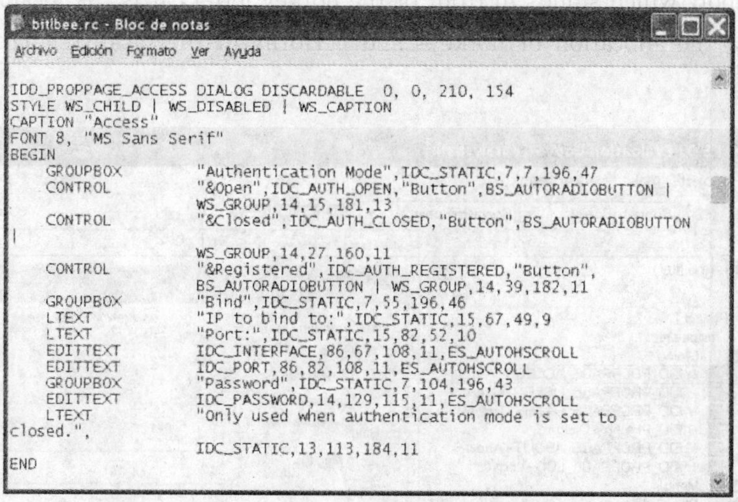
bitlbee.rc - Bloc de notas
Archivo Edición Formato Ver Ayuda
IDD_PROPPAGE_ACCESS DIALOG DISCARDABLE 0, 0, 210, 154
STYLE WS_CHILD | WS_DISABLED | WS_CAPTION
CAPTION "Access"
FONT 8, "MS Sans Serif"
BEGIN
GROUPBOX "Authentication Mode",IDC_STATIC,7,7,196,47
CONTROL "&Open",IDC_AUTH_OPEN,"Button",BS_AUTORADIOBUTTON | WS_GROUP,14,15,181,13
CONTROL "&Closed",IDC_AUTH_CLOSED,"Button",BS_AUTORADIOBUTTON | WS_GROUP,14,27,160,11
CONTROL "&Registered",IDC_AUTH_REGISTERED,"Button", BS_AUTORADIOBUTTON | WS_GROUP,14,39,182,11
GROUPBOX "Bind",IDC_STATIC,7,55,196,46
LTEXT "IP to bind to:",IDC_STATIC,15,67,49,9
LTEXT "Port:",IDC_STATIC,15,82,52,10
EDITTEXT IDC_INTERFACE,86,67,108,11,ES_AUTOHSCROLL
EDITTEXT IDC_PORT,86,82,108,11,ES_AUTOHSCROLL
GROUPBOX "Password",IDC_STATIC,7,104,196,43
EDITTEXT IDC_PASSWORD,14,129,115,11,ES_AUTOHSCROLL
LTEXT "Only used when authentication mode is set to closed.", IDC_STATIC,13,113,184,11
END

Figure 3 Translation of a resource file with NotePad

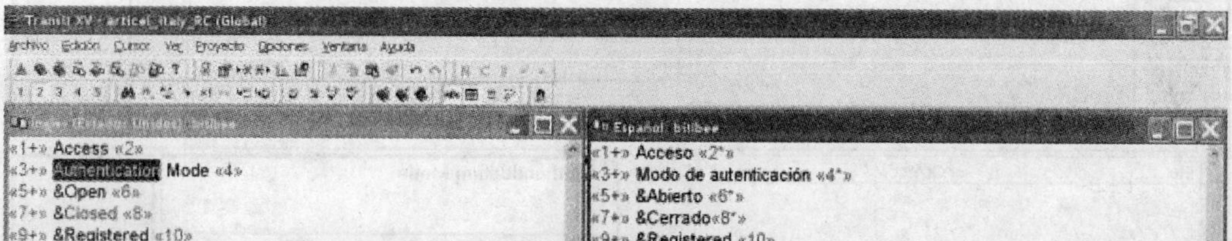
«1+» Access «2»
«3+» Authentication Mode «4»
«5+» &Open «6»
«7+» &Closed «8»
«9+» &Registered «10»
«11+» Bind «12»
«13+» IP to bind to: «14»
«15+» Port: «16»
«17+» Password «18»
«19+» Only used when authentication mode is set to closed. «20»
«21+» Users «22»
«23+» Known users «24»
«25+» Current users «26»
«27+» &Remove «28»
«29+» &Kick «30»
«31+» &Refresh «32»
«33+» &Refresh «34»
«35+» Paths «36»
«37+» Config path «38»
«39+» &Browse... «40»
«41+» Message of the day file «42»
«43+» &Browse... «44»
«45+» &Edit... «46»
«1+» Acceso «2*»
«3+» Modo de autenticación «4*»
«5+» &Abierto «6*»
«7+» &Cerrado«8*»
«9+» &Registered «10»
«11+» Bind «12»
«13+» IP to bind to: «14»
«15+» Port: «16»
«17+» Password «18»
«19+» Sólo cuando el authentication mode is set to closed. «20»
«21+» Users «22»
«23+» Known users «24»
«25+» Current users «26»
«27+» &Remove «28»
«29+» &Kick «30»
«31+» &Refresh «32»
«33+» &Refresh «34»
«35+» Paths «36»
«37+» Config path «38»
«39+» &Browse... «40»
«41+» Message of the day file «42»
«43+» &Browse... «44»
«45+» &Edit... «46»
authentication: autenticación [A]
Closed: Cerrado [B]
No se encontró equivalencia aproximada.
Seg:20 Pos:11
Ins
Sin traducir
d: Alt+0100

Figure 4 Translation of a resource file using Transit

Are translation-memory tools any better? Figure 4 shows a screenshot of the Transit translation memory suite. Here we have the same file being translated, with source and target text, dictionary and memory database. Translators working with this environment cannot see or edit the code, so their duty is to translate text. Even if they have the ampersand symbol, which stands in front of the hotkey letter, it is the localization engineer who should test the allocation of hotkeys and perform all the tasks related to layout and function.

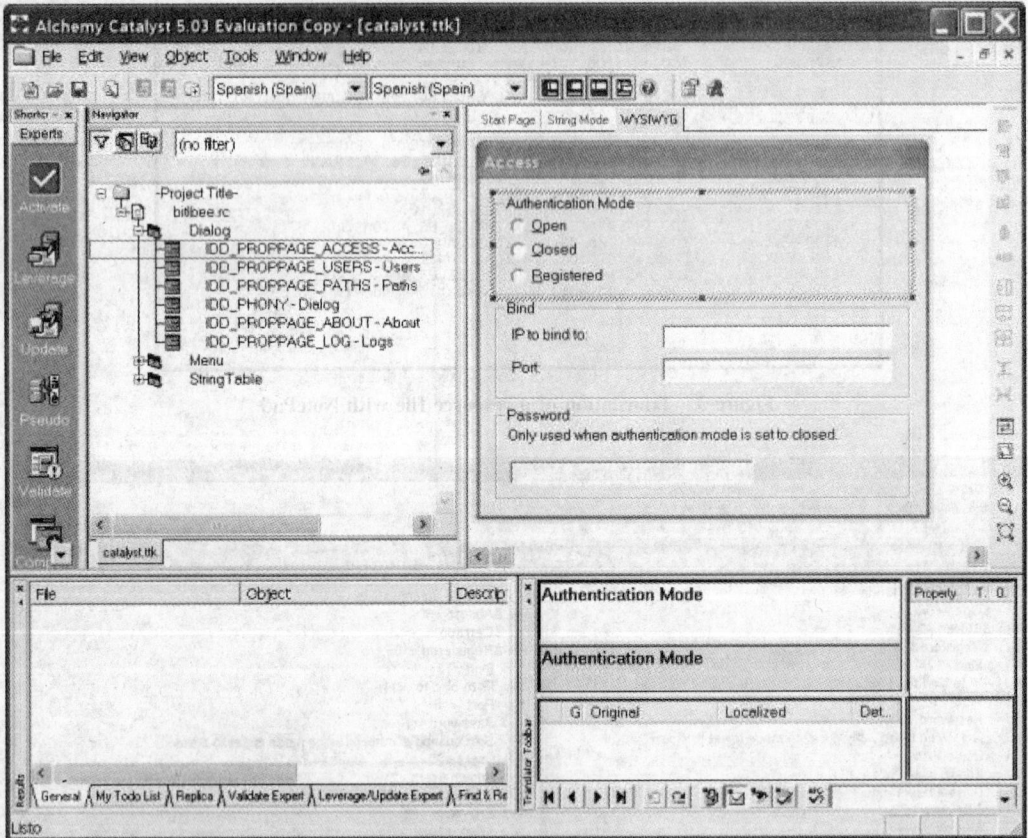

Figure 5   Localization of a resource file using Catalyst

So what are the tools developed for localizing software? In Figure 5 we can see the same file being translated with Catalyst, which is specifically designed for this kind of work. This is perhaps like the translation memory, except that here we can see what the dialogue box looks like; we have its visual context. And just below the dialogue box we have the active segment ("Authentication Mode") where we can type our translations and see immediately if the target text fits into the box. We can assign unique hotkey combinations to each function and resize the dialogues if we need to allocate more space for our translation.

Tasks become considerably easier when you get the right tool for the job.

5   Machine Translation

Machine translation (MT) is probably the translation technology with the most sway over the popular imagination. The first serious attempts to create MT systems date from the late 1940s, when United States and the USSR both funded projects to move rocket technology out of German, and then to spy on each other. It is often said that the initial expectations were very naive, which would be why when the early projects were almost completely abandoned in the US following the negative ALPAC report in 1966.

However, the early approaches were based on quite sophisticated concepts of code-breaking, and there is little evidence that the aim was to produce high-quality output that would be of immediate use. Indeed, the main limitations of the day were on the capacity to store and retrieve huge amounts of lexical, morphological, syntactic and semantic information. The funding evaporated when the Cold War went through a relative thaw.

Several generations later, MT is readily available and relatively functional. The transfer-based Syst ran system can be used for free on several websites. Its many unhappy matches and almost complete inability to handle proper nouns can result in hours of fun for bored linguists or enthusiastic revision classes. However, the system is extremely useful for gist translations from languages you know nothing about. It allows users to identify the texts or fragments of interest, which they can then have translated by other means.

In other circumstances, MT systems produce high quality translations in very restricted contexts. This can be done by limiting the lexical and grammatical structures of the source text (controlled language) and fine-tuning the system to work only with a specific text type. A classic case is French-English weather reports in Canada, for which an MT system has been in continuous use since 1984. In other circumstances, a company may develop a highly standardized central language and fixed document templates, enabling MT to be used successfully in conjunction with controlled writing of content (in fact a form of internationalization) and careful revising of MT output (cf. Lockwood, 2000, on the heavy machinery producer Caterpillar, where content is written in "Caterpillar English"). The Translation Service of the European Commission similarly uses its own version of Systran to give acceptable results on formulaic texts between cognate languages (especially from French to Italian or Spanish).

There are important technical differences between these examples. The Canadian weather reports and the use of EU Syst ran are based on correspondences between language pairs (a "transfer" architecture), whereas the use of controlled writing (as at Caterpillar) enables MT to go from one language to many languages at the same time (thanks to an "interlingua" architecture). From the translator's perspective, however, the consequences are the same.

Machine translation systems are not replacing human mediators. This is first because the prime use of MT is only to locate the texts and fragments requiring human translation. Second, if MT output is to be used professionally, it requires human revision. And third, the future development of quality MT output requires serious attention to controlling writing of the input, which is an area that some translators may want to move into. Indeed, the better MT systems work (and current statistical models seem able to offer a better future), the more texts will be processed, and the more work will be created for human translators.

Whatever happens, do not let a client tell you that you have been replaced by a machine. If they say that a text has already been translated automatically and you only have to correct the errors, look for another client. It will usually take you less time to translate from scratch rather than identity and correct the errors. And your quality will be higher.

6　Advantages and Disadvantages for Translators

Technology is not an option in today's professional world; it is a necessity. Years ago one talked about Computer-Aided Translation (CAT). That now seems a redundancy. Virtually all translating is aided by computers. Further, the most revolutionary tools are quite probably the everyday ones that are not specific to translation: Internet search engines, spell checkers, search and replace functions, and revision tools have had a huge impact on all forms of written communication. On countless levels, the advantages presented by technology are so great that they cannot be refused. Translation memories perform the most repetitive tasks so that translators can concentrate on the most creative aspects of translation. The intelligent use of machine translation should mean that our best human efforts are focused where they are most needed. However, technology is not perfect, and translators must be very aware of those imperfections. Here, in closing, we offer a list of those aspects where critical awareness seems most needed.

Each new technology requires new investment, not just in purchasing tools but also in learning how to use them. In all cases, the investment you put in should be less than the benefits you expect to gain. This means, for example, that the kind of text corpora that linguists use in order to study language are generally not cost-beneficial tools when applied to professional translation. They address problems that are more easily solved with a quick web search, and the kinds of quantitative data bases they use have little to do with those developed by translation memory tools. Or again, there is little need to take a course in a particular translation-memory suite if you already know how to use a rival brand. All the products are similar in their underlying technology, and you should be able to find your own way from one to the other. As a general rule, inform yourself before buying anything or signing up for courses. Demonstration versions of all tools are usually available on the web for free, many of them with online tutorials, and translators' forums can give you numerous pointers about the relative advantages and drawbacks of each tool.

Investment in a certain technology can be essential if you are to move from one segment of the translation market to another. The jump is usually made when a client or intermediary offers you work requiring knowledge of a certain tool. You then have to learn very fast, but you are at least sure that you have the right tool for the available job.

Even within large projects, the cost of technology tends to form a set of internal barriers. For example, in a localization project, the project managers (responsible for the overall organization) usually have very powerful, expensive tools with advanced project-management options. The language project managers (responsible for a specific version of the product) have tools that allow them to perform advanced processing, such as automatic terminology checking and the preparation of the packages they send to translators. At the end of the line, the translators have the cheapest and most restricted versions of the software, sometimes called "light" versions, with which they can only replace language strings and perform some basic editing and proofreading tasks. Since code is protected, only the people with the original source files and the powerful tools are able to edit the layout or the content of the source text. By limiting the functions of the tools assigned to each member of the workflow chain, technology has become one way to control the actions and responsibilities of translators.

All these barriers can, of course, be overcome. Translators can and do move into high-tech sectors; some do become project managers, marketing experts, or owners of companies. In general, the way to advance within the profession usually involves more conceptual control over technology, not less. Too often, the dominant industry workflows impose their own specific technologies and processes. Only when translators are critically aware of the available tools can they hope to be in control of their work.

选文二　信息时代的翻译工具

冯志伟

导　言

　　作者为教育部语言文字应用研究所研究员、中国传媒大学博士生导师,主要研究领域为应用语言学和计算语言学。

　　本文提出,在今天这样一个多语言网络的信息时代,如何有效地使用现代化手段来突破人们之间的语言障碍,成为全人类面临的共同问题。作者进一步指出翻译是克服语言障碍的有利手段。信息时代的翻译工具有:机器翻译系统、因特网上的语言翻译资源、CD-ROM上的语言翻译资源、计算机辅助术语管理系统、双语对应语料库、翻译记忆软件和本土化软件工具、机助翻译系统。译者掌握了信息时代的这些翻译工具,就可以大大地提高翻译的效率,满足信息时代对翻译的迫切需要。

一、信息时代对于翻译的需求

语言是人类交际、思维和认知的重要工具。但是,由于语言的差异而造成的语言障碍,却给人类带来极大的困扰。为了克服语言的障碍,曾经有人提出使用"人类通用语言"(lingua franca)来替代各种不同语言的想法。但是,这样的想法显然是很难实现的,即便有了这样的通用语言,它也代替不了各种不同的语言。因为语言是民族文化的象征,放弃民族语言就意味着放弃民族的文化。如果全人类都讲一种通用的语言,各具特色的、丰富多彩的民族文化也就黯然失色了。这显然不是一件好事。英语在英国和美国占绝对的统治地位,目前世界上讲英语的人数已经超过 112 500 000,大约有 90% 的科技出版物是用英语写的,在各种专业性的国际会议上,英语几乎成为与会者公认的共同语言。在德国,98% 的物理学家和 83% 的化学家用英语公布他们的新发现,大多数诺贝尔奖金获得者来自广泛使用英语的国家,英语似乎已经成为当代世界的 lingua franca。可是,在英国的威尔士,人们还在讲威尔士语,在美国的某些地区,还有很多人在讲西班牙语。至于像加拿大和瑞士这样的双语和多语国家,像欧洲联盟和联合国这样的组织,多语言的使用(multilingualism)已经成为了日常生活中的基本原则和普遍现象。因为多语言的使用,不同语言之间的翻译就非常重要了,翻译的需求会变得越来越迫切和尖锐。我们以欧洲联盟(European Union,以下简称欧盟)的多种语言翻译为例来说明这个问题。按照欧盟的前身欧洲经济共同体 1957 年首脑会议通过的关于语言多样化的决议,各成员国都有平等使用本国语言的权利,各成员国的官方语言即成为这个组织的工作语言。当时只有 6 个创始国,开会时只使用 4 种语言,语言问题还不十分突出。1995 年欧盟扩大到 15 个国家,官方语言增加到 11 种(比利时、奥地利没有自己独特的语言,爱尔兰官方语言为英语、爱尔兰语,卢森堡因其官方语言为德语、法语和卢森堡语,没有要求使用卢森堡语),可能的语言翻译方向有 110 种,语言问题开始突显出来。按照规定,在召开欧盟的正式会议时,这 11 种语言就是会议的工作语言。也就是说,欧盟在召开正式大会时应当提供 11 种语言的翻译服务,大会文件要译成 11 种语言,由此增加的翻译工作量之大,财政支出之高是可以想见的。据统计,欧盟每个正式会晤至少需要 33 个翻译人员,才能完成 11 种语言间高达 110 种可能的互译;每年欧盟大小会议共 1 万多个,为此要付出 15 万个翻译人/日,全年翻译的文件达 113 万页以上。每次为期 5 天的欧洲议会起码需要 450 名翻译人员。目前欧盟雇用的常年翻译(in-house translator)有 460 人,临时翻译(external freelance translator)1 500 多人。即便如此,仍不能满足所有成员国的所有语言要求,这支庞大的翻译队伍如今越来越难以应付巨大的工作压力,已陷入捉襟见肘和穷于应付的困境。整个欧盟在 1997 年用在翻译方面的支出(包括口头翻译和术语工作的支出)高达 20 亿欧元,而这项开支还不包括欧盟使用 EC - SYSTRAN 机器翻译系统每年翻译 20 万页文件的费用。根据欧盟资助的一项叫做 ASSIM 的研究报告,整个欧盟和欧洲经济区(简称 EEA)的 18 个国家翻译市场的总营业额,在 1997 年高达 37.5 亿欧元,其中 20% 是翻译软件和声像多媒体翻译产品的营业额,而这个地区的翻译市场的翻译人员已经达到 10 万人之多。语言的困扰随着欧盟成员国的增加而愈加尖锐:一方面,所有成员国的代表当然有权使用本国的语言表达各自的意见;另一方面,由此增加的翻译工作量和财政支出却并非是所有成员国乐于承担的。从 2004 年 5 月 1 日开始,欧盟成员国已经扩大到 25 个,这就意味着欧盟正式会议的工作语言至少有 21 种,可能的语言翻译方向进一步增加到

420 种,而每增加一种新的语言,就需要增加 250～300 名翻译人员,一场会议的同声传译至少需要 60 名翻译人员。欧盟每天都有七八百名翻译人员在进行同声传译工作。现在欧盟就因同声传译跟不上,笔译错误层出不穷而叫苦不迭。一旦 21 种官方语言同时互译,其后果将更加混乱,而用于翻译方面的财政支出将大幅度提高。据报道,2004 年由于 10 个新成员国的加入,文件翻译总量达到 206.5 万页,2005 年更是高达 237 万页,其支出进一步上升,对欧盟各成员国无疑会增加了更大的负担,在语言方面也带来了更多的矛盾与困扰。2004 年 5 月,欧盟不得不通过一项新的议案,规定所有欧盟成员国在欧盟会议上的文件都不得超过 15 页 A4 纸,以减轻翻译人员的工作量。随着信息技术的进步和网络的发展,因特网(Internet)逐渐变成一个多语言的网络世界。目前,在因特网上除了使用英语之外,越来越多地使用汉语、西班牙语、德语、法语、日语、韩国语等英语之外的语言。从 2000 年到 2005 年,因特网上使用英语的人数仅仅增加了 126.9%,而在此期间,因特网上使用俄语的人数增加了 664.5%,使用葡萄牙语的人数增加了 327.3 %,使用中文的人数增加了 309.6%,使用法语的人数增加了 235.9%。因特网上使用英语之外的其他语言的人数增加得越来越多,英语在因特网上独霸天下的局面已经打破,因特网确实已经变成了多语言的网络世界;因此,网络上的不同语言之间的翻译自然也就越来越迫切了。

信息时代,科学技术的发展日新月异,新的信息、新的知识如雨后春笋不断增加,出现了"信息爆炸"(information explosion) 的局面。现在,世界上出版的科技刊物达 165 000 种,平均每天有大约 2 万篇科技论文发表。专家估计,我们目前每天在因特网上传输的数据量之大,已经超过了整个 19 世纪的全部数据的总和;我们在 21 世纪所要处理的知识总量将要大大地超过我们在过去 2 500 年历史长河中所积累起来的全部知识总量。随着知识突飞猛进的增长,翻译市场供不应求的局面也就越来越严重了。根据国际权威机构对世界翻译市场的调查显示,全世界翻译市场的规模 1999 年只是 104 亿美元,2003 年为 172 亿美元,而 2005 年则达到了 227 亿美元。随着因特网应用范围的扩大和国际电子商务市场的日渐成熟,到 2007 年,仅网页的翻译业务将达到 17 亿美元的规模。目前,我国翻译能力严重不足,我国翻译市场的规模尽管已经超过了 100 亿人民币,但是现有的国内翻译公司只能消化 10% 左右。由于无法消化大量从国际上传来的信息流,我们的信息不灵,就有可能使我们在国际竞争中失去大量的机会。在这种情况下,传统的手工翻译已经难以满足不断增长的翻译需求,我们很有必要在翻译工作中使用电子工具来提高翻译的效率,电子翻译工具将使翻译工作者如虎添翼。事实上,国外很多翻译工作者已经使用各种电子翻译工具了。根据欧盟资助的 ASSIM 研究项目在 1997 年的报道,在他们所采访的翻译工作者中,50% 以上的人使用电子词典,1/3 的人使用翻译记忆系统。我国内地和香港也有不少的翻译工作者开始使用电子翻译工具。电子翻译工具将可能成为翻译工作者不可缺少的重要工具。

二、机器翻译系统

机器翻译(machine translation)是使用电子计算机把源语言(source language)翻译成目标语言(target language)的一门新学科。这门新学科也同时是一种新技术。它涉及语言学、计算机科学、数学等许多部门,是非常典型的多边缘的交叉学科。在语言学中,机器翻译是计算语言学的一个研究领域;在计算机科学中,机器翻译是人工智能的一个研究领域;在数学中,机器翻译是数理逻辑和形式化方法的一个研究领域。机器翻译要把这些不同的学科结合起来,综合地进行研究。机器翻译要求不同学科的专家通力合作,取长补短,相得益彰。目前机器翻译产品虽然不能达到很高的质量,但是,它可以帮助人们及时地获取信息,克服语言的障碍。有人把机器翻译比喻为达摩克利斯剑(sword of Damocles)。达摩克利斯是希腊传说中的叙拉古国王狄奥尼西奥斯的朝臣。据传说其被迫坐在上悬宝剑的餐桌旁,宝剑由一根头发系住,以此来暗示命运的险恶。这些人把机器翻译比喻为翻译工作者的达摩克利斯剑,以表示机器翻译现状和前景的险恶,这样的比喻是不恰当的。机器翻译是翻译工作者的重要的工具,不能把它比喻为翻译工作者的达摩克利斯剑。不少人对机器翻译存在着一些误解。例如,有人说,美国的机器翻译系统曾经把英语翻译成俄语,结果闹出了大笑话。例如,机器把英语的成语 The spirit is willing, but the flesh is weak(心有余而力不足)翻译成俄语之后,这个句子的意思却变成了 The vodka is good, but the steak is lousy(伏特加很好,而肉却令人恶心)。类似的笑话被那些反对机器翻译的人们翻来覆去地引用。这种种笑话全都是伪造的谎言,不足为信。有人说,"机器翻译费钱费时,派不上什么用场",把机器翻译贬得一无是处;有人说,"如果机器翻译打破了语言障碍,那么,所有的翻译人员就只好失业了",把机器翻译说得神乎其神。这样的看法都是片面的。尽管目前机器翻译的技术还不完善,但是,它给翻译工作者开辟了一个新的活动领域,对于翻译工作者还是很有用的。这样的机器翻译系统对一些较简单的翻译任务还是可以胜任的。比如,机器翻译系统的应用常常集中完成下列翻译工作:

(1) 那些粗略翻译就足够的工作;

(2) 那些人工译后编辑(post-editing)可用于提高机器翻译输出质量的工作;

(3) 能够产生高质量译文的受限子语言领域的翻译工作。

网络中信息的获取是一种"信息采集"的任务,只要有非常粗略的翻译,读者就会感到满意。例如,Syst ran 多语言机器翻译系统,如果只是为了获取信息,其译文还是可以接受的(Syst ran 的网站是:http://www. syst ransoft. com,读者可以一试)。

我们来看下面摘自 Syst ran 机器翻译系统的英汉机器翻译的英文原文和汉语译文:

SYSTRAN Translation from English to Chinese(翻译日期:11 – March – 2004)

英文原文:

Austrian Airlines Group has announced that it will include Shanghai in its flight service network beginning from April 29th with the operation of three flights a week from Pudong International Airport to Vienna. At the same time the number of flights from Vienna to Beijing will also be increased from four to six this summer. According to a company official, 120,000 Chinese tourists visited Austria last year, and the figure is expected to rise 20 percent annually.

汉语译文:

奥地利航空公司小组宣布,它包括上海在它的飞行服务网络起点从 4 月 29 日以三次飞行的操作每星期从浦东国际机场到维也纳。同时飞行的数量从维也纳的向北京并且将被增加从四到六这个夏天。根据公司官员,120 000 个中国游人去年访问了奥地利,并且图被预计年年上升 20%。

这样的机器翻译的译文是大致可以看懂的,从这种粗糙的译文中,我们可以知道奥地利航空公司将增加从上海到维也纳的航班,这个消息对于那些打算到奥地利去旅游的人肯定是会有帮助的。尽管在汉语的译文中,把英语 figure 这个多义词错误地翻译为"图",而正确的翻译应当是"数字",译文中还有不少的语法错误,但是,译文整体的含义还是清楚的。译文的信息对我们是有用的。这种"全自动的低质量的机器翻译"可以说目前已经成为现实了。但是,在目前的技术水平下,"全自动高质量机器翻译"(fully automatic high-quality translation,简称 FAHQT)还难以实现,这样高的目标已经被放弃了。歧义问题(ambiguity)、句法复杂性问题(syntactic complexity)、习惯用语问题(idiom)和指代消解问题(anaphora resolution)都是机器翻译研究中的难题。由于这些问题的存在,机器翻译的译文质量还不高。因此,我们还应该采用其他的电子翻译工具。

三、因特网上的语言翻译资源

因特网不仅给翻译工作提供了信息交流和信息传递的手段,也给翻译工作提供了宝贵的信息资源。要想在网络上找到一些数据易如反掌,可是,要想在网络上找到你所需要的确实而可靠的信息却不是一件简单的事情,往往容易陷入大海捞针的困境。目前网上搜索的策略有三种:第一种策略是通过 URL (Uniform Resource Locator)进行单位搜索以便根据单位的名称找到相关信息;第二种策略是通过主题树(subject tree)进行主题搜索以便根据主题的类别找到相关信息;第三种策略是通过搜索引擎(search engine)进行单词搜索以便根据具体的关键词或短语找到相关信息。

因特网上的语言资源都是联机(online)的语言资源。这些联机的语言资源主要包括:

(1) 联机的图书馆目录和虚拟书店。如通过 OPAC (http://catalog. loc. gov)可以查询主要的图书馆,通过 Amazon (http://www. amazon. com)可以浏览网络上的虚拟书店;

(2) 通用百科全书。如,通过 Britannica online (http://www. britannica. com)可以查询联机的大英百科全书。http://www. britannica. com;

(3) 专业百科全书。如,通过 PC Webopedia (http://www. pcwebopedia. com)可以查询联机的专业百科全书;

(4) 通用单语词典。如,通过 Merriam-Webster (http://www. m-w. com)可以查询联机的普通词典和类属词典;

(5) 通用多语词典。如,通过 OneLook (http://www. onelook. com)可以联机查询多语言词表、词典和数据库,通过"金山词霸"(http://cb. kingsoft. com)可以联机查询汉英-英汉双向词典;

(6) 多语言术语数据库。如,通过 Termite (http://www. itu. int) 可以查询国际通信联盟 ITU (International Telecommunication Union) 联机的多语言术语数据库,通过 Eurodicautom(http://europa. eu. int/eurodicautom)可以查询欧盟翻译服务部联机的术语数据库;

(7) 电子报纸和杂志文献。如,通过查询西班牙的电子报纸 ABC (http://www. abc. es),德国的电子报纸 Die Welt (http://www. welt. de),美国的电子杂志 Newsweek (http://www. newsweek. com),可以检索到有关的背景信息;这些电子工具给翻译工作者插上了翅膀,让他们在网络的天空中翱翔。翻译工作者可以有效地检索遍布全世界的书目数据,从而找到他们所需要的书籍和资料。

四、CD - ROM 上的语言翻译资源

在 CD - ROM（只读光盘）上的语言翻译资源是脱机（offline）的语言翻译资源。CD - ROM 的存储量很大，32 卷的不列颠百科全书可以存储在一个小小的 CD - ROM 中，如果使用 CD - ROM，翻译工作者就用不着与网络连接，他们只需要带有光盘驱动器（CD - ROM drive）的计算机，就可以使用 CD - ROM 上信息资源。有的 CD - ROM 还有超链接（hyperlink）的功能，从而把光盘上不同的条目链接起来，便于用户进行搜索。例如：

（1）CD - ROM 上的百科全书：如，中国大百科全书 CD - ROM，Britannica Concise Encyclo-pedia 的 CD - ROM；

（2）CD ROM 上的百科词典：如，Const ruction Installation Encyclopedia；

（3）CD - ROM 上的普通词典：如，Oxford English Dictionary （OED）的 CD - ROM，Bibliorom Larousse 的 CD - ROM；

（4）掌上电子词典：如，市售的各种电子词典。

五、计算机辅助术语管理系统

绝大部分的专业文献翻译是技术文献翻译，如信息技术、制造技术、生物技术、商业、医药等领域的翻译。我们不能要求翻译工作者同时也是这些领域的专家，门门精通，样样内行。但是，我们希望翻译工作者在进行专业技术的翻译之前，对于所翻译的专业领域基础知识有大致的了解，尽快地掌握相关的知识和信息。在专业技术文献的翻译过程中，最令人头疼的问题是术语的翻译。为了找到准确得体的术语，翻译工作者往往要花费大量的时间。使用计算机辅助的术语管理（Terminology Management）系统，大大地减轻了翻译工作者查询术语的时间。目前，许多跨国公司也使用计算机辅助术语管理系统进行"本土化"（localization），以便经济有效地建立和管理术语，消除因纠正术语错误而造成的非生产性时间和成本，确保在产品和服务整个生命周期中的全体从业人员都能准确而一致地使用术语，支持分散的术语编辑团队，把翻译工作者、术语专家、编辑、校对和用户结合为一体，经济地在公司的组织内外发布术语，集中维护关键术语资产。世界领先的计算机辅助术语管理系统 Trados'MultiTerm（http://trados. com）的主要功能包括：建立术语数据库，输入术语数据，检索术语数据，输出术语数据，在 Multi'Term 和词语处理器之间交换术语数据。

六、双语对应语料库在翻译中的应用

为一个或多个应用目标而专门收集的、有一定结构的、有代表性的、可被计算机程序检索的、具有一定规模的语料的集合叫做语料库（corpus）。由于语料库可以代表真实的语言现象，因此，它可以根据真实的语料来帮助翻译工作者判断译文是否准确。双语对应语料库（parallel corpus）中，既包括源语言的文本，又包括对应的目标语言的文本，可以帮助翻译工作者对源语言和目标语言进行比较，提高翻译的质量。例如，

（1）使用语料库来检查译文的可接受程度；

（2）从现存的网络资源中搜索有用的语料库或者建立适合自己要求的语料库；

（3）使用 WordSmith（http：//www1. oup. com/elt/catalogue/Multimedia/Wordsmith）软件从语料库中检索数据和编写词表；

（4）使用 Alta Vista（http：//altavista. com）软件来搜索文献和编制词语索引。

下面是《圣经》的汉英对应语料库（http：//www. o-bible. com/b5/int. html）的片段，

其中，[hb5]表示汉语繁体字和合本，[kjv]表示英文钦定本（King James Version），[bbe]qd 表示英文简易本（Bible in Basic English）：

1：1 [hb5]起初神创造天地。

　　[kjv] In the beginning God created the heaven and the earth.

　　[bbe] At the first God made the heaven and the earth.

1：2 [hb5]地是空虚混沌，渊面黑暗，神的灵运行在水面上。

　　[kjv] And the earth was without form, and void; and darkness was upon the face of the deep. And the Spirit of God moved upon the face of the waters.

　　[bbe] And the earth was waste and without form; and it was dark on the face of the deep：and the Spirit of God was moving on the face of the waters.

1：3 [hb5]神说，要有光，就有了光。

　　[kjv] And God said, Let there be light：and there was light.

　　[bbe] And God said, Let there be light：and there was light.

1：4 [hb5]神看光是好的，就把光暗分了。

　　[kjv] And God saw the light, that it was good：and God divided the light from the darkness.

　　[bbe] And God, looking on the light, saw that it was good：and God made a division between the light and the dark.

1：5 [hb5]神称光为昼，称暗为夜。有晚上，有早晨，这是头一日。

　　[kjv] And God called the light Day, and the darkness he called Night. And the evening and the morning were the first day.

　　[bbe] Naming the light, Day, and the dark, Night. And there was evening and there was morning, the first day.

对比双语语料库，我们可以看出英语译文中，[kjv]的译文比较典雅，而[bbe]的译文则比较通俗。通过这样的比较，有利于提高翻译的质量。

七、翻译记忆软件与本土化软件工具

"翻译记忆"（Translation Memories，简称 TMs）软件能够保存和重复使用翻译工作者已经翻译好的译文。这些译文对于新的翻译文件来看，是"似曾相识的记忆"，这使我们想起我国古诗中的名句："似曾相识燕归来。"翻译记忆软件在内容修订和更新的全过程中能保存和重复使用译文。如果有新的资料需要翻译，可以重复使用原来存储在翻译记忆中的译文。原来的译文与新的资料之间要进行匹配，或者是精确匹配（exact match），或者完全匹配（full match），或者是模糊匹配（fuzzy match），翻译记忆软件可以根据匹配的不同水平来决定翻译策略。

翻译记忆与机器翻译不同,机器翻译软件是一种软件系统,它自己进行翻译,提供质量不高的译文草稿。而翻译记忆软件保存和重复使用人工翻译工作者的译文,保证了译文的质量,减少了翻译的开支,降低了翻译的成本,避免了重复的翻译,而且,还可以保证翻译的一致性,特别是保证术语翻译的一致性。翻译记忆是企业重要的知识资产,作为知识资产的翻译记忆库,可以在公司内得到最大程度的应用和重复使用。中央翻译记忆库中保存的译文越多,降低的成本也就越多。我们可以采用集中管理翻译记忆库的方法,来提高翻译记忆库的使用效率。例如,TRADOS 公司的翻译记忆系列产品 Translation's Workbench (http://www. trados. com)。本土化(localization)是商品适应本土市场要求的过程。在本土化过程中,除了翻译工作之外,还要考虑本土地区的文化习俗。本土化软件有必要把与翻译有关的各种功能结合起来,实现"所见即所得"(What You See Is What You Get,简称 WYSIWYG) 的服务。例如,Corel 公司的本土化软件 Catalyst (http://alchemysoftware. ie),以及本土化软件 Passolo (Pass Software Localizer) (http://www. passolo. com)。

八、机助翻译系统

由于机器翻译的质量还不能尽如人意,因此,目前可以采用"人助机译"(human-assisted machine translation,简称 HAMT)的办法或者"机助人译"(machine-aided human translation,简称 MAHT)的办法。在 HAMT 中,可以由人来进行译前编辑(pre-editing)或译后编辑(post-editing),或者进行人机交互(interaction),主要的翻译工作基本上是由机器来完成的。因此,这样的机器翻译有时也叫做"全自动机器翻译"(full automatic machine translation,简称 FAMT)。在 MAHT 中,借助于电子词典和翻译记忆等电子翻译工具,源语言的分析和解码工作都是通过翻译人员手工完成的。有时,可以用"机助翻译"(computer-assisted translation 或者 computer-aided translation,简称 CAT)这个术语来统称 HAMT 和 MAHT,因为两者都要使用计算机,只是前者的翻译工作主要由机器来完成,后者的翻译工作主要由人来完成。在机助翻译中,应当综合地使用上面所述的各种翻译工具来提高翻译的质量。例如,我们可以使用计算机辅助术语管理系统,在翻译前进行候选术语的抽取和术语搜索。候选术语的抽取和术语搜索的目的在于决定在术语数据库中究竟应该包含一些什么样的候选术语。当源语言中的术语确定之后,术语搜索的目的就是确定目标语言中的恰当的术语以便准确地表示概念。术语搜索可以利用各种语言资源(因特网上的资源和术语数据库)。例如,如果在术语数据库中已经存在单词术语 thermal 和 layer,我们发现在术语数据库中没有 thermal layer 这个多词术语,我们就要把这个术语看做候选术语,使用计算机辅助术语管理系统把它加入到术语数据库中。在翻译过程中,我们可以使用计算机辅助术语管理系统进行自动术语查询。自动术语查询实际上就是在术语平面上进行术语的机器翻译。例如,在英汉机器翻译中,当源语言中出现 flowchart 和 flow diagram 这两个同义术语时,计算机能够自动地把它们在目标语言中统一地翻译成"流程图",而无须翻译人员进行手工翻译。在翻译后,我们可以使用计算机辅助术语管理系统进行术语一致性检查和不合格术语检查,也可以编制检查程序来检查术语的一致性。例如,如果我们的系统倾向于把 thermocline 翻译成"温跃层",而翻译人员手工把它翻译成"温变层",检查程序应当自动地把它更正为"温跃层",以便保持术语的一致性。另外,还要把那些不合格的术语标出来,以便引起人们的注意。在机助翻译中,我们也可以使用翻译记忆技术和双语对应语料库的资源,使用联机的语言资源和 CD‑ROM 上的语言资源。如果我们掌握了信息时代的这些翻译工具,就可以大大地提高翻译的效率,满足信息时代对翻译的迫切需要。

【延伸阅读】

[1] Austermuehl, F. *Electronic Tools for Translators*. St: Jerome Publishing, 2001.

[2] Bedard, C. Translation Memory Seeks Sentence-oriented Translator …. *Traduire*, 2000: 186. http://www. terminotix. com/eng/info/mem _ 1. htm. Visited 7 September 2005.

[3] Esselink, B. *A Practical Guide to Localization*. Amsterdam/Philadelphia: John Benjamins, 2000.

[4] Lockwood, R. Machine Translation and Controlled Authoring at Caterpillar//Robert C. Sprung (ed.), *Translating into Success: Cutting-edge strategies for going multilingual in a global age*(pp. 187–202). Amsterdam/Philadelphia: John Benjamins, 2000.

[5] Megale, F. *Diritto d'autore del traduttore*. Napoli: Editoriale Scientifica, 2004.

[6] Jurafsky, D. , & Martin, J. 自然语言处理综论. 冯志伟, 孙乐, 译. 电子工业出版社, 2005.

[7] 冯志伟. 机器翻译研究. 北京:中国对外翻译出版公司, 2004.

[8] 冯志伟. 应用语言学新论——语言应用研究的三大支柱. 北京:当代世界出版社, 2003.

【问题与思考】

1. 各种电子工具是如何影响和拓展人们的能力的?
2. 根据文章,译员与客户之间是如何进行联系和交流的?
3. 在机器翻译存在的时代中,译员们面临哪些有利条件和不利条件?
4. 人们对机器翻译存在的误解主要是什么? 如何克服它们?
5. 译者如何充分使用因特网上的语言翻译资源?
6. 如何更好地使翻译记忆软件与软件工具本土化?

第二章 翻译的电子工具

导 论

近年来,随着互联网,尤其是智能手机的飞速发展和普及,翻译工作者可资使用的电子工具愈来愈多。与传统的翻译工具,如双语词典、文化词典、背景词典等相比,电子工具具有便捷、功能强大等优点。这无疑会大大促进翻译工作者的翻译工作,提高翻译速度和翻译质量。

究其本质,翻译电子工具可以从根本上提高翻译工作者的翻译能力,即双语语言能力、百科知识能力、专业知识等。既可以帮助译者更好地理解原文,又可以帮助译者尽可能地道、准确地用目的语表达原作的意义、意图、思想等。可以毫不夸张地说,今日之翻译已经离不开电子翻译工具的参与。

翻译的电子工具数量庞大、名目繁多。何少庆(2010)将译者的辅助工具主要分为:网络工具、桌面词典、在线翻译、机器辅助翻译等。[①] 在这种时代背景下,翻译学科面临两个新的课题,即:

(1) 从实践层面上看,如何充分利用电子工具提高翻译质量?

(2) 从理论层面上看,翻译的研究范式发生了什么变化?

当然,由信息技术和互联网带所引发的翻译电子工具的发展不只引发了翻译范式的变化,也为翻译教学和翻译培训带来新的革命。在这种背景下,翻译教学和翻译培训在内容和方法上也应当做相应的调整,以适应时代和市场的变化和需求。

本章共选取了三篇文章。Jose Ramon Biau Gil 所撰的文章 Teaching Electronic Tools for Translators Online 认为,在挑选网上翻译课程的学生时,应该重视备选学生的计算机能力,对于翻译技术课程而言,更是如此。John Hutchins 撰写的 Multiple Uses of Machine Translation and Computerized Translation Tools 重点探讨了电子工具对机器翻译的作用,并介绍了许多具体的运用。孙鸿仁教授的论文《信息时代与翻译实践》着重介绍了信息时代的电子翻译工具的内容、特征以及使用方法。

---

① 何少庆:从译者生存状况调查报告看辅助翻译工具的应用[J],浙江师范大学学报(社科版),2010(2):102-103.

选 文

选文一 Teaching Electronic Tools for Translators Online

José Ramón Biau Gil

导 言

　　本文写于 2006 年，收录于 Anthony Pym 等学者编著的 *Translation Technology and its Teaching* 一书。

　　作者 Jose Ramon Biau Gil 现任教于西班牙的洛维拉·依维尔基里大学（Rovirai Virgili University），其研究兴趣包括：翻译与译员技术、本土化与翻译等。与 Anthony Pym，Carmina Fallada 等人合编 *Innovation and E-learning in Translator Training*（2003），并写过多篇与翻译技术有关的论文。本文谈及网上培训、翻译技术、网上课程、学习工具与资源、教学方法、练习示范等内容。作者认为，对于不善于使用计算机的学生而言，面对面的教学方式更为有效，而计算机水平高的学生则可以借助于计算机技术独立地解决问题。以此背景为基础，翻译课的练习需要做出相应的调整。

1　On Online Training

There is a huge demand for online courses. Nowadays, studying is not something that people do before entering the labor market; it is a lifetime activity. Today's professionals are ready to invest in training, but they must combine it with other adult responsibilities such as working full-time and raising children. The traditional university face-to-face teaching system thus fails to provide an adequate means of training for this sector of potential students. On top of that, online training is suitable not only for practicing professionals, but also for other profiles (traditional young students included), so the scope of student intake is very wide.

There is also a strong supply of online courses. In an effort to catch up with the times and attract more students, most universities offer now virtual or semi-virtual courses. This is as true in the field of translation as it is in any other field of professional training.

2　On Translation Technologies

Personal computers and the Internet have brought about a shift in the way translators work. Twenty years ago most freelance translators used a typewriter or dictated translations to a secretary; ten years ago they had a computer with a word processor; nowadays most translators need to know how to use translation-memory software and terminology managers, and must be expert Internet users. They might also have replaced the secretary with a voice-recognition software system. Telecommuting is now a reality within the profession, since electronic means of communication mean that customers and translators no longer need to be in the same geographical area, and members of the same translation team may live and work in different places. The Internet (and, by extension, computer proficiency) is not only a source of information or a tool for translations, but also the platform for communication with clients, agencies and fellow translators.

3   Online Courses at Tarragona

The Intercultural Studies Group at the Universitat Rovira i Virgili in Tarragona currently offers two certificate courses in 100% online mode. One of those courses is the "Online Postgraduate Certificate in Technical Translation and Electronic Tools". Here we use data from the way that course was taught between October and December 2002. There were 12 students, from Bolivia, France, Spain, the United Kingdom, the United States and Venezuela. The course tasks were based on the English-Spanish language pair, so all students were fluent on both languages and were expected to work in both directions. English was the language of instruction, but Spanish was also used when interacting with the students.

The course comprised 50 hours of learning time, distributed over ten weeks. Of those 50 hours, 5 (10%) were devoted to the translation market, 15 (30%) to translation strategies, 15 (30%) to CAT tools and 15 (30%) to translation projects. The module topics were as follows:

- Advanced Internet searches
- Revision tools with MS Word
- Terminology management with MS Excel
- HTML basics: Creating a simple website with Netscape Composer
- HTML for translators: Identifying translatable text inside code
- Using Translation Memories:
- Trados
- WordFast
- DejaVu

4   Learning Tools and Resources Available for Students

Although there are many online learning platforms available (WebCT, Blackboard,

Moodle), this course was based on very simple technology allowing maximum accessibility.

There was a course website with all the lessons and exercises available in web format. If the exercises to be done in a specific file format (Excel, PowerPoint), they were posted in that format.

There was also a non-moderated e-mail discussion list, which was the main means of communication between teachers and students. All the participants could send messages to the list, and the messages would be forwarded automatically to all course participants (teachers and students). Messages were also automatically posted to a website, so it was possible to read messages even if students had no access to their own e-mail account temporarily.

From the course website there was a link to the Shared Files, a web-based application (BSCW) to put and share files on the Internet without the need for any extra tool or knowledge. An Internet connection and a web browser was all the students needed. Students posted their work, and teachers posted their feedback. The Shared Files were also used to share some off-topic materials, such as articles on translation not used for the lessons, personal pictures and jokes.

A chat channel was made available from the course website. Students were free to use it at any time as a means to communicate with each other, apart from the scheduled sessions with the trainers.

According to replies to a questionnaire given to students after the course, the website was easy to use: none of the students said it was difficult to use or that they would have liked more time to get used to the learning environment.

Time for the sessions was calculated based on the experience of face-to-face classes.

5　Pedagogical Approach

The course was very practical, making students translate texts and otherwise practice the lesson contents. Tasks were set at the end of each lesson. The basic interaction pattern was as follows:

For each lesson, the teacher sent a message to the list specifying what had to be read and which exercises the students should do, and gave a deadline for the exercises. If students had doubts or comments on the activities, they would send another message to the list, and the teacher or another student would reply. This developed discussion threads. When students finished the exercises, they posted them to the Shared Files, teachers revised the tasks and posted the feedback in the Shared Files. This led to discussion on the exercises and the feedback (difficult points, applications in the market, investment in technology, questions on the feedback, ethical issues, etc.). Finally, the teacher would send another e-mail indicating further readings and activities, thus starting the cycle again.

As the course advanced, the session threads overlapped. Students also sent e-mails and opened new lines of discussion based on their own needs and interests. All this enriched the communication between all the course participants and gave an added value to the list.

6　The E-mail List

We analyzed the topics of all the e-mails sent to the list. It was found that the e-mails could be grouped into the following four general areas, following the classification used by Fallada (2003) and adapted from Schlager (2003: 7). The description of each of the categories is as follows:

- Pedagogy: messages directly related to course contents.
- Technology: messages on technology issues not directly related to the course contents.
- Management: messages on the overall functioning of the course (pedagogy and technology excluded)
- Social events: messages with personal information, organization of local meetings or information relevant to translators.

Many e-mails did not fall neatly into one category or another. When an e-mail had two topics, for instance, we used the following criteria to allocate them to a category:

- Position: if there was more than one topic in one single e-mail, the first topic was picked.
- Length: if there was more than one topic in one single e-mail, the lengthiest topic was picked.

If the two previous criteria contradicted, length had priority. The results of this analysis are shown below.

Category	Percentage of total
Pedagogy	38
Technology	26
Social events	21
Management	15

Here we see that, of all the messages sent to the e-mail list, only 38% were on class issues. That could be seen as negative, since it means that more than half the e-mails were on issues other than the specified business of the course. However, the course organizers had actually fostered the sending of non-pedagogical messages. Although the course syllabus included some technology, the educational goal was not to focus on that alone but to expand the technological horizon of both students and teachers. Thus, comments on software not used for our course were very much welcome. Also, we expected some extra-curricular questions regarding computer skills, as this was a course dealing with computer programs and we did not want people to be silent when facing a problem.

Management e-mails dealt with the overall functioning of the course. In a face-to-face course with local students, teachers and students may share the same experience and assumptions on how the course should work. In an online environment (new to some of the participants) with people from several countries, rules and guidelines had to be made explicit, in our case by emailing to the list.

The justification for having off-topic social messages in our discussion list is very simple: to fight student distress. When studying online, many students feel isolated, which may lead to them dropping out of the course (Palloff and Pratt 1999: 29). By fostering social messages, we expected to build a greater sense of community, and that this would help students stay motivated. The social e-mails were thus thought to have a positive effect on the overall pedagogical results of the course participants, apart from making the experience more enjoyable for everyone.

When looking at the number of e-mails on technology sent to the list, we found that both low-tech and hi-tech students sent the same number of messages. However, this did not mean that both groups needed the same amount of teacher support. There was a notable difference in the way students interacted. Students with good computer skills did the exercises and then sent comments to the list, adding extra value to the task by talking about their experience and raising awareness on interesting issues. Students with low computer skills sent questions on how to do the tasks, since the written lessons and tasks on the web were not clear enough for them. Also, some of the questions were sent more than once and some questions needed more than one message to be answered. Further, despite the teachers' efforts to have all the messages sent to the list, some students sent private e-mails to the teachers asking for help on technology issues. Those messages are not represented in our statistics.

7　The Sample Exercise

Two chat sessions were organized. The first session was set up as an open discussion on practical issues such as prices and the advantages and drawbacks of specific tools. All the students were invited to participate. The second session was designed to provide individualized, synchronic support to two students who needed extra help with the following exercise.

Students were expected to do advanced searches on the Internet. By restricting the search of two terms to a specific country domain (. es,. uk,. ar, etc.), they had to find out which term was used more widely in a given country. All the necessary steps were available in a web-based lesson. Some students did the task and sent comments, others asked the list for help and received replies to most of their questions. There were, though, two students who did not manage to complete the activity. For them, we set up a chat session in order to work synchronically, to identify the problems and to find a solution.

The chat session lasted just over one hour. At the end of it, the students managed to do the assigned task, but failed to apply the mechanics to other similar searches. Both students were then invited to come to the teacher's office to have a face-to-face session: only one was able to accept, as the other lived on a different continent. The teacher saw the student working on the computer and identified the student's problems quickly (missing quotation marks, commas, spaces, Boolean operators in the wrong place, etc.). The teacher made the student aware of the importance of commas and spaces when doing advanced searches, and performed the search before the student's eyes. After that, the student was able to apply the concepts to other searches. The whole session took less than 20 minutes. The Tarragona program runs the same activity in a face-to-face environment for Masters students, who usually spend one hour to learn the concepts (equivalent to reading the lesson in the online environment) and do the tasks.

8 Conclusions

In the online course, students with low computer skills needed to spend much more time than expected in order to attain the course objectives. Moreover, they needed more time from the teacher, who was obliged to provide a lot of individualized attention to each of the students with low computer skills.

From this general experience, we can conclude:

• For students with low computer skills, a face-to-face environment is more fruitful than an online environment.

• Students with good computer skills tend to be very independent learners: they can manage technological problems on their own.

• Students with low computer skills are dependent learners: they need a lot of external help, usually requested from the teacher. These students tend to seek "the human factor", that is, a person to help them, rather than find solutions by themselves.

• Economically speaking, the teachers' income needs to be calculated to compensate for the time commitment involved in online education.

• Blended learning environments (combined face-to-face and online sessions) cover a wider range of students' needs and abilities.

9 Adjustments

On the basis of this experience, some modifications have been made to the course design:

• The number of exercises on electronic tools has been reduced so that students have extra time to download, install and interact with these new programs, since the learning curve is longer in online environments. The original program, based on experience in the face-to-face environment, proved to be too ambitious for the average profile of students in the given amount of time.

• Prospective students are given more detailed information on the skills they are expected to have in order to finish the course successfully.

• Teachers are now paid according to a formula that accounts for the number of students they teach as well as the hours of course content.

10 Final thoughts

Online education involves efforts that are different from those demanded by face-to-face classes. The same activity may have very different timing depending on whether it is offered in a face-to-face, blended or online environment.

To be an effective online learner or teacher, one must be familiar with computers, be ready to interact with them, and be very independent at solving potential problems, as participants do not share the same physical space. Moreover, communication skills are crucial for the course to move forward smoothly. Students with low computer skills may have problems with the means of delivery, and this is likely to affect their performance. In courses on technology, the ability to interact with a computer is even more important. It is thus crucial to check the student's initialcomputer literacy so as to make sure they can get the most out of the course.

选文二 Multiple Uses of Machine Translation and Computerized Translation Tools

John Hutchins

导 言

本文载于 2009 年召开的 ISMTCL: International Symposium on Data Mining and Sense Mining, Machine Translation and Controlled Languages, and their application to emergencies and safety critical domains 论文集。

作者 John Hutchins 的研究兴趣主要在于机器翻译及其翻译工具。其主要作品包括: *Machine translation: past, present, future*(此书于 1993 年被译为汉语,题目为《机器翻译:过去、现在、未来》),*An introduction to machine translation* 等,并有十几篇论文发表。

作者首先扼要介绍了机器翻译的历史,之后介绍了 20 世纪 70 年代、80 年代以及 90 年代初译者常用的翻译工具。同时,作者还介绍了 20 世纪 90 年代以来翻译工作者可以使用的网络翻译工具。"语音翻译"部分涉及较早的"语音翻译软件"及其用途。接着,作者指出,网络翻译工具新发展应该是开放的杂合系统。最后,作者认为,机器翻译融合了信息检索、信息提取与分析、问题解答、总结以及技术编程。

1　Traditional Uses

Machine translation (MT) has a long history—it is 60 years since Warren Weaver's memorandum of July 1949 launched research on the topic. For most of that history—at least 40 years—it was assumed that there were only two ways of using MT systems. The first was to use MT to produce publishable translations, generally with human editing assistance ("dissemination"). The second was to offer the rough unedited MT versions to readers able to extract some idea of the content ("assimilation"). In neither case were translators directly involved—MT was not seen as a computer aid for translators.

The first MT systems operated on the traditional large-scale mainframe computers in large companies and government organizations. The outputs of these systems were then revised (post-edited) by human translators or editors familiar with both source and target languages. There was opposition from translators (particularly those with the task of postediting) but the advantages of fast and consistent output has made large-scale MT cost-effective. In order to improve the quality of the raw MT output many large companies included methods of "controlling" the input language (by restricting vocabulary and syntactic structures)—by such means, the problems of disambiguation and alternative interpretations of structure could be minimised and the quality of the output could be improved. Companies such as Xerox used MT systems with a "controlled language" from the late 1970s—many companies followed their example, and the Smart Corporation specializes to this day in setting up "controlled language" MT systems for large companies in North America. In a few cases, it was possible to develop systems specifically for the particular "sublanguage" of the texts to be translated (as in the Meteo system for weather forecasts). Indeed, nearly all systems operating in large organizations are in some way "adapted" to the subject areas they operate in: earth moving machines (Caterpillar), job applications (JobBank in Canada), health reports (Global Health Intelligence Network), patents (Japan Patent Information Office), health and social affairs (Pan American Health Organization), police data (ProLingua), software (SAP), and many more. These large-scale applications of MT continue to expand and develop, and they will do so into the foreseeable future.

Included in such expansion will undoubtedly be the further application of MT to the localization of products. Localization became a specialist application of MT and translation memories in the early 1990s. Initially stimulated by the need of software producers to market versions of their systems in other languages, simultaneously or very closely following the launch of the version in the original language (usually English), localization has become a necessity in the global markets of today. Given the time pressures, the many languages to be translated into, MT seemed the obvious solution. In addition, the documentation (e. g. software manuals) was both internally repetitive and changed little from one product to another and from one edition to the next. It was possible to use translation memories and to develop "controlled" terminologies for MT systems. The process involves more than just translation of texts. Localization means the adaptation of products (and their documentation) to particular cultural conditions, ranging from correct expression of dates (day-month-year vs. month-day-year), times (12-hour vs. 14-hour), address conventions and abbreviations, to the reformatting (re-paragraphing) and re-arranging of complete texts to suit expectations of recipients.

The second use ("dissemination") was initially rather reluctantly conceded by MT researchers. With the coming of MT software on microcomputers or personal computer (PC) systems the situation changed. Although intended for professional translators for the production of publishable translations (e. g. the systems in the early 1980s from ALPS and Weidner), they were soon followed by systems (many from leading Japanese manufacturers of PCs) which were clearly intended both for translators and for non-translators ("occasional translators") mainly interested in the "assimilation" function. Such PC systems now cover an increasingly wider range of language pairs and run on a wide range of operating systems. As long as desktop PCs continue to be manufactured and used, this method of delivering MT will continue. What has always been uncertain is how purchasers have been using these systems. In the case of large-scale (mainframe) "enterprise" systems it has always been clear that MT is used to produce drafts which are then edited by bilingual personnel. This may also be the case for PC systems, i. e. it may be that they have been and are used to create "drafts" which are then edited to a higher quality. On the other hand, it seems more likely that users are "occasional translators" who want just to get some idea of the contents (the basic "message") of foreign texts and are not concerned about the quality of translations. This usage is generally referred to "assimilation" (in contrast to the other aim: "dissemination"). We know (anecdotally) that some users of PC MT systems have trusted them too much and have used "raw" (unedited) MT translations as if they were as good as human translations—probably by users unfamiliar with the target language and unaware of the problems of translation by computer. However, it is an unfortunate fact that we do not know in any detail how PC systems have been and are being used. We know that sales of systems continue to be high enough for manufacturers to remain in business over many years, but it is suspected by many observers that purchasers rarely use systems after their initial enthusiasm, once they learn how poor the quality of MT output can be.

The MT engines of both mainframe (client-server) and PC systems are overwhelmingly "general purpose" systems, i. e. they are built to deal with texts in any subject domain. As mentioned, "enterprise" systems (particularly controlled language systems) usually concentrate on particular subject areas. By contrast there are few PC-based subject-specific systems; exceptions are versions of the English/Japanese Transfer system for medical texts and for patents. On the whole, however, PC systems deal with specific subjects by making available subject glossaries, which can be ranked in preference by users. For some PC systems the range of dictionaries is very wide, embracing most engineering topics, computer science, business and marketing, law, sports, cookery, music, etc. How much they are used in practice is of course unknown.

2　Aids for Translators

For most of MT history, translators have been wary of the impact of computers in their work. They obviously did not want to be "slaves" to mainframe MT output—post—editing what they could do more quickly and accurately than the machines. Many saw MT as a threat to their jobs—little knowing the inherent limitations of MT. During the 1980s and 1990s, the situation changed. Translators were offered an increasing range of computer aids. First came text-related glossaries and concordances, word processing on increasingly affordable microcomputers, then terminological resources on computer databases, access to Internet resources, and finally (most significantly of all) translation memories. The idea of storing and retrieving already existing translations arose in the late 1970s and early 1980s, but did not come to fruition until the availability of large electronic textual databases and with facilitating bilingual text alignment. The first commercial translation memory systems came in the early 1990s (Trados, Transit, Deja Vu, WordFast, etc.) All translators are now aware of their value as cost-effective aids, and they are increasingly asking for systems which go further than simple phrase and word matching—more MT-like facilities in other words. With this growing interest, researchers are devoting more efforts to the real computer-based needs of translators. As just two examples there are the TransSearch and TransType systems: the first a sophisticated text concordancer, the second exploiting translation memories by predicting the words a translator may select when translating a text similar to ones already translated.

3　Special Devices, Online MT

From the middle of the 1990s onwards, mainframe and PC translation systems have been joined by a range of other types. First should be mentioned the obvious further miniaturization of software: the numerous commercial systems for hand-held devices. There are a bewildering variety of "pocket translators" in the marketplace. Many, such as the Ectaco range of special devices, are in effect computerized versions of the familiar phrase-book or pocket dictionary, and they are marketed primarily to the tourist and business traveller. The dictionary sizes are often quite small, and where they include phrases, they are obviously limited. However, they are sold in large numbers and for a very wide range of language pairs. As with PC systems, there is no indication of how successful in actual use they may be—it cannot be much different from the "success" of traditional printed phrase books. (Users may be able to ask their way to the bus station, for example, but they may not be able to understand the answer.) Recently, since early in this decade, many of these hand-held devices have included voice output of phrases, an obvious attraction for those unfamiliar with pronunciation in the target language.

With the widespread and growing use of mobile telephones, there are an increasing number of manufacturers providing translation software for these devices. MT is an obvious extension of their text facilities. The range of languages is so far not very wide, limited on the whole to the "commercially dominant" languages: English, French, German, and Spanish. In some cases, the translation software is built-in. But now, more frequently, the translation software is accessed from Internet database servers which can therefore provide large dictionaries and some linguistic processing. The next obvious development is the use of mobile devices as terminals for online MT services.

This has indeed been one of the most significant changes since the middle of the 1990s: the availability of free MT services on the Internet. Online MT services appeared in the early 1990s but they were not free. In 1988 Syst ran in France offered a subscription to its translation software using the French postal services Minitel network. At about the same time, Fujitsu made its Atlas English-Japanese and Japanese-English systems available through the online service Niftyserve. Then in 1992 CompuServe launched its MT service, initially restricted to selected forums, but which proved highly popular, and in 1994 Globalink also offered an online subscription service—texts were submitted online and translations returned by e-mail. A similar service was provided by Syst ran Express. However, it was undoubtedly the launch of AltaVista's Babelfish service in 1997 (based on the various Syst ran MT systems) that caused the greatest publicity. Not only was it free but results were (virtually) immediate. Within the decade, the Babelfish service has been joined by FreeTranslation (using the Intergraph system), Gist-in-Time, ProMT, PARS, Microsoft Windows Live Translator, and many others; in most cases, these are online versions of already existing PC-based or mainframe systems, and primarily rule-based. The exception has been the latest entrant, the Google Translate, based on the latest developments in statistical MT—the coverage of languages is expanding rapidly beyond competitors, and the text resources are vast. The great attraction of online MT services was (and is) that they are free to users (even if not to providers)—it is evidently the expectation of the developers is that free online use will lead to sales of PC translation software (when available), although the evidence for this has not been shown; or that it will encourage the use of the fee-based "valued-added" post-editing services offered to users (e. g. by FreeTranslation). Whether any of this has in fact happened is not known.

While online MT has undoubtedly raised the profile of MT for the general public, there have, of course, been drawbacks. To most users "discovering" online MT services the idea of automatic translation has been (and is) something completely new—despite the availability of PC translation software. Attracted by the possibilities, many users "tested" the services by inputting for translation sentences containing idiomatic phrases, ambiguous words and complex structures, and even proverbs and deliberately opaque sayings. A favourite method of "evaluation" was back translation ("to-and-fro" translation), into another language and then back into the original—a method which might appear valid to the uninitiated but which is not satisfactory. Not surprisingly, they found often that the results were unintelligible, they found that MT was liable to much "faulty" and "inaccurate" results, that MT suffered from many limitations—all well-known to company users and to purchasers of PC software. Numerous commentators have enjoyed finding fault with online MT and, by implication with MT itself. Users have undoubtedly been gravely disappointed by the poor quality; there is no doubt that the less knowledge users have of the language of the original texts the more value they attach to the MT output.

However, we know very little (indeed almost nothing) about who uses online MT and what for. We do not know their ages, backgrounds, knowledge of languages, we do not know how many translate only into their native language, how many use online MT to translate into an unknown foreign language, how many are translators using MT as rough drafts, how many use the subject glossaries available, and so forth. Almost all that we do know are the surprising facts that translation of web pages is very much a minor use (no more than about 15% at best), that the average length of texts submitted is just 20 words, and that more than 50% of submissions are one-or two-word phrases. It had been anticipated that longer texts would be submitted—the general maximum length of 150 words is clearly no impediment—and that much of the translation would be of web pages. The surprisingly low submission of texts longer than a few words seems to suggest that online MT is being used primarily for dictionary consultation—despite the availability of many free online dictionaries—and perhaps therefore by people with some familiarity with foreign languages. Whatever ways people are using them, overall usage of online MT continues to increase exponentially (e. g. FreeTranslation from 50,000 in 1999 to 3.4 million in 2006; the totals for Babelfish are much higher).

The translation of web pages—a facility provided by PC systems before online MT services came—has complications in addition to the obvious problems of rendering the often colloquial and culture-dependent nature of the texts. Many web pages include text in graphic format, which no MT system can deal with, and therefore often much of the webpage will be untranslated. This may account for the low usage of webpage translation on online MT systems. It is thus all the more surprising that so many website developers and owners recommend users to online MT services for translation of their web pages. It is clear that they do not appreciate the poor results of any MT version, nor are they aware of consequent negative impacts on their company or products.

A recent development is systems designed for website localization. As mentioned above, localization became a specialist application of MT and translation memories in the early 1990s. The extension into website localization was an obvious move—which came, however, not until after 2000. The most significant development has been the introduction of specialized systems, notably IBM Websphere, which is designed for Internet service providers and for large corporations to supply and edit translations of their own web pages localised to their specific domain, as well for cross-language communication with customers and for providing "gist" translations internally.

The limitations of MT when dealing with colloquial and elliptical "normal" language—as opposed to the formal written texts of books and magazines—is highlighted by its problems with electronic mail. Just as most PC systems have provided facilities for translating web pages, many seek to embrace e-mail text as well—with what success or user satisfaction is unknown. Few researchers have focused specifically on this type of text; they have been mainly in Japan and Korea; and even fewer have marketed such systems. An exception is Translation, which offers online translation of e-mails for companies. Subscriptions vary according to the level of service, and whether web-based or located on a client-server system.

Even more challenging perhaps is the language of social networking sites. Some tentative attempts have been made which highlight and illustrate the similarities of such texts with spoken language and the similarities of their shared problems. But the huge possibilities of devising MT for social networking in general appear to have not yet been tackled.

4 Speech Translation

As mentioned earlier, an increasing number of phrase-book systems offer voice output. This facility is also increasingly available for PC based translation software—it seems that Globalink in 1995 was the earliest—and it seems quite likely that it will be an additional feature for online MT sometime in the future. But automatic speech synthesis of text-to-text translation is not at all the same as genuine "speech-to-speech translation," the focus of research efforts in Japan (ATR), the United States (Carnegie-Mellon University), Germany (Verbmobil project) and Italy (ITC-irst, NESPOLE) for many years since the late 1980s. The research in speech translation is beset with numerous problems, not just variability of voice input but also the nature of spoken language. By contrast with written language, spoken language is colloquial, elliptical, context-dependent, interpersonal, and primarily in the form of dialogues. MT has focused on well-formed, technical and scientific language and has tended to neglect informal modes of communication. Speech translation therefore represents a radical departure from traditional MT. Complexities of speech translation can, however, be reduced by restricting communication to relatively narrow domains—a favourite for many researchers has been business communication, booking of hotel rooms, negotiating dates of meetings, etc. From these long-term projects no commercial systems have appeared yet. There are, however, other areas of speech translation which do have working (but not yet commercial) systems. These are communication in patient-doctor and other health consultations, communication by soldiers in military (field) operations, and communication in the tourism domain.

The potentialities of health-communication applications are obvious, particularly for communication involving immigrant and other "minority" languages. However, there are different views of the most effective and most appropriate methods. In some cases, communication can be one way, e. g. a "doctor" or "medical professional" (nurse, paramedic, pharmacist, etc.) asks the "patient" a question, which can be answered nonverbally or by a simple "yes" or "no." In other cases, communication may be two-way or interactive, e. g. patient and doctor consulting a screen displaying possible "health" conditions. Or communication may be via a "phrasebook"-type system with voice input to locate phrases and spoken output of the translated phrase and/or with interactive multimodal assistance. Nearly all systems are currently somewhat inflexible and limited to specific narrow domains. Speech translation itself may be only one factor in successful health-related consultation since cultural and environmental issues are also involved; and whether medical personnel should be the initiators and "in control" is another issue. However, before even such issues of usability and appropriateness can be resolved, the robustness of speech translation even in highly constrained domains has to be satisfactory—the weakest point is still automatic speech recognition, even though domain-specific translation itself is also still inadequate.

In the military field, the MT team at Carnegie-Mellon University developed a speech translation system (DIPLOMAT) which can be quickly adapted to new languages, i. e. languages where the US Army is deployed (Serbo-Croat, Haitian Creole, Korean). The system was based on an example-based MT approach; spoken language was matched against phrases (examples) in the database and the translations output by a speech synthesis module. An evaluation "in the field" concluded that the speech components were satisfactory but the MT component was not adequate-translation was far too slow in practice, and a feedback ("back translation") module enabling users to check the appropriateness of the translation introduced additional errors. Further development was not pursued. However, in the same domain, another system on a hand-held PDA device has been more successful it seems. This device (Phraselator, from VoxTec, initially funded by DARPA) contains a database of phrases in the foreign language which the English-speaking user can select from a screen. Output is not synthesised speech but pre-recorded by native speakers. The device has been used by the US Army in various operations in Croatia, Iraq, Indonesia, including civilian emergency situations (e. g. the tsunami relief in 2005), by the US navy, by law enforcement officers, etc. A wide range of languages is now covered and the device and its software are now more widely available commercially.

One of the most obvious applications of speech translation is the assistance of tourists in foreign countries. Many of the organizations mentioned earlier are involved in developing systems (ATR in Japan, ITC-irst in Italy, and Carnegie-Mellon University in the USA). Many groups are utilizing the BTEC corpus of Japanese/English tourism and travel example expressions; but most have extended investigation to Chinese and English, Arabic and English and Italian and English. A welcome feature of this activity is the collaborative efforts and the exchange of resources by research groups, e. g. at the International Workshops on Spoken Language Translation since 2005. In many cases, translation is restricted to "standard" phrases extracted from corpora of dialogues and interactions in tourist situations. However, in recent years, researchers have moved to systems capable of dealing with "spontaneous speech," i. e. something more like real-life applications. Despite the amount of research in an apparently highly-restricted domain it is clear that commercially viable products still lie some way in the future. In the meantime, for some years yet, the market will see only the voice-output phrase-book devices and systems mentioned above.

5 Rapid Development, Open Source, Hybrid Systems

One of the advantages of statistical machine translation (SMT)—the current focus of most MT research—is claimed to be the rapid production of systems in new language pairs. Researchers do not need to know the languages involved as long as they have confidence in the reliability of the corpora which they work with. This is in contrast to the slower development of rule-based MT (RBMT) systems which require careful lexical and grammatical analyses by researchers familiar with both source and target languages. Nearly all commercially available MT systems (whether for mainframe, client-server, or PC) are rule-based systems, the result of many years of development. Statistical MT has only recently appeared on the marketplace. The LanguageWeaver company, an offshoot of the research group at the University of Southern California, began marketing SMT systems in 2002. It began with Arabic-English and has now added many other language pairs. (Many users of these systems are US government agencies involved in information gathering and analysis operations—see below.)

Increasingly, resources for statistical MT (components, algorithms, etc.) are widely available as "open source" materials. The Apertium system from Spain has been the basis for freely-available MT systems for Spanish, Portuguese, Galician, Catalan, etc. There are other open source translation systems (less widely used), such as GPL Trans, but it is to be expected that more will be available in the coming years.

Many researchers believe that the future for MT lies in the development of hybrid systems combining the best of the statistical and rule-based approaches. In the meantime, however, until a viable framework for hybrid MT appears, experiments are being made with multi-engine systems and with adopting statistical techniques with rule-based (and example-based) systems. The multi-engine approach involves the translation of a given text by two or more different MT architectures (SMT and RBMT, for example) and the integration of outputs for the selection of the "best" output—for which statistical techniques can be used. The idea is attractive and quality improvements have been achieved, but it is difficult to see this approach as a feasible economic method for large-scale or commercial MT. An example of appending statistical techniques to rule-based MT is the experiment (by a number of researchers in Spain, Japan, and Canada) of "statistical post-editing." In essence, the method involves the submission (for correction and improvement) of the output of an RBMT system to a "language model" of the kind found in SMT systems. One advantage of the approach is that the deficiencies of RBMT for less-resourced languages may be overcome.

The languages most often in demand and available commercially are those from and to English. The most frequent pairs (for online MT services and apparently for PC systems) are English to/from Spanish and English to/from Japanese. These are followed by English to/from French, English to/from German, English to/from Italian, English to/from Chinese, English to/from Korean, and French to/from German. Other European languages such as Czech, Polish, Bulgarian, Romanian, Latvian, Lithuanian, Estonian, and Finnish are more rarely found on the market. Until the middle of the 1990s, Arabic to/from English and Arabic to/from French were also rare, but this situation has changed for obvious political reasons. Other Asian languages have also been relatively neglected: Malay, Indonesian, Thai, Vietnam and even major languages of India: Hindu, Urdu, Bengali, Punjabi, Tamil, etc.

And African languages (except Arabic dialects) are virtually invisible. Many are among the world's most spoken languages. The reason is a combination of low commercial viability and lack of language resources (whether for rule-based lexicons and grammars or for statistical MT corpora).

6　Minorities, Immigrants

The categorization of a language as a "minority language" is determined geographically. In the UK, world languages such as Hindi, Punjabi and Bengali are minor, because the major language is English. In Spain, the languages Basque and Catalan are both "minor" because the official language is Castilian Spanish. In the context of the European Union, languages such as Welsh, Irish, Estonian, Lithuanian are "minor," whether official languages of a country or not. From a global point of view, "minor" languages are those which are not "commercially" or "economically" significant. The language coverage of MT systems reflects this global perspective, and so the problems and needs of "minority" languages were virtually ignored. Recently they have had more attention—in Spain with MT systems for Catalan, Basque, and Galician; in Eastern Europe with systems for Czech, Estonian, Latvian, Bulgarian, etc.; and in South and South East Asia with MT activity on Bengali, Tamil, Thai, Vietnamese, etc. This growing interest is reflected in the holding of workshops on minority-language MT. The problems for minority and immigrant languages are many and varied: there is often no word-processing software (indeed some languages lack scripts), no spellcheckers (sometime languages lack standard spelling conventions), no dictionaries (monolingual or bilingual), indeed a general lack of language resources (e. g. corpora of translations) and of qualified/experienced researchers. Before MT can be contemplated, these resources must be created—and the Internet may help to some extent with glossaries and bilingual corpora.

One specific target of MT for immigrants or minorities has been the translation of captions (or subtitles) for television programmes. Probably the most ambitious experiment is at the Institute for Language and Speech Processing (Athens) involving speech recognition, English text analysis and caption generation in English, Greek and French. Usually, however, captions in foreign languages are generated from caption texts produced as a normal service for the deaf or hearing impaired by television companies. A group at Simon Fraser University in Canada has investigated the translation of English television captions into Spanish and Portuguese, and a group at the Electronics and Telecommunications Research Institute in Korea are developing Caption Eye/EK, an MT system for translation English television captions into Korean. In both cases, translation is based on pattern matching of short phrases (in systems of the example-based MT type.)

Apart from minorities and immigrants, there are other "disadvantaged" members of society now beginning to be helped by MT-related systems. In recent years, researchers have looked at "translating" into sign languages for the deaf. The problems go, of course, beyond those encountered with text translation. The most obvious one is that signs are made by complex combinations of face, hand and body movements which have to be notated for translation, and have to be mimicked by a computer-generated avatar. In most cases, conventional rule-based approaches are adopted, but there have also been experiments with hybrid statistical and example-based methods. Most research has focused on translation of English text into American Sign Language and into British Sign Language, but also there are also reports involving German sign language.

7 Information Retrieval, Information Extraction, and Other Applications

Translation is rarely an isolated activity; it is usually a means for accessing, acquiring and imparting information. This is clearly the case with many examples already mentioned: translation in health-related communication, translation of patents and technical documentation, translation of television subtitles, etc. MT systems are therefore often integrated with (combined or linked with) various other NLP activities: information retrieval, information extraction and analysis, question answering, summarization, technical authoring.

Multilingual access to information in documentary sources (articles, conferences, monographs, etc.) was a major interest in the earliest years of MT, but as information retrieval (IR) became more statistics-oriented and MT became more rule-based the reciprocal relations diminished. However, since the mid 1990s with the increasing interest in statistics-based MT the relations have revived, and "cross-language information retrieval" (CLIR) is now a vigorous area of research with strong links to MT: both fields are concerned with the retrieval words and phrases in foreign languages which match (exactly or "fuzzily") with words and phrases of input "texts" (queries in IR, source texts in MT), and both combine linguistic resources (dictionaries, thesauri) and statistical techniques. There are extensions of CLIR to multilingual retrieval of images and spoken "documents," to retrieval of broadcast stories which are "similar" to a given input English text (not just a query).

Information extraction (or "text mining") has had similar close historical links to MT, strengthened likewise by the growing statistical orientation of MT. Many commercial and government-funded (international and national) organizations have to scrutinize foreign language documents for information relevant to their activities (from commercial and economic to surveillance, intelligence, and espionage). The scanning (skimming) of documents received-previously an onerous human task—is now routinely performed automatically. Searching can focus on single texts or multilingual collections of texts, or range over selected databases (e. g. via syndicated feeds) or the whole Internet. The cues for relevant information include not just keywords such as "export," "strategic," "attack," etc. (and their foreign language equivalents), but also the names of persons, companies and organizations. Since the spelling of personal names can differ markedly from one language to another, the systems need to incorporate "transliteration" facilities which can convert, say, a Japanese version of a politician's name into its (perhaps original) English form. The identification of names (or "named entities") and the problems of transliteration have become increasingly active fields in the last few years.

Information analysis and summarization is frequently the second stage after information extraction. These activities have also, until recently, been performed by human analysts. Now at least drafts can be obtained by statistical means-methods for summarization have been researched since the 1960s. The development of working systems that combine MT and summarization is apparently still something for the future. The major problems are the unreliability of MT (incorrect translations, distorted syntax, etc.) and the imperfections of current summarization systems (which seek "indicative" contents in paragraph-initial sentences, sentences containing "important" lexical clues, sentences including specific names, etc.) Combining MT and summarization would be a desirable development in many areas—not just for information gathering by government bodies but also for managers of large corporations and for most researchers with no knowledge of the original language. Such potential users of MT rarely want to read the whole of a document; what they want is to extract information for a specific need.

The field of question-answering has been an active research area in artificial intelligence for many years. The aim is to retrieve answers in text form from databases in response to (ideally) natural-language questions. Like summarization, this is a difficult task; but the possibility of multilingual question-answering is attracting more attention in recent years.

Finally, the impetus in large corporation to produce documentation in multiple languages in as short timescales as possible has led to the closer integration of the processes of authoring (technical writing) and translating. This is true not only where companies have decided to adopt "controlled languages" for their documentation—as we have seen above—but also where writers make use of rough translations as aids. Surveys of the use of Syst ran at the European Commission have shown that much of its use is by administrators and other officials when writing documents in languages they are not fully fluent in—a draft translation from a text in their own language is used as the basis for writing in another. Perhaps this is what some users of online MT and of PC systems are doing; the translation systems are aids to writing in another relatively poorly known language.

This survey has not exhausted all the applications that have been envisaged for MT; we may mention suggestions for combining MT and photocopiers, MT and document scanners, MT and cameras (e. g. for reading menus and road signs), and finally—in a reversion to MT's origins—the use of MT techniques for decipherment.

What these examples of MT applications illustrate is that MT technology is being used not just for "pure" translation but increasingly as an aid to bilingual communication in an ever-widening range of contexts and situations, and embedded in a multiplicity of multilingual, multimodal document (text) and image (video) extraction and analysis systems. Whenever there is a need for communication and contact across languages, there will be a potential use for MT—the applications seem unending.

选文三　信息时代与翻译实践

孙鸿仁

导　言

选文原刊载于《中国科技翻译》2001 年第 3 期。

作者孙鸿仁为绍兴文理学院教授,主要论文包括《英语从属语式探讨:标记性》、《从标记性看虚拟语式类型的确定》等。

选文以对"St. John wort"和"Johnnie Cochran"的理解为例,探讨如何使用互联网实现对这两个短语的正确理解。作者首先指出,当下,译者不只应该具备三个水平,即汉语水平、英语水平和语言本身以外的知识水平,还应该具备第四个水平,即电脑水平。接着,作者认为,译者使用互联网有三个层次,即"人与机器对话"、"人与网络对话"、"人与人对话"。然后,作者用以上两例说明如何借助于互联网实现对这两个短语的理解。

《中国翻译》曾刊载马建德先生的一篇文章,文中指出,鲁明先生将"St. John wort"译为"圣约翰麦芽汁"为误译,正确的译名应是"灌叶连翘"。据马先生称,该文是"就事论事的一点看法",但其论理缜密,令人佩服。同时也不禁促人感叹译事之艰难。

鲁明先生确实误译了。然而,鲁明先生在英文、中文和专业知识方面的综合能力,应该是高的,因为他是在《光明日报》的专栏上撰文介绍美国草药界利用西药的成分检定法鉴定草药所含成分情况时出现了误译。换个人来翻译,似乎也难以不出错。

20 世纪,科技日新月异,信息急增骤长,知识更新加快,科技成果转化周期缩短。"30 年来的世界科技成果比历史上两千年科技成果的总和还要多,这意味着知识进入了一个急剧发展和爆炸时代。科技成果商业化的周期大大缩短,从发明到应用,电磁波通讯用了 26 年,集成电路用了 7 年,激光器只用了 1 年"。据 Burton & Kebler 对信息半衰期的分析,社会科学的半衰期是 5 年,即现有的社会知识在 5 年后有一半的信息已经老化,而因特网的信息半衰期只有 6 个月。

合格的翻译工作者应该具有"三个水平",即汉语水平、英语水平和语言本身以外的知识水平,这是基本要求。在这三者中,语言水平在总体上总是不断提高的。也就是说,随着翻译实践活动,驾驭中英两种语言的能力总是会不断地得到加强,水平会逐步提高。但是,一个人的能力毕竟有限,人脑存储知识的能力,即容量也是有限的。知识在经过"原始积累"之后,则需要一个"更新、淘汰、更新……"的周期性循环。从动态变化方面进行考察,如果说语言、历史和文化等方面的知识是静态的(static),"淘汰率"较低,那么科学技术知识则是动态的(dynamic),其淘汰率高而"半衰期"短。介于其间的是政治和经济方面的知识。现在我们所谓的"知识爆炸"、"信息爆炸"等,在很大程度上与科技知识相关度更高。在当今的时代,新词不断涌现,而旧词又被赋予新义,对翻译工作者提出了更高的知识要求。知识的无限膨胀和人类个体有限的知识"存储能力"之间,出现了空前的矛盾。因此,信息时代的翻译工作者,如果仅通过传统、常规的方式"积累"知识,熟悉所涉及的专业领域,就无法跟上知识更新的节奏,也难以满足信息时代对翻译工作的要求。

马先生论证了"St. John's wort"应译为"灌叶连翘",但这只能属于"个案",难以重复。他在本例的成功,得益于他在这方面有所专长,且是这一领域的有心人。正如马先生所言,"由于工作需要,笔者常接触一些国外药学方面的杂志,并注意到近来英、美等国在对草药的报道中,多次讨论过一种名为'St. John's wort'的草药。"如果没有这一段经历,即使是具有一般的医学知识,也未必能道出"St. John's wort"的正确译名,因为单靠经历和经验的积累,已难以解决信息时代的翻译问题。今天我们可以解决"St. John's wort"这个词的释义,而明天又会有更多的新词、新义,需要我们去正确翻译。在全球信息时代的今天,科技翻译工作者的出路何在?

蒸汽机的出现使人类体能得到了极大解放,带来了产业革命。计算机的发明,使人类智能得到极大的延伸,促进了信息革命。而因特网则将我们带入了全球信息时代。在世纪交替的今天,积累、存储、提取和更新知识,不但可以在现实世界中进行,而且可以在更为广袤的虚拟世界(virtual world)中实现,因此"三个水平"已难以满足全球信息时代的要求。合格的翻译工作者还应该有一定的"电脑水平",具有使用电脑的能力,即利用电脑获取、存储、提取信息的能力,进行检索和咨询的能力。

知识在激增、"爆炸",同时也在迅速地老化。原有专业知识,无论多么深厚,若想跟上时代不落伍,都需要不断更新。对科技翻译工作者而言,仅仅"具有专业知识"是远远不够的。还应知道哪里可能有更多、更新的专业知识,知道如何利用、提取这些知识。在这种情况下,解决问题只能走出传统、利用电脑,进入数字和虚拟世界。

由于经历和经验的限制,在现实世界中无法解决问题的时候,亦即经过"人与人"和"人与纸质媒介"的对话(咨询)后仍无法走出困境时,我们可进入"虚拟世界"咨询。

笔者认为,这种咨询可分三个层次。首先"人与机器对话",进而"人与网络对话",最后是更高层次的"人与人对话":通过网络,把问题摆在世界面前,借助世界的智力解决某一专业或文化翻译中的难题。这不是梦想,而是现实。

以解决"St. John's wort"译名为例。我们可以首先进行常规的检索、咨询;在无法得到合理的答案之后,我们可以借助电脑,进入虚拟世界,即使没有马先生的阅历,也可以轻松地搬倒"麦芽汁"。

首先,我们可以进行"人机对话",查阅多媒体电子工具书,以"St. John's wort"作为关键词进行检索。这种检索非常方便,鼠标点击之间,我们就可以得到有关"St. John's wort"图文并茂的答案。有了这样的查询结果,我们绝不可能把作为"麦芽汁"的"wort"(infusion of malt that is fermented to make beer)和作为植物的"…wort"混淆起来。

如果不满意,或者希望对"St. John's wort"及其药用情况作更为详尽的了解,我们启动浏览器,登上因特网,进行"人网对话",检索"St. John's wort"。我们可以利用"yahoo!","Sohu","infoseek"等搜索引擎(search engine)进行查找,也可以直接点击电子百科全书提供的网址。例如,点击 *Compton's Interactive Encyclopedia* 在"St. John's wort"词条下提供的网址 http://www. botanical. com/botanical/mgmh. html,转瞬间我们可以看到以下概要:

St. John's wort

Botanical:Hypericum perforatum(LTNN.)

Family:N. O. Hypericaceae

Description

MedicinalAction and Uses

Preparations and Dosages

——Parts Used——Herb tops,flowers.

——Habitat——Britain and throughout Europe and Asia.

通过超级链接,我们可立刻阅读到有关"St. John's wort"的详细内容。若用搜索引擎进行查找,只需几秒,就可以找到一系列相关网址。轻轻点击其中一条,如 http://www. usphanmacist. com/NewLook/,我们可以读到下列内容:

St. John's wort and the

Treatment of Depression

Historically,St. John's wort has been used as an herbal remedy for depression,anxiety, dieresis, gastritis and insomnia. Recent studies demonstrate that the extract, primarily hypericin, is a strong, and nearly irreversible, inhibitor of monoamine oxidase types A and B.

St. John's Wort Botanical and Chemical Properties: St. John's wort (Hypericum perforatum L.), belonging to the family Hypericaceae and also known as Klamath weed, amber touch-and-heal, goatweed and rosin rose, is an aromatic shrubby perennial plant with numerous bright yellow flowers that bloom from June to September. The blooms are said to be at their brightest and most abundant around the day traditionally celebrated as birthday of John the Baptist (June 24).

从这条信息中，我们不但能了解 St. John's wort 的功用、用途、来源和学名，而且还能看到它的来源和别称，如"Klamath weed"，"amber touch-and-heal"，"goatweed"和"rosin rose"等，这在较大的工具书中都是可以查阅到的。

电脑和因特网不但是科技翻译的得力工具，也是文学翻译的好助手。翻译当代文学作品，同样会遇到信息时代给我们带来的问题。

不久前笔者读一本 1998 年出版的美国通俗文学作品 *Full Dress Gray*，其间曾遇到样一个看似简单的句子"He is a good lawyer, but he is no Johnnie Cochran."句子后半句译成"……但比不上约翰尼·考克兰"，或"……但他算不上出类拔萃"等，都说得过去。但是，若不搞清楚 Johnnie Cochran 是何许人，无论怎样翻译，都不能完整地传递原文意义。此时，传统工具书或百科全书，由于其滞后性，对 Cochran 已经是无能为力。在现实世界中进行"面对面"的咨询，也很难得到正确结果。

借助电脑查阅电子百科全书，问题便可以迎刃而解。鼠标点击之间，便查到出自 Johnnie Cochran 之口的引语"If it doesn't fit, you must acquit"以及对作者的介绍：

Johnnie L. Cochran, Jr. (b. 1937), U. S. lawyer in closing defense statements to jury, September 27, 1995, p. A1, (Sept. 28, 1995), Cochran was part of O. J. Simpson's defense team; Simpson was charged with murdering his wife, Nicole, and her friend, Ron Goldman. Cochran's point was that the evidence against Simpson did not make sense. He had just referred to the bloody gloves that were found at the murder scene; Simpson showed difficulty when he was ordered to try on the gloves during the trial. In October 1995, the jury found Simpson not guilty.

通过"人机对话"，我们轻松搞定 Johnnie Cochran 的身世：美国律师，参加了指控橄榄球星辛普森杀妻案件的辩护。

面对信息时代，传统工具书的局限性已经显露，因为大型百科类工具书一般都要滞后十来年，无法满足信息时代翻译工作者的需求。相反，大型电子或数字百科全书的出版周期短，更新快，滞后少，而且可以在网上更新下载（update download），至少每月一次，这无异于月月有新的"修订版"、"增补版"发行。对于"有纸"出版，这是根本无法做到的。因特网提供的信息几乎是"实时"的，这就最大限度地克服了传统读物的滞后缺陷。

电脑的出现正在改变着我们的生活，影响着与语言学相关的研究领域。机器翻译，自然语言理解，语料库语言学，人工智能等等，无不随着电脑的出现和不断完善而得以发展。翻译工作者，不论是科技的，还是人文的，有必要也有能力利用电脑与网络，神游虚拟世界，去获取、探索数字世界和网络世界中无穷无尽的信息资源和知识宝库。作为语言工作者，我们更有着得天独厚的条件。

【延伸阅读】

[1] Carmina, F. P. A Comparative Study of Community Building in Online and Face-to-Face Courses. Minor dissertation. Departament de Filologia Anglogermanica, Universitat Rovira i Virgili, 2003.

[2] Palloff, R. , & Pratt, K. *Building Learning Communities in Cyberspace*：*Effective Strategies for the Online Classroom*. San Francisco：Jossey-Bass Publishers, 1999.

[3] Schlager, M. , Fusco, J. , & Schank, P. Evolution of an On-line Education Community of Practice//K. A. Renninger & W. Shumar (eds.), *Building Virtual Communities*：*Learning and Change in Cyberspace*. New York：Cambridge University Press.

[4] Truscott, L. K. , Ⅳ. *Full Dress Gray*. New York：William Morrow & Company Inc, 1998.

[5] *The Columbia Dictionary of Quotations*. New York：Columbia University Press, 1998.

[6] 马建德. "圣约翰麦芽汁"到底是何物？中国翻译, 1999(4).

[7] 邓琮琮. 科技副部长敲打中关村老总. 中国青年报, 1999 - 11 - 14.

[8] 桂诗春. 再论科学研究方法. 全国大学英语教学学术研讨会主基调报告. 北京：1999(10)：22 - 27.

【问题与思考】

1. JOSE RAMON BIAU GIL 在文中提到的"网上翻译课程"讨论的话题有哪些？

2. 学生的计算机水平与"网上翻译课程教学"有着密切关系，这对我们的翻译教学有何启发？

3. 机器翻译的工具主要有哪些？

4. John Hutchins 认为，翻译不是孤立的活动，你是如何理解的？

5. "纸质时代"的翻译工具和"信息时代"的电子翻译工具有何异同？

6. "信息时代"的电子翻译工具对译者提出了哪些新的要求？

【研究与实践】

伴随着 20 世纪中期以来电脑以及互联网的迅猛发展，翻译的电子工具也在日新月异地进步。结合国内外对该领域所作的研究，撰文综述该领域几十年来的发展，尤其关注每个时期电子工具的优劣，以及对翻译范式所产生的影响。

第三章　翻译词典的类型及其使用

导　论

　　翻译既是两种语言之间的交流，也是两种文化之间的交流。所以，翻译实践既离不开双语词典，亦离不开有关双文化的词典，诸如大百科全书、语言背景知识词典、典故词典等。可以说，任何翻译实践都离不开词典的参与。如何正确地使用词典是每一位翻译工作者必备的技能。

　　信息化时代，词典已经不再局限于大部头的纸质版本，而是更多地进入了电子时代。在这一大背景下，词典的属性发生了很大变化，这对翻译实践有何影响？如何正确地使用电子时代的词典？这都是当下比较有益、有趣的话题。本章选取了三篇文章将从这一路径展开讨论。

　　Roda P. Roberts 撰写的论文 *Translation Pedagogy：Strategies for Improving Dictionary Use* 旨在讨论译者，尤其是翻译班的学员如何充分利用词典以提高翻译质量。此前，这一领域被许多人忽视，并指出其原因。该文的核心在于，作者提出了四种使用词典提高翻译质量的策略：熟悉词汇的各种形态，熟悉各种词典，熟悉每个条目的各种格式，将语篇分析、译文与查阅词典结合起来。作者结合实例讲解如何应用这些策略。想必这些策略对翻译工作者、翻译教师和学员都会大有裨益。Gilles-Maurice de Schryver 和 David Joffe 的论文 *On How Electronic Dictionaries Are Really Used* 探讨了真实场景下如何使用电子词典。作者结合日志文件跟踪每位电子词典使用者的每个行为，包括每次查阅词典的日期与时间、找到的词汇排序、未找到的词汇、观察词汇的长期记忆等。最后可以将这些内容交给词典编纂者，借此可以建立适合个人的电子词典。Batia Laufer 的论文 *Electronic Dictionaries and Incidental Vocabulary Acquisition：Does Technology Make a Difference？* 则从电子翻译词典对学生的影响这一角度展开论述。

选　文

选文一　Translation Pedagogy: Strategies for Improving Dictionary Use

Roda P. Roberts

导　言

本文发表在期刊 *TTR*: *Traduction*, *Terminology*, *Redaction* 1992 年第五期上。

Roda P. Roberts 是渥太华大学(University of Ottawa)的教授,其研究领域涉及翻译理论和术语学,参编 *The Critical Link 2*: *Interpreters in the Community* 一书。其论文主要有 *Using Dictionaries Efficiently*; *Translation and the Bilingual Dictionary* 和 *The Use of Corpora in Bilingual Lexicography* 等。作者首先论述了正确使用双语词典对于学翻译的学生的重要性;接着作者介绍了四种提高词典使用效率的策略;最后,作者重点推荐了几本他认为比较实用的词典,并做了简要分析。

Introduction

Bilingual dictionaries are obviously indispensable working tools for translators and translation trainees. And yet, there is widespread dissatisfaction with such dictionaries expressed in the literature on translation. This love-hate relationship existing between translators and bilingual dictionaries, which has been explored in some depth by Ingrid Meyer (1987:18 – 36), is based on the presumption that there is such a thing as an ideal general bilingual dictionary or at least an ideal general bilingual dictionary for translators. In other words, the attitude has been, and still is, that if the bilingual dictionary is not the perfect tool for translators, it is the fault of lexicographers. Thus, much attention has been focused recently on better adapting such dictionaries to meet translators' needs.

However, as the 1987 Euralex Colloquium "Translation and Lexicography" revealed, different types of translators have different needs, and it will clearly be difficult, if not impossible, to produce a general bilingual dictionary that satisfies them all. The same, in fact, can be said of all types of dictionaries, unilingual and bilingual, general and specialized. So, although we can and should justifiably expect lexicographic improvements, we should also begin to reflect more seriously on improving methods of dictionary use among translators and especially among translation trainees.

Although there has been much development over the last twenty years or so in the teaching of translation techniques and approaches, strategies of dictionary use have not figured prominently among them. For instance, there are no exercises for teaching appropriate dictionary use in Jean Delisle's Analyse du discours comme mtthode de traduction, although there are a couple that indicate the problems that dictionaries can pose to the unwary. For example, the first exercise in this manual, intended to show the difference between equivalences at the level of linguistic meaning ("transcoded equivalents") and equivalences at the level of message meaning ("translated equivalents"), consists in having students translate isolated words and phrases using dictionaries, and then seeing how the same words and phrases may be rendered differently when they form part of a text (Delisle, 1980: 131 – 135). While such an exercise is very useful in underlining the limitations of dictionaries, it does not show students how to deal with these limitations. Similarly, Claude Tatilon, in Traduire. Pour une pidagogie de la traduction, indicates the problems that the translation of lexical items can pose without providing any guidance on making the best use of dictionaries to solve them (1986: 45 – 57). It is this void in translation didactics that this paper intends to fill.

1 Importance of Teaching Dictionary Use to Translation Students

The first question that needs to be addressed is why there is this void. There is little doubt that students both in professional translation courses and in academic translation courses[①] have constant recourse to dictionaries, which they use incompetently. So the need for teaching dictionary use seems obvious. And yet it has not been addressed by translation didacticians.

The reasons for this state of affairs seem to lie both in the theoretical foundations underlying current translation pedagogy and in the perceived lacks in dictionaries. Both these points are made forcefully by Delisle (1988: 46 – 48): (a) Translation in the proper sense of the word is not transcoding. Transcoding establishes equivalences at the level of language as a system by matching words. Translation, on the other hand, establishes equivalences of utterances in context or in situation; in other words, translation equivalents arise out of the use of language in a given situation. (b) Bilingual dictionaries provide transcoded equivalents, not contextual equivalents, and are therefore improperly called "translation dictionaries." Moreover, all dictionaries, bilingual and unilingual, provide only the most common significations of words; they do not explore all the semantic possibilities of words

---

① According to Delisle (1988: 26 – 27), the purpose of a professional translation course is to teach students to manipulate language so that they can make it carry a given meaning in a given situation, while that of an academic translation course is to help students to improve their language skills.

used in context. They are thus limited in their usefulness.

However, while there is no denying that "translation is an exercise in interpretation, an intelligent analysis of the text" (Delisle, 1988: 48), and not just a matter of substituting one word for another, there is also little doubt that recent advances in lexicography are invalidating some of the traditional criticisms of dictionaries. Since dictionaries are increasingly corpus-based, they are not necessarily limited to the most common significations. And the corpus approach also implies that lexicography, like translation, deals with words in context, or more specifically the meaning of lexical items in texts (R. R. K. Hartmann, 1989: 12). This can be illustrated by taking as an example the word sympathetic, used by Delisle to illustrate the inadequacies of the transcoded equivalents and common significations generally found in bilingual dictionaries. Delisle points out, quite rightly, that the commonly cited equivalent comprihens if does not work in all contexts, and certainly not in the following excerpt from a letter by a senior civil servant: "While I am more than sympathetic to the recommendations of the social worker, we have to remember that ... " However, in addition to covering several significations of the word sympathetic, the Harrap's Standard French and English Dictionary specifically includes the phrase to be sympathetic to a proposal. This shows that today's bilingual dictionaries go well beyond the single equivalent per entry word and increasingly present words and their translation in context. In fact, modern dictionaries supply contextual information in a number of different ways: through examples (many of them taken from computerized corpora), context words and field labels. In addition, partial definitions, usually in the form of synonyms, are also provided to guide users in their choice of equivalents. These lexicographic trends are clearly revealed in the following (partial) entry for popular in the Collins/Robert French-English English-French Dictionary (1987):

popular ... (a) (well-liked) person, decision, book, sport populaire; (fashionable) style, model a la mode, en vogue, he is ~ with his colleagues ses collegues l'aiment beaucoup, il jouit d'une grande popularitS aupres de ses collegues; he is * with the girls il a du succes or il a la cote * aupres des filles; I'm not very * with the boss just now * je ne suis pas ties bien vu du patron or je n'ai pas la cote aupres du patron en ce moment; (Comm.) this is a very ~ colour cette couleur se vend beaucoup; it is ~ to despise politicians mepriser les hommes politiques est a la mode, c'est la mode de mepriser les hommes politiques.

Moreover, this entry, which is typical of good modern dictionaries, covers three out of the four possible types of lexical information that Claude Tatilon has identified as being important in translation (1986: 7 - 12, 49 - 53): referential information—provided by the partial definitions; pragmatic information—supplied by the style labels; and stylistic information—provided here by the field label Comm. If there is no indication of what Tatilon calls "dialectal information," it is because it is not applicable in this case. Since, as Tatilon points out, "ce qui est a traduire, c'est l'information lexicale d'un enonc6," an entry such as this provides an excellent starting point for translation students.

However, the more information is packed into dictionaries, the greater the dilemma of these students, for they are unable to find what they need in the mass of information provided. This is not surprising in light of the fact that dictionary use, like translation, is itself an exercise in interpretation. But there now exists the paradoxical situation of dictionaries, on the one hand, becoming more suitable for translation purposes, and translation students, on the other hand, unable to take advantage of lexicographic improvements. Instead of vainly trying to wean our students away from dictionaries or castigating them for poor use of dictionaries, the time has come for us, teachers of translation, to train students in the use of dictionaries—both bilingual and unilingual—for translation purposes.

2　Strategies for Improving Dictionary Use

Strategies for improving dictionary use can be subdivided into four main categories on the basis of the four following objectives: (a) familiarization with different types of lexical items; (b) familiarization with different types of dictionaries; (c) familiarization with dictionary entry formats; and (d) illustration of ways to combine text analysis, translation and dictionary consultation. These four categories represent the four main problems facing translation students: knowing what to look up in a dictionary; knowing where to look for lexical information; knowing how to interpret lexical information provided; and knowing when and how to consult dictionaries during the translation process.

2.1　Familiarization with Different Types of Lexical Items

The reason why, in many cases, dictionary consultation gets off to a bad start is that students are often incapable of identifying complex lexical items in the source language text. This is particularly true when the source language is the student's second language. The classic example of students rendering simple soldat by simple soldier (instead of private) is a good illustration of the problem.

Students have to be made aware of the kind of bonding words can have. While they do not need to know all the degrees of bonding that may exist, they must be taught to distinguish between compounds (e. g. simple soldat above), idioms (e. g. to keep one's eyes peeled) and collocations (e. g. poser une question), for these three categories are often treated very differently in general dictionaries. Compounds are often presented as headwords in unilingual English dictionaries; compounds and idioms are sometimes grouped into separate subdivisions in entries for simple lexical items in bilingual dictionaries. Finally, collocations, when they are presented, are normally mixed in with free combinations in the examples section. Thus, students must first learn to identify these different types of lexical items before they can search for them appropriately in dictionaries.

The best way to introduce students to types of lexical items seems to be by analyzing with them specific examples of each premarked in a text (see Appendix 1). This analysis should lead to a short theoretical presentation, accompanied by further examples. This must be followed by the scanning of a number of source texts by students, with the goal of identifying compounds, idioms and collocations therein. It seems advisable to use reasonably general texts for this purpose, since highly specialized texts have relatively few idioms. It is important to follow up each scanning exercise with a discussion, so that students who have made errors in identification can understand why. These discussions should also bring out one more general point: that the dividing line between different types of lexical items is seldom clearcut, which is why what one dictionary may classify as an idiom, another may consider a collocation. Despite this problem, however, apreliminary identification of different types of lexical items will allow for more effective dictionary consultation, for they are often treated differently in different types of dictionaries.

2. 2　Familiarization with Different Types of Dictionaries

The ubiquitous general bilingual dictionary, on which translation students rely so heavily, is only one of many different types of dictionaries which can and should be used in translation. The problem seems to be that very few students are aware of anything beyond the general bilingual and general unilingual dictionaries—and only one of those at that! A presentation of a variety of useful dictionary types, followed by workshop sessions in which models of different types are examined, would go a long way towards increased use of the variety of dictionaries available.

There exist a number of dictionary typologies that can be drawn on for the presentation.① However, the instructor should limit his comments to the kinds of dictionaries most useful for translation in the students' working languages (which, in Canada, would generally be English and French). Given the popularity of the bilingual dictionary among translation students, it might be best to begin by introducing students to different varieties of these. Thus, a distinction should be made between the general bilingual dictionary (e. g. the Collins/Robert or the Harrap's referred to above) and specialized bilingual dictionaries (e. g. Fernand Sylvain's Dictionnaire de la comptabilitd et des disciplines connexes). Another distinction that needs to be made is that between specialized dictionaries, which are limited to one field, and special purpose dictionaries, which are limited to one aspect of language such as dialect, slang, idioms or collocations (e. g. J. van Roey et al. 's Dictionnaire des faux amis anglais-frangais, 2001 French and English Idioms,

---

① Among the more useful typologies are Sidney Landau's classification of dictionaries in general in Dictionaries. The Art and Craft of Lexicography (pp. 6 - 22), and Ali Al-Kasimi's typology of bilingual dictionaries in particular in Linguistics and Bilingual Dictionaries (17 - 31).

Brueckner's French Contextuary and Dictionnaire français-anglais de locutions et expressions verbales). Finally, it should be pointed out that not all bilingual dictionaries are bidirectional (English-French and French-English), but that many unidirectional dictionaries contain a reverse index, which points the user to the part of the dictionary where he may find the information he needs. Consideration of bilingual dictionaries should be followed by a similar examination of unilingual English and French dictionaries, which should include not only the categories discussed above but also others. For example, there are unilingual dictionaries for foreign language learners—as opposed to native speakers (e. g. Collins Cobuild English Language Dictionary) and unilingual dictionaries for younger native speakers (e. g. Dictionnaire CEC Jeunesse) which often contain clearer definitions, more information on collocations, and more examples of words in context than unilingual dictionaries intended for the general public. Translation students in Canada must also be introduced to unilingual Canadian dictionaries such as the Gage Canadian Dictionary and the Penguin Canadian Dictionary for English, and the Dictionnaire du français plus for French. Dictionaries of synonyms, which are of great help to translators, especially at the revision stage, should also be presented at this stage. A final point applicable to both bilingual and unilingual general dictionaries must be made: that pertaining to size, which is calculated in terms of the number of words covered. Students should be warned of the dangers of using any general dictionary smaller in size than a college dictionary, unless there is a special reason for doing so (e. g. consultation of a learner's dictionary for collocational information), and should be introduced to semi-abridged and unabridged dictionaries, which they may never have used.

Presentation and examination of these various types of dictionaries should be followed by practical exercises of various kinds. For example, students can be given a source text, with a certain number of lexical items of various kinds underlined and asked to consult two dictionaries to find the meaning of these and two dictionaries to find possible equivalents. By limiting the number of dictionaries that they may consult, the instructor forces them to choose the most pertinent ones. Thus, for instance, if the lexical item is a compound, they are more likely to find its meaning in a semi-abridged or unabridged dictionary than in a college dictionary. The results of the dictionary search should be discussed in class, so that students are made aware not only of different types of dictionaries but also of differences in quality between dictionaries of a certain type. Another exercise, which could be integrated into a normal translation assignment, could consist of having students submit an annotated translation, indicating every lexical item checked in a dictionary, along with the titles of the dictionaries consulted (see Appendix 2, Note 1 for an example). This particular exercise would also prepare them for translation in a professional milieu, where new translators are often asked to indicate the sources of their information.

But dictionary consultation involves more than finding a dictionary that provides information on a given item. It involves above all finding pertinent information without undue waste of time. In order to be able to do this, students should be familiar with dictionary entry formats.

2. 3 Familiarization with Dictionary Entry Formats

Entry formats differ considerably not only from one type of dictionary to another, but also from one dictionary of a certain type to another. For example, while many bilingual specialized (field) dictionaries provide, in addition to the entry word and the target language equivalent, a definition and cross-references to quasi-synonyms and other related words, others do not. While it would be too time-consuming to examine jointly in class the entry formats of all the dictionaries that could be useful to the translation student, it seems important to take the time to study at least those of current general bilingual dictionaries, for many student errors can be attributed to a poor reading of information in such dictionaries. The four main English-French French-English dictionaries which translation students tend to use are the following: the Collins/Robert, M.-M. Dubois' Dictionnaire français-anglais anglais-français published by Larousse (1981), the Harrap's Shorter French-English English French Dictionary (1987), and the Harrap's New Standard referred to above. So analysis could be limited to these four. In fact, since the Harrap's Shorter is a one-volume edition of the four-volume unabridged Harrap's New Standard, examination of two college dictionaries (the Collins/Robert and the Larousse) and one unabridged dictionary (the Harrap's New Standard) would suffice. Prior to analysis of these dictionaries, students should be required to read the introductions, which are unfortunately quite inadequate, except in the case of the Collins/Robert.

The analysis, which could be guided by a series of questions, may be based on sample dictionary entries chosen by the professor on the basis of specific lexical items identified in a source text. However, the source text as well as the lexical items examined need to be carefully chosen in order to allow students to find answers to all the questions the instructor needs to ask to focus attention on specific entry elements. These questions should cover the type of lexical items presented as subentries rather than main entries, the exhaustivity of the senses covered, the ordering of senses, the type and number of examples presented, the ordering of examples, the inclusion of collocations and idioms, the headword under which collocations and idioms are presented and their place in the entry, the way contextual information is presented, meaning discrimination devices and stylistic discrimination devices used. A series of sample questions are presented in Appendix 3. The answers could be prepared as a homework exercise and form the basis of a subsequent class discussion, or the questions could be worked on as a small-group exercise in the classroom, with each group focusing more particularly on one particular dictionary. This introductory analysis could be followed up by annotations of a certain number of lexical items in a translated text. These annotations would be more detailed than those discussed in Section 2. 2 above. Not only would they indicate the dictionaries in which the lexical item was looked up, but they would also contain a rationale for the choice of translation, on the basis of such criteria as contextual information, meaning discrimination devices, stylistic discrimination devices and examples of usage found in dictionaries (see Appendix 2, Note 2 for an example). These annotations would allow the instructor to ensure that students were interpreting their dictionaries correctly, if not using them efficiently.

2. 4　Illustration of Ways to Combine Text Analysis, Translation and Dictionary Consultation

Efficient dictionary use involves knowing when to consult dictionaries, which one to consult at a given stage and how to integrate dictionary information with textual information. This skill, essential for the translation student, is one that can be acquired more easily through guidance and supervised practice than through trial and error. At this point, students need to be guided through the three stages of translation—analysis of source text, translation, and revision of the translation—using a concrete example, and shown how to combine dictionary consultation with each stage.

Should dictionary use be encouraged from the start of the first stage? Or does dictionary consultation at this point impede textual analysis? Lexical items in a text fall into three main categories: those that students know well and whose precise meaning is obvious in the text, those that students know vaguely and which they are tempted to look up directly in a bilingual dictionary for the purpose of translation, and those that students do not recognize. Immediate use of dictionaries to resolve problems with the latter often results in inadequate analysis of the context. This was demonstrated by an exercise done in the framework of a course on documentary research methods in the first year of a translation programme.

Students were given a number of short but complete contexts, each containing a lexical item that they knew only vaguely or that they did not know at all, with a partial translation of each passage: they were asked to translate the lexical item in question, using dictionaries if necessary, justifying the equivalent in terms of both dictionary information and context. The classic example of the danger of using dictionaries at too early a stage was the following sentence:

J'ai passe mes vacances dans une pourvoirie.

I went to a for my holidays.

Allowed the free use of dictionaries, more than 60% of the students ignored the context (the fact that pourvoirie had to be a place where one could go for a holiday), and came up with the totally nonsensical equivalents suppliers, outfitters or outfitting operation, on the basis of hasty dictionary consultation. The starting point for them all was a general bilingual dictionary, in which they found nothing—only Harrap's Standard contains this term and it is clearly marked "historical." Some then turned to on-line term banks, in which they found outfitters and outfitting operation. The rest turned to unilingual French dictionaries and, finding no non-historical definition in most of them (since pourvoirie in the sense presented above is Canadian), used suppliers, which is the general equivalent provided for pourvoyeur by the Collins/Robert. Not once did they think of the inappropriateness of these equivalents in the context.

On the basis of this experience, it would seem advisable to withold dictionaries during the stage of analysis, until the students have read the text thoroughly and attempted to figure out the meaning of different lexical items in context. Students should be asked to underline those lexical items that they do not understand completely and then shown how the problems they pose can often be solved or at least delimited by a thorough study of syntactic and semotactic markers in the context and by an analysis of the situational parameters of the text. ①

Discussion following such analysis should reveal which lexical items still remain vague in the students' mind and they should be limited to looking up only these items in a suitable dictionary. At this point, a suitable dictionary would obviously be a unilingual source language (SL) dictionary, for, despite the addition of some partial definitions in a few bilingual dictionaries such as the Collins/Robert, the purpose of the latter is not to provide users with detailed indications of the meanings of SL items. Depending on the general or specialized nature of the SL items, students would be guided to a general or appropriate specialized dictionary. Their selection of the appropriate meaning and their comprehension of the definition provided could be verified by having them paraphrase the source text (ST) sentence containing the difficult lexical item and seeing whether that paraphrase made sense within the text.

Once the analysis of the ST is completed, the actual work of translation begins. Here again, students should be encouraged not to turn blindly to dictionaries for answers. They should be reminded of Peter Newmark's adage that for non-standardized language there is rarely only one correct equivalent, although for standardized language there often is only one (1981: 16). Among the lexical items they feel they cannot render, they should be helped to make a distinction between standardized terms, collocations and idioms and non-standardized lexical items. They should then be allowed to consult appropriate bilingual dictionaries only for the former at this point. They should then be required to reexpress the lexical information contained in the rest of the text without having a target language (TL) equivalent at their fingertips. Only when they have attempted such a paraphrastic translation and when the resultant text has been discussed should they be allowed to use their bilingual dictionaries to find a more concise and perhaps stylistically more appropriate way of rendering certain lexical items. Having already worked through a paraphrastic translation, they should be better able to judge whether a dictionary-proposed equivalent does fit into the overall context, not only of the ST but also of the target text (TT).

---

① See E. A. Nida and C. Taber, The Theory and Practice of Translation (pp. 56 - 63) on the marking of meaning. This section also includes exercises in identifying syntactic and semotactic elements in English sentences which help to identify the specific meaning of a polysemous lexical item. See also R. P. Roberts, "Le Role du contexte et de la situation en traduction" (Actes du 2' colloque sur V enseignement fonctionnel du frangais et de la traduction en Amerique latine, 180 - 192).

At the third stage of revision, students should be asked to put away their bilingual dictionaries and work only with unilingual TL dictionaries of various kinds. It is at this point that they will verify in a general unilingual dictionary the precise meaning of TL equivalents provided by the bilingual dictionary which they are unsure about. It is also at this point that they may turn to collocational dictionaries or learner's dictionaries to ensure, for instance, that they have used the usual verb with a given noun. This is when they will turn to dictionaries of synonyms in an attempt to vary the vocabulary used or to find the most exact synonym to render a nuance or a register. A final reading of the TT will be followed by a check of the TT against the ST to ensure that improvements in the vocabulary of the TT have not led to any omissions, additions or distortions of the ST.

This first in-class translation exercise, intended to show appropriate dictionary consultation during the entire translation process, can be followed up occasionally by spot checks of dictionary use during specific stages. For instance, students could be asked to undertake at home the analysis of an ST intended for a sight translation exercise in class and to look up the meanings of only a given number of terms identified in advance. Their contextual analysis of other lexical items should then be quickly verified before the start of sight translation. Another exercise, intended to oblige students both to limit their dictionary use and to use their dictionaries efficiently, is that of sight translation practised more or less as in interpreter training programmes. Students are handed an ST which they have not seen before, given a short period of time to read it, analyze it, and find any necessary equivalents, and then asked to translate the text aloud into a tape recording machine. Translation students, in contrast to interpretation students, may be given more preparation time and allowed to use any dictionaries they like during this period. However, given the limited period of preparation, they will soon learn to use dictionaries only when strictly essential. They will thus better learn the role of dictionary consultation in the translation process.

3　Analysis of Some Basic Special Purpose Dictionaries Useful to English/French Translators

While introducing students to a large variety of dictionaries, the professor will no doubt orient them towards those he finds the most useful. Presented below is a schematic analysis of some special purpose dictionaries that I recommend more particularly.

3.1　Learners' Dictionaries

As indicated in 2.2 above, learners' dictionaries, while limited in vocabulary, provide clearer semantic information and more detailed syntactic information than general unilingual dictionaries for native users. They are therefore particularly useful for translators.

3.1.1　Collins Cobuild English Language Dictionary (London, Collins, 1988)

This is a learner's dictionary of English, which is nevertheless of use also to native English speakers. It is undoubtedly the best English learner's dictionary on the market.

Special features

• Simple explanation of meanings, with the word being explained normally included in the explanation in such a way that you can see how it is typically used in English (e. g. barbarity: ① Barbarity is extremely cruel behaviour ... ② A barbarity is an extremely cruel and shocking act. Cf. Random House Webster's: barbarity: ① brutal or inhuman conduct; cruelty; ② an act or instance of cruelty.)

• Each new usage of the headword clearly separated, (e. g. compare includes six subdivisions dealing with the following usages: ① to compare two or more things, ② to compare someone or something to someone or something else, ③ something compares favourably or unfavourably with something else, ④ something is large, small, etc. compared to or with something else, ⑤ something does not compare with something else, and ⑥ something is beyond compare. Cf. Random House Webster's which makes nine subdivisions, but on the basis of senses that are sometimes hard to understand from the definitions provided; e. g. "to appear in quality, progress, etc. as specified. ")

• Inclusion of many collocations (e. g. under anchor are found the verb + noun collocations drop anchor, cast anchor, and weigh anchor. Cf. Random House Webster's, which does not include any of these collocations).

• Systematic inclusion of examples taken from actual modern usage, e. g. anchor, in the abstract sense of "mainstay," is illustrated by two examples in the Collins Cobuild—the anchor of marriage; your material body is the anchor of consciousness—while Random House Webster's has none at all.

• Structural information in a separate column, not found in any general use unilingual dictionary (e. g. ampere: count noun, usually after numeral).

Use

• For Anglophones: verification of collocations and of usage.

• For Francophones: explanation of meanings, awareness of collocations, and appropriate insertion of words in sentences.

3.1.2　Robert mithodique. Ed. J. Rey-Debove. Paris, Le Robert, 1988

There is no real equivalent of the Collins Cobuild in French. The closest is the Robert mithodique, which is more geared towards those learning French as a mother tongue than second language learners. However, it does have certain features that make it specially interesting for translation students.

Special features

• Simpler definitions than in most general purpose unilingual dictionaries (e. g. debat

1. action de ddbattre une question; cf. Petit Robert 1: action de d£battre une question, de la discuter).

• Simple, non-literary examples, which often include many common collocations (e. g. under debat, in the sense of "action de d6battre une question" are found not only eclaircir un dSbat and entrer dans le cceur du debat—which are also included in the Petit Robert 1—but also ouvrir, ranimer, trancher le debat).

• Inclusion of antonyms in a given sense division, immediately after the definition and synonyms, rather than at the end of the entry (e. g. debile:

① qui manque de force physique. V. Deficient, faible, frele [...] Contr. Vigoureux. Cf. Petit Robert 1 débile: 1.... 2.....3..... Ant. fort, vigoureux).

• Additional remarks which cover special difficulties and exceptions related to the headword, not normally found in general purpose unilingual dictionaries (e. g. effronte: se dit surtout des enfants et des jeunes personnes).

Use

• For Anglophones: simple explanation of meanings, awareness of collocations and of particular difficulties related to the headword.

• For Francophones: verification of collocations and of usage.

3. 2   Dictionaries of Collocations

"Proper words in proper places make the true definition of style," according to Jonathan Swift (1720). Certainly, the use of appropriate word combinations shows awareness of the idiomatic nature of language. Moreover, the fact that collocations do not necessarily coincide from one language to another make the use of collocation dictionaries essential for translators.

3. 2. 1   The BBI Combinatory Dictionary of English. Eds. M. Benson et al. Amsterdam/ Philadelphia, John Benjamins, 1986

This dictionary presents a large variety of both lexical and grammatical collocations for a series of headwords (primarily nouns, adjectives and verbs). Since its purpose is solely to present collocations, it contains far more such combinations than even unabridged English dictionaries such as the Webster's Third.

Special features

• Collocations presented in their most obvious form (e. g. to detonate a bomb), and not as part of examples (e. g. They detonated the bomb and destroyed the bridge in Longman Dictionary of Contemporary English) or as part of the definition of the entry word, e. g. detonate: to cause (a bomb, mine, etc.) to explode—in the Collins English Dictionary.

• Clear separation of different types of collocations within a given entry, e. g. bomb: ① to detonate, explode, set off; drop; fuse a ~ (verb+noun collocations);.... ⑩ a ~

explodes, goes off (noun+verb collocations).

• A number of synonymous collocations provided (cf. bomb above).

• Indication of meanings of polysemous entry words to enable users to choose the appropriate collocation for a given meaning, e. g. body ("substance") ("firmness") ① to give ~ to ("group") ("unit") ② an advisory; deliberative; elected; governing; study-...

• Examples provided to illustrate usage of certain collocations, e. g. body ... ③ in a ~ (they presented their petition in a ~).

• Inclusion of some phrases transitional between collocations and idioms (e. g. bird: as free as a bird) and of important fixed phrases (e. g. business: to mix business with pleasure), which are often neglected by dictionaries of idioms.

Use

• For Anglophones: verification of collocations when writing in or translating into English.

• For Francophones: awareness of idiomatic word combinations in English.

3. 2. 2　Les Mots et les ide'es, Dictionnaire des termes cadrant avec les id4es. Ed. U. Lacroix. Paris, Fernand Nathan, 1956

This dictionary, dated as it is, is still really the only dictionary of collocations in French. It consists of noun headwords followed by the main verbs, adjectives and nouns used in combination with them.

Special features

• Grouping together of different collocational types (e. g. blessure: Causer, provoquer, panser, envenimer une blessure. Couvrir, cribler de blessures. Une blessure se ferme, fait souffrir, se rouvre. -QUAL.: profonde, grave, dangereuse [...] blesser grievement, legerement, gravement, affreusement, cruellement.)

• Cross-references to synonymous headwords with similar collocations, (e. g. billet: Voir argent, lettre)

Use

• For Anglophones: awareness of idiomatic word combinations in French.

• For Francophones: verification of collocations when writing in or translating into French.

3. 3　Dictionaries of Neologisms

New words and new senses are constantly added to the existing vocabulary. Since many of them prove to have only a short life span, traditional dictionaries tend to ignore such items until they become more established. However, translators do not enjoy the luxury of waiting for neologisms to become established, for the latter often find their way into texts. Thus, they need to be aware of dictionaries of neologisms to which they can turn when they come up with a blank in their usual general unilingual dictionaries.

3.3.1 The Longman Register of New Words. Volume Two 1990. Ed. John Ayto. Harlow, England, Longman, 1990

This dictionary, although published in England, covers lexical items culled from newspapers and journals from many areas of the English-speaking world, including the US and Canada. It is therefore international in scope.

Special features

• Simple definitions provided (e. g. contra noun someone, especially from the right wing, who opposed another).

• Authentic examples (often more than one per lexical item) provided to show sense and usage, (e. g. contra: Tory contras opposed to Heseltine can no longer refer to him without revulsion. To call him "a tart" as the Daily Mail did on Friday shows how close to panic they are.)

• Notes on usage (e. g. abortuary noun, American derogatory)

• Entries also on evolution of grammatical and syntactic uses of existing words (e. g. accused noun [...] A subtle but significant change is taking place in the grammar of the noun accused. Hitherto it has been used only with the definite article the, but now there are signs that it is turning into an ordinary countable noun, capable of being preceded by an indefinite article).

Use

• For Anglophones: awareness of new meanings and new words in English; awareness of changes in English usage.

• For Francophones: awareness of new meanings and new words in English.

3.3.2 Dictionnaire des mots contemporains. Ed. Pierre Gilbert. Paris, Le Robert, 1980

This dictionary completes and expands on information found in the Petit Robert.

Special features

• Simple definitions provided (e. g. abandonnique adj. Qui dprouve une crainte maladive d'etre abandonné)

• Authentic examples (often more than one per lexical item) provided to show sense and usage, (e. g. abandonnique adj. Le caractere un peu difficile de cet enfant risque de lasser tres vite des parents nourriciers. II en changera sans cesse, il deviendra "abandonnique," comme disent les psychiatres).

• Usage notes (e. g. aeroglisseur: Rem. 2: Ce terme tend a remplacer ranglicisme hovercraft', il s'emploie concurremment avec naviplane).

• Cross-references to other related articles (e. g. cross-references to aeroglisseur and hovercraft in the entry for naviplane).

4　Conclusion

What dictionaries to use, how to get the most out of dictionaries and how to use dictionaries efficiently in the translation process are all, in my opinion, integral components of translation pedagogy. But where and when should these components be covered? In most professional translation programmes, which often include not only translation courses but also a documentation course, it is generally taken for granted that dictionary use will be integrated into the latter. While this is possible at least in the case of two of the objectives presented above (familiarization with different types of dictionaries and with dictionary entry formats), this solution is often unsatisfactory. Since such a course is sometimes given by a documentalist or librarian rather than a translator, the practical connection between the actual translation process and dictionary use may not be adequately made. In any case, there are still many professional translation programmes that do not have a distinct documentation course and academic translation courses are rarely, if ever, complemented by such a course. Thus, it seems logical to include dictionary use exercises into the first translation course offered.

In order not to delay introduction of translation per se in a translation course, it might be a good idea to begin with the fourth objective, that of illustrating ways in which to combine text analysis, translation and dictionary consultation. Working through the translation of a text in class, with controlled consultation of a limited number of dictionaries proposed by the instructor, will allow the latter to present simultaneously the various stages of the translation process and the role of dictionaries in the process, while at the same time introducing students to some basic dictionaries and helping them to decipher essential information therein. This can be followed by more specific work on each of the four objectives, either in the form of exercises complementary to translation, or in the form of annotations to translations.

Whatever form it takes, improvement of dictionary use is a must for students learning translation. For, as all translation teachers will acknowledge, students have neither the knowledge nor the willpower to stay away from dictionaries completely. Nor is complete abstention from dictionary use desirable, for it is only by using lexicographic tools that students can expand their lexical knowledge to the point where they need to consult dictionaries less. What is essential therefore is not to avoid the issue of dictionary use either in the name of theoretical principles or in the hope that it will be dealt with elsewhere by someone else, but to make dictionary use an integral component of translation pedagogy.

Appendix 1

Identification of different types of lexical items in a text

Petite capitale ayant donné son nom à un territoire où la France tiendrait à l'aise au moins trois fois, Québec étendit un jour son autorité sur près des trois quarts du continent nord-américain. Fondée en 1608 par le Saintongeais Samuel de Champlain sur une étroite bande de terre au pied du cap Diamant, elle prit bientôt d'assaut son rocher pour se répandre sur le plateau où, dès le début, les communautés religieuses construisirent leurs monastères, leurs couvents, leurs collèges.

J. Archambault, *Le Québec tel quel*
(Québec, Éditeur officiel du Québec, 1975, p. 65)

à l'aise: idiomatic expression
étendre l'autorité sur: collocation
bande de terre: compound
prendre d'assaut: idiomatic expression
communauté religieuse: compound

Appendix 2

Annotated Source Text and Translation

Source text

Petite capitale ayant donné son nom à un territoire où la France tiendrait à l'aise au moins trois fois, Québec étendit un jour son autorité sur près des trois quarts du continent nord-américain. Fondée en 1608 par le Saintongeais Samuel de Champlain sur une étroite bande de terre au pied du cap Diamant, elle prit bientôt d'assaut(1) son rocher pour se répandre sur le plateau où, dès le début, les communautés religieuses construisirent leurs monastères, leurs couvents, leurs collèges.

Le Québec tel quel, p. 65

Translation

Quebec City, a small capital which gave its name to a territory into which France could easily fit three times over, once extended its authority over almost three-fourths of the North American continent. Founded in 1608 by Samuel de Champlain, a native of Saintonge, on a narrow strip of land at the foot of Cap Diamant, it soon took over the cliff and spread onto the plateau, where, from the beginning, religious orders built their monasteries, convents and colleges.

Note 1: prendre d'assaut

• Meaning checked in Lexis. Expression found (with difficulty) only in one example under prendre. No separate definition. Meaning also checked in Dictionnaire des expressions et locutions figuries. Expression under assaut with following definitions: "entrer de force dans (un lieu)" and "prendre de haute lutte."

• Possible equivalents checked in Collins/Robert. Found expression under assaut with equivalents "to take by storm, to assault." There were also examples of more figurative uses, but none were close to context and therefore their translations were considered non-pertinent. Possible equivalents also checked in 2001 French and English Idioms. Expression not found under assaut or prendre.

Note 2: Equivalent "assault" (see Note 1 above) does not seem figurative enough. Equivalent "take by storm" researched for suitability. Webster's 3rd provides definition of by storm (under storm), but example with take by storm ("take an audience by storm") does not correspond to ST context. Collins Cobuild provides two definitions, each with an example, for take by storm but neither fits ST context. Therefore translation provided paraphrases idea of "domination" found in prendre d'assaut.

Appendix 3

Sample questions intended to draw attention to dictionary formats

Questions based on the source text found in Appendix 1. Answers in brackets following questions.

1.1　Is Saintongeais found in the Petit Robert 1? (Yes, but only in an appendix.)

1.2　Why do you think it is not a regular entry in this dictionary? (Because it is a proper noun and language dictionaries do not include many proper names as regular entries.)

1.3　In what kind of dictionary are you likely to find proper nouns as main entries? (A dictionary of proper nouns such as Petit Robert 2 or an encyclopedic dictionary such as the Petit Larousse)

2.1　Is bande de terre found in the Petit Robert 1 and in Lexis? (bande de terrain found in PR1, but nothing in Lexis.)

2.2　Is communauts religieuse found in the Petit Robert 1 and in Lexis? (Yes, in PR1. In Lexis, found only congregation religieuse.)

2.3　Where you did find these compounds, were they listed as separate entries? (No; bande de terrain found under bande in PR1; communaute' religieuse found under religieux in PR1; congregation religieuse found under religion in Lexis.)

2.4　Where were these compounds listed in these entries? (In the pertinent meaning division, along with other examples of usage.)

2.5　Is a definition provided for these compounds? (No, just for the element under which the compound is listed.)

3.1　Why is congregation religieuse found under religion and not under religieux in Lexis? (There is no full entry for religieux—just a cross-reference to religion.)

3.2　Is there a full entry for the noun rocher in Lexis? (No, just a cross-reference to the entry for roche.)

3.3　What can be deduced from the answers to the two preceding questions? (Lexis groups together words that are semantically and morphologically related.)

4.1   Is bande de terre found in the Collins/Robert, Larousse, and Harrap's Standard? (Yes; under bande and terre in CIR and under bande in Larousse. Not in Harrap's.)

4.2   Is communaute religieuse found in the Collins/Robert, Larousse, and Harrap's Standard? (Only in Harrap's under religieux.)

4.3   Where were the compounds that were found listed in the entry? (In the pertinent meaning division, along with other examples of usage, except in the Collins/Robert entry for bande, where bande de terre was listed in a separate section which covered several compounds beginning with bande)

选文二   On How Electronic Dictionaries Are Really Used

Gilles-Maurice de Schryver   David Joffe

导 言

本文收录于 2004 年 Computational Lexicography and Lexicology 会议简报中。

Gilles-Maurice de Schryver 是比利时根特大学(Ghent University)非洲语言与文化系的教授,其研究兴趣主要包括:电子时代词典编纂的概念与工具、语言技术与计算机智慧等。Gilles-Maurice de Schryver 是一位高产的学者,著书 20 余部,撰文逾百篇。与本书主题有关的书籍包括:*Special Issue on IJL's Silver Jubilee: Key Issues, Key Scholars, and Their Impact on Lexicography*(2012),*A Way with Words: Recent Advances in Lexical Theory and Analysis* (2010) 等。相关论文有:*Introducing a New Lexicographical Model: AlphaConceptual, Digitizing the Monolingual Lusoga Dictionary: Challenges and Prospects;Trends in Twenty-five Years of Academic Lexicography* 等。David Joffe 是 TshwaneDJe Human Language Technology 公司的创办者。

作者首先介绍了"电子词典应用"的最新进展,接着作者提及"即时反馈和模糊即时反馈",然后,作者重点分析了一个电子词典项目(即 The Sesotho sa Leboa Dictionary Project) 的日志文件,并对网上的反馈信息进行研究。

1   Introduction: Research on (Electronic) Dictionary Use

Within the framework of Wiegand's dictionary research (Worterbuchforschung), research on dictionary use (Worterbuchbenutzungsforschung) is the first of four sub-fields inmetalexicography. In one of his monographs, Wiegand (1998) devotes nearly a thousand pages to the issue, citing 86 previous studies on the way. In the same year, Hulstijn & Atkins (1998) list some 50 papers revolving around empirical research into dictionary use; their study itself being part of an edited collection entitled "Using Dictionaries" (Atkins, 1998). Around a dozen brief summaries of articles on dictionary usage may also be found in Dolezal & McCreary (1999). Mainly in the more recent contributions, the virtues of computer-controlled investigations are emphasized, as these enable an unobtrusive monitoring of dictionary use. With the popularisation of electronic dictionaries, an increasing number of scholars have pointed out the potential of especially Internet dictionaries to generate free implicit feedback, retrievable from log files attached to such dictionaries (De Schryver, 2003a: 160 – 161).

Although the proposal to draw upon log files in order to improve dictionaries was already expressed in the mid-1980s (Abate, 1985; Crystal, 1986), and although numerous researchers have reiterated this idea in recent years (Hulstijn & Atkins, 1998; Sobkowiak, 1999; Docherty, 2000; Harley, 2000; Sato, 2000), very few reports have been published of real-world dictionaries actually making use of this strategy. Notable exceptions are Lofberg (2002) and Proszeky & Kis (2002). Instead, electronic dictionaries cum log files seem to be more popular in research environments focusing on vocabulary acquisition (Hulstijn, 1993; Knight, 1994; Hulstijn & Trompetter, 1998; Laufer, 2000; Laufer & Hill, 2000). When it comes to electronic dictionaries, statements regarding log files are often hypothetical, such as in: "A log file of user access and queries is kept that should serve to give insight on how such a service is used" (Popescu-Belis et al., 2002: 1144 [emphasis added]). What is true for log files, is also true for the utilisation of direct feedback, whereby users are encouraged to comment online on dictionary articles and to suggest new items (Dodd, 1989; Carr, 1997; Considine, 1998; Harley, 2000; Nesi, 2000; Warburton, 2000), i.e. reports on what is done with this type of feedback are hard to come by.

2 Simultaneous Feedback (SF) and Fuzzy SF

Since 1997 a methodology is being worked out whereby the results of studies of actual dictionary use are directly integrated into the compilation of a reference work (De Schryver, 1999). Feedback from the envisaged target user group is systematically and continuously obtained while compilation is still in progress. In practical terms this process, known as Simultaneous Feedback (SF), "can be understood as entailing a method in terms of which the release of several small-scale parallel dictionaries triggers off feedback that is instantly channeled back into the compilation process of a main dictionary" (De Schryver & Prinsloo, 2000: 197).

Whereas the original concept was developed within the confines of printed dictionaries, work on an electronic adaptation, known as Fuzzy SF, was begun in 2001 (De Schryver &

Prinsloo, 2001). In Fuzzy SF, traditional means for gathering feedback such as participant observation or questionnaires are replaced with the computational tracking of all actions in an electronic dictionary. Ultimately, the idea is that an automated analysis of the log files will enable the dictionary to tailor itself to each and every particular user. At present, the analysis of the log files is still largely done manually, in part with the aim to draw up typical user profiles that will then be fed into the projected adaptive and intelligent dictionary of the future (cf. De Schryver, 2003a: 188 – 190).

3　The Sesotho sa Leboa Dictionary Project (SeDiPro)

One electronic reference work that is currently being compiled within the framework of Fuzzy SF is the Sesotho sa Leboa Dictionary Project (SeDiPro), a bilingual dictionary between Sesotho sa Leboa (a Bantu language spoken in South Africa) and English. This dictionary has been made available on the Internet (http://africanlanguages. com/sdp/), and with approximately 25,000 items on the Sesotho sa Leboa side and 28,000 in the English search index, as well as a linguistics terminology list of over 300 items, it is currently the largest freely-available African-language Internet dictionary. It is also the first African-language Internet dictionary allowing for some low-level fuzzy searches and for which the entire interface can be set to an African language in addition to English. The latter is not merely a small extra or a political move, but a fully functional component. Indeed, "the terminology list contains a world's first for an online dictionary, namely the customization of the output of part-of-speech (POS) tags, usage labels and cross-references depending on the language chosen" (De Schryver, 2003b: 12). This customization is realised in real time on the Internet.

Unlike in the great majority of current electronic dictionaries, dealing with feedback, whether implicit or explicit, has been a central component right from the start in SeDiPro. Since the first day the dictionary was posted online, a well thought out log file has been unobtrusively keeping track of all aspects of dictionary use, while an online feedback form has allowed for a more traditional and open way of receiving feedback.

The software used is TshwaneLex (see Joffe & De Schryver, 2004), a modern dictionary compilation program developed by TshwaneDJe HLT (http://tshwanedje. com/). Using TshwaneLex, the dictionary contents are exported to a MySQL (http://www. mysql. com/) database that is stored on a Linux/Apache web server (http://www. apache. org/). The online dictionary software is implemented using the scripting language PHP (http://www. php. net/). The PHP scripts generate the HTML-based search interface, log users' searches, query the MySQL database and generate the search results. In order to track the number of unique visitors (and to track return visits), each visitor is associated with a unique 128-bit identification number (visitor ID) that is saved in the log file each time that user performs a search. The visitor ID is generated the first time a user uses the dictionary, and it is stored using a cookie in the user's web browser software, allowing the ID to be retrieved again during subsequent searches or visits. This method, which is commonly used on the Internet, has the advantage of being unobtrusive and transparent to the user (as opposed to, for example, a user registration system with login and password, as is the case for ELDIT). However, it is not foolproof. Some users periodically clear the cookies stored by their browser, and other users even block cookies altogether. One can also not distinguish between multiple users who share a computer, or determine when a single user has made use of multiple computers (e. g. a student who uses a computer lab). Nonetheless, the technique is reliable in the majority of cases, providing an error margin of probably not more than 15%.

4　Analysing the SeDiPro Log Files

SeDiPro was made available on 22 April 2003, and what follows is a brief analysis of the main dictionary log files of the first six months, referred to as months 1 to 6 below. A total of 21,337 lookups were made by 2,530 different visitors during those six months. Although this corresponds to an average of 8.4 lookups per visitor, the actual distribution is Zipfian, as shown in Figure 1, with the great majority of users only performing a few searches each, and a minority up to several hundreds of searches each.

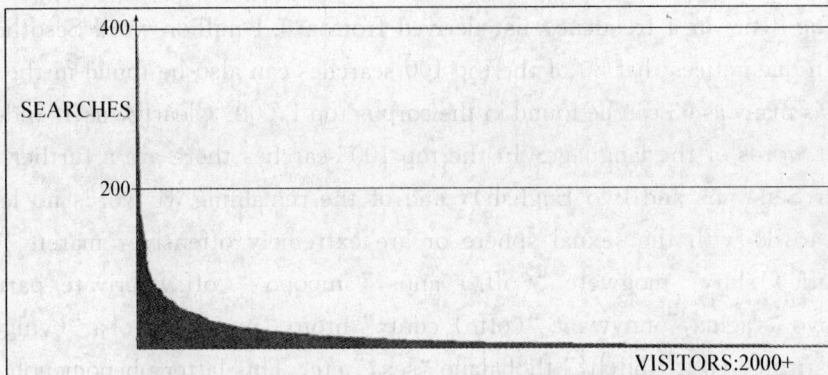

Figure 1　Distribution of the number of searches per visitor

Per day, an average of 16.8 visitors carried out 116.6 lookups: 40.8 (i. e. 35%) in the direction Sesotho sa Leboa to English, and 75.8 (i. e. 65%) in the reverse direction. Lookups during weekends were markedly less frequent than during weekdays. With each passing month, both the number of searches and the number of visitors increased, as can be seen in Figure 2.

Monthly

Month	Total searches	Sesotho sa Leboa	English	Unique visitors
1	1308	512	796	138
2	2261	915	1346	282
3	5892	2266	3626	851
4	3607	1109	2498	482
5	4596	1647	2949	529
6	3673	1025	2648	427

Figure 2 Distributions of the number of searches and visitors per month

The peak for month 3 is mainly the effect of a series of local media releases in several South African newspapers starting on 3—4 July 2003, and lasting for a week. In contrast, the official academic launch two weeks earlier, on 20 June 2003, had no great impact on the stats. When one studies the origin of all searches per domain or country one may conclude that the large majority of the lookups are also made from within South Africa.

Apart from such general facts about electronic dictionary use, the logs also enable one to examine more closely what people actually look up. This could for example be linked to the following research question: "Are the top 100 searches also the top 100 in a corpus?" If it would turn out that there is indeed a large overlap, this finding would provide substantial support for the practice of including or omitting lemma signs in a dictionary based on frequency considerations (and by extension for corpus-based lexicography in general).

If one compares the top 100 Sesotho sa Leboa searches with the ranks of the corresponding items in a frequency list derived from a 6.1-million-word Sesotho sa Leboa corpus, then one notices that 30 of the top 100 searches can also be found in the corpus top 100, while as many as 63 can be found in the corpus top 1,000. Clearly, users indeed look up the frequent words of the language. In the top 100 searches there are a further six foreign words (four Setswana and two English), and of the remaining 31 words no less than 17 either have to do with the sexual sphere or are extremely offensive: marete "testicles," masepa "(off.) shit," mogwete "(off.) anus," mpopo "(off.) private part (vagina; penis)," nnyo "vagina," nnywana "(off.) cunt," ntoto "penis," nyoba "(vulgar) fuck," sefebe "prostitute; (off.) bitch," thobalano "sex," etc. This latter phenomenon might very well be the case for all (Internet) dictionaries. The following note was for example added to the yearly top 50 of the Cambridge Dictionaries Online (http://dictionary.cambridge.org/): "The list had to be edited slightly for prurient content." One may therefore conclude that genuine frequent words are looked up on the one hand, and then those words that only mother-tongue speakers know, but, as they are taboo, never pronounce in public.

An analogous study of the top 100 English searches reveals a similar pattern, with 18 of the top 100 searches also in the BNC top 100 (Leech et al., 2001) and 62 in the BNC top 1,000. A single item in the top 100 searches is misspelled, while 6 of the remaining 37 searches again belong to the same sexual/offensive sphere: bitch, fuck, penis, sex, shit and vagina.

The most frequently looked for word in both sides of the dictionary is the same concept: hello and dumela respectively. As a matter of fact, numerous users seem to "greet the dictionary" on arrival (other frequent variants are (good) morning and thobela respectively), and after having gone through their lookups, they also "say" goodbye and šepela (gabotse) respectively.

Not all lookups are successful, of course. Quite a number of English words are searched for in the Sesotho sa Leboa side and vice versa. A surprisingly high percentage of words are also consistently misspelled and/or mistyped in both languages, and a large number of items from neighbouring African languages (especially from Setswana and isiZulu), as well as from Afrikaans and Dutch, are found in the logs. Not-founds that are repeatedly searched for and that should have been included in the first place, are added during updates of the online dictionary. Care is taken not to react blindly on incidental peaks however. Compare in this regard the sudden popularity of so-called terrorist-related concepts following September 11, 2001, as recorded and analysed by for instance Google (http://www.google.com/press/zeitgeist/9-11.html) and Cambridge Dictionaries Online (http://dictionary.cambridge.org/top20/top20_0901.asp). Two substantial updates of SeDiPro were effected, the first on 30 July 2003, the second on 4 September 2003. Although no more than a dozen, respectively around one hundred, changes/additions were made, the impact on the hit rate was impressive. The percentage of successful searches in the English side, for example, went from 67% to 72% after the first update, and then to 75% after the second update. Examples from the first update include the addition of "fuck" as translation equivalent of nyoba, to supplement the more formal "have sexual intercourse," or the inclusion of Inthanete "Internet" which had not yet been lemmatized. During the second update more abstract concepts as well as multi-word units (MWUs) were included, for example "devaluation" was added as an equivalent of phokotso, while MWUs such as ka kua ga "across" or ya/tsa/wa/... gauta "golden" were lemmatised. The latter necessitated the creation of a new convention; in other instances new words had to be coined following consultation and fieldwork. As such, the online dictionary could be viewed as a service to the community.

On another level, especially relevant within the framework of Fuzzy SF, one can zoom in on particular users, and study their search strategies. Research questions may include: "How do users look up?" and "What do users do when a search fails?" As the log files are written in such a way that they automatically track and summarise all aspects of each and every visitor, one may for example study look-up behaviour when the exact spelling is not known. One series of searches is: ... chinese √¶ indian √¶ arab √¶ foreigner ×¶ foreigner ×¶ outsider √¶ foreigner √¶... Here the user struggled with the spelling of "foreigner", then tried the related word "outsider," which returned the article for lephatle. As the latter article also mentions "foreigner" in its translation equivalent paradigm, the user now saw the correct spelling, and went on to search for it directly. The beginning of the above series is also rather typical in the logs, as items from a single onomasiological field are looked up. In some cases, users even type in single search strings such as "eye, ear, nose, mouth, tongue, hand, arm. "

The online dictionary has several dozen regular visitors. In Figure 3 the searches made by one such visitor, between 19 June and 12 September 2003, are shown. During the studied period this visitor performed 168 searches, looked up in both Sesotho sa Leboa and English, and did not use the dictionary on weekends (grey). Hlogo (automatically re-routed from hlogo) "head; prefix; heading; principal" being rather polysemous, it is not surprising it was looked for repeatedly; yet the two searches for "woodpecker" suggest that there was no long-term retention for the ways to express this item in Sesotho sa Leboa.

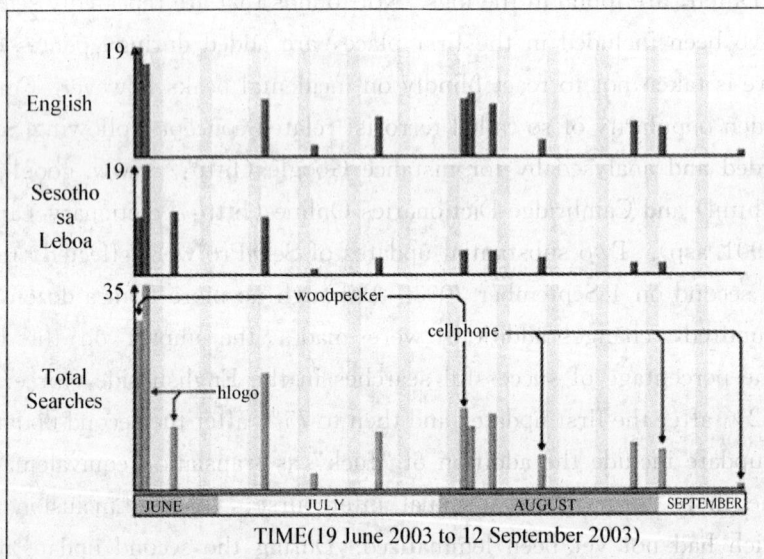

Figure 3　Zooming in on the searches across time by one particular visitor

5　Analyzing the SeDiPro Online Feedback Forms

In addition to the unobtrusive logging of the dictionary users' actions, as briefly discussed in the previous section, users are invited to provide the compilers with direct feedback. To that end, an online dictionary feedback form (offered in both Sesotho sa Leboa and English) is available, and all this feedback is automatically date stamped and logged. A total of 52 messages were received during the first 6 months, or thus on average two per week. In Table 1 the topics of these messages, as well as where the authors come from and the languages in which they write, are summarized.

Table 1　Summary of the analysis of the online feedback forms

Topic [N=52]	%	Affiliation [N=52]	%
		Expected	
		Academic(. ac)/Education(. edu)	38. 5
Support for the project		Less expected	
Congratulations	31. 7	Company(. com)/Organisation	32. 7
Expressing disbelief	8. 7	(. org)	
		Surfer	21. 2
Regarding SeDiPro itself		Professional translator	5. 8
General contents	11. 5	Government employee	1. 9
Useful tips	10. 6		100. 1
Questions on specific word use	7. 7		
Extra grammar/synonyms	3. 8	**Language [N=52]**	**%**
please			
Interface	5. 8		
In other dictionary media as well			
please		English	87. 5
Electronic dictionary(on CD etc.)	8. 7		
Paper dictionary	3. 8	Sesotho sa Leboa	6. 7
More languages please	7. 7	Afrikaans/Dutch	5. 8
	100. 0		100. 0

Four out of every ten messages is written in support of the project. In some cases the users even express outright disbelief, such as in "OH MY GOODNESS. Very incredible that this is indeed available! Please continue improving upon this wonderful work. Most of all, thank you for even beginning this project!!!! Many thanks!!!!" or "Thank you a million—never would I have thought I'd see my language first, translated to English and secondly, on-line. This is remarkable and I hope this site is exposed to a lot of 'ba geso' [our people] out there! Re a leboga ka kudu! [We thank you very much!]." Apart from being gratifying, it is important to realise that, in a country officially eleven-lingual, so far the majority of the people have just been paying lip service to all things relating to multilingualism. Another four out of every ten messages deals with the dictionary itself. On the one hand there are general remarks and useful tips, on the other hand there are questions that deal with specific words or requests for more data categories. An example of the first is "I strongly believe that the Northern Sotho word seriti has more to do with dignity or aura than just personality," and of the second "Can I ask you for a translation of the word 'cellphone'". Surprisingly, 5.8% of the messages deal with aspects of the interface, with people commenting on computational features. In 12.5% of the messages people express their wish to acquire a stand-alone electronic and/or a hardcopy version. Lastly, in 7.7% of the messages users point out that they would like to see analogous dictionaries for the other South African languages, and request that these be compiled.

Each and every message is followed up, a reply is sent in all cases (which sometimes results in real discussion), and the dictionary is adapted whenever necessary. In line with the idea to be a service to the community, attending to the formal feedback receives higher priority than implementing changes prompted by trends seen in the log files. Users also take the compilers—and with this perhaps even the concept of Simultaneous Feedback—seriously. In Figure 3, the first search for "cellphone" (on August 15) was unsuccessful. During this user's next visit (on August 28), the feedback form was filled in with a request that the compilers come up with a translation equivalent for this word. Already four days later (on September 1) this user checked again, yet the matter was still being researched. Three days later an acceptable translation (mogalathekeng) was found and uploaded. A third search for "cellphone" (on September 12) then returned a hit. As far as the call for Internet dictionaries in other South African languages is concerned, planning of ZuDiPro, the isiZulu equivalent of SeDiPro, has begun. On the whole one observes a very good correspondence between the formal feedback received through the online feedback forms, and the informal feedback obtained by means of an analysis of the log files. This is a satisfying sign indeed and indicates that modifying and adapting dictionary contents based on log-stat trends is a feasible strategy.

When one focuses on the origin of the feedback forms, one sees that 38.5% originate from the academic and higher education spheres. One would have expected this percentage to be even higher, given that 82% of all African-language Internet dictionaries are provided (and mainly used) by tertiary institutions, with only 13% by dotcoms and another 5% being private efforts (De Schryver, 2003b: 9). The large percentage of visitors from dotcoms, organizations and individual surfers is thus surprising. Lastly, 87.5% of the messages are written in English, with only 6.7% in Sesotho sa Leboa and another 5.8% in Afrikaans or Dutch. One would have wished the African-language part to be larger.

6 Conclusion: Truly Unobtrusively Improving Dictionary Contents and Studying Dictionary Use

A real electronic dictionary used in a natural setting with no manipulation of research variables whatsoever was presented in this paper. It was shown how a combination of informal log-file analysis and the processing of formal online feedback forms may lead to improving dictionary contents and to a study of (electronic) dictionary use in a truly unobtrusive way.

With specific reference to a Sesotho sa Leboa Internet dictionary, it was indicated that the general trend during the first six months has been one of a growing number of lookups by a growing number of users—already reaching unexpected heights for an African language. Most visits remain local, and being mentioned in the popular press, unlike an academic launch, results in huge spikes in the stats. While the distribution of the number of lookups per visitor is Zipfian, most visitors tend to look up frequent items on the one hand, and sexual/offensive items on the other. Revisions and improvements of the dictionary may successfully be based on a semi-automatic analysis of log files, in combination with follow-ups on feedback received electronically. With the discussed tracking function, any number of individual users' look-up strategies may be monitored across time, which is especially relevant for studying vocabulary retention and for drawing up user profiles needed for the projected intelligent and adaptive Fuzzy SF dictionary of the future.

More basic plans include smart re-routers for frequently misspelled and/or orthographically challenging words, whereby the software would not merely re-route but also point out the correct spelling. The selection of items to re-route ought to be based on frequencies derived from the log files, and in the case of frequently looked up foreign words a link to a dictionary in that particular language could also be offered. More than ever, dictionaries are becoming a service to the community.

选文三   Electronic Dictionaries and Incidental Vocabulary Acquisition: Does Technology Make a Difference?

Batia Laufer

导 言

本文发表于 2000 年的欧洲词典学会年会的论文集中。

作者 Batia LAUFER 是以色列海法大学(University of Haifa)的教授,研究领域主要涉及二语词汇习得,著有 *Vocabulary in a Second Language*: *Selection*, *Acquisition and Testing*; *A Teacher's Grammar of the English Verb*; *Similar Lexical Forms in Interlanguage* 等书籍,其代表论文有: *The contribution of dictionary use to the production and retention of collocations in a second language*; *Incidental Vocabulary Acquisition*: *the effects of Task Type*, *Word Occurrence and Their Combination* 等。作者首先指出论文的写作背景:研究电子词典对于词汇学习的影响具有十分重要的意义,同时对于教育工作者的决定也大有裨益。接着作者声明其研究问题、实验对象、实验方法。最后,根据实验结果,作者得出其结论。

1   Background

At the EURALEX symposium in Zurich, Henri Bejoint stated that if dictionaries are instruments for the acquisition of meaning, "the process remains so mysterious that one's recommendations cannot really be based on scientific evidence" (ZuriLEX '86 Proceedings:

146). Fourteen years later, there is a body of studies, albeit a modest one, which has investigated how much vocabulary is acquired incidentally when learners consult a dictionary during a reading activity. The conclusion that seems to have emerged is that people who use a dictionary almost always acquire more words than people who read without a dictionary. Without a dictionary, readers approach the unknown vocabulary through a combination of guessing and ignoring the unfamiliar words. If words ignored, i. e. unattended to, they are unlikely to be remembered. If guessing is attempted, it cannot always be carried out, which leads either to non retention of the word or to retention of incorrect meaning, if it was guessed incorrectly (Laufer, 1997). On the other hand, when words looked up in a dictionary, some of them are retained (Luppesku and Day, 1993, Knight, 1994). Looked up words were shown to be remembered better than words inferred from context (Mondria, 1993), or words whose meaning is given by the teacher (Hulstijn, Hollander and greidanus, 1996).

The advent of electronic dictionaries has raised the inevitable question whether electronic dictionaries have a similar effect to that of paper dictionaries and glosses and what type of electronic glossing techniques will produce the best results in vocabulary learning. Most studies, however, compared the effect of different types of glosses (paper, electronic textual, electronic pictorial, electronic and video) on reading comprehension, translation, on the number of words looked up by the learners, the length of time on task and the effect of gloss type on the reported satisfaction of dictionary users (Leffa, 1992; Roby, 1991, 1999; Aust, Kelly and Roby, 1993; Lomicka, 1998; Nesi, 1999). Fewer studies investigated incidental vocabulary learning via computer glosses (chun and plass, 1996; plass, chun, Mayer and Leutner, 1998; Lyman-Hager, Davis, Burnett and Chennault, 1993; Laufer and Hill, 2000), and, to my knowledge, only Lyman-Hager et al. (1993) specifically compared vocabulary retention resulting from the use of paper and electronic dictionaries. And yet, researching the effect of electronic dictionaries on vocabulary learning is important as it may influence pedagogical decisions with regard to recommendations of dictionaries for learners.

2　The Study

2. 1　Research Questions and Test Items

The paper investigates incidental vocabulary acquisition during a reading task in two conditions: paper gloss condition and electronic gloss condition. It addresses two questions:

1. Which type of gloss, paper or electronic, will result in higher scores on vocabulary learning test?

2. Which types of looked up information in the electronic dictionary (L1 translation, L2 definition, example of usage, or combinations of these) are associated with better vocabulary learning scores?

Ten low frequency words and expressions were selected for investigation: rigmarole, wrath, grist, not one whit, sanitize, privy to, morally derelict, curb, inflammatory, deeply ingrained. In this study, vocabulary learning was considered to be the recall of word meaning. The target words were pre-tested on a group similar to the experimental group and were found to be unfamiliar.

2.2　Subjects and Procedure

The subjects were two parallel groups of advanced university learners of English as a foreign language in Israel, one group in each condition. Students in condition one (n=31), the paper gloss condition, received a 621 word text and a set of ten multiple choice comprehension questions. The ten target words were highlighted by being typed in bold print and glossed in L1 on the margin of the text. The task of the students was to read the text and answer the ten comprehension questions. Students in condition two (n = 24), the electronic dictionary condition, read the same text on computer screen and answered the same ten comprehension questions on paper. The target words were highlighted. The learners were told that, in the course of reading, they could look up information about the highlighted words by clicking on them with the mouse and then choose the options or options that would best clarify the meaning of the word in the text. Whenever the word was clicked on, a window appeared on the screen with three options: translation, definition in English, examples of usage. The three main options and their various combinations offered seven look up possibilities (translation + definition, translation + example, definition + example, etc.). In practice, however, only three look up patterns were selected by students: translation only, translation + definition, translation + definition + example. Students could return to look up the same word as many times as they wished. While they were looking up the words, the log was recording every mouse click. The results screen (available to researchers only) displayed the following information: which words were selected, what dictionary information was looked up, the number of times each word was selected and how much time was spent on the entire task.

After the completion of the task, the work sheets were collected and the students were unexpectedly given a list of the ten target words and asked to provide the L1 equivalents or English explanations for these words. Two weeks later, the same test was repeated. The scoring was done as follows: a word that was not translated, or translated wrongly received zero points. A correct response received two points. A semantically approximate response received one point. Thus, a student could receive a maximum of 20 points (10 words x 2 points) if all the responses were correct.

While the tests provided us with the retention scores, the log files showed which look up options were selected for which word, and how each option contributed to word retention, i.e. whether the looked up word was later retained.

3 Results

The difference between paper and electronic dictionary (research question 1) was examined by comparing the mean vocabulary retention scores of the two groups. Table 1 presents mean retention scores on the immediate and the delayed tests and the t-tests results comparing the means in the two conditions. Table 2 presents the above results as well. This time, however, the retention scores of the electronic group were calculated for words which were looked up in L1 only. This was done in order to eliminate the variable of additional L2 dictionary information which was available in the electronic gloss, but not in the paper gloss. Of the 24 students in the electronic gloss condition, 17 used Hebrew glosses only.

Table 1 Paper and electronic glosses: the effect on word retention—All electronic dictionary selections (Maximum retention score=20)

	Paper gloss (n=31)	Electronic gloss (n=24)	Difference
Immediate recall	M=3.87(19%) Sd=4.19	17.52(87.6%) Sd=4.29	T=9.66 p<.000 01
Delayed recall	M=0.88 Sd=1.72	4.8(24%) Sd=3.6	T=3.9 p<.001

Tables 1 and 2 show that both on the immediate recall test and the delayed test, the computer group achieved significantly higher retention scores than the paper gloss group. This was true for learners who consulted a variety of dictionary information and for learners who consulted L1 glosses only.

The effect of selected dictionary information on learning (research question 2) was examined by comparing word retention scores in all the look-up patterns. For each word, we calculated the number of times it was looked up in each of the three patterns that students adopted: L1 only, L1 + L2 definition, and L1 + L2 definition + L2 example. Then the number of correct test responses was calculated for each pattern and converted into percentage.

Table 2 Paper and electronic glosses: the effect on word retention—Only L1 selection

	Paper gloss (n=31)	Electronic gloss (n=17)	Difference
Immediate recall	M=3.87(19%) Sd=4.19	14.59(73%) Sd=4.65	T=10.72 p<.000 01
Delayed recall	M=0.88(4%) Sd=1.72	3.82(19%) Sd=3.52	T=2.94p p<.05

Table 3 presents the following information: the mean number of look ups in each of the three look up patterns for all the words; the mean retention percentage, i. e. the percentage of correct test responses for each look up pattern; the results of ANOVA comparing the retention scores of three look up patterns. The maximum mean of look ups per option could be 24, if all 24 students looked up all the 10 words using this option.

Table 3 shows that the preferred dictionary look-up pattern is translation of the unknown words (14. 3 out of 24). The immediate recall does not seem to be significantly affected by the type of information selected even though the scores are higher for words looked up in both languages. The long term recall scores, however, are significantly higher when a combination of translation, definition and example is selected.

Table 3　Look up patterns and word retention

Dictionary information look up	L1 only	L1+ L2 definition	L1+ L2 definition +L2 example	Difference
Mean number of selections	14. 3	1. 1	0. 4	
Retention rate Immediate recall	M=82. 91% Sd=14. 45%	M=90% Sd=20%	M=100% Sd=0%	F=0. 9 Not significant
Retention rate Delayed recall	M=27. 09% Sd=23. 24%	M=0%	M=100% Sd=0%	F=18. 5 P<. 001

4　Conclusion

In the two research conditions, the new words were highlighted in the texts thus drawing learners' attention to them. And yet words looked up in an electronic gloss were retained better than words glossed in the margin of the text. Why is an electronic gloss superior to a paper gloss for acquiring new vocabulary? One reason may have to do with the visual impact produced by a word which embedded in a window and appears in a prominent position on the computer screen.

A marginal gloss in a paper text may not have the same prominence, and may therefore fail to create a memory trace to the word. Another explanation relates to the "involvement hypothesis" proposed by Laufer and Hulstijn (forthcoming 2001). The hypothesis states that tasks which create a need for a word, elicit search for its meaning and "evaluation" (decision involving processes of selection and combination) will have a better effect on the retention of the words than tasks which do not induce the three above mentioned elements of involvement. In our study, the paper group did not have to search for the meanings of the words as these were provided in the margin. The computer group, on the other hand, was actively involved in searching for the meanings of the target words.

With regard to the effect of look up patterns on learning, it is sometimes claimed that multiplicity of information (translation, definition, and example) may provide several retrieval routes to the words and would therefore benefit retention (cf. Plass et al., 1998). Our results which seem to support this position, should, nevertheless, be interpreted with caution. Thought the delayed recall scores were highest in L1 + definition + example condition, this look up pattern was observed only with two words (out of 10) and four students (out of 24). Furthermore, words looked up in L1 + L2 definition were not remembered at all on the delayed test while words looked up in L1 only were remembered in 27% of cases. The data of the study together with the results of Laufer and Hill (2000) suggest that, in most cases, combining dictionary information in two languages reinforces retention. The beneficial effect of this combination may lie in the richness of semantic encoding; it may lie in the prolonged attention that multiple items of information require; or it may lie in both.

【延伸阅读】

[1] Al-Kasimi, A. M. *Linguistics and Bilingual Dictionaries*. Leiden: E. J. Brill, 1977.

[2] Delisle, J. *L'Analyse du discours comme me'thode de traduction*. Ottawa: University of Ottawa Press, 1980.

[3] Hartmann, R. R. K. Lexicography, Translation and the So-called Language Barrier// M. Snell-Hornby, et al. (eds.), *Translation and Lexicography* (pp. 9 - 20). Kirksville, Missouri: NMSU.

[4] Landau, S. I. *Dictionaries: The Art and Craft of Lexicography*. New York: Charles Scribner's Sons, 1984.

[5] Meyer, I. Towards a New Type of Bilingual Dictionary. Ph. D. dissertation. University of Montreal.

[6] Newmark, P. *Approaches to Translation*. Oxford: Pergamon Press, 1981.

[7] Nida, E. A., & Taber, C. *The Theory and Practice of Translation*. Leiden: E. J. Brill, 1974.

[8] Tatilon, C. *Traduire. Pour une pédagogie de la traduction*. Toronto: Editions du GREF.

[9] Abate, F. R. Dictionaries Past & Future: Issues and Prospects. *Dictionaries*, 1985, 7: 270 - 283.

[10] Dodd, W. S. Lexicomputing and the Dictionary of the Future//G. James (ed.), *Lexicographers and Their Works* (pp. 83 - 93). Exeter: EUP, 1989.

[11] Hulstin, J. H., & Atkins, B. T. S. Empirical Research on Dictionary Use in Foreign-Language Learning: Survey and Discussion//B. T. S. Atkins (ed.), *Using Dictionaries: Studies of Dictionary Use by Languages Learners and Translators* (pp. 7 - 19). Max Niemeyer verlag: Yubingen, 1998.

[12] Laufer, B. & Hill, M. What Lexical Information do L2 Learners Select in a Call Dictionary and How does it Affect Word Retention? *Language Learning &*

Technology，2000，3(2)：58－76.

［13］Aust，R.，Kelley，M. J.，& Roby，W. B. The Use of Hyper-reference and Conventional Dictionaries. *Educational Technology Research & Development*，1993，41：63－73.

［14］Chun，D. M.，& Plass，J. L. Effects of Multimedia Annotations on Vocabulary Acquisition. *The Modern Language Journal*，1996，80：183－198.

［15］Hulstin，J. H.，Hollander，M. & Greidanus，T. Incidental Vocabulary Learning Advanced Foreign Language Students：The Influence of Marginal Glosses，Dictionary Use，and Reoccurrence of Unknown Words. *The Modern Language Journal*，1996，80：327－339.

［16］Knight，S. Dictionary Use While Reading：The Effects on Comprehension and Vocabulary Acquisition for Students of Different Verbal Abilities. *The Modern Language Journal* 1994，78：285－298.

［17］Laufer，B. The Lexical Plight in Second Language Reading：Words You don't Know，Words You Think You Know and Words You Can't Guess//J. Coady & T. Huckin（eds.），*Second Language Vocabulary Acquisition：A Rationale for Pedagogy*（pp. 20－34）. Cambridge：Cambridge University Press，1997.

词典推荐：

［1］Brueckner，J. H.，et al. *Brueckner's French Contextuary*. Englewood，NJ：Prentice-Hall，1975.

［2］Benson，M.，et al. *The BBI Combinatory Dictionary of English*. Amsterdam/Philadelphia：John Benjamins，1986.

［3］Atkins，B.，et al. *Collins and Robert French-English English-French Dictionary*. London/Paris：Collins/Le Robert，1987.

［4］*Collins Cobuild English Language Dictionary*. London：Collins，1988.

［5］Hanks，P. *Collins Dictionary of the English Language*. London & Glasgow：Collins，1986.

［6］Boulanger，J.-C.，et al. *Dictionnaire CEC Jeunesse*. Montreal：CEC，1986.

【问题与思考】

1. Roda P. Roberts 介绍的 4 种提高词典使用效率的策略有哪些？
2. 你认为文章中推荐的词典对你有用吗？为什么？
3. 概念解释
   Simultaneous Feedback：
   Fuzzy Simultaneous Feedback：
4. The Sesotho sa Leboa Dictionary Project 的设计原理是什么？
5. Batia Laufer 的研究方法是什么？

第四章　翻译的网络资源

导　论

在全球化和数字化的背景下,"一部词典打遍天下所有翻译"的时代一去不复返了。"互联网"使翻译实践、教学和研究正在经历着前所未有的革命性的变化。

信息通信技术是每位翻译工作者的必备工具。其中,网络资源更是让翻译者如虎添翼。所以,当下,要想成为一名称职的译者,应该学会充分利用互联网提供的无限的网络资源。在提高翻译准确度的同时,恰当有效地使用网络资源既可以节省翻译的时间,又可以节省购买其他翻译参考用书的费用。

可资翻译使用的网络资源主要有:在线词典、搜索引擎、翻译软件、双语文献资源、在线机器翻译、翻译网站等。

网络资源对翻译的影响主要体现在三个方面:

1. 对于翻译实践而言

借助于网络资源,译者可以大大提高翻译质量和翻译效率。具体来讲,首先,通过查找相关网站,译者可以最大限度地准确理解原文意义、原文作者的意图、原文创作的时代背景、文化负载词意义、原作者的生平等。其次,可以提高译文的地道性和准确度。最后,译者借助于网络资源可以检验译文的质量。

2. 对于翻译教学而言

翻译教学不只像以前一样教会学生一些翻译技巧,同时,还应该教授学生如何更充分地利用网络资源提高学生的语言知识和语言技能、丰富学生的百科知识、准确理解原文、修改自己的译文等。

3. 对于翻译研究而言

互联网时代,翻译实践活动发生了重大变革,其研究范式也应该随之变化。如何描述这一背景下翻译实践活动,并根据这些描述找出一些共性,以期对翻译实践作出评估。

本章选取了三篇文章。Snezhina Gileva 撰写的文章"Using the Web as a Linguistic Tool in Translation Practice"重点探讨了译者如何将网络视为一个超大的语料库以提高翻译质量。王军礼所著《网络资源在翻译中应用》一文则主要介绍了翻译的主要网络资源,给出了常用网站的网址,并对其特点简要论述,对于翻译工作者的翻译实践具有极强的实用性。最后,Heather Fulford 的论文"The uptake of online tools and web-based language resources by freelance translators: implications for translator training, professional development, and research"给出了自由译员可以使用的网上翻译工具和资源,接着给出了一份对于 400 名译者所作的问卷调查,并给出了其调查结果。

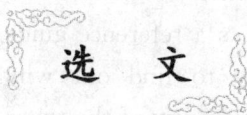

选 文

选文一　Using the Web as a Linguistic Tool in Translation Practice

Snezhina Gileva

导 言

作者 Snezhina Gileva 是保加利亚索菲亚大学的老师,主要研究计算机语言学。其著作 *Literature and the Net* 于 2000 年以电子书的形式出版。

本文主要探讨译者如何将网络作为一个多语语料库以辅助翻译实践。作者首先介绍了网络可以给译者提供多种语言参考的工具。之后,阐明了字典在翻译时存在的不足,并简要概述了常用的几种翻译语料库。接着,作者试图证明,网络实际上就是一个语料库,以及这种语料库对翻译的作用。最后,作者用一个小型"实地试验"来证明其观点。

1　Introduction

Internet, in its capacity of a global information environment, represents a unique source of linguistic information, unfortunately, still not fully utilized by translators. The wide use of the net in everyday translation practice makes it possible not only to solve multiple linguistic problems but also to improve significantly the quality of translation. Precisely for that reason we can be positive that in the near future the ability to use the linguistic capabilities of the net will become such an essential skill as the use of computers is nowadays.

There are several main areas in which Internet is invaluable to the translator:

• Quick access to a vast range of reference information materials: electronic dictionaries, encyclopaedias, glossaries, and various terminological resources.

• Use of the net in its capacity of a universal multilingual corpus for extracting diverse linguistic information.

• Acquisition of background information about the source and the target texts.

• Operational connection: Internet is a medium for communication that facilitates the fast exchange of information with customers, making the translator quite independent and globalizing the range of translation services.

The main topic of this paper shall be the investigation of the possibilities of the web as a multilingual corpus. First, we shall go over the potentials of the web as a reference guide offering multiple tools for linguistic references. Then we shall try to find out why dictionaries are not a sufficient source of information and make a short overview of the types of corpora used in translation. In addition, we shall try to prove that the web is actually a corpus and find out what its potentials as such are with regard to translation. Finally, we shall perform a small field test consisting of a translation problem and an attempt to find its answer in the web using first Google and then BNC.

2 The Web as a Linguistics Reference Guide

Undoubtedly, the main advantage of the net as a reference guide is the wealth of specialised glossaries and dictionaries from all possible fields of knowledge. Practically all well-known publishing houses offer electronic versions of their dictionaries and encyclopaedias on a CD-ROM, and many of them like Merriam Webster, Encyclopaedia Britannica, Larousse, Hachette, Meyers, Brockhaus, Garzanti, etc. also have free online versions of their products. Most often the access to the big dictionaries is in online mode but the majority of the specialised glossaries can be downloaded and used offline. Of special interest are dictionaries of slang, idioms, differences between British and American English, reference guides of grammar, style and many other.

The diverse choice of dictionaries and encyclopaedias is yet not the most valuable thing Internet has to offer to the translator. The modern search engines are also widely used as front-end solutions for linguistic queries on the net. Practically we can look at the whole set of pages present online as acolossal corpus covering all imaginable fields of knowledge.

Here it is worthwhile mentioning how the search engines actually work. Each such system is basically a huge database containing copies of websites scattered all over Internet. A robot program (called web crawler) travels around the web, collecting hypertext links and feeding them into this database. All pages are automatically indexed and when a user runs a query in the search engine, the program searches not across all pages on the net but looks up the key words in an alphabetic index and returns a link to the page on which the keyword is present.

The practice of using the web in translation practice has allowed to increase radically the quality of the end product, especially when translating from one's mother tongue into a foreign language and in fields where the terminology is updated virtually every day like telecommunications, business and finance, international relations etc. Moreover, even the most experienced translators inevitably come across unknown terms, neologisms, professional slang etc. that cannot be found even in the most recent dictionaries. In situations like that Internet is invaluable. Typing a few words in the search engine window is often worth several trips to the library and long hours of consultations with experts.

3　Why Dictionaries Are Not Enough?

In this line of thought the question arises why dictionaries are not sufficient resources for lexical information and why should translators complicate matters further by introducing additional information sources. The reasons can be briefly summarised in the following way (Varantola, 2000:172):

• Dictionary-makers usually aim at context-free descriptions of word use, whereas dictionary users resort to dictionaries to solve a context-dependent problem.

• Translators certainly need equivalents, but they also need reassurance; for this reason translators do not like to find equivalents that they do not recognize.

• Translators often need information relating to longer stretches of text rather than a single lexical item.

• Translators try to find non-dictionary type information in dictionaries because it is not readily and systematically available in other sources.

It has been estimated that up to 50% of the total time for performing a particular translation task may be spent while trying to find relevant lexical information. We can therefore argue that the more varied tools language professionals have at their disposal, the better their decisions and work will be (Varantola, 2000: 173).

4　Corpora in Translation

Speaking about linguistic tools, it is worth mentioning that an increasing number of scholars in translation studies have begun to consider seriously the corpus-based approach as a feasible perspective for studying translation in an original and systematic way. Contrastive linguists have also recognized the value of translation corpora as resources for the study of languages, and translator trainers have begun to design general and specialized corpora to aid the comprehension of source language texts and improve production skills (Laviosa, 1998: 1).

There are several types of corpora as we know them but the ones which attracts greatest attention in translation are multilingual and aligned parallel corpora.

4.1　Annotated vs. Unannotated

If corpora is said to be unannotated it appears in its existing raw state of plain text, whereas annotated corpora has been enhanced with various types of linguistic information. Naturally, the usefulness of a corpus is increased when it is annotated. For example, the form "gives" contains the implicit part-of-speech information "third person singular present tense verb." However, in an annotated corpus the form "gives" might appear as "gives_VVZ," with the code VVZ indicating that it is a third person singular present tense (Z) form of a lexical verb (VV). Such annotation makes it quicker and easier to retrieve and analyse information about the language contained in the corpus. (McEnery & Wilson, 2004, Encoding and annotation, para. 2)

4.2 Sample vs. Monitor Corpus

When talking about corpora, in most cases we mean bodies of text having finite size, for example, 1,000,000 words. However, there is another type of corpora called monitor corpora, which are constantly being updated and extended, like John Sinclair's Collins COBUILD corpus. According to McEnery and Wilson the main advantages of monitor corpora are:

• They are not static—new texts can always be added, unlike the synchronic "snapshot" provided by finite corpora.

• Their scope—they provide for a large and broad sample of language.

Their main disadvantage is:

• They are not such a reliable source of quantitative data (as opposed to qualitative data) because they are constantly changing in size and are less rigorously sampled than finite corpora.

Apart from monitor corpora, most often the case is that a corpus consists of a finite number of word. Usually this figure is determined at the beginning of a corpus-building project. An exception is the London-Lund corpus, which was increased in the mid-1970s to cover a wider variety of genres.

4.3 Monolingual vs. Multilingual Corpora

Apart from monolingual, there are also corpora containing texts from several different languages which are called multilingual and an increasing amount of work in being done on the building of such corpora.

First we must make a distinction between two types of multilingual corpora: the first can be described as small collections of individual monolingual corpora—they contain completely different texts in those several languages, which are not translations of each other.

The second type of multilingual corpora attracts most attention and is known as parallel corpora. This refers to corpora which hold the same texts in more than one language. The parallel corpus dates back to the famous Rosetta Stone and mediaeval times when "polyglot bibles" were produced which contained the biblical texts side by side in Hebrew, Latin and Greek, etc.

In order for such corpora to be useful, it is necessary to indicate which sentences in the source language are translations of which sentences in the target language, possibly even which words are translations of each other. A corpus which has this additional information is known as aligned corpus. If we take the sentence "The boy loves the girl" in such a corpus it should be aligned next to "Der Junge liebt ein Madchen," at a higher level of organisation even "the" can be aligned next to "der. " This is not always a simple task because due to the specific features of the languages often one word in the source text may be translated with more than one word in the target text (e. g. "raucht" in German and "is smoking" in English), not to mention the stylistic and syntactic differences between languages which may complicate matters even further.

Annotated parallel corpora are rare and those which exist tend to be bilingual rather than multilingual. However, two EU-funded projects (CRATER and MULTEXT) are aiming to produce genuinely multilingual parallel corpora. The Canadian Hansard corpus is annotated, and contains parallel texts in French and English, but it only covers a restricted range of text types (proceedings of the Canadian Parliament). However, this is an area of growth, and the situation is likely to change dramatically in the near future. (McEnery & Wilson, 2004, Multilingual corpora, para. 4)

5 Is the Web Really a Corpus?

Due to the versatile nature of texts that need translation often even the most voluminous corpora cannot offer sufficient information to solve a translation problem. The web is far from the ideal of an orderly annotated corpus but has one undeniable advantage over other collection of texts—it is huge. I use the term "collection of texts" because in order to name the web a "corpus" we first need to try to prove its status as such. McEnery and Wilson outline four main characteristics of a corpus: finite size, sampling and representativeness, machine readable form and a standard reference.

They write:

• The term "corpus" also implies a body of text of finite size, for example, 1,000,000 words. This is not universally so—for example, at Birmingham University, John Sinclair's COBUILD team have been engaged in the construction and analysis of a monitor corpus. This "collection of texts" as Sinclair's team prefer to call them, is an open-ended entity— texts are constantly being added to it, so it gets bigger and bigger. " (Mc Enery and Wilson, 2004, Definition of a corpus, para. 1)

If we apply that definition to the nature of the web, it turns out that it is basically what we call a monitor corpus—one that has no finite size but grows constantly. If we look it that way, the web is actually the biggest possible monitor corpus.

Undoubtedly, all texts on the web are machine readable. Moreover, their primary existence is in electronic form and although many of the web documents have hard copies, most of them are available only on the hard disks of computers.

According to McEnery and Wilson "a corpus represents a standard reference to the language variety it represents" and "provides a yardstick by which successive studies can be measured."

However, outside very specialised domains we do not really know what existing corpora might be representative of (Kaligarriff & Grefenstette, 2003: 340) and although the web cannot really be called a yardstick, it may be a very lucrative source of information, which structured in an appropriate way, may present a linguistic playground not worse than that offered by other well-known corpora.

As far as sampling and representativeness are concerned, I would allow myself to quote Adam Kaligarriff and Gregory Grefenstette, who in their paper, "Introduction to the Special Issue on the Web as Corpus"(2003), adopt a very straightforward approach to this question. They disagree with the definition of McEnery and Wilson claiming that these authors mix the question "What is a corpus?" with the question "What is a good corpus?". It is indeed true that many of the corpora used for literary, linguistic or language-technology studies do not fit into the McEnery-Wilson definition, especially in the part "sampling and representativeness." Kaligarriff and Grefenstette give an example with a corpus consisting of the complete works of Jane Austen, which is neither a sample, nor representative of anything else. Finally they come up with the following definition "A corpus is a collection of texts when considered as an object of language and literary study." So far this definition is the most suitable one establishing the status of the web as a corpus and also fitting best into the concept of this paper.

6 Potential Uses of the Web in Translation

In recent years the web has become a most useful tool for translators as a place where they can easily look up how a certain word or phrase is used. Since queries to standard search engines allow for restrictions to a particular language and, via the URL domain, to a particular country, it has become easy to obtain usage information which has been buried in books and papers prior to the advent of the web. In addition to simply browsing through usage examples one may exploit the frequency information (Volk, 2002: 6). Here we will summarize several examples how a translator may profit from the web.

One of the most common cases in translation practice is checking the translation variant one already has in mind. For example, can we translate "Spontanpramie" as "special bonus" or "key ratio" as "Schlusselzahlen"? The simplest way is to type the corresponding keyword in the Google site (after enclosing the search items in quotation marks "") to get a quick answer. The decision of the translator in this case is based predominantly on frequency information. If there are enough occurrences of the word or phrase in question in Google and if they come from reliable sources one may safely conclude that this is a good candidate for the target translation term. Of course, on the web everything is relative, and what we call "enough occurrences" and "reliable sources" may vary greatly from one search item to another. In addition, the number of hits in Google only show if the word or combination of words actually exists in language, only after carefully examining the context in which the word occurs (e. g. Shlusselzahlen very often appears in contexts like "Verwendung von Schlusselzahlen fur Eintragungen im Fuhrerschein") we can decide if this is the correct term or not.

This method allows to also check the correct translation of proper nouns and names of institutions. For example, if one does not know how to translate the name of Sofia University "Cb. KnuMeHT Oxpmackm" and hesitates whether to use the actual name of the patron saint St. Climent of Ochrid or transliterate it as St. Kliment Ohridski, one can always use Google to find out that the latter is much more frequent. Names of institutions can also pose a problem but it is in the web where we can find out that the German "Direktion fur Hochschulbildung" and the French "Direction des enseignements superieurs" are equivalent to the English "Department for Higher Education" (as a structure within a ministry).

Another case is when we do not have a translation variant (e. g. how to translate the German word "Pistenflitzer" in English) or our variant has not been confirmed (special bonus does not express well the implicit meaning of Spontanpramie as a term opposed to annual, performance-related bonus). In that case the translator needs to find texts from the corresponding thematic domain where he or she stands a good chance of finding the necessary term (key words may be "bonus," "reward" and "compensation"). Practically all search engines allow advanced search options where you can limit the search scope to a particular language (e. g. only sites in German) or to one domain area (e. g. sites ending in. bg are hosted in Bulgaria,. ch in Switzerland etc.)

6. 1　Translation of Compound Nouns

In 1999 Grefenstette used the web to show how one can locate the correct translations of German compound nouns if the potential translations of their constituent parts were known. He selected a number of German compounds from a machine-readable German-English dictionary. The requirement was that every compound had to be decomposable into two German words found in the dictionary and the English translation also had to consist of two words. However, for each segment of the words in question there was more than one translation possible. For example, the German noun Aktienkurs (share price) can be segmented into Aktie (share, stock) and Kurs (course, price, rate) both of which have multiple possible translations. By generating all possible translations (share course, share price, share rate, share course,...) and submitting them to Alta Vista queries, Grefenstette obtained frequency results for all possible translations. He tested the hypothesis that the most frequent translation is the correct one. He extracted 724 German compounds according to the above criteria and found that his method predicted the correct translations for 631 of these compounds (87%) which is an impressive result given the simplicity of the method (Volk, 2002: 6).

6.2　Mining the Web for Parallel Texts

Translation memory systems have become an indispensable tool for translators in recent years. They store parallel texts in a database and can retrieve a unit (typically a sentence) with its previous translation equivalents when it needs to be translated again. Such systems come to their full use when a database of the correct subject domain and text type is already stored. They are of no use when few or no entries have been made. However, very often previous translations exist and have been published on the web (e. g. documents in the administrative sphere, or common EU documents in multiple languages). The idea is to find these translation pairs, evaluate them, download and align them and, finally, feed them into a translation memory.

In 1999 Philip Resnik developed a method for automatically finding parallel texts in the web. Initially he ran queries on Alta Vista by asking for parent pages containing the string "English" and "German" in anchor text within a fixed distance of each other. This generated many good pairs of pages such as those reading "Click here for English version" and "Click here for German version" but of course also many bad pairs.

Then he made use of the fact that the translations and the originals are very similarly arranged in terms of HTML structure. He used a statistical language identification system to discover if the documents are in the suspected language. Then he submitted 192 pairs to human judgement and 92% of the pages judged as good by the human experts were judged as good by his system as well.

In the second phase of the experiment he expanded his scope of research by looking not only for parent pages but also for sibling pages (linked pages which are translation of each other). For the language pair English-French he obtained more than 16,000 page pairs.

7　Web and Other Corpora in the Translation Process

A corpus of finite size cannot always offer sufficient information for disambiguating complicated translation questions. Even the British National Corpus with its 100 million words is often ill-equipped for that purpose. On the other hand, the web has a potential to be invaluable for linguistic research due to its width, breadth, up-to-dateness and universal availability.

A simple search conducted in Google and BNC was meant to illustrate the suggestion that relatively simple search techniques for querying the web can be used for solving quite complex translation problems. The translation pair came from an academic certificate written in Bulgarian. The source text was "u3flbpxan M3nuTu no" (=[the student] has passed exams in/on [several subjects]) followed by a list of subjects attended and marks of the student. The two translation variants that offered themselves were "passed exams on" and "passed exams in. " Preposition usage is one of the trickiest things in translation and since it was not quite clear which preposition was more appropriate in that case a search on both Google and BNC was designed to solve the problem.

Initially a full-text search in Google was done for the two phrases. The results were:

Query	Results (Hits in Google)
passed exams in	735
passed exams on	224

However, there was a lot of "noise" in the results like:

... The number of passed exams in nine rural schools in the area where ...

... average score of the passed exams (in words and in figures); ...

... In 1999 I passed exams in Moscow State University ...

... have passed exams in one sitting to become a memeber of ...

AND

... (Both passed exams on November 6, call signs pending)...

... a student who took and passed exams on the same day ...

... 270 candidates who have passed exams on paper ...

... graduated from Bergen school in 1707; MA in 1727. Religion, passed exams on Oct. 22, 1714 ...

which clearly did not fit into the formula:

passed + exams + <preposition> + <name(s) of subjects>

Despite that everything pointed to the fact that the first variant was the more common of the two.

To confirm the results, I decided to do a second search using the main form of the verb "to pass" in order to collect more results. Again a full-phrase search in Google was used. The results were:

Query	Results
"pass exams in"	1,460 hits
"pass exams on"	1,550 hits

Once again only frequency information was not enough and not quite representative to demonstrate clearly that either one or the other of the prepositions was the correct one in that case.

For that reason a third search on Google was conducted including the word "subjects" to the above-mentioned search phrase. The reason to do that was to find web pages that mimic the original academic certificate, i. e. pages containing the phrase "passed exams in OR on" followed by a list of subjects. The results were:

Query	Results
"pass exams in" + subjects	199
"pass exams on" + subjects	30

With the search query structured in that way, the word "subjects" may appear anywhere on the page, not necessarily in close proximity to the search phrase. What turned out was that in the first case "subjects" was much closer to "pass exams in." e. g.

"pass exams":

- in a number of subjects
- in four core subjects
- in the following national subjects
- in all subjects of the curriculum

In the second case the results looked like that:

- ... Candidates must pass exams on Windows architecture and services plus programming languages of ... the person who trains others in these subjects through Microsoft ...

- ... They will be required to pass exams on driving and the Rukhnama in order to get ... academic year, students can choose to sit three exams in the subjects of their ...

- ... Where only a few subjects in a JAR-66 module are covered by the ratings ... Existing licence holders need not pass exams on Human Factors (module 9) and Aviation ...

Bearing in mind the frequency of occurrence and the proximity search results, the conclusion imposed itself that in our case the preposition IN was the more appropriate of the two.

However, after closer observation of the results, it turned out that there was a fine separation between the use of IN and ON in that particular case. ON appeared mainly in combinations with nouns or phrases denoting specific areas of knowledge and fields of expertise like:

- to pass exams on the US Constitution
- to pass exams on the latest Microsoft Technologies
- to pass exams on two different instruments
- to pass exams on earlier release versions of Oracle

while IN, in most cases, collocated with names of subjects as they are defined in the school curriculum (Mathematics, Physics, Biology, Chemistry etc.) and although there were examples like "to pass an exam on Maths" they were not very common. Despite the simplicity of the search method the results were convincing enough to show that both prepositions had their domain of usage.

What were the results in BNC? For that particular query were used both the online version of BNC and the downloadable SARA client. Unfortunately, only one single entry in the corpus matched the queries which were conducted. The results were the following:

Query	Results
"passed exams in"	K5J 2150 Michael Wittet: CA who passed exams in German prison camp
"passed exams on"	No matches
"pass exams on"	No matches
"pass exams on"	No matches

The following search queries have been tested as well:

• pass=VVB + {exam[s]} + prp-to which no results were returned

• Pass + {exam[s] } returned eight matches but they excluded exactly the part of speech I was interested in—namely the preposition.

The results from BNC were insufficient to solve the problem at hand but there is no doubt that BNC and other well-known corpora offer options for linguistic research incomparable to any online search engine. There are, of course, projects like WebCorp, KwiCFinder, Gsearch etc. , which try to facilitate the process of searching the web for grammatical constructions, still this ultimate linguistic goal has not be fully achieved. However, when faced with no time and, in most cases limited budget, the most obvious place to search for an answer to a translation problem is the net.

8   Conclusion

Corpora have been a part of the translation practice and training for a good number of years. Their use has proved beneficiary irrespective of whether the text sources are monolingual, bilingual or even aligned parallel corpora. As a new medium for the existence of information Internet provides an additional stimulus to the development of translation. It offers a much larger number of opportunities for corpus research since it exceeds in size any previously compiled corpora. Unfortunately, online search engines are suited not for linguistic but for general knowledge queries. Yet, currently the web is the first and the most obvious place where most translators look for linguistic information, and, not quite surprisingly, in most cases they are able to find it there.

The objective of the paper is not to make sweeping generalizations about the usefulness of the web as a corpus or juxtapose it to BNC and other corpora. The task is to show that in translation practice, by using relatively simple search techniques and in within a very limited time span, one can find an answer to quite tricky questions by using the web as a huge multilingual corpus. It is my deepest conviction that this largest and most up-to-date collection of texts should be used to its full potential in translation studies and as well as in other linguistic fields.

选文二　网络资源在翻译中的应用

王军礼

导　言

本文发表于 2007 年《中国科技翻译》第 2 期。

作者王军礼是宁夏医科大学外国语教学部的教师。本文首先简单介绍了翻译与网络资源密不可分的关系,接着,作者详细介绍了翻译中能够利用的网络资源,例如,在线词典、搜索引擎、在线机器翻译、翻译论坛和翻译博客等。此外,作者还探讨了译者如何使用这些网络资源,以及这些网络资源对于译者的主要作用。

美国翻译家和翻译理论家尤金·奈达在他的书中提到,翻译是一项复杂而迷人的工作。I. A. 理查兹(1953)甚至认为翻译可能是宇宙历史过程中最为复杂的活动。翻译活动的复杂性在于它不仅涉及语言转换问题,更重要的是它还涉及人文、历史、地理、文学、科学技术、宗教等诸多因素。作为译者,面对这诸多领域,能够掌握其中一两个领域都是非常艰难的事情。要做好翻译,译者不但要通晓中外语言,而且还要有充足的信息资源以供参考。传统的参考资源包括各科词典、百科全书以及其他一些相关资料。由于资金因素,一般译者很难完全具备这些传统参考资料,即使配备了,翻阅起来既费时费力又影响翻译的效率。

电子计算机与现代通信技术相结合,为人类提供了一个全新的信息环境,即网络环境。随着网络和电脑的普及以及信息技术的发展,网络为人们提供了大量丰富的信息资源,同时也为翻译活动创建了一个超级信息平台。网络资源已成为译者不可或缺的帮手,不仅为译者节省资金,而且可以大大促进翻译效率,提高翻译质量。网络信息资源具有使用方便、成本低廉、内容丰富、形式多样等特点。译者只要具备一定的计算机技能和网络知识就可以有效获取翻译所需的信息资源。目前能够在翻译中利用的网络资源包括在线词典、搜索引擎、在线机器翻译、翻译论坛、翻译博客等。

1　在线词典

传统词典长期以来一直是译者的必要工具之一。然而,不论这些字典编得有多好,它们都有先天的不足。首先,传统词典的编撰一般都需要三五年甚至更久,然而语言时时刻刻都在发展变化,新词语不断出现。所以词典总是滞后于语言的发展变化。其次,词典的义项解释有其局限性,再全的词典也不可能包罗万象。翻译一个词要依赖其语境和文化等因素,单凭词典的解释来做翻译是不可靠的。另外,传统词典使用起来比较麻烦。笔者做了一个试验,用传统词典查一个词平均需要 32.5 秒(不包括阅读时间),而利用网络词典查一个词平均需要 16.8 秒

（不包括阅读时间）。很明显，利用传统词典比网络词典要多花将近一倍的时间。在线词典具有使用方便、种类丰富、更新快的特点。网络词典的更新速度比印刷版词典快，一般网络词典是按天、按周、按月或按季更新的，在新颖性方面具有很大优势，印刷型词典无法与之相比。所以在线词典为译者带来极大方便。翻译中常用的在线词典主要有以下一些：

1.1 词霸搜索（http://www.iciba.com）

词霸搜索是由金山软件公司开发的。收录词典 198 本，既有综合性词典，如《简明英汉词典》，也有专科性词典，如《朗文英汉综合电脑词典》等。共计有词条：英汉 450 万条，汉英 340 万条，日汉 12 万条，汉日 2 万条，汉汉 10 万条。其界面简洁，操作方便。

1.2 dict.cn（http://sh.dict.cn）

dict.cn 采集了大量各行业的专业英语网络资料和英汉人工翻译双语材料，并做了大量程序分析整理（包括使用中文分词，词频统计，英中、中英相互关联词义生成，词条解释由程序利用自定义参数优化等）。部分词条由人工释义（包括对程序生成的解释修改）而成。每个词条下都有若干英汉、汉英句对供译者参考。

1.3 谷词（http://www.godict.com）

谷词提供详细解释、专业解释和简单解释三种搜索方式，能满足不同的搜索要求。在详细解释中包括某一词条的全部义项、用法（甚至包括俚语用法）、例句、相关短语以及词性变化等。专业解释中列出该词在不同科技领域里的专业意义。因此它是翻译科技文章和著作的一个有效在线词典。

1.4 华建多语词典（http://www.hjtrans.com/online_dict/dict.htm）

华建词典目前提供英文单词的基本词义、词组、例句、同/反义词功能，以及英文词组的查询。中文单词只有基本词义的翻译，目前提供常用中文短语的查询功能。例如："多语言实时对讲系统"功能。用户可以分别查"多语"、"在线"、"词典"，但是不能查询"多语在线词典"。另外，如果输入错误，系统会提示错误然后给出相近词义。目前还没有提供模糊查询。华建在线词典的一个特点是它提供词条的所有可能的短语搭配，为译者提供了语境参考。

1.5 朗文当代英语词典网络版（http://www.idoceonline.com）

该词典简称 LDCE，收录了 10 600 个单词和短语，另配许多精美图片，它释义简明易懂，包含了关于现代英语在词义与用法方面的大量信息。界面简洁，查询简单，直接在输入框中输入单词即可。另外，还可以对释义中出现的任意单词双击，词典自动对该单词进行查询，即具有超链接的检索功能。

以上是一些具有代表性的在线词典。总之，目前的网络在线词典琳琅满目，应有尽有，其中还不乏一些具有特色的在线词典，比如俗语词典、俚语词典、成语词典以及其他一些专业性很强的词典。译者可以根据自己翻译的内容使用相应的词典，也可以通过搜索引擎找到自己需要的专业性在线词典。

2 搜索引擎

搜索引擎是因特网上的一种信息检索工具,它通过因特网接收用户的查询请求,在其索引库进行检索,然后向用户反馈其感兴趣的信息所在的网址列表。目前网络上使用最多的搜索引擎是用软件的方式实现与全球计算机自动链接,将对方服务器上的主页信息自动取回,并进行排序或索引,形成一个庞大的主页信息数据库。通过搜索引擎提供的链接,用户马上就可以登陆相关网页,进行信息查询。译者可以充分利用搜索引擎来找到需要的信息。目前最受欢迎的搜索引擎有 Google、雅虎、百度、搜狐、天网搜索等。为了更好地利用这些搜索引擎,译者必须掌握基本的信息搜索方法和技巧,可参阅一些网络信息检索书籍。

雅虎(http://www.yahoo.com)是万维网上最早、最著名和使用最普遍的网页导航指南,是最著名的目录索引、搜索引擎的开山鼻祖之一。雅虎收录了大量的学术资源,供译者参考。

Google (http://www.google.com)以精密度高、速度快成为最受欢迎的搜索引擎,是目前搜索界的领军网站。其界面自带翻译功能,可进行中英文网页互译,译文可参考性很高,这一功能可以给译者提供极大的帮助。

百度(http://www.baidu.com)的商业化全文搜索引擎,其功能完备,搜索精度高,几乎可以与 Google 相媲美,是国内技术水平最高的搜索引擎。这些搜索引擎可以完美地应用到翻译实践当中。

2.1 搜索翻译模板

翻译工作中,译者可能会碰到各种各样的文体,特别是比较困难的应用文体翻译。应用文体的翻译目的性很强,往往要求译者知道它的目标受众,并重视目的语受众对语言、文体和社会文化的期待,翻译时根据翻译目的和译文读者的文化语境,注重文本的功能传达,尽量创作出地道的译文。应用文具备功能性强、简洁性、格式规范这三个特点。应用文体式繁多,海报、广告、商务信函、合同、标书、各类公函、旅游英语等都属于应用文体之列,各体式都有明确的目的。如果译者对某个应用文体式、术语等不太有把握,就可以通过搜索引擎找到相应的应用文,参照其格式和术语的表达方式来完成翻译工作。比如,笔者曾接到一份英文工程标书汉译的任务,由于对标书的格式及语言不太熟悉,于是笔者在百度搜索中输入关键词"标书范本",搜索之后找到了很多的链接,点击标书网(http://biaoshu.com.main.htm),选择工程施工类标书下载以便参考,然后顺利完成翻译任务。如果是中文应用文英译,也可在 Google 中搜索相应的英文应用文体式。

2.2 检验译文的准确性

译员在工作中往往涉及到自己不熟悉的领域,然而这些工作必须要完成。这个时候,译员可能担心翻译出来的译文不够准确,或者虽然准确地译出了原文的意义,但却未能准确使用相关领域的专业术语,造成译文不地道。在这种情况下,译员可以利用搜索引擎来检验译文的准确性和规范性。译者可将自己不太有把握的译文关键词输入到百度、搜狐、Google 等搜索引擎中去搜索。如果该关键词或短语在检索结果中被广泛使用,而且根据其结果中的上下文,可以判断其意思与原文一致,说明这种译法地道;如果在检索结果中没有出现译文关键词,则说明这种译法是错误的。所以,网络在某种程度上如同一个超大型的语料库,可以用来检验译文的准确与否。因为如果译文准确地道,那么它在网络这个语料库中的出现频率就应该相对大一些。

这里以"农业生态环境"一词的英译作为实例来说明问题。笔者通过查阅中国期刊全文数据库的一些相关论文发现,该词的英译文至少有四种:"agricultural ecological environment","agro-ecological environment","agricultural eco-environment","agricultural ecology environment"。将这四种译法分别输入 Google,检索结果显示:第一种译法有 0 项结果;第二种译法有 508 项结果;第三种译法有 42 项返回结果,而且多数在中国期刊的摘要中出现,极可能是中国人自己的译法;第四种译法有 36 项返回结果,而且这一表达方式也只出现在中国期刊的摘要中。通过比较,发现"agro-ecological environment"使用的频率远远高于其他三种译法,并且多出现在英语作为母语的文章中,所以可断定,"农业生态环境"最准确地道的译法应该是"agro-ecological environment"。

2.3　查找专有名词

专有名词表示"独一无二"的对象,即所指对象单一、固定,基本上包括人名、地名、节日名称、机构名称、报刊杂志、书名、电影名、商标名称等。正因为专有名词是固定、约定俗成的,所以在翻译它们时不能闭门造车,而应当借鉴前人的翻译成果,保证译名的准确性,不出现张冠李戴的情况。专有名词的翻译面广、量大,各行各业的译员都会经常碰到。在手头资源有限的情况下,运用网络资源是做好专有名词翻译的重要手段。利用搜索引擎,不但可以找到常见人名、地名的译名,而且能够查询到一些鲜为人知的人名、地名的译名。笔者在参与翻译《最高决策者》一书时遇到很多人名,但是不敢随意按照发音翻译了事,所以利用百度搜索引擎,经过检索,都找到了相应的中文译名。比如"Arnold Piso",分别在搜索框中输入 Arnold 和 Piso,检索到很多网页,发现它们对应的中文译名分别为阿诺德和皮索,所以这个人名可译为"阿诺德·皮索"。一些小地方的名称也可以通过网络找到相应的译名。

机构名称的翻译也是译者经常遇到的,因为其名称的固定性,译者不能轻易按字面翻译。参阅网络资源是一个稳妥、有效的方法。目前,一般的机构都有自己的网站,译者可以通过搜索引擎找到它们的网站,首页一般会有该机构的英文名称,而且有些网站也有自己的英文版。比如笔者在翻译"中国国家认证认可监督管理委员会"时,找到该机构的网站,首页上有英文版链接,点击之后得到该机构的英文译名为"Certification and Accreditation Administration of the People's Republic of China"。当然,我们可以利用 Google 等其他搜索引擎来完成专有名词的翻译。

2.4　搜索背景知识

翻译是一个理解与表达的过程。翻译中的理解以忠实地表达原作的意义并尽可能再现原作的形式之美为目的,因此,它要求具有准确性、透彻性及全面性。不仅从微观上要细致到句法和词法,还要从宏观上把握原作产生的社会、历史和文化背景等。这就是常说的背景知识,它涉及语言和上下文以外的因素,即交际情景和有关的政治、历史、地理、军事、经济、文化、教育、科学、卫生道德、宗教、风俗习惯等情况。这些知识往往在一般的语言词典和综合词典中难以查到。翻译所涉及的内容有时相当广泛,因为作者与译者的经历、所处的国情或社会文化背景不可能相同,反映在原作中的内容也就不易为译者所理解,这时译者对背景知识的了解就非常重要。

网络中的内容无所不包，应有尽有。所以译者可以利用搜索引擎，查找自己有疑问或者不确定的背景知识，从而更好地完成翻译任务。如翻译一篇有关麦当劳历史的英文文章，可以在"百度"或者 Google 中输入关键词"麦当劳＋历史"，便可找到许多有关麦当劳历史的链接，点击链接之后就可浏览到麦当劳的历史背景知识，这对于后面的翻译工作有很大的帮助。

3 在线机器翻译

目前，网络上有很多专门提供在线翻译服务的网站。同时，许多翻译软件公司在自己的网站上都提供在线机器翻译服务，为客户提供免费的在线翻译服务。虽然目前这些在线机器翻译的译文质量还不是很高，但是这种自动翻译对于那些只想粗略了解一下译文大致内容和信息的客户来说已经足够了。

3.1 Worldlingo

Worldlingo 是一个专业的在线翻译网是笔者觉得非常好用的网站。其网址为：http://www.worldlingo.com/zh/microsoft/computer translation.html。它支持多国语言，以满足不同使用者的需要，而且该网站的翻译系统十分强大，可以将英、汉、法、德、日、韩等语言的网页或者文本进行相互的自动翻译。译者在翻译专业性较强的文章时，可以在网站页面上的"科学"选项里选择适合的专业词库。该网站拥有汽车技术、航空、化学、计算机和数据处理、经济和商业等专业词库。

3.2 金桥翻译（http://www.netat.net）

这个在线翻译网站只支持将英文、日文的网页翻译成简体或繁体中文，虽然不及Worldlingo，但对于一般的使用而言已经足够了。而且它可以用上下对照的方式显示翻译前后的网页。这种显示方法对那些认真谨慎、需要对译文进行核对的用户是非常方便的。

3.3 译海网（http://www.gb.transea.com）

译海网可以翻译文本或网页，支持英文、简体中文、繁体中文、俄文互译。译海网翻译的准确性较高，界面操作简单。但是使用译海网必须先在其网站注册，而且每次翻译时，都必须先登陆。在线机器翻译的译文是大致可以看懂的，当然，文笔一点也不美，句子断断续续，表达方式也很拙劣，但是可以交流信息。

4 翻译论坛

论坛是随着网络这一媒体的出现而产生的一个新名词，一般也称之为 BBS。BBS 是英文Bulletin Board System 的缩写，按照字面翻译为"公告板系统"。随着网络技术的提高和社会生活的需要，论坛逐渐发展，突破了传统的传递信息的模式，建立起互通信息的快捷渠道，成为网上交互联络的主要手段。论坛的这种交互作用，完全突破了时空局限，在信息传递与交互方面发挥着巨大作用。

利用网络论坛进行翻译理论研究和实践可以说是一大创举,它有效利用了论坛这一载体的各种优势。目前,一些翻译论坛办得非常系统全面,人气指数很高。译者可以通过网络论坛寻找翻译资料,比如专业词汇、口译常用句式、翻译技巧、翻译心得等。翻译论坛同时也吸引从事翻译实践及理论研究的学者或爱好者在论坛上发表自己的科研成果、学术论文等,并且参与翻译问题的讨论。译者在碰到翻译上的难题时可将问题提到网络论坛上供广大网友讨论。有高水平的翻译学者参与,还会提供专家的解答。它支持多国语言,可会诊,帮译者解决翻译中遇到的难题。在组织大型项目的翻译时,又可利用网上的翻译人才资源进行合作。译者还可以在论坛上获取最新的翻译资讯,了解翻译发展的现状,把握翻译发展的趋势。

许多专门的翻译网站都设有翻译论坛,其中比较受欢迎的有以下一些:中国翻译协会主办的网站中国翻译网(http://www.chinatranslation.com)的翻译论坛,该论坛栏目比较全面,包括各种小语种,在线人数比较多;翻译中国的翻译论坛(http://www.fane.cn/forum.asp),该论坛有 49 859 名注册会员,主要侧重于英汉互译。中国翻译家联盟的翻译论坛(http://www.translator.com.cn/dvbbs)也很有特色,其界面简单明快,操作方便。当然还有许多其他翻译论坛,只要译者多留心,还会找到更加专业、更适合自己的论坛。

5　翻译博客

Blog 是 web log 的缩写,中文是"网络日志",而博客(blogger)则是写 blog 的人。具体说来,博客这个概念解释为使用特定的软件,在网络上出版、发表和张贴个人文章的人。不过和个人网站不同,blog 显然没有技术的门槛,就像无需自己造纸也有纸用,blogger 无需掌握建站的各种知识,就能拥有自己的 blog 网站。和 BBS 中到处散落的文本相比,blogger 能很好地从整体上展示自己。blog 是传统笔记和现代论坛(BBS)的有机结合。它既有传统笔记随时记录感想、思考,摘抄有用信息的功能,又具有类似网络论坛分享和交流的作用。浏览者可对博客的文章或观点发表留言和评论,共同探讨、共同提高。博客也可加入自己感兴趣的博客圈,与其他博客进行广泛的交流和信息共享。所以,blog 使互联网的通讯功能、信息功能和交流等功能得到进一步加强,使其更个性化、开放化、实时化和全球化。

翻译博客是指与翻译相关的博客。这些博客一般都是专门从事翻译理论研究和工作的人员,具有一定的理论修养和实践能力,甚至有些博客是著名高校的翻译学教授或者著名翻译家。他们将自己的心得体会、翻译技巧、理论思考等发表在其 blog 上面。一方面,这是自身经历和思考的翔实记录;另一方面也可供浏览者参考、讨论和交流。翻译学习者或工作者都可以利用 blog,通过与其他博客探讨和交流,解决自身遇到的问题。

据中国互联网络信息中心(CNNIC)《2006 年中国博客调查报告》对整个博客市场容量的描述显示:截至 2006 年 8 月底,中国博客作者规模已达到 1 750 万,其中活跃博客作者(平均每个月更新一次以上)接近 770 万,注册的博客空间数接近 3 400 万,而博客读者则达到 7 500 万以上,其中活跃博客读者高达 5 470 万人。目前,中国的门户网站,比如新浪、搜狐、网易都有博客栏目,还有专门的博客网站,如:中国博客网(http://www.blogcn.com),博客中国(http://www.blogchina.com),博客动力(http://www.blogdriver.com)。其中也有许多翻译博客圈,即由翻译博客组成的团体,为博客就相关翻译问题的交流提供了一个更为便利的平台。作为译者,利用翻译博客不但可以提高理论修养、学习翻译技巧,而且可以直接向其他博客请教,解决翻译实践中遇到的问题和困难。

6　结　语

综上所述,我们已深刻体会到网络资源给翻译带来的巨大便利。作为一名译员,往往受到时间的制约,不可能为"一名之立"而"旬月踟蹰"。传统的资料搜集手段已经远远不能适应现代社会快节奏生活的需要。而且,翻译是跨行业、综合性的工作,译者不可能做到样样精通,然而有时还必须涉足自己不熟悉的领域或专业。因此,需要我们充分利用信息技术革命带来的种种便利,充分利用无限丰富的网络资源,吸收借鉴他人的劳动成果,提高我们的翻译效率和译文质量。

选文三　**The Uptake of Online Tools and Web-based Language Resources by Freelance Translators: Implications for Translator Training, Professional Development, and Research**

Heather Fulford

导　言

本文发表于 2004 年举办的"第二届国际翻译实践、研究与培训资源研讨会"会议公报上。

作者 Heather Fulford 博士任教于英国拉夫堡大学。Heather Fulford 博士研究兴趣广泛,除了语言和翻译技术之外,还涉及创新传播、网址设计与开发等。其主要论文包括:*Translation Tools: An Exploratory Study of Their Adoption by UK Freelance Translators*, *Machine Translation*; *Translation and Technology: A Study of UK Freelance Translators*; *The Internet and the Freelance Translator* 等。

文章首先交代了互联网背景下翻译范式的变化:翻译需求大大增加,网上电子文本格式知识急剧增加为译者的检索提供了可能。接着,作者概述了自由译员可用的网上服务,并介绍了调查方法。最后,作者讨论了其发现。

1　Background

It has been suggested that the Internet is "significantly affecting the way translators work today," in both the "way they handle orders" as well as "how they search for linguistic and encyclopaedic information" (Austermuhl, 2001: 38). Indeed, Austermuhl goes on to assert that the impact of the Internet on the "research habits" of translators has been so considerable as to warrant being denoted a "paradigm shift." Elsewhere, in a discussion referring specifically to translators working alone on a freelance basis or in small groups, the Internet has been hailed as a "lifeline" for translators, rendered particularly attractive to them because of its cheapness and ease of use (Carter-Sigglow, 1999).

It is certainly true that the advent of the Internet, and the World Wide Web in particular, has put at the disposal of translators an ever-increasing array of online tools and web-based language resources. These tools and resources offer opportunities for supporting translators at various points in their workflow, including work procurement, topic research, client liaison, terminology identification and verification, and the production of draft translations.

As well as the increasing availability of online tools and language resources for the translation community, a number of other factors arguably point to the appropriateness of, and indeed need for, the Internet as a facility for freelance translators to utilise during various aspects of their work today. Such factors include:

1.1 Demand for Translation Services

It is widely acknowledged that the demand for translation services is growing (Andres Lange and Bennett, 2000: 203; Austermuhl, 2001: 4), fuelled by developments such as industry globalization, "intensified international competition" (Austermuhl, 2001: 4), efforts towards closer collaboration between European countries and the growth of the EU, the expansion of the Internet, software localization initiatives, and technological innovations, such as DVDs with multilingual content. In addition to the growth in demand for translation services, there are also increasing requirements made of translators to produce high-quality translations in ever-shorter time periods (Andres Lange and Bennett, 2000: 203). Online tools and language resources provide facilities to help translators produce and deliver their assignments more swiftly than was previously possible. Moreover, the Internet access to an extensive range of document and terminology resources to help translators check and improve the quality and accuracy of their output.

1.2 Knowledge Growth

There has been a growth in knowledge in the past few decades, especially in the sciences, engineering and technological domains. This growth has often been accompanied by a plethora of new terms, as well as an increase in the quantity of both paper-based and electronic texts produced to disseminate that knowledge (Fulford, 2001: 260). The World Wide Web comprises a massive repository of documents and databases which translators can use for resolving terminology queries, and for identifying and verifying new term coinages and their foreign-language equivalents. Furthermore, it can act as a rich store of background information and reference material to assist translators in the subject field research tasks associated with the production of translation assignments.

1. 3 Electronic Business Developments

A final factor worthy of mention with regard to translators and Internet is the rise of electronic business in the past few years. It has been widely reported that owners and managers of small businesses have been particularly keen to embrace e-business developments, such as setting up web sites, communicating with clients and suppliers via e-mail, and conducting business transactions online. These developments have given them an unprecedented opportunity to compete on a level playing field with larger enterprises (Daniel, Wilson and Myers, 2002: 253), to engage in low-cost marketing activities, and to extend their geographical reach to a wider (potentially worldwide) customer base (Aldridge, Forcht and Pierson, 1997: 161; Herbig and Hale, 1997: 98; Kiani, 1998: 185). For the freelance translator, the Internet provides a means to liaise with clients, to advertise their translation services via web sites, and to attract clients from a wider geographical area. The text-based nature of the "translation product" renders it a particularly suitable candidate for electronic business operations.

Whilst the various factors outlined above indicate the potential usefulness of a number of online tools and language resources to translators, there is, in fact, very little empirical data available to indicate which of the various online services are actually being employed by translators. The purpose of this paper is to help address this gap by presenting some empirical evidence of Internet adoption by freelance translators. This evidence has been gathered by means of a major survey conducted among translators based in the UK, to which some 400 responses have been received to date from freelance translators. The findings point to some important implications for the design of curricula for trainee translators, for continuing professional development provision for practising translators, and for further research into the design and development of online services for translators.

The survey reported here forms part of a wider three-year research project into the adoption of ICT (Information and Communications Technologies) by UK translators. The project is funded by the EPSRC (Engineering and Physical Sciences Research Council).

The paper is structured as follows: First, an overview of the online services available to freelance translators is provided (Section 2). The survey methodology is then outlined (Section 3). An overview of the findings of the part of the survey relating to Internet use is presented in Section 4, followed by a discussion of those findings (Section 5). Finally, some concluding remarks are made and some indications given of areas for further research (Section 6).

2 Internet Services for Freelance Translators: An Overview

As Austermuhl has noted, translators have "heterogeneous information needs" (Austermuhl, 2001: 53). For freelance translators, such information needs might include specialist terminology, background information about particular subject fields, client details, information about colleagues and their translation specialisms, and details of potential future work providers. In today's Internet era, there are many Internet services available to translators to help meet those wide-ranging information needs.

The Internet services available to translators may be divided into three broad categories:

■ Data and information repositories: These include, on the one hand, repositories of linguistic and/or terminological data, such as online dictionaries, glossaries and terminological databases. On the other hand, there are, on the World Wide Web, repositories of information encoded in language, including, for example, online documents such as newspapers, specialist journals, publicity material, and organizational web pages.

■ Information retrieval and processing programs: These programs include search tools (e. g. search engines) for tasks such as terminology query resolution and document searching. Included also are online machine translation systems for producing draft or information-only translations.

■ Communication tools: These tools include e-mail and messaging programs, file transfer applications, and online discussion groups.

Within each of the above three broad categories, there are first, tools and resources that have been designed and developed specifically for translators to use during the process of translation (e. g. multilingual terminological databases produced for translators). Second, there are tools and resources that have been designed for non-translation purposes (whether general or specialist purpose), but which may, nevertheless, be incorporated by translators into their workflow. Included in this latter group are general-purpose dictionaries, specialist journals, search engines, and e-mail applications. A comprehensive study of the adoption of Internet services by translators, such as the one presented in this paper, needs to consider both the translation-specific and the more general tools and resources available to translators.

In order to illustrate the range of Internet services available to translators today, a summary is provided in Table I below of some of the online tools and language resources that might be integrated into various stages of the freelance translator's workflow.

Finding linguistic or terminological data

Online dictionaries

Merriam-Webster Online YourDictionary. com

Meta dictionaries

Onelook

Terminological databases

Eurodicautom

TIS (Council of the EU)

Search engines

Google

Metacrawler

Finding background information（topic research）

Encyclopaedias

Encyclopaedia Britannica

Encarta

Newspaper archives

Worldnews

Databases

CORDIS

Resource gateways

RefDesk

Search engines

Google

Metacrawler

Producing draft / information-only translations

Online machine translation

Babel Fish Translation

Finding translation work

Online marketplaces

Aquarius

Proz

Promoting translation services

Web site creation software

Dreamweaver

MS Frontpage

Communicating with colleagues

Electronic mail

MS Outlook

Eudora

Electronic mailing lists & discussion groups

LANTRA-L

3　Survey Context and Method

The survey discussed in this paper forms part of the exploratory phase of a larger three-year study, which has been established to gain insights into the contemporary working practice of translators, considering in particular their adoption of ICT into the translation workflow. The project aims to identify and examine translators' strategies for integrating computer-based tools and language resources into their workflow, and to assess the impact those tools and resources are having on translation working environments. The specific focus of this paper is on those parts of the project survey relating to the adoption of Internet services by freelance translators.

3.1 Questionnaire Development and Validation

In order to conduct the survey, a draft questionnaire was developed. This questionnaire was based on a review of the relevant literature to identify the range of tools and language resources available to translators today. Since there are few published academic papers explicitly addressing the adoption of information and communications technologies (ICT) by translators, the literature was used primarily as a guide to generate ideas and insights, rather than as a source of specific questions and item measures that could be utilized directly in this study. The resultant questionnaire was organized into the following sections:

Translator profile: demographic data; details of translator training and qualifications; ICT knowledge and skills.

ICT uptake and usage: tools and language resources adopted to date.

Internet usage: uptake of web-based technologies, and general Internet tools to date.

ICT strategy: perceptions of general ICT; perceptions of translation technologies; business planning and strategy issues.

The draft questionnaire was initially validated through a series of pre-tests, first with some experienced researchers, and then, after some modifications, it was re-tested with some translators. The pre-testers were asked to critically appraise the questionnaire, focussing primarily on issues of instrument content, question wording and validity, before providing detailed feedback. The pre-tests were very useful, as they resulted in a number of enhancements being made to the structure of the survey and the wording of specific questions. Having refined the questionnaire, a pilot study exercise was also undertaken, which provided valuable insights into the likely response rate and analytical implications for the full survey.

3.2 Questionnaire Distribution

There is no official register of translators in the UK. Consequently, an exhaustive list of UK translators was not available for use in the study. For the purposes of this study, however, the sample used for the survey was drawn from a database of 1,400 UK-based translators obtained from the membership database of an appropriate professional body. Questionnaires were mailed to the translators in the database of that professional body.

4 Survey Findings

To date, 590 responses to the survey have been received and logged. Of these responses, 152 were eliminated during a pre-screening exercise on the grounds that the respondents reported that translation is not currently their principal activity, but rather an activity they combine with other undertakings, such as teaching, training, or interpreting. Of the remaining 438 responses, 390 were from freelance translators, and it is the responses of these freelance translators that are the focus of the discussion in this paper. In comparison with other studies of translators undertaken in recent years, both the response rate to this survey and the sample size generated for analysis were encouraging: the sample for Translator's Workbench Project survey, for instance, comprised a total of 110 translators (Fulford, Hoge and Ahmad, 1990); and the more recent LETRAC project survey sample consisted of just over 100 "individual translators" (Reuther, 1999).

In this section, some of the findings of the survey are presented, beginning with an overview of the respondents in the sample.

4.1　Profile of Survey Respondents

With regard to educational background, 92% of the respondents had university-level qualifications, with 53% of them having postgraduate-level qualifications. A high proportion of the sample (82%) had specific qualifications in translation, such as a first degree, master's degree, or a postgraduate-level diploma in translation studies.

With regard to the length of translation experience, responses ranged from 1 to 51 years (median: 12 years) spent working in the profession. The most common subject areas translated were business/commerce (78%), technical domains (54%), and legal issues (53%). Productivity varied considerably, ranging from 50 to 100,000 words per week (median: 6,000 words). A further measure of productivity showed variations from 0.5 to 84 hours per week (median: 25 hours) dedicated to translation-related tasks. The findings relating to length of translation experience and translator productivity are summarised in Table 1 below.

Table 1　Length of experience and productivity

	Mean	Median	Mode
Years established	13.95	12	4
Translated words/week	7,284	6,000	1,0000
Hours translating/week	25	25	40

In addition to translation services, some of the translators in the sample offered other services such as linguistic consultancy (15% of the sample), subtitling/dubbing (15%), website localization (14%), or language training courses (provided by 24% of the respondents).

The majority of translators in the survey sample were female (63%), and the distribution of ages in sample was as follows: 20—29 years (4%), 30—39 years (23%), 40—49 years (30%), 50—59 years (26%), and 60 and over (17%).

4.2 ICT Skills

Responses to questions about ICT knowledge revealed that the vast majority (85%) of the translators in the sample were self-taught, and most had no formal ICT qualifications. Among those who had formal ICT qualifications, half of them held a professional certificate, while only a few (15%) had a degree in computing or an ICT-related subject. These findings about ICT skills seem to accord broadly with those reported in the LETRAC project survey (See Reuther, 1999).

4.3 ICT Uptake and Usage

Whilst the focus of this paper is on those findings of the survey relating to the uptake of online tools and resources, a brief summary is provided here of the respondents' general ICT adoption and usage.

All of the freelancers in the sample were using computer-based tools to support document production processes (such as word processing software), and 40% were making use of tools to support business management processes (such as spreadsheet packages, databases or accounting applications). Approximately one third of the translators in the sample were using tools to support terminology management and translation creation (including packages for creating and managing personal terminology collections, and computer-assisted translation tools, such as translation memory). There was little evidence from the findings of translators supporting collaborative work with the use, for instance, of groupware or project management software.

4.4 Internet Connection

Of the 390 respondents, 97% used an Internet connection or some other network service giving access to the Internet.

The majority (66%) of freelance translators in the sample accessed Internet services via a dial-up connection, with only 31% using broadband services or a LAN connection. Figure 1 below summarizes these findings.

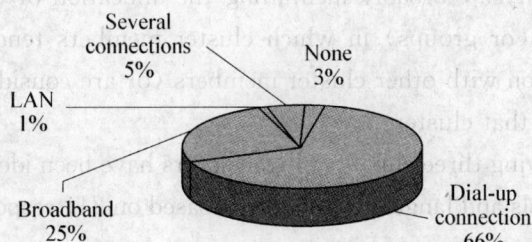

Several
connections
5%

None
3%

LAN
1%

Dial-up
connection
66%

Broadband
25%

Figure 1 Types of network connection

Further analysis of Internet connections indicated that there was no significant relationship between the types of Internet connection employed and the extent of usage of online tools and language resources.

4.5 The Uptake of Online Tools and Language Resources

In this section, the findings relating to the uptake of online services are presented.

The overriding majority (93%) of freelance translators in the sample used e-mail. A high proportion (85%) used online search engines. A small minority of respondents (3%) were making use of online machine translation systems. A few were using usenet groups (6%), and a similar proportion (6%) were making use of specialist gateways. There was widespread use of some web-based language resources, such as online dictionaries and glossaries (78%), and multilingual terminology databases (59%). Furthermore, quite extensive use was being made of document archives, such as newspaper archives (51%), but less use of other online resources such as academic journals (30%), and electronic libraries (27%). A number of possible reasons can be advanced for the differences among the respondents in their uptake of, for example, newspaper archives (51%) and academic journals (30%), including cost issues, levels of resource awareness, and factors such as perceived usefulness of each resource.

As with many studies conducted in an organizational context, the adoption of the survey format restricts the range of issues and constructs that can be explored. It must also be recognized that the results of a survey of this kind are based on statistical analysis and are, therefore, identifying general trends, and measuring "association" rather than "causality." These limitations highlight the need for further research to be conducted that adopts different methods. In particular, there is a need now for a more qualitative study that will allow the statistical patterns and relationships identified in this survey to be more fully explored, and it is hoped, explained empirically. It is precisely this sort of qualitative investigation that forms the next phase of the present research project.

The analysis of the responses is currently being extended to permit the identification of groupings of translator types according to their adoption of, and familiarity with, a range of online tools and language resources. This analysis is being undertaken using the statistical technique of cluster analysis, broadly facilitating the allocation of individual translators to one of several clusters (or groups) in which cluster members tend to share a number of characteristics in common with other cluster members (or are considered in statistical terms to be closely aligned to that cluster).

To date, the following three clusters of translators have been identified in the analysis of the uptake of online tools and language resources (based on 241 responses deemed to be valid for cluster analysis purposes):

Cluster 1: Translators make *extensive use* of e-mail, and *some use* of search engines and online dictionaries and glossaries. They show *some awareness* of a broad range of other online terminology resources (such as multilingual terminology databases or online encyclopaedia) and document archives (77 translators in this cluster).

Cluster II: Translators make *extensive use* of e-mail and search engines, and *some use* of online dictionaries and glossaries, terminology databases, mailing lists, and to a limited extent use document archives. They show *some awareness* of a range of other online terminology resources, online communication tools (such as online discussion groups and online translation marketplaces), and a wide array of document facilities (such as academic journals, archives, electronic databases, and electronic libraries), but do not demonstrate an awareness of online MT systems (81 translators).

Cluster III: Translators make *extensive use* of e-mail, search engines, and online dictionaries and glossaries. They make *some use* of a wide range of other online terminology resources (such as multilingual terminology databases and online encyclopaedias), document facilities (such as academic journals, archives, electronic databases, and electronic libraries), and online communication tools (such as online mailing lists, discussion groups, and translation marketplaces). They also show *some awareness* of online MT systems, usenet newsgroups and specialist gateways (83 translators).

Further analysis of the three clusters revealed, perhaps inevitably, that the younger, least-experienced translators holding a university qualification in translation (particularly a bachelor's or master's degree) were more likely to be found in cluster III. No clear statistical relationships were found between membership of the clusters and levels of productivity, such as weekly word counts.

4.6 Translator Home Pages

The survey also included a section enquiring about the use translators are making of web sites to promote their own translation services. The findings here showed that only 21% of the sample had their own home page. One might suppose that newcomers to the translation profession would run a home page in order to establish themselves in the freelance arena and attract clients, whereas those who had already been operating an established translation business for some years might not need to do this. The data from this survey, however, did not show any such relationship. Indeed, further analysis of the data here revealed that the uptake of home pages varied little with length of translation experience. Similar findings were found when looking at relationships between home page and age of translators in the sample.

Having presented a summary of the survey findings relating to the uptake of online services, a brief discussion of those findings is provided in the next section of the paper.

5　Discussion

As indicated in the summary of findings above, the three clusters contained a broadly similar number of translators. They suggest three groupings of translators: first, those who largely utilise general-purpose online tools for terminology retrieval purposes, and who make some use of online versions of conventional lexical and terminology resources, such as dictionaries and glossaries. They have not ventured far into exploring new resources and new tools. Second, there are those who use general-purpose online tools and quite a broad range of online resources for terminology retrieval; they also, to some extent, use other specialist facilities such as mailing lists, but again have not ventured far into the exploration and adoption of these. Third, there are those who use general-purpose online resources, a broad range of online terminology resources, and who also utilise online document archives, as well as a range of different collaborative tools such as mailing lists, discussion groups and online marketplaces. Those in the third grouping thus show a greater awareness, and higher level of uptake, of a broad range of resources than those in grouping one or two. This suggests that those in the third grouping are incorporating online services into a greater range of tasks and processes in their workflow.

Overall, the findings seem to suggest that the translators in the sample are making more use of online services for information retrieval, particularly terminology retrieval, purposes, than they are either for supporting collaborative work, or for marketing and work-finding purposes. Possible reasons for this are being explored in the next phase of the research project.

It was evident from the findings that younger, less experienced translators holding university degrees in translation tended to be using a broader range of Internet services than their more established counterparts. Assuming that these newcomers to the profession acquired their knowledge of Internet services through their university training, it is clear that universities have been adapting and tailoring their courses to reflect the increasing availability of Internet-based facilities to support various aspects of the translation workflow. Given the changing nature of the translation profession, coupled with general advances in online services and virtual working environments, it will be important for these academic institutions to continue to adapt and innovate in order to prepare their student translators for future web-based collaborative workflows. Examples here might include group translation projects and the use of shared translation memory.

Whilst the findings of the exploratory survey presented in this paper have helped to provide a picture of the adoption of Internet services by UK-based freelance translators, they raise a number of questions regarding reasons for adoption or non-adoption. Such questions include:

■ Cost issues and availability of free services: is cost a motivating factor for freelance translators when selecting an Internet service?

■ Perceived usefulness: what is the perceived usefulness of various Internet services, and how does their usefulness compare with more conventional tools and resources?

■ Ease of use: how easy do freelance translators find Internet services to use? What problems have they encountered when using them to date? Do their experiences to date influence their willingness to adopt further services?

■ External factors: to what extent do clients require, or encourage, the use of certain Internet services? What role do team-working environments play in encouraging the adoption of Internet services?

■ Online translator communities: what role do online translator communities play in encouraging the adoption of online services?

These questions are among those now being investigated using a more qualitative-based study, including in-depth interviews with individual translators.

The findings of the survey indicated that although some translators are aware of a number of Internet services, they have not adopted them into their workflows. This discrepancy between usage and awareness highlighted another area for further investigation in the next phase of the research project: why have translators not moved from awareness to usage? Furthermore, the survey findings suggested that translators tend to be aware of some Internet services and not others. From the point of view of translator training and ongoing professional development, it will be important to identify the factors that influence awareness of each type of service: how have translators become aware of certain services, for example?

A final issue that the survey raises is that of the benefits being gained by translators from the various Internet services they have adopted. Again, this is now being explored in the next phase of the project. It is anticipated that the findings regarding benefits will be of particular importance to translator trainers and providers of ongoing professional development materials to help guide and inform their future planning of courses or modules on Internet services. Moreover, a wider understanding of benefits being realized from Internet services could be useful for sharing successful practice strategies among existing professional translators.

Whilst the survey has focused on UK-based translators, it is envisaged that the survey instrument now designed, developed and validated, could be employed for replication studies among translator communities in other countries. Indeed, undertaking comparative studies among translators in other countries would represent an interesting avenue for further research.

6 Conclusions

In this paper, an overview of online tools and language resources for translators was presented. A study was outlined in which the uptake of these online services by freelance translators in the UK was explored. The findings of that study suggested that translators are making more use of online services for information retrieval, particularly terminology retrieval, purposes, than they are either for supporting collaborative work, or for marketing and work-finding purposes. Further research in this area will include the deeper exploration of the reasons for uptake (or non-uptake) of various online services by the translation community in the UK, as well, it is hoped, as further comparative studies of uptake beyond the UK.

【延伸阅读】

[1] Kilgarriff, A. Web as corpus//Rayson, P., et al. (eds.), Proceedings of the Corpus Linguistics 2001 Conference, UCREL Technical Papers: 13. Lancaster University.

[2] Kilgarriff, A., & Grefenstette, G. Introduction to the Special Issue on the Web as Corpus. *Computational Linguistics*, 2003, 29 (3): 333 - 47. Retrieved November 26, 2004, from http://www-mitpress.mit.edu/journals/pdf/coli 29 3 333 0.pdf

[3] McEnery, T., & Wilson, A. Corpora and Translation: Uses and Future Prospects. *UCREL Technical Papers*, 1993.

[4] Resnik, P., & Smith, N. A. The Web as a Parallel Corpus. *Computational Linguistics*, 2003, 29(3): 349 - 380.

[5] Tymoczko, M. Computerized Corpora and the Future of Translation Studies. *Meta*, 1998, vol. 43, 4 (98): 652 - 659.

[6] Varantola, K. Translators and Disposable Corpora//F. Zanettin, S. Bernardini, & D. Stewart (eds.), *Corpora in Translator Educaion* (pp. 55 - 70). Manchester: St Jerome, 2003.

[7] Varantola, K. Disposable Corpora as Intelligent Tools in Translation//Tagnin, S. E. O. (eds.), *Cadernos de Traducao* (pp. 171 - 189). Florianopolis: NUT, 2002, 1(9).

[8] 沈固朝. 网络信息检索:工具·方法·实践. 北京:高等教育出版社,2004.

[9] 孙建军. 网络信息资源搜集与利用. 南京:东南大学出版社,2000.

[10] 王勇. 搜索引擎与翻译. 中国科技翻译,2005,(1):2.

[11] 冯志伟. 机器翻译研究. 北京:中国对外翻译出版公司,2004:752.

[12] Aldridge, A., Forcht, K., & Pierson, J. Get Linked or Get Lost: Marketing Strategy for the Internet. *Internet Research: Electronic Networking Applications and Policy*, 1997, 7(3):161 - 169.

[13] Lange, A.C., & Bennett, W. S. Combining Machine Translation with Translation Memory at Baan//R. C. Sprung (ed.), *Translating into Success: Cutting-edge Strategies for Going Multilingual in a Global Age*. Amsterdam/Philadelphia: John Benjamins Publishing Company, 2000.

[14] Austermuhl, F. *Electronic Tools for Translators*. Manchester: St. Jerome Publishing, 2001.

[15] Carter-Sigglow, J. The Internet and the Single Translator. Twenty-First International Conference on Translating and the Computer, ASLIB, London, 1999.

[16] Daniel, E., Wilson, H., & Myers, A. Adoption of E-Commerce by SMEs in the UK: Towards a Stage Model. *International Small Business Journal*, 2002, 20 (3): 253 - 270.

[17] Herbig, P., & Hale, B. Internet: The Marketing Challenge of the Twentieth Century. *Internet Research: Electronic Networking Applications and Policy*, 1997, 7 (2): 95 - 100.

[18] Kiani, G. R. Marketing Opportunities in the Digital World. *Internet Research: Electronic Networking Applications and Policy*, 1998, 8(2): 185 - 194.

[19] Reuther, U. LETRAC Survey Findings in the Industrial Context. *Deliverable*, 1999, D2. 2.

【问题与思考】

1. 你认为作者列举的网络对翻译的价值的研究课题是不是很全面？如果不全面，请问还有什么领域是可以研究的？

2. 选文二为什么将网络视为翻译工作者的必要工具？

3. 网络资源对于翻译有何作用？

4. 选文二的哪些网络资源对于您的翻译实践有益？

5. 网络时代背景下，为何翻译需求增加了？

6. 选文二中介绍了哪些可供自由译者使用的网络翻译工具？

第五章　翻译记忆研究

导　论

在同一类文本的翻译过程当中，译者经常会碰到文章内容前后是重复的，虽然重复的比重各有不同。这时，如果译者能够充分利用已经翻译的材料，就可以大大节省时间、提高翻译效率、保持翻译文体和风格的一致。通俗来讲，这种可以重复利用的已经翻译过的内容就是翻译记忆。翻译记忆（Translation Memory，简称 TM）是计算机辅助翻译技术（Computer-Aided Translation，简称 CAT）的核心技术之一，肇始于 20 世纪 90 年代中后期。

翻译记忆的工作原理：

方梦之先生在其《中国译学大辞典》（2011：332-333）中将"翻译记忆"的工作原理描述为："用户利用已有的原文和译文，建立起一个或多个翻译记忆库，在翻译过程中，系统将自动搜索翻译记忆库中相同或相似的翻译资源（如句子、段落），给出参考译文，使用户避免无谓的重复劳动，只须专注于新内容的翻译。"[①]当然，对于给出的参考译文，译者可以完全照搬，也可以修改后使用，如果觉得不满意，还可以弃之不用。[②]

翻译记忆的分类：

苏明阳（2007：71）将翻译记忆系统分为三类：翻译记忆模型、翻译记忆检索、翻译记忆编辑环境。

1. 翻译记忆模型是翻译记忆的储存方式，它又分为数据库模型和引用模型。就前者而言，翻译记忆以"翻译单元"的形式储存，源语言句段与目标语言句段精确对应。而后者并不将源语言句段与目标语言句段成对保存为翻译单元，而是利用"双语文本字符串"检索技术检索并引用其在文中出现的位置。

2. 翻译记忆检索分为基于字符串的匹配检索和语言学知识增强匹配检索。基于字符串的匹配检索较为传统，它是利用"编辑距离"比较字符串之间的相似程度。这种检索方式仅考虑到语言的形式而不涉及语言的意义，所以其精确度不高。利用语言学知识增强匹配检索可以提高翻译记忆检索的精确度。

3. 翻译记忆编辑环境是指译者进行翻译工作的文字处理程序环境。依据翻译编辑环境的不同，翻译记忆系统可以分为嵌入式和独立式两类。[③]

---

① 方梦之，《中国译学大辞典》，2011. 上海：上海外语教育出版社.
② 王金铨，翻译记忆（TM）——计算机翻译技术的新发展[J]. 现代图书情报技术，2004(5)：14.
③ 苏明阳，翻译记忆系统的现状及其启示[J]. 外语研究，2007(5).

114

翻译记忆可以很大程度地提高翻译质量,节省翻译时间和翻译成本,提高翻译术语的连续性。所以,翻译记忆比较适合于科普类、法律类等文本。但是,翻译记忆也有其局限性,主要体现在对于不同语境的适应性上的灵活处理,比如对于同一词汇的翻译比较单一死板,尤其是对于文学翻译,特别是诗歌翻译。

本章选取了三篇文章。Ahmed Saleh Elimam 撰写的"The Impact of Translation Memory Tools on the Translation Profession"一文主要探讨了翻译记忆对于翻译职业的影响。在 Vincent Vandeghinste 的论文"Removing the Distinction Between a Translation Memory,a Bilingual Dictionary and a Parallel Corpus"中,作者除了介绍机器翻译的研究方法以外,重点论述了如何消弭翻译记忆、双语词典和平行语料库之间的差异。第三篇选文"Removing the Distinction Between a Translation Memory,a Bilingual Dictionary and a Parallel Corpus"重点介绍当下机器翻译发展的新动态及其对翻译记忆的影响,并提出"机器翻译辅助的翻译记忆"(MT-assisted TM)以及两种翻译记忆的模式,即 utility model 和 hive model。

选 文

选文一 The Impact of Translation Memory Tools on the Translation Profession

Ahmed Saleh Elimam

导 言

本文于 2007 年 1 月发表于 *Translation Journal*。

作者 Ahmed Saleh Elimam 现任教于曼彻斯特大学,主要研究句式结构对可兰经诗文命题意义的影响。发表的论文有 *Clause-Level Foregrounding in the Translation of the Quran into English*:*Patterns and Motivations*;*Marked Word Order in the Quran*:*Functions and Translation* 等。作者主要探讨了翻译记忆对于译者、翻译机构和客户的利弊;同时,作者重点论述了翻译记忆带来的译者翻译方法的变化。

In order to conserve time, money and quality, Computer Assisted Translation (CAT) tools, including Translation Memory (TM), have become very popular with translators, translation agencies, and clients. While TM has its advantages and disadvantages for the translator and the translation bureau, it has advantages and virtually no disadvantages for clients.

First, as far as the translator is concerned, the great advantage of TM is in the area of translation quality. The quality is likely to improve in terms of consistency, both in the same document and across documents. TM saves pairs of terms or strings of texts, and reproduces them when the same SL term or string comes along in any other position in the document being translated. This, therefore, helps the translator to maintain consistency by always using the same equivalent for the same term or string. In other words, the translation becomes more efficient and consistent. In addition, a translator can always use the same TM with future translations, albeit from the same client, and hence achieve consistency in terms of terminology and style across translation jobs.

Second, "Terminology mining is said to account for 75 percent of a translator's time" (Arntz & Picht, 1989: 234 in Austermuhl, 2001). TM saves the translator's time by sparing him/her the need to look up the terms and words again if they are repeated in the text, especially in the case of large documents, or in another translation from the same client or in the same field of specialization. The translator will translate repeated terms and strings only once and TM will "translate" them whenever they come up again in the SL which, therefore, saves time. TM also spares the translator from the need to strain his/her memory to remember how he/she translated a certain term or string before or the need to go back through the document, albeit in long documents, to locate it. On the other hand, if TM is provided with the translation job, he/she will simply choose the equivalent used in the TM without need to "researching" which equivalent to use especially where synonymous or semi-synonymous equivalents exist, which is quite often the case. For example, the translator may "not know whether to use 'sexually Transmitted Disease' or 'sexually Transmitted Infection'," and this is where the role of TM comes in to decide which equivalent has been used before and to maintain consistency. Consistency means better quality which, in turn, means the client will be happy with the translation and will thus be more likely to consider the translator for future jobs.

Third, by saving the translator's time, TM increases his/her productivity which can lead to an increase in income. Further, more and more clients now are not only aware of but also require that their work be translated by TM software. In other words, the use of TM makes a translator more competitive by being distinguished from the others who do not use TM, and more likely to receive work. Finally, TM is quite portable. A translator can, literally, move easily around with all his/her translation resources on a CD or a "Memory Stick."

However, TM has its own disadvantages for a translator. First of all, he/she will have to invest a considerable amount of money to obtain the software and to put some time and effort into learning how to use it. Furthermore, especially at the early stages of use, the translator will always need to refer to the manual or ask experienced colleagues about the technical difficulties he/she may encounter, which means loss of valuable time.

In most programs using TM, a translator will only see a few sentences, strings or one paragraph on the screen at a time during the translation process. Therefore, he/she will only be able to work on that sentence, string or, at best, paragraph level and therefore may be translating out of context. As a result he/she may need to change some of his/her translations afterwards, which again means wasting some more time depending on how many corrections he/she needs to introduce in the translation. There may also be a risk of too much consistency in the translation. TM can adversely affect the translator's search for other, and perhaps better, equivalents and restrict him/her to use the same equivalent throughout the document even if there is a better alternative. In addition, if the translator delivers the TM together with the job, this can make the client less dependent on the same translator for future work, since the client can always give a new translator the TM they have received from previous translations together with the job. In other words, while promising a translator an opportunity of more work, TM still carries with it some inherent risks.

For the translation bureau, which manages the translation project for the client, TM also has some pros and cons. On the positive side, as has already been pointed out, more clients now request that their work be translated using TM. This means that having TM will help the bureau secure jobs that could have been lost otherwise. More work means more income. Furthermore, in cases of large translations which are normally divided among several translators, agencies can better proofread and project-manage the work with the use of TM. In the case of a ST being translated to more than one language, a bureau can manage the different target texts (TT's) quite easily and update its own TM accordingly. Other advantages of TM include the fact that agencies will be able to offer competitive prices for translation and can recruit several translators for the same job without fearing loss of consistency when all use the same TM. The only disadvantage of TM for agencies, in my opinion, is that a bureau will have to invest in the purchase of the software and its yearly updates and this outlay is usually high.

From a client's point of view, TM gives them the freedom to use different translators and translation agencies for future translation tasks. Consistency with previous translations is still maintained since clients can always request TM to be handed over with the translation and can later provide it to new translators to use and update. More important is that the client may be able to negotiate a lower fee when they provide TM along with the text to be translated. They may only pay full price for no matches but less (60% to 70%, for example) for fuzzy matches and even less for complete matches (30%, for example). The turnaround time, a major concern for clients, will be quicker because translators work faster and agencies manage the project more effectively. In short, the client has everything to gain and nothing to lose.

From the above one can say that TM may only be used with technical documents where there is a certain amount of repetition. For example, manuals, brochures and balance sheets contain a considerable number of repetitions and also need to be updated quite often. This is where TM comes in to achieve consistency and efficiency. On the other hand, TMs are not likely to be used with literary texts where the context plays a more important role compared to non-literary texts. Literary texts are also characterized by their figurative language which makes them difficult to translate with TM. Finally, literary texts do not seem to have the same amount of repetition as technical texts.

The Impact of TM on the Translator's Working Methods

Pros and cons aside, let us now look at the impact of TM on the translator's working methods. Austermuhl (2001) thinks that "more than any other professionals, translators are feeling the long-term changes brought about by the information age. The snowballing acceleration of available information, [and] the increase in intercultural encounters ... have resulted in drastic and lasting changes in the way translators work." Therefore, the question now for translators is not whether to use electronic tools or not but rather which tools to buy, learn, and use. Electronic dictionaries, glossaries and other resources have an edge over hard copies because they are easy to update and research. In fact some encyclopaedias and scientific journals are no longer published in print but are only delivered digitally (ibid: 102).

With the domination of English over other languages in the world of business, science, and technology, it is not surprising that more translators are now needed than ever before. The volume of translations being carried out each year from English into other languages is huge and worth billions of dollars. In addition, the expansion of the Internet and the computerization of the global economy have changed the way business is being conducted and emphasize the need for more effective and, undoubtedly, faster methods of translation, making full use of the huge amount of data available online. The influence of specialization and diversification, often referred to as the "information explosion", is also obvious as the amount of information available is now far greater than ever before and beyond the capacity of the available human brainpower to handle.

With TM the translator switches from the traditional method of looking up words and terms in hard-copy dictionaries, manuals and other written materials and perhaps maintaining hard-copy glossaries, to the world of online resources. A translator can tour national libraries, virtual bookstores, multilingual databases, newspaper and magazine archives, and other sites online, available at his/her fingertips, build up his/her own glossaries and attach them to the TM to enhance its performance. In addition, by developing his/her IT skills, a translator switches from translating only hard-copy documents to the fields of software localization, web page translation, and handling different electronic formats. He/she becomes more competitive because of the range of services he/she offers. As a knowledge-based activity, translation requires new strategies and a "paradigm shift in methodology. This shift must embrace practice, teaching and research" (Austermuhl, 2001). A translator is no longer someone sitting at a desk with a pen in hand，sheets of paper before him/her and a number of dictionaries within reach. He/she has become a person using a computer，or perhaps carrying a laptop，on which He/she has installed，among other things，several online dictionaries and glossaries. The translator is also someone who uses TM software and has very good IT skills. Translators now receive work electronically in different formats. This is in short the effect of TM on the work of the translator.

In conclusion，TMs have become popular with translators，agencies and clients because they save time and promote better quality and efficiency. Unlike translators and agencies who derive some gains but also some losses from the use of TM，clients only have gains：shorter turnaround，lower cost，and less dependency on the translator/translation bureau. Of all the advantages they have brought about to the translator，TMs have had a great impact on the way translators work now. Translators are now able to make better use of the available resources：electronic dictionaries and glossaries，and spelling checkers. TMs have equipped translators to handle the information explosion in all areas of human endeavor more efficiently than the human brain alone ever could.

选文二　Removing the Distinction Between a Translation Memory，a Bilingual Dictionary and a Parallel Corpus

Vincent Vandeghinste

导　言

本文摘于 2007 年在伦敦召开的"翻译与计算机大会"会议公报。

作者 Vincent Vandeghinste 是荷语鲁文天主教大学计算机语言学中心博士后研究员，学术兴趣主要集中于机器翻译。其所撰论文有：*Bottom-up Transfer in Example-based Machine Translation*；*Very Large Aligned Treebanks for Syntax-based Machine Translation*；*Top-down Transfer in Example-based Machine Translation* 等。

在引言部分，作者介绍了几种机器翻译研究范式：rule-based machine translation, statistical machine translation, example-based machine translation, context-based machine translation, data-oriented translation 等。在第二部分，作者介绍了另外一种机器翻译研究方法，即METIS-II，重点指出其优点；当然，它也有缺点，比如它所用资源非常有限。以这种方法为基础，作者提出了一种全新的方法，即 Parse and Corpus based machine translation，简称 PaCo-MT。除了简介其原理以外，作者还使用图示讲解了该方法的两种路径。第四部分是关于译者的后期编辑。第五部分是该文的核心，即，消弭翻译记忆、双语词典和平行语料库之间的差异。

1 Introduction

In machine translation (MT) research, traditionally a distinction is made between three paradigms: rule-based machine translation (RBMT), statistical machine translation (SMT), and example-based machine translation (EBMT).

RBMT relies on a large set of hand-crafted rules, which makes the development of new language pairs very costly, and improving existing systems becomes a tedious tasks, as these rule sets can become very large and complex. An RBMT system makes use of a dictionary to bridge the gap between the source language lexical items and the target language, together with a number of transfer rules or a complex interlingual representation, to map the source language sentence structure onto the target language sentence structure.

EBMT and SMT are data-driven approaches, and claim to be much faster in development, as they do not rely on hand-crafted rules. Instead, these approaches rely on large parallel corpora, which therefore become the bottleneck in developing new language pairs or new technical domains, as they are often unavailable, or not large enough. A difficult issue in working with parallel corpora is the alignment of the source and the target language. Whereas sentential alignment does not seem to pose too many problems, alignment within a sentence is a much more difficult task.

The ideas behind EBMT are often linked to ideas about translation memories. An EBMT system tries to match its input sentence with the source language side of a parallel corpus, and the aligned target language side of the corpus will generate the target language sentence. The difficulty for such systems lies in how this matching process is done in the case of partial matches, and how to solve overlapping partial matches and recombine the target side of the mapping fragments.

This is not the case for SMT, in which the generated sentence will be based on statistics derived from the aligned parallel corpus, making abstraction of the cases which are contained in the parallel corpus.

In recent years, hybrid machine translation systems have been starting to emerge. Within the METIS-II-consortium the idea arose to avoid some of the problematic issues of the previous approaches, and develop a prototype for a new translation method (Dologlou et al., 2003; Dirix et al., 2005; Vandeghinste et al., 2006), which relies heavily on the target language generation side, combining techniques from RBMT, SMT, and EBMT. The system was implemented for four language pairs: Dutch to English, Modern Greek to English, Spanish to English, and German to English. A more detailed description is given in Section 2.

Another hybrid machine translation system is the Matador system (Habash and Dorr, 2002; Habash, 2003, 2004), which is somewhat similar to the METIS-II approach, in that it does not require parallel data. It translates from Spanish to English, and relies heavily on target language generation. It is aimed at language pairs lacking resource symmetry. It employs symbolic and statistical target language resources, and requires a source language parser and a translation dictionary, but no transfer rules or complex interlingual representation. On the target side, rich symbolic resources like lexical semantics, categorial variations and subcategorization frames are used to overgenerate multiple structural variations from a syntactic dependency representation of the source language sentence, where all terminal nodes are translated by the dictionary. The overgeneration is constrained by several statistical target language models, including surface n-grams and structural n-grams.

Context-based Machine Translation (CBMT) as described by Carbonell et al. (2006) is another approach somewhat similar to the METIS approach. It does not require parallel corpora either and relies heavily on the target language side. It has been implemented for Spanish to English translation, and requires an extensive target language corpus, and a full-form dictionary. It does not contain transfer rules or interlingual representations, but instead relies on long n-grams. The principle is to produce many long n-gram candidate translations by finding those long n-grams that contain as many as possible of the potential word and phrase translations from the dictionary, and as few as possible other content words. These n-grams are matched with the target language corpus, and the highest scoring translation candidate is selected by the decoder. While this is in such a statistical approach, the general idea behind it is not within the classical SMT paradigm, but justifies its classification together with the METIS system and the MATADOR system.

A somewhat different approach using ideas from both SMT, RBMT, and EBMT is called Data-oriented Translation (DOT), which was first proposed by Poutsma (1998), and the first large scale implementation of this approach was done by Hearne (2005). DOT still requires parallel data, but this time, it concerns parallel treebanks, in which alignments have been made on several levels in the trees. By using linguistically motivated trees, combined with using translation examples, and statistical techniques like data oriented parsing (Scha, 1990; Bod, 1992), this approach borrows from the three different MT paradigms.

The prototype presented in this paper is based on the METIS-II approach, which will be described in the next section.

2 The METIS-II Approach

The aim of the METIS-II approach is to allow development of MT systems for low resource languages. Therefore, we restricted ourselves to using only limited tools, which are available for lots of languages, or which can be easily adapted to the languages in focus.

The METIS-II approach also tries addressing some of the weak points of the classic approaches. Only a limited set of rules is used, and no parallel data, except for the dictionary. All entries in the dictionary are lemmas, which is a useful abstraction over word forms, as it reduces dictionary size and data sparsity.

The METIS-II system is a hybrid system based on the ideas of EBMT systems, but without using a parallel corpus.

In a first step, shallow source language analysis is applied. The sentence is tokenized, tagged, lemmatized, and chunked. This results in a shallow parse tree.

Then the lexical entries in the sentence are looked up in a bilingual dictionary. Special care is taken in the lookup of complex entries, which might be discontinuous. Separable verbs are also looked up (which is not only relevant for Dutch, but also for German). In this process, only lemmas and part of speech tags are used.

Through a limited (50) number of transfer rules, the sentence structure is mapped onto the target language, generating a number of translation candidates.

These candidate translations are weighed by matching them with the target language corpus. For METIS-II, we used the British National Corpus. First we try to find matches for the lowest level chunks. The corpus lookup provides us with information about lexical selection and word order.

Each chunk from the source language tree is considered a bag: an unordered list. We retrieve from the corpus all chunks with the same chunk type containing as many lemmas as possible from the bag. According to how well these chunks match the bag, we give them a weight. By considering several translation alternatives and matching them with the corpus, different alternatives get different weightings, allowing us to select the one with the highest weight. Word order is determined by the matched corpus chunks. For words that are in the bag but not in the corpus chunk, we look for a slot in the corpus chunk with the same part of speech, and replace that word with the word from the bag.

At higher levels in the shallow parse tree, we use the heads of lower level chunks, which should have been resolved at this point.

Matching the sentence with a monolingual target language corpus has the advantage of not needing a parallel corpus, which is a scarce resource for most language pairs. Whereas the difficulty of EBMT systems is to find matching source language fragments, this is moved to finding matching corpus segments in the target language, based on the translated words in the dictionary. The difficult issue of sub-sentential alignment is avoided.

For a detailed description of the METIS-II approach, take a look at Dirix et al. (2006) for the description of the Dutch to English approach. Other language pairs developed in METIS-II are German to English (Carl et al., 2007), Spanish to English (Badia et al., 2005), and Greek to English (Markantonatou et al., 2006).

In this paper we describe a new prototype, which is based on the METIS-II paradigm, but whereas METIS-II was restricted to using only limited resources, as it was developed as a new methodology for MT systems for lesser resourced languages, this new system will use all resources that are available for the language pair at hand.

Another difference with the METIS-II system lies in the integration of a postediting interface with the system, such that each of the human-edited translations is fed back into the system, using that information for future translations.

3 The New Prototype

In the prototype which we describe in this paper, we want to scale up the METIS-II approach. We will not limit ourselves anymore to using only linguistic resources. This time, we will use all resources we can get.

We will still use the METIS-II approach, but add a lot of information coming from parallel aligned treebanks, in a similar way as the DOT approach described earlier.

In Figure 1, we show the general architecture of the new prototype, which is called PaCo-MT (Parse and Corpus based MT).

This prototype is built for the language pairs Dutch-English and Dutch-French, in both directions. In the rest of this paper, we will only focus on the Dutch-English language pair, but the same principles are applied when translating from Dutch into French or vice versa.

When a sentence is entered into the system, this sentence goes through a source language parser, resulting in a full parse tree analysis of the source language.

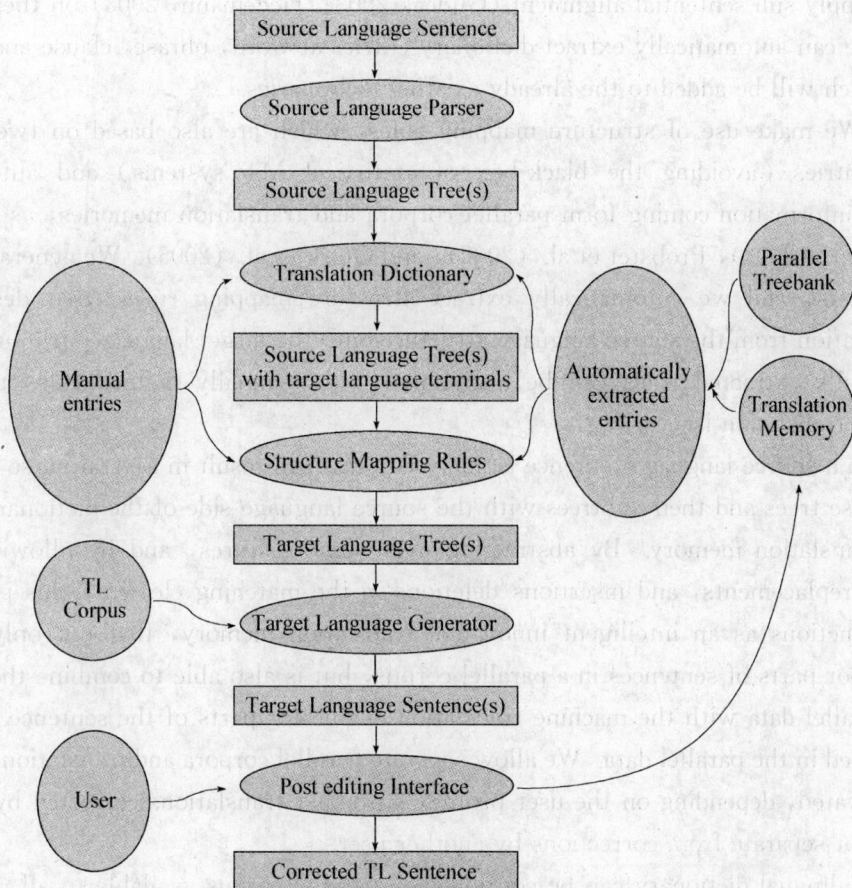

Figure 1 Architecture of the prototype

The Alpino parser (Van der Beek et al., 2005; Van Noord, 2006) is used when translating from Dutch. It is chosen because it is a wide-coverage parser with a high accuracy and it is freely available.

The PET parser (Callmeier, 2000) combined with the ERG-grammar (Copes-take and Flickinger, 2002) will be used when translating from English. The PET parser is chosen because it is optimized for speed, and they are both freely available. Besides this, they are based on the HPSG paradigm (Pollard and Sag, 1987, 1994), and so is Alpino, which will result in comparable structures for both source language and target language trees.

To go from source to target language we use two paths:

(a) We make use of a translation dictionary (containing words, phrases, clauses, and full sentences), which is based on two sources: manual entries and automatically extracted information coming from parallel corpora and translation memories. We use a Dutch-English dictionary from the METIS-II project. We are collecting parallel corpora like Europarl (Koehn, 2005), Acquis Com-munautaire (Steinberger et al., 2006), and the Dutch Parallel Corpus (which will be available soon). A translation company provides us with real translation memories and translated texts.

We apply sub-sentential alignment (Gildea, 2003; Tiedemann, 2003) on these parallel data so we can automatically extract dictionary entries at word, phrase, clause and sentence level, which will be added to the already existing dictionaries.

(b) We make use of structure mapping rules, which are also based on two sources: manual entries (avoiding the black-box of statistical MT systems) and automatically extracted information coming form parallel corpora and translation memories, as is done in Lavoie et al. (2002), Probstet et al. (2002), and Quirk et al. (2005). We generate parallel parse forests, and we automatically extract structure mapping rules, that describe the transformation from the source language structure onto the target language structure. These automatically extracted rules can be augmented with manually defined rules to address remaining translation issues.

When a source language sentence is analysed, this can result in several parse trees. We match these trees and their subtrees with the source language side of the dictionary/parallel corpus/translation memory. By abstracting over some features, and by allowing partial matches, replacements, and insertions/deletions in the matching element, this part of the system functions as an intelligent innovative translation memory, that not only matches sentences or parts of sentences in a parallel corpus, but is also able to combine the outcome of the parallel data with the machine translation engine for parts of the sentence which are not matched in the parallel data. We allow separate parallel corpora and translation memories to be activated, depending on the user profile, such that translations corrected by one user can be kept separate from corrections by another user.

The bilingual dictionary can be considered a parallel corpus available to all users, and mainly contains single words. Full phrases, multi-words and discontinuous dictionary entries are allowed as well. Translations leading to structural changes in the dependency tree can be coded through dictionary entries.

At this point in the processing procedure, we have an intermediate tree representation in which all leaf nodes (or sometimes higher level nodes) are translated into the target language. Parts of this tree structure are already in the target language structure, as they result from the target side of the parallel corpus or the dictionary, while other parts of the tree structure are still in the source language structure. These parts should be converted into the target language structure, through the structure mapping rules.

Alternative target language trees are generated in the previous processing steps, each with a weight representing the confidence. These weights are adapted through information gathered from the monolingual target language corpora: how well does the tree fit the target language?

The target language corpus is preprocessed with the respective parser and grammar for that language, resulting in a target language treebank. For Dutch as target language, we use the Lassy treebank (van Noord et al., 2006) and the Alpino tree-bank, (http://www.let.rug.nl/~vannoord/trees/) which are both publicly available. For English as TL, we use the Redwoods treebank (Oepen et al., 2002). We extend these treebanks with the respective sides of the parallel data, and will possibly extend them with more automatically annotated monolingual treebanks, as the need arises.

Lexical selection amongst several translation alternatives is based on co-occurrence metrics (Dunning, 1993; Church and Hanks, 1990; Evert, 2004; Evert and Krenn, 2004), and frequency metrics taking into account the syntactic environment of the word (which are similar to what we already did in Dirix et al. (2006)). This allows us to decide which of the translation alternatives for e. g. an adjective are most likely to go together with a specific noun, etc.

Target language generation needs to be performed based on the obtained target language trees. In the target language corpus database, we store (sub-)tree structure patterns combined with surface string information like word order for these trees, allowing us to generate target language word order as derived from the target language corpus. The better a tree matches a tree in the target language corpus, the higher the weight this translation will get, in the list of generated translations. This is a refined version of the target language generation component in Dirix et al. (2006).

4　Human Post-editing

The output of our system is sent to a post-editing interface, in which the human post-editor can adapt the translation:

• The post-editor can choose another translation candidate, be it on the sentence level or on any lower levels in the tree.

- The post-editor can make changes to the text, by simple typing.
- The post-editor can move words or phrases.

Because the sentence was automatically generated, and by tracking the post-editor's changes to the sentence, we have a number of ways in improving our system automatically. The newly generated parallel sentence, which is aligned at sub-sentential level can be fed back into our translation dictionary. Like in a traditional translation memory, this sentence will now be automatically generated when the same input sentence is given. The different phrases of this sentence will also be put into the dictionary. As the sentence was automatically generated, we have a detailed sub-sentential alignment which allows this. Apart from that, the corrected target language sentence will also be added to the target language treebank, so this information becomes available when trying to match future similar sentences.

We can also adapt the weights in our dictionary for the current user/text to improve consistent translation. The automatically extracted transfer rules (or their weights) can also be updated as a consequence of human post-editing, in a similar way as Font Llitjos et al. (2007).

5 Removing the Distinction Between a Translation Memory, a Dictionary, and a Parallel Corpus

In the METIS-II system, we started the development of a translation dictionary format in which we could not only represent single word entries, but also complex entries leading to structural changes in the target language. For this purpose, we use XML.

In example (1) you can see how a single word entry, with only one translation alternative looks in our dictionary.

```
(1) <dict-entry id="19">
    <source>
       <token id="1" pos="ADJ" lemma="blauw"/>
    </source>
    <target>
       <trans-unit id="1">
          <token id="1" pos="AJ?" link="1" lemma="blue"/>
       </trans-unit>
    </target>
 </dict-entry>
```

Each dictionary entry consists of two main parts. In the <source> part, the source language side of the entry is described, through one or more <token>-tags, which can be grouped to higher level linguistic units in <chunk>-tags.

In the <target> part, the target language side of the entry is described, consisting of one or more <trans-unit>s, each representing a translation alternative for the source language token(s).

In the <token> entries, you can see a pos feature. On the source side this contains the restrictions to which the entry must comply in order to generate the translation candidates. On the target side, this contains part of speech information which applies to the token. In the source language tag set (Van Eynde, 2005), features are represented between brackets. For instance, a singular (ev) non-diminutive (basis) common (soort) noun (N) in standard case (stan) gets the tag N(soort, ev, basis, zijd, stan). When no brackets are used, this indicates that there are no restrictions on the features of the source side.

On the target side, question marks are used for underspecification, as the CLAWS5 tagset uses the third character to represent the features. For instance, NN1 represents singular nouns, whereas NN2 represents plural nouns.

Underspecifications are due to the fact that we use lemmas, which are under-specified for features like number, case, etc.

The link feature is used on the target side only, to indicate which part of the target side is a translation of which part in the source side.

For the translation of more complex entries, for instance, the translation of Dutch's morgens into English in the morning things are a bit more complicated. As shown in (2), the Dutch phrase is an NP chunk, which is represented by the <chunk>-tag. This tag contains the feature ref to indicate which <token>s belong to the chunk. This Dutch NP is translated into an English PP, consisting of the preposition in and the NP, consisting of the tokens *the* and *morning*. To indicate that the target language PP is a translation of the source language NP, the link feature in the target language PP refers to the source language NP. Note that the source language pos features contain the restriction that they need to be in genitive case, which avoids translating Dutch de morgen (in standard case: the morning) into English in the morning which would be incorrect.

```
(2) <dict-entry id="4">
      <source>
        <token id="1" pos="LID(gen)" lemma="de"/>
        <token id="2" pos="N(gen)" lemma="morgen">
        <chunk id="c1" ref="1-2" label="NP" head="2"/>
      </source>
      <target>
        <trans-unit id="1">
          <token id="1" pos="PRP" lemma="in"/>
          <token id="2" pos="ATO" lemma="the"/>
          <token id="3" pos="NN1" lemma="morning"/>
          <chunk id="c1" ref="1-c2" label="PP" link="c1"
```

```
        head="1"/>
    <chunk id="c2" ref="2-3" label="NP" head="3"/>
        </trans-unit>
    </target>
</dict-netry>
```

Thinking about how to represent this structural change in the METIS-II dictionary, resulted in a format in which we represent both sides of an entry as a tree. The link values allow us to represent lower level alignment in these trees.

If our dictionary can be used to map a source language tree onto a target language tree, which is what we do, then it would also be possible to use the dictionary to map full source language sentences in much the same way onto full target language sentences, which is necessary when translating idiomatic phrases or proverbs.

And, if we can translate full sentences using the dictionary, why would we not add human post-edited sentences to this dictionary. For these sentences, we have lower level alignments, as they were originally generated by our system. When the post-editor does not make any typing changes, but merely changes the selected translation candidates and moves around words or phrases, this does not pose any problems.

We not only add these full sentences to the dictionary, but also all their aligned parts. When some parts are already in the dictionary, we update the weight for the selection as made by the post-editor. This ensures that the system will learn immediately from the post-editor's behaviour.

Because of the fact that our dictionary grows fast, we need to have a fast way of matching our sentence with the source language side of the dictionary. We can use classic EBMT methods for this.

And when we can use aligned post-editing information in the improvement of our system, there is no reason why we cannot import already existing translation memories or parallel corpora, hence removing the distinction between a dictionary, a translation memory, and a parallel corpus. For this, we would need to parse both sides of the translation memory or parallel corpus and align them at a sub-sentential level.

6 Conclusions

In the METIS-II system, the only parallel data which is used is a bilingual dictionary. Since we wanted to be able to model complex dictionary entries which lead to structural changes in the tree representation of the sentence under translation, we set up an XML dictionary in which we can map source language trees onto target language trees. While this was initially only intended for use with idioms and proverbs, there was no principle reason why we could not use this set up in much the same way as a traditional translation memory.

In the Paco-MT system, which is still in its development phase, we are no longer tied to the METIS-II restriction of using low resources. Therefore we can use existing, available data, and the most logical spot to incorporate this data in our system is in the dictionary.

We also wanted an adaptive system which learns from interaction with the human post-editor. Apart from a growing target language corpus (a by-product of the corrected sentences which are added to this corpus), the amount of parallel data grows as well. Since this parallel data is based on our MT output, it is aligned with the source language. By immediately feeding back this information into the dictionary, the system will learn immediately.

In the way that we represent all parallel data in what was originally our dictionary, we have removed the distinction between a translation memory, an aligned parallel corpus, and a traditional bilingual dictionary.

选文三 Beyond Translation Memory: Computers and the Professional Translator

Ignacio Garcia

导 言

本文发表于 2009 年的 *The Journal of Specialized Translation* 第 12 期上。

Ignacio Garcia 博士是澳大利亚西悉尼大学人文与语言学院的高级讲师,主要教授翻译记忆和机器翻译系统。他在该领域发表了多篇论文,比如 *Is Machine Translation Ready Yet?*; *Beyond Translation Memory*: *Computers and the Professional Translator*; *Power Shifts in Web-based Translation Memory* 等。

本文中,作者首先指出新时期翻译作为一种职业所具备的特征。接着,作者简单介绍了翻译记忆的兴起与发展。之后,作者列举了翻译记忆带来的变化,尤其是翻译记忆在网络时代的应用。此后,作者用了大幅笔墨介绍当下机器翻译发展的新动态及其对翻译记忆的影响。并且作者提出了一个新概念,机器翻译辅助的翻译记忆(MT-assisted TM)。最后,作者提出了两种翻译记忆的模式,即 utility model 和 hive model。

1 Introduction

The digital age has affected all professions, but change has been felt by translators more keenly than most. Like the rest of the "knowledge sector," translators are obliged to work on computer screens and do their research using the web. Unlike their colleagues however, they have been propagating this new work environment and fomenting change precisely by their role in translating it. The most significant tool used until now by translators in the digital work environment is Translation Memory software, or TM. By putting the developments of the last 20 years in historical perspective and with particular attention to events over the last two, this article argues that TM is reaching its use-by date. It also examines the strong re-emergence of Machine Translation (MT) in response to TM's inability to cope with the increasing translating needs of today's digital age. Furthermore, this paper foresees the closure of the cycle which began when translation became an "independent" profession, and an approaching future in which translation may once again be the realm of the gifted amateur or keen bilingual subject specialist.

2　Translation as a Profession

Translation as a profession is only a recent development. For most of written history, translators were bilinguals with a particular ability or inclination to transfer text between languages, mentored (or not) by more experienced masters. They typically made their living from another primary activity, and applied their knowledge and insights to transferring key texts. Thus, physicians translated medical texts, public servants translated laws or treaties, theologians translated scripture, writers and poets translated literature, and so forth. This model continued unaltered well into the 20th century; it still persists in some sectors and is actually gaining ground in others.

Translation as an "independent" profession only emerged towards the mid-twentieth century, when the old model could not cope and formal training within educational institutions took over from the previous guild-like approach. As the complexity of the translation task became better appreciated and its theoretical foundations were laid, the field was opened to a new professional class. Unlike their historical counterparts, modern translators were linguists trained in the craft of transferring meaning from one language to another, and they acquired specialized topic knowledge as an adjunct to their primary skill as text interpreters and rewriters.

Since the late 1980s the most dynamic sector of the translation profession has been that linked to translating digital content—translating for the screen, not for the printer; translating for localization, not for publishing. Localization, in its classic late nineties definition, means the linguistic and cultural adaptation of a product or service into another language or locale. It has translation at its core, but equally involves associated engineering and managerial tasks.

From the nineties onward, this shift went hand-in-hand with increasing demand, as the Information Technology industry realised that the task of translating user interfaces, user assistance, web pages, video games etc. far exceeded the capacities of its bilingual staff. This was the age of the Language Services Providers (LSP) that employed translation technology, the internet, and pools of professional translators and revisers to process large jobs efficiently and competently. Without professional intervention, the industry would have choked in the linguistic mess that the amateurs had been creating. Preparing candidates for this profession is what authors such as Gouadec (2007), McKay (2006) or Samuelsson-Brown (2004) and a large number of university courses are all about.

3　TM Beginnings

The Information Revolution did not just generate more work for translators, but also new tools aimed at boosting their productivity. One particular tool soon achieved prominence—and it was not machine translation (MT), as many pundits had been predicting since the 1950s. While computer sophistication and language algorithms were not yet enough for useful MT, the humble PC had abundant processing power and memory aplenty for a low tech off-shoot of MT: translation memory (TM).

Essentially a data base application, TM allowed for recycling of past translations that afforded increased productivity and consistency, while its filters could handle digital file formats that word processors could not. TM became the interface between LSPs and freelance translators, allowing them to collaborate in large-scale translation projects.

TM was useful for most kinds of translation tasks, but came into its own with localization. Ownership of and proficiency with an industry-compatible TM software suite soon became indispensable for aspirants to this kind of work. In fact, during its early phase, the main impetus in developing the technology came mostly from keen freelancers (Jochen Hummel and Iko Knyphausen of Trados, Emilio Benito of Deja Vu), although emerging localization agencies (Star-Transit) or big corporations (IBM Translation Manager) also played a role.

Over time however, what had commenced as a translator's tool became something that language vendors imposed on their pool of freelancers, and finally—once major translation buyers became aware of the benefits—was in turn imposed on language vendors by corporations.

Over the course of the nineties, TM technology matured: applications became more stable and more powerful. They incorporated terminology management systems, alignment, and terminology extraction tools, then quality control (QC) and project management features, and eventually the capacity for batch handling of multiple files and formats, and simultaneously using several memories and glossaries. The evolution of this technology can be traced best by following reviews of individual products in industry journals (for example Benis, 2003; Wassmer, 2003).

3.1　Focus on Segments

The role of the technical translator changed as a direct result of TM technology.

Translators were no longer focused on translating texts, but segments, which were often displayed in the editing window in nonsequential fashion. When matches were found, the translator would have the option to accept them after checking and/or editing (but not translating). Rejected or empty segments would of course require old-fashioned translating from scratch, but always within the narrow context of the TM editor, rather than a "whole-text" approach (Hennessy, 2008).

This was a radical departure from the canonical translator's role, and to a large extent ignored by translation research, training institutions and professional bodies. Nevertheless, users soon became accustomed, finding that after a period of adaptation they could achieve higher productivity.

For a brief honeymoon period, translators who embraced the new technology enjoyed the benefits of significant time savings and almost exclusive access to high-tech jobs. Moreover, the translation solutions they generated stayed on their hard drives, and over time increased in value as linguistic resources. This heyday involved what has been termed the "interactive mode."

However, freelancers soon lost control of this technology to the emerging translation bureaus, which would eventually be known as Language Service Providers (LSPs). Now, translators were no longer accessing their own resident translation memories at will, but rather dealing with a "pre-translated" file emailed or downloaded from an LSP. Under this mode, freelancers would receive a bilingual file with matches both exact and fuzzy, plus terms from the existing databases already inserted in the target section. This "pre-translation" mode allowed LSPs to share the minimum information required, thus centralizing resources and preventing collaborators from sharing them with other competing LSPs or clients. With little effort, LSPs could now multiply individual productivity gains by leveraging the memories and glossaries generated by hundreds of (mostly freelance) translators.

Wallis (2006) has studied how translators respond to these two ways of engaging with TM, and found that although there was not much difference productivity-wise, translators tended to prefer and to work more comfortably in the original interactive mode. But user-friendliness was not the critical issue. What galled freelancers was the fact that external databases contained segment matches they had not generated themselves. This meant more time checking and editing, yet entailed mandatory price reductions—the infamous "Trados discounts," so-called because of the pre-eminence of Trados among the big players. A search for "Trados discounts" in the archives of any mainstream translator's list (TM oriented or not) will reveal some very interesting threads.

By the turn of the century, it was the translation departments of big corporations that would take the technological initiative from LSPs. Now, corporate clients would retain their own memory and glossary repositories, and commission translations from possibly several competing LSPs—pushing prices down and obliging LSPs to conform to the chosen TM application or format.

3.2 From Hard Drive to Server

As computer power and broadband connectivity increased, moving the databases from hard-drives to servers become feasible. Over the last few years, both language buyers and language vendors have keenly joined in. The pre-translation mode is rapidly being phased-out in favour of the emerging web-interactive mode, whereby translators now log in to the databases via their browser. Although access is still only one segment at a time, there is now the possibility of leveraging segments in real time, as and when they are created by other translators working remotely on the same project.

No empirical studies have been done yet on how this emerging web-interactive mode suits the translators who are shoehorned into it. Just by looking at the technology, and as confirmed by some anecdotal evidence, it appears to disadvantage them in at least four ways. Firstly, it imposes the tool they must use: whereas the pre-translation mode allowed a translator to work using, say, a Trados-compatible tool rather than Trados itself, with web-based technology this is no longer feasible. Secondly, on anecdotal evidence it slows the respective response times for opening each segment, searching the data base(s) and returning results, and closing (uploading) completed segments (tool developers might dispute this point, but comments from translators suggest otherwise). Thirdly, it makes it difficult for translators to build up their own linguistic assets, although in some cases with extra effort they might perhaps circumvent this. Lastly, it clearly gives LSPs access to performance-related information that most self-employed professionals would like to keep confidential: hours spent, translation speed, work patterns.

The web-interactive mode is therefore not serving freelance translators well—on the contrary, it seems to have deteriorated their working conditions (Garcia, 2007). With payment on a per-word basis (for the most common languages at least), it contributes to continual downward pressure on rates as the expansion of internet services affords access to translators from countries with lower costs of living (see Chan, 2008 for an interesting view of the overlap between localization and the economy).

LSPs meanwhile have gained much broader control over the translation process. The sector has witnessed various mergers and acquisitions, developed complex systems to automate translation processes which previously relied on phone calls and e-mail, and off-shored many engineering tasks to developing countries. And yet LSPs are struggling now too, while a look at globalization journals (ClientSide News for example) indicates that language buyers are also unhappy with the current status quo—despite the chips having seemingly fallen all their own way.

The principal stumbling block is that, notwithstanding all the undeniable productivity gains from improvements in TM technology, translation remains a "manual" activity. At this stage of web development, translation needs are growing exponentially with the emerging

"Web 2.0" community, and even with state-of-the-art technology and processes the present paradigm is inadequate. This is because key tasks must still be performed by capable humans, who are slow and expensive in comparison to machines.

3.3　Translating for the Web

Whether we choose to use the Web 2.0 tag (O'Reilly, 2005) or not, the cyber-scape of today is vastly different to that of the nineties. Software developers are moving data, computing tools, and even software development itself from the hard drive to servers in data macro-centres—or the "cloud," if you prefer the latest vogue metaphor (Haynie, 2008). Instead of residing on the user's own hard drive, applications are now increasingly accessed through a web browser in a trend known as SaaS or "Software as a Service" (SIIA, 2001).

As for the way people use the web, that has also dramatically changed. It is not just the producer-centric venue of a decade ago, through which corporations and institutions could market goods and services to potential customers via hypertext files on "static" pages. Now it also has a user-centric layer where we can connect with real and virtual "friends" to exchange ideas and opinions, or pursue common causes and interests. Computer operation was once a career, but nowadays practically anyone can book travel and accommodation, communicate instantly with text, voice, or video, download or upload text, audio and video from or to websites, buy and sell, join groups, operate banking accounts—and the list is growing.

Meanwhile, concerns at not dealing with a physical "shopfront" are vanishing, as consumers discover they can access quality services cheaply, sometimes even for free. Consequently, in just a few years, we have imperceptibly grown accustomed to transacting our business and even social lives though mouse clicks. The technology is inexpensive and transparent, and has opened up a brand new world full of possibilities ... as long as we speak English, or one of the major languages.

Effectively, the web has drastically lowered the space/time barrier. The accessibility barrier (the cost of the hardware) also keeps falling. The language barrier, however, remains. As remarked earlier, the amount of content contributed by producers and users far exceeds the translation industry's capacity to cope. Localization is geared to producing quality output, but is relatively slow and only affordable to big players on big projects. It simply cannot keep pace with an environment that puts a premium on cheapness and speed.

For some twenty years, the industry made impressive progress on the back of TM. But just as the master/apprentice model collapsed under the weight of the mid-20th century scientific-technical revolution, the localization model that subsequently emerged is failing now itself in the face of web-driven demand.

When the hard-drive was at the core of the computer revolution, the localization industry had power and purpose. Now, with the personal computer becoming little more than a browser terminal, TM technologies and current localization processes are not enough.

Recent developments point to some trends that may play a big role in the translation of digital content as we enter into the next decade. For now, we can predict that TM will still have a role over the next decade, but mostly in support of new generation MT.

4 Free, Unassisted MT

To become fully connected, planet web has a language barrier to break through—and on past performance, if the localization industry is unable to help, it will do it on its own. Trying, as Yoda might say, it is.

The first attempt, so far, has been machine translation (MT), in the shape of web-based, fully automated MT such as that offered since the late nineties by Babel Fish, and more recently by Google Translator or Microsoft Windows Live. MT embodies the trinity of our brave new web world: free, instantaneous, and easy to use. In the latest versions, you can set your browser for Google Translate to produce a page in your language (if among the 13 languages/29 language pairs now supported by its MT engine) at the click of a button. Similarly, if you are consulting an article in the Microsoft Knowledge Base that has not been translated, the page offers you a machine translated version, and asks for feedback. Laughable? You might be surprised. According to a study by Wendt (2008: cited in Clientside News by Dillinger & Gerber, 2009), Microsoft found little difference in usefulness ratings between the source in English and the MT version in Spanish, Portuguese and Arabic, with some machine translated articles into Chinese gaining a greater rating than the original. A study by Intel also reported in Clientside News (Gerber, 2008) examines customer satisfaction with its own knowledge-base performance. The figures show 53% positive responses for the original English, with French, German, Italian and Turkish "human" translations ranging between 34% and 40%. By comparison, raw Spanish TM output scored 43%. If these studies are reliable, they certainly call the current expenditure on translation QA into question.

It goes without saying that MT quality can be a somewhat elastic concept within certain limits, and depends on several variables: source processing, engine preparation, engine type (rule-based, statistical, or some kind of hybrid), language pair combination (Wilks, 2005). Only in the most restrictive environments is it likely to produce output that is "publishable" under old notions of quality, but with the speed we now desire, assessment is tempered by fitness for use: if users are satisfied with results, anything more is a waste of resources.

According to a recent TAUS (2009) report, automatic translate buttons in search portals get more than 50 million hits a day. The free MT model advanced by Google and other big commercial applications will certainly be maintained, since its market value does not depend on the selling of licences, but on advertising revenue from searching eyeballs (DePalma, 2007). Its quality can only improve in the coming years, given already heavy research funding by the US Department of Defence (Bemish, 2008), advances in retrieving useful bilingual text from the internet (see, for example, the Cross-language Information Retrieval model in Lu, 2007), and the increasing amount of clean, TM-generated bilingual text that can be used to train its engines.

Bilingual seed data will of course keep growing in quantity and quality, driven by initiatives such the Translation Automation User Society (TAUS) and its Data Center to which significant language buyers (Adobe, Microsoft, Oracle, Sun Microsystems) and vendors (Lionbridge, Jonckers, SDL, Welocalize) have already pledged to contribute. All this will further propel the inexorable march of linguistic assets from hard drive to enterprise server to industry-shared repositories.

While unassisted, free MT can be useful for gisting purposes, it is still the general consensus that it is not yet up to the standard required to be used for dissemination. But this situation can be greatly improved when MT is properly assisted.

5　Beyond TM: MT-assisted TM

For now and the foreseeable future, stand-alone, unassisted MT is not yet the solution. However, the big players in localization are already taking assisted MT very seriously indeed.

Back in March 2008, when Google had just launched its new SMT engine, Common Sense Advisory was proposing that LSPs should pre-process texts using Google Translate, and then decide whether to post-edit or discard and translate from scratch (DePalma, 2008). So far no LSP has admitted to trying this, but there is no cause for embarrassment since this basic strategy is already attracting significant interest.

Using careful controlled authoring (now of course enhanced by authoring tools), customized MT engines with the most up-to-date glossaries and memories, and human post-editing, adherents believe MT is now reaching a stage where it can produce TM quality output faster than TM itself for many types of texts. Taking the best of both worlds, they propose a workflow whereby the source text is first pre-translated with TM, with remaining empty segments processed by MT. The human translator who would once have translated the incomplete segments now post-edits the final result.

Big language buyers (including Microsoft) tend to think the tipping point at which MT output will help rather than distract translators has been reached, and have commenced implementing such TM-assisted MT systems. There are still no empirical studies to measure its success, but this is the standard course of events nowadays in most fields: first the technology is developed, then applied, and only then will there be studies to inquire if that application made sense. That said, there is some interesting preliminary work in TM/MT that examines how translators deal with fuzzy matches versus machine-translated segments (Guerberof, 2008; O'Brien, 2006).

As we move into the next decade, what has begun as a pilot by a few heavyweights could well become mainstream for the whole of the localization industry. A recent study commissioned by SDL found that of 40 of clients surveyed, 40 percent were likely to use MT "now" for either technical documentation or support and knowledge-based content (SDL Research, 2008). At the freelance level, MT output for translators using TM was hitherto deemed to be more distracting than helpful. At the beginning of the decade, some tools already came with MT plug-ins (Wordfast version 3, SDLX version 4, Trados version 5), but the concept did not find favour and was consequently neglected in subsequent versions. This is changing now. SDL Trados 2007 offered access to its in-house SDL Automated Translation feature in late 2008 (SDL, 2008), and the feature remains, now with easier access, in the new SDL Trados Studio 2009. MultiTrans signed an agreement to offer access to the Syst ran MT engine early in 2009 (Multicorpora, 2009).

From outside the traditional localization industry, Google announced in June 2009 its Translator Toolkit, a web-based TM tool that went a step ahead in this direction by offering the filling in of target segments with Google Translate as default—translating from scratch rather than postediting just an option. This started as a beta release with only English as a source language and no fuzzy matching, thus not suitable for professional translation. Seen as a ploy by Google to engage unpaid translators to provide parallel texts to feed into its SMT (Zetzsche, 2009; van der Meer, 2009), the Google Translator Toolkit illustrates, however, how fast MT is gaining ground.

Soon, if not already, professional translators in the localization industry will no longer translate texts (like their literary counterparts) or segments (as in the TM heyday), but just post-edit machine output. Recent research comparing translating by post-editing MT versus translating directly from the source text showed the post-edited output was judged to be of higher clarity and accuracy if not of better style (Fiederer & O'Brien, 2009). The new key figures will be the technical writers that produce the consistent controlled source text that ensures accurate TM results, and the data base managers and reviewers that tend the TM corpus.

The new model will continue improving its cost effectiveness by reducing demands on those doing the post-editing, and this will almost certainly see the deputizing of competent bilinguals in place of professional translators. The present cycle will then presumably close, as translation loses its professional status and returns to its millennial amateur paradigm.

5.1　Beyond TM: Translation as a "Utility"

The introduction of MT-assisted TM may help extract more productivity out of the traditional localization mode. After all, TM has been its foundation, and this is the next step—albeit a radical one—in the path the technology has followed since its inception. While MT-assisted, TM will contribute to incrementally advancing productivity, it will only alleviate the problem rather than offer the necessary solution.

The advent of SaaS has provided cost savings and enhanced tracking systems that can manage translation with minimal human intervention, and LSPs are already making full use of it. But interestingly, this technology also offers the possibility of bypassing LSPs altogether. This concept has been under test for some time, for instance through portals such as ProZ (or Translators' Cafe, or Aquarius or others).

Yet web users typically expect more: they want translation to be as close to instantaneous and free as possible, and if the localisation industry can't or won't deliver, sheer demand almost guarantees someone else will ... Livetranslation. com, for example, offers fast, small-volume, user-friendly human translation on-demand. Here the client posts a source text to the site and, with payment arranged, a translator-on-duty performs the translation and uploads it in the time taken to type it. It seems ideal for natural language applications beyond the present capabilities of unassisted MT. It may sound trivial, but Microsoft is taking it seriously enough, with plans to configure its Knowledge Base so that if users are unhappy with results from its un-assisted MT engine, they can access this premium "human" service instead(Livetranslation, 2008).

Indeed, this mode seems tailor-made for customer support/knowledge-based content, where the translator can be assisted with the corporation's latest available terminology and memories, as well as for natural language applications like e-mail/instant messaging which unassisted human translation could handle well. At least for the languages and areas of greater demand, one can easily imagine future translators being paid by the hour rather than the word, and working on-site under call-centre conditions rather freelancing from home.

TAUS has already named this trend "translation as a utility," but it might also be called "translation-on-tap," or "off-the-wall" by analogy with public utilities such as water or electricity.

5.2 Beyond TM: "Hive" Translation

Late in 2007, the social networking site Facebook asked its bilingual users to translate their site for free, and succeeded. The Spanish, French and German sites became available by January 2008, and many others since. It required planning, certainly, and a sophisticated technical platform, but it was translation by amateurs—albeit bilinguals with a privileged knowledge of the subject matter. Facebook's experiment came at a very critical moment when competing site MySpace was translating its own site by following the standard localization processes, and Skyrock, Hi5 and others also seeking to grow outside the English market.

What Facebook actually did was crowdsource its translation, and on the strength of the results, if it had followed the usual localization industry processes the task would probably have not been performed any faster orbetter. Crowdsourcing itself was around well before wired popularized the term (Howe, 2006) and had already been used in several other industries (see Kleemann, 2008). Big players have also crowdsourced particular pockets of content they thought could be suitable. Google in fact relied and keeps relying on crowdsourcing to translate its interface into many "minority" languages. Not to mention the "suggest a better translation" feature through which Google Translate requests crowd contributions towards its SMT engine.

What is significant is that Facebook and all these other sites are commercial concerns that have appropriated an altruistic concept that originated in the free/open source software (FOSS) sector. Here, since there were no funds to localise, translation by volunteers was the only means. Indeed, much early research into computer assisted collaboration on linguistic tasks, even involving MT in its processes, was initiated within these FOSS areas (Murata, 2003; Shimohata, 2001).

Businesses are now looking at this development with great interest, as can be inferred by the attention generated in the professional press and consulting firms (Multilingual, ClientSide News, Common Sense Advisory, Byte Level Research, The Gilbane Report and others). TAUS calls this "community" translation, and Common Sense Advisory dubs it CT3 (community translation + collaborative technology + crowdsourcing). We propose the term "hive" translation, since the unbounded nature of cyberspace associations clearly transcends old notions of "community."

Translators have not reacted much as yet, other than with the occasional complaint about amateur translation that writes the Spanish hacer as aser. However, it is precisely these obvious errors that will be quickly seized upon and corrected by other "hive" members. Professional translators will have to deal seriously with collaboration in the next decade.

Even within the traditional localization framework, in 2007 Common Sense Advisory was already proposing a need to replace the traditional translate-edit-proofread (TEP) print/Taylorist era model with a "collaborative translation" model better suited to our instant communication era. Thus, translations would be undertaken in parallel rather than consecutively, with as many translators and subject matter experts as possible, while doing away with editing/proofreading roles, with the idea being to avoid mistakes from the outset rather than detect them at the end (Beninatto & DePalma, 2008).

The typical role of the professional translator is further challenged in new scenarios currently under test. These projects include the use of wikis, as in the Cross-Lingual Wiki Engine (CLWE) introduced by Huberdeau, Paquet & Desilets (2008), which allows for content authoring and translation that do not rely on one master language or the use of professionally trained translators in environments no longer bound by tight coordination.

6 Professional Translators Post-2010

Translation as performed by the localization industry is expensive and time consuming. The industry itself is being sidelined by technological advancement, and is proving slow to react. Change, as noted by Bower and Christensen (1995) can be incremental (from the inside) or disruptive (through the intervention of external forces), and Joscelyne and van der Meer (2007) have already given examples of how these two forces are shaping localization into the next decade. The same forces are also recasting the role of professional translators.

Most translation done for localization is likely to follow the MT-assisted TM model, with the translator thus becoming a de-facto post-editor. Some professional translators will still be needed to fill this role, and are still likely to work within the traditional TEP model under their current freelance status.

The "utility" model could well cater for small projects, or projects in specialised areas. It would also employ professional translators using MT-assisted TM for texts written in some kind of managed authoring environment, or translating directly when dealing with the colloquial language of e-mail and instant messaging. In a typical situation, the use of on-site resources will entail professional translators working in low-paid, call-centre conditions.

The "hive" model does away with professional translators altogether in preference to a mass of volunteers/amateurs. This model brings back the pre-professional era when translators were simply bilinguals with good subject knowledge, and the ability or inclination to transfer meaning between languages. This model would be supported by a few professionally trained translators occupying key terminological or QC roles in the background.

One can easily imagine both "utility" and "hive" approaches merging, and volunteer bilinguals helping their fellow virtual "friends" with the same goodwill as we might give directions to a foreign tourist in the street. Google's forthcoming Wave offers the possibility of inviting a robot, Rosy (as in Rosetta Stone) to the conversation, and Rosy will machine translate words as they are being typed. For web interactions too complex for Rosy to handle, the requester could send a message that a volunteer could translate, with or without MT-assisted TM or payment. If Google is also the agent or provider of this additional service, it can clearly capture the data to improve Rosy's next performance.

What place would the bulk of today's professional translators occupy? This paper argues that, as soon as 2010, translation for localization will be pushed into simple MT post-editing, while other sectors will see a shift toward call-centre conditions and a return of the amateur.

As Internet becomes a true utility, translation is not the only profession to experience the stress of the digital age. Translators will still be needed, but their working conditions into the next decade will be quite dissimilar to those of the nineties.

【延伸阅读】

[1] Austermuhl, F. *Electronic Tools For Translators*. Manchester: St. Jerome Publishing, 2001.

[2] Baker, M. *In Other Words: A Coursebook on Translation*. London/New York: Routledge, 1992.

[3] Delsile, J., et al. *Translation Terminology*. Amsterdam/Philadelphia: John Benjamines Publishing Co., 1999.

[4] Whitelock, P. & Kilby, K. *Linguistic and Computational Techniques in Machine*

Translation System Design. 2nd edtion. London：UCL Press，1995.

［6］Carbonell，et al. Context-based Machine Translation. AMTA 2006：Proceedings of the 7th Conference of the Association for Machine Translation in the America，"Visions for the Future of Machine Translation". pp. 19－28. Cambridge，Massachusetts，2006.

［7］Dirix，P.，Vandeghinste，V. & Schuurman，I. A New Hybrid Approach Enabling MT for Languages with Little Resources. In Proceedings of the 16th Meeting of Computational Linguistics in the Netherlands. CLIN—2005，Amsterdam，2006.

［8］Evert，S. The Statistics of Word Cooccurrences：Word Pairs and Collocations. PhD dissertation. University of Stuttgart，2004.

［9］Habash，N. The Use of a Structural N-gram Language Model in Generation-Heavy Hybrid Machine Translation. In Proceedings of the Third International Conference on Natural Language Generation (INLG04). Birghton，2004.

［10］Habash，N.，& Dorr，B. Handling Translation Divergences：Combining Statistical and Symbolic Techniques in Generation-heavy Machine Translation. In Proceedings of the 5th Conference of the Association for Machine Translation in the Americas：Machine Translation：From Research to Real Users，London，UK. Springer-Verlag，2002.

［11］Benis，M. Much More Than Memories. *ITI Bulletin*，2003，November—December：24－29.

［12］Garcia，I. Power Shifts in Web-based Translation Memory. *Machine Translation*，2007，21(1)：55－68.

［13］Guerberof，A. Post-editing MT and TM. A Spanish Case. *Multilingual*，2008，19(6)：45－50.

［14］O'Brien，S. Eye-Tracking and Translation Memory Matches. *Perspectives：Studies in Translatology*，2006，14(3)，185－204.

［15］Wallis，J. Interactive Translation vs. Pre-translation in the Context of Translation Memory Systems：Investigating the Effects of Translation Method on Productivity，Quality and Translator Satisfaction//*MA in Translation Studies*. Ottawa：University of Ottawa.

【问题与思考】

1. 对于译者而言，翻译记忆有何利弊？
2. 对于翻译机构或翻译公司而言，翻译记忆有何利弊？
3. 选文一提及的机器翻译研究方法有哪些？
4. 请评述选文一作者提出的新的机器翻译研究方法。
5. 在选文一作者看来，新时期翻译记忆有何新的特点？
6. 试比较 utility model 和 hive model 的异同。

第六章 翻译语料库的使用

导 论

    基于语料库的翻译研究开创了新的翻译研究方向，它是建立在语料库语言学和描述翻译研究基础之上的一种新的研究范式，是通过计算机检索和数据统计，采用定量与定性相结合的方法对翻译现象进行描述，并在充分描述的基础上揭示翻译本质。基于语料库的翻译研究是一种定量和定性相结合的实证性研究，大致可以分为两大类：理论性研究和实践性研究。语料库语言学是一门学科更是一种研究方法，它以大量真实文本为研究素材，主要通过概率统计的方法得出结论，因此语料库语言学从本质上讲是实证性的。语料库语言学的应用非常广泛，包括句法词法分析，编纂词典和参考书籍，外语教学，机器翻译及文本校对等等。语料库不仅为纯翻译研究提供了有力的工具，而且在应用翻译研究中也大有作为。随着语料库的发展，很多研究者也开始尝试将它融入翻译研究并应用于翻译教学，为现代翻译教学提供了新方法和新思路。同时，语料库语言学的发展对语言研究以及翻译研究产生了巨大的影响。本章的部分选材介绍了语料库与语言研究及翻译研究的现状，并且对当前的一些语料库进行了简单的描述。所选的文章主要讨论了翻译语料库的建构、语料库在翻译实践中的运用、翻译的普遍性研究，同时还指出翻译的语料库研究对翻译实践的意义。在各类翻译语料库中，平行语料库和类比语料库为最常见的两类语料库。从语料库代表性的角度来看，平行语料库、类比语料库和多语语料库各自都有优缺点，研究应当充分考虑各类语料库的优势和适用性，根据研究目的和内容合理选择语料库类型以达到最佳的研究效果。另外，语料的代表性是需要关注的一个重要问题。目前翻译理论界在语料库的收录对象和内部结构方面都有比较大的分歧，而翻译理论难以指导语料库翻译研究。只有解决好了语料的代表性问题，语料库翻译研究才能更好地健康发展。本章的选材对语料库的应用翻译研究作了一个概述性介绍，以便我国研究者对其形成比较全面的了解和认识，更好地拓展我国翻译研究的新视野。

选 文

选文一 Corpora and Translation：Uses and Future Prospects

Tony McEnery　Andrew Wilson

导　言

本文重点讨论了语料库的种类及其在翻译研究中的具体运用。作者在文中阐述了语料库的概念和属性，并着重讨论了它在两大领域的运用：人工翻译与机器翻译。随着可用语料库的数量的增加，其影响力也日趋增大。它在 21 世纪的语言学发展中会发挥更大的作用。

1　Introduction

Although corpora have been an object of study for some decades, the nineteen eighties saw an increased interest in their use and construction. With this increased interest and awareness has come an expansion in the application areas for which corpus based approaches have been deemed relevant. This paper will seek to define the concept of a corpus, and discuss its relevance to two application areas in particular, automatic and manual translation.

2　Corpora

A corpus, simply defined, is a large body of text. Corpora may exist in machine readable form or in their natural state as written texts or recorded speech, but increasingly the term "corpus" is used to refer to the machine readable variety.

Machine readable corpora have a number of advantages over other forms of storage. Firstly, and most importantly, machine readable corpora may be searched and manipulated in ways which are simply not possible with the other formats. Secondly, machine readable corpora can be swiftly and easily enriched with additional information. But so far corpora have been discussed as though they are an undifferentiated mass. This is not the case: corpora can be adapted in many ways. In the following sections the varying forms that a corpus may take will be discussed, begining with one basic distinction which bifurcates the concept of the corpus; should they be unannotated or annotated?

Unannotated corpora are corpora which are left in their "raw" (or "pure") state. These corpora may be of use for many purposes, but it is important to note that retrieval from such a corpus may take a more linguistically expert user than would otherwise be required. Also, programs manipulating and processing such data will either be:

(a) More "intelligent," to be able to identify some of the implicit linguistic categories and relations. Even where such an intelligent program is successful, it inevitably leads to an increase in cost and processing time.

(b) Less useful—the programs may not succeed in identifying this implicit information, and consequently their functionality is limited.

Thus although untagged corpora have their uses, the range of functionality for automated retrieval and manipulation of corpora is greatly enhanced by the provision of annotation in a corpus.

Annotated corpora are corpora to which additional information (especially linguistic information) has been added (Leech, 1992). This usually involves the attachment of some kind of coding to the machine readable language material itself.

Many types of linguistic information may be encoded in a corpus:

2.1 Part of Speech

Part-of-speech (or POS) tagging, also known as grammatical tagging, entails the assignment of a part of speech to every lexical item in a corpus. One automatic POS tagging suite, CLAWS (Garside, 1987), uses a set of part-of-speech codes (up to 169 codes in size) to mark such information in texts. An example of one of these codes is "NN1," used to denote a singular common noun. A POS tag is attached to each word in the corpus by means of a symbol such as an underscore. So in an annotated corpus the sequence "dog_NN1" may be read as being composed of two parts—the word "dog" and the part of speech "singular common noun." The following shows an example of POS tagging from the Lancaster-Oslo/Bergen (or LOB) corpus:

EXAMPLE OF PART-OF-SPEECH TAGGING FROM LOB CORPUS

^another_DT new_JJ style_NN feature_NN is_BEZ
the_ATT wine-glass_NN or_CC flared_JJ heel_NN '_'
which_WDT was_BEDZ shown_VBN teamed_VBN
up_RP with_IN pointed_JJ '_' squared_JJ '_' and_cc
chisel_NN toes_NNS '_'
^colour_NN is_BEZ highly_RB important_JJ in_IN
choosing_VBG autumn_NN footwear_NN '_' ^the_ATI
autumn_NN range_NN of_IN shades_NNS is_BEZ almost_RB
bewildering_JJ '_' and_CC there_EX are_BER some_DTI
exciting_JJ new-comers_NNS '_' such_IN as_IN"
conker_NN calf_NN and_CC charcoal_NN '_' rocco_NN
and_CC Russian_JNP violet_NN '_'

Key：

ATI	article neutral for number
BEDZ	was (past sing. form of the verb BE)
BER	are (present plural form of the verb BE)
BEZ	is, 's (-s form of the verb BE)
CC	coordinating conjunction
DT	singular determiner
DTI	determiner neutral for number
EX	existential there
IN	preposition
JJ	general adjective
JNP	adjective with word-initial capital
NN	singular common noun
NNS	plural common noun
RB	general adverb
RP	adverb which can also be a particle
VBG	present participle of lexical verb
VBN	past participle of lexical verb
WDT	WH-determiner

［In this text，IN indicates the second part of the two-word syntactic idiom such as which has the function of IN.］

POS annotation can be important in translation for several reasons. Firstly, it may be used as a preliminary to the disambiguation of homographs. It cannot differentiate word senses, but it can disambiguate word function and sometimes this can amount to the same thing：for example，booted as an adjective means "wearing boots" but as a verb means "kicked." In an empirically-based machine translation system such as that proposed by Brown et al. (1990)，which employs a translation model using bilingual alignment at the word level，this provides additional information about where alignments are and are not likely to constitute "correct" translations. Secondly，a syntactic idiom such as the subordinator so that cannot always be translated through a simple word-to-word alignment. In German，for example，the English so that (2 words) may be translated as damit (1 word). POS tagging which uses "ditto tags" 1 facilitates the alignment of many-to-one and one-to-many examples such as this.

2.2 Syntactic Structure—Parsing

Parsing involves the assignment of surface structure to a text，normally using a form of phrase structure grammar. Typically the constituents are indicated using labelled brackets rather than tree-like structures，though sometimes an attempt is made to provide some graphic realization of structure (cf. Marcus and Santorini，1992). The following is an example of a type of parsing using a very small set of constituent types; for this reason, it is sometimes known as "skeleton parsing" (Leech and Garside, 1991).

EXAMPLE OF SKELETON PARSING FROM THE SPOKEN ENGLISH CORPUS

[N the_AT first_MD book_NN1 [[N he_PPHSI N][V took_VVD

[P from_II [N the_AT library_NN1 N]P]V]]N][V was_VBDZ

[N[G Darwin_NP1 'S_S' G]['_" [N Origin_NN1 [P of_IO

[N Species_NN N] P] N] '_" [Fr [N which_DDQ N] [V inspired_VVD

[P of_IO [Tg becoming_VVG [N a_AT1

geologist_NN1 N] Tg] P]N]P]V]Fr]]N]V]'−'

Syntactic constituents are bounded by labelled square brackets. POS tags are linked to their words by the underscore character.

The tagset used in this example is the "CLAWS2" tagset. This is a later version of the CLAWS1 (or LOB) tagset illustrated above. The symbols for the various parts of speech are broadly similar to the CLAWS1 tags, for example common noun tags still begin with NN and adjectives with J.

The symbols for the syntactic constituents in this example are:

Fr	relative clause
N	noun phrase
P	prepositional phrase
Tg	-ing clause
V	verb phrase

Where unlabelled brackets occur, this indicates a constituent-type which is not included in the reduced set of constituents employed in skeleton parsing. Such indeterminacy is allowed for in the parsing guidelines used by the human analysts.

Most corpus-based research on machine translation has relied on alignment at the word level, or alternatively at the sentence level which is easy to perform on the basis of punctuation. However, Brown et al. (1990) recognize the potential of alignment at the level of syntactic constituents, which may enable the induction of a computational phrase structure grammar and hence subsequently alignment and translation at the level of the grammatical constituent. Clause-level alignment is also important in a bilingual knowledge base approach to machine translation such as is advocated by Sadler (1989).

2.3 Word Sense

In addition to POS tagging and parsing, it is also possible to annotate semantic features in corpora. Two types of semantic annotation may be identified: the representation of word senses, normally using some form of sense classification (rather like a thesaurus), and the marking of more structural semantic relations such as agent/patient structures. The latter type of annotation is not often encountered at present, but is likely to increase in the near future. Word sense annotation is also quite rare, but is an active area of current research. This form of tagging has not been carried out to any large extent on corpora in other languages, but deserves to be as it enables large quantities of structured lexical data to be extracted.

The following is an example of semantic word-tagging, taken from the automatic content analysis described by Wilson and Rayson (1991):

EXAMPLE OF WORD SENSE TAGGING

AT1	The	Z5
MC	one	N1
NN1	disadvantage	A5.1−
IO	of	Z5
JJ	woolen	O1.1
NN2	clothes	B5
VBZ	is	A3+
CST	that	Z5
PPHS2	they	Z8
VM	can	A7+
VV0	become	A2.1
JJ	uncomfortable	O4.2−
II	in	Z5
RG	very	A13.3
JJ	hot	O4.6+
NN1	weather	W4

In this example, the text is read vertically. The first column contains the POS tags, the second column the words of the text, and the third column the semantic tags. The semantic tags are composed of: (a) an upper case letter indicating general discourse field; (b) a number indicating a first subdivision of this discourse field; (c) (optionally) a decimal point followed by a further number to indicate a finer subdivision and; (d) (optionally) one or more pluses or minuses indicating opposites and degrees of intensity on a semantic scale.

For example, the tag O4.6+ indicates a word in the field "Physical Objects and Properties" (O), in the subcategory "Physical Attributes" (O4), in the sub-subcategory "Temperature" (O4.6) and "hot" (+) rather than "cold" (-).

Word sense annotation is a crude basis for translation per se. A translation based on the fact that in L1 belongs to the same thesaurus class as w2 in L2 does not necessarily entail that w2 is a good translation of w1. However, word sense annotation can be of use in creating term banks and multilingual thesauri from large quantities of text, to function as translation tools in other approaches to machine and machine-aided translation. The use of measures such as mutual information further enables the extraction of collocations at the level of semantic rather than lexical information.

2.4 Anaphoric Relations

Anaphoric annotation indicates the co-reference of noun phrases and pronominals in text. This is an important, but not frequently encountered type of annotation. It has been carried out successfully over some 100,000 words of English by Lancaster University in collaboration with IBM T. J. Watson Research Center, New York. Again, it has not to our knowledge been carried out on corpora in languages other than English, but its potential in modelling pronominal reference suggests that it ought to be.

An example of this form of annotation is as follows:

ANAPHORIC ANNOTATION OF AP NEWSWIRE

{21 (4 Civic Center 4) Director 21}} {21 Frank E. Russo Jr. 21}

said <21 he was confident (4 the s31.5 million coliseum 4)

would be ready to open as scheduled.

"There's no turning back now", <21 he said.

Tickets for (167 (7 the Whalers 7)' first game in (25 <7 their

home city 25) in two years 167) have been selling briskly.

The use of the same index number in the above indicates the co-reference of constituents. In the following, the letter n is used to represent an index number in the actual notation:

(n n) OR [n ...]enclose a constituent (normally a noun phrase) entering into an equivalence chain

<n indicates a pronoun with a preceding antecedent

{ nn } } enclose a noun phrase entering into a copular relationship with a following noun phrase

Anaphoric annotation is of particular value in research on automated pronoun translation. In order to translate a pronominal which does not enter into a one-to-one relationship with a pronominal in the target language, one requires two sets of information:

(a) The antecedent of the pronominal, where one exists.

(b) The number and gender of the antecedent.

Pronominals typically inherit number and gender from their antecedents. Sometimes it is easy to translate from one language to another: for example, English she aligns unproblematically with French elle as feminine singular (nominative). However, the French translation of English they depends on whether the plural group is all female, or includes one or more male person. This may not always be clear from the text, but if the English pronoun refers to a phrase the girls then it is obvious that it should be translated as elles and not ils. Anaphoric annotation enables empirical research to be carried out into automatic pronoun resolution, including the examination of exceptions to general rules, and thus it will then be possible to attempt to overcome this particular translation problem.

3　Parallel Corpora

Parallel corpora are, in a very real sense, best characterized as the "Rosetta Stone" of modern corpus linguistics. These are corpora which hold the same text in more than one language. Typically, at present, these parallel corpora are bilingual rather than multilingual.

There is a general paucity of annotated parallel corpora. A very few do exist, such as the Canadian Hansard (a parallel corpus in French and English of the proceedings of the Canadian Parliament) and a corpus of IBM Technical Manuals (English and French), but they tend to be of limited value because of restrictions of domain and availability.

Research is limited to these corpora and language pairs alone, e. g. Brown et al. (1990, forthcoming), which is hardly satisfactory. Further, their potential for yielding large automated lexicons (Garside and McEnery, forthcoming), as will be discussed later, remains largely unexploited.

But before any further discussion of the use of the corpora can gainfully take place, one necessary refinement of the form taken by a parallel corpus needs to be considered—alignment.

4　Parallel Aligned Corpora

It is clear that simply having a corpus composed of two parallel subcorpora poses as many problems as it solves. Which sentences are translations of which? Below that level, which word (or words) are translations of which word (or words)? An aligned corpus tackles this problem, by aligning sentences which are mutual translations of one another. It may also, below the sentence level, align word units that are translations. So within a corpus we may see the sentences "C"est magnifique, mais ce n'est pas la guerre and "It is magnificent but it is not war" aligned together. Below that level we may see further alignments. C "may be aligned with It," la guerre "may be aligned with war" and mais "may be aligned with but. "

This form of alignment may be achieved with a high degree of accuracy automatically, using such statistical techniques as mutual information. These techniques are currently being refined within project ET 10-63 (Section 6). It is intended to further develop these techniques in the future. To give two examples of techniques that may be used to improve alignment not exploited by ET 10 − 63:

(a) Using part-of-speech tagging to align at the level of grammatical function rather than at word string level.

(b) Smoothing any skewed probabilities by using statistics not only from the current corpus, but other successfully aligned corpora.

5 Uses of Parallel Aligned Corpora

The uses of parallel aligned corpora are potentially many, but two obvious areas would be machine translation and lexicon construction.

5. 1 Machine Translation

Brown et al. (1990, forthcoming) attempt to build upon the success of probabilistic methods in other areas of language processing and apply them to the problem of machine translation. They have produced a probabilistic machine translation system trained on an aligned French-English corpus. This system chooses the most probable translation sentence in the target language given a sentence in the source language using two probability models: a trigram language model based on three-word sequences, originally developed for a speech recognition system, and a translation model derived from the word-level alignment of their English and French parallel sub-corpora and information about word positions within the corpus sentences.

Sadler (1989) proposes an alternative approach in which a very large bilingual database is constructed, with each language parsed using a form of dependency grammar. The resulting units are then aligned between the languages involved. Translation is carried out by isolating possible units in the source text, retrieving these units and their translations in the database, and combining the retrieved translation units. The work carried out by Tsujii (1992) on machine translation also requires parallel aligned corpora for its operation.

5. 2 Lexicon Construction

It is possible to extract correspondences between languages not only at the word level, but also above the level of the word. Multiword units would also be retrieved from a parallel aligned corpus, making multilingual dictionary building an easier task.

If the corpus is machine readable, it can also be scanned for frequent collocations. With a specialized corpus it is also possible to construct terminology databases.

Multilingual parallel aligned annotated corpora open up many possibilities for future development. Yet their full potential may only become known when an end user has the opportunity to actively exploit such a corpus. That presupposes the existence of one.

6 The ET 10-63 Project

ET 10-63 is a project under the EC's EUROTRA programme currently running at IBM Paris, C2V Paris, Essex University and Lancaster University. Its aim is to develop a large, part-of-speech tagged, bilingual parallel aligned corpus of EC telecommunications texts and carry out work on lexicon building techniques, including term extraction and argument frame extraction.

This project has developed a data model to store parallel aligned bilingual corpora as databases (e. g. McEnery and Daille, 1993). This has the advantages that:

(a) A standard for corpus storage may be created.

(b) The powerful query languages used with databases, such as SQL and other relational query languages, can be used to retrieve linguistic information from annotated corpora.

(c) Data may be shared more readily between sites, as the data model remains constant.

A new proposal has recently been formulated, called the MACE project. MACE seeks to extend and widen the scope of this research, taking it beyond the bilingual domain, and producing the first multilingual parallel aligned POS-annotated corpus. Greek, French, Italian and English are the languages that the corpus hopes to cover. The corpus will be based upon the Official Journal of the EC, as this is an excellent source of parallel texts. Also, the Official Journal is available in all of the official languages of the EC, so the corpus would be readily extensible beyond its original four core languages.

The ET 10-63 model will be extended in the near future to cover the form of corpora proposed within the MACE project so that a standard for the storage of multilingual parallel aligned corpora can be achieved.

7 Conclusion

This paper has outlined the nature of corpora, and has concentrated specifically upon the applications of corpora within the field of translation studies. This influence is growing as the availability of relevant corpora increases. It would seem that this trend is set to continue, especially when it is considered that corpora are seen to be an increasingly significant part of the CEC's strategy for the development of linguistic engineering in the next decade as is stated in the Technical Background Document for the LRE Call for Proposals 1992: "The availability of large, duly classified and annotated text corpora is a sine qua non for any linguistic R&D work." CEC (1992: 15)

Hence the presence of corpora in translation studies, as well as other areas of linguistic study, seems destined to become ever greater.

Notes:

1. A scheme whereby a multi-word sequence such as so that, which has a single syntactic function, is assigned just one part of speech and each constituent word in the idiom is differentiated only by an index (cf. Blackwell, 1987).

2. This is not, however, always the case. The most important exceptions are anaphoric islands (cf. Oakhill and Garnham, 1992) and conceptual anaphors (cf. Oakhill et al., 1992).

151

选文二　Corpora in Translation Practice

Federico Zanettin

导　言

Federico Zanettin 是意大利佩鲁贾外国人大学(*Universita per Stranieri di Perugia*)的教授。本文的目的是探寻语料库语言学和翻译实践之间的关系。翻译与语料库的相关性,特别是与双语平行语料库的相关性是通过对比语料库和翻译记忆,或是通过比较不同类型的语料库和更传统的参考工具(即字典)进行评测的。本文提出可供译者使用的语料库资源可呈梯次被排列放置,如从健全、稳定的语料库(如大型参考语料 BNC)到虚拟、短时性的语料库(如 DIY 网络语料库)。本文最后提出一些建议以使专业译员更广泛地使用语料库和语词索引软件。

1　Introduction

The translator's workplace has changed dramatically over the last ten years or so, and today the computer is undoubtedly the single most important tool of the trade for a translator regardless of whether he or she is a literary translator working for a small publisher, a technical translator working for a translation agency or a legal translator. Today, translators compose their texts on the computer screen, often receive their source texts in electronic format and sometimes their translations will only live as digital information as in the case of web site localization.

The specific hardware and software resources individual translators will resort to will vary depending on the task to be done. While in the case of most literary translators the translated text will probably take shape by means of a general purpose word processor, in the case of technical translators the target text will be produced with the help of the most sophisticated "translator workbench," equipped with all sorts of CAT tools, translation memory and terminology systems, and localization software.

The computer has also flanked, if not substituted, other technological supports in providing access to traditional tools and resources. Translation aids such as monolingual and bilingual dictionaries, terminologies and encyclopedias are now available not only on paper but also in electronic format. Colleagues and expert informants can now be consulted via e-mail and newsgroups besides via telephone, fax and face-to-face encounters. The storage capacity and processing power of personal computers have made access to linguistic and content information easier and quicker than ever before, and the Internet has opened up highways of communication and information retrieval. The problem is now not finding a piece of information, but finding the right and reliable piece of information without wasting too much time.

Corpora and concordancing software can be a way of gaining access to information about language, content, and translation practices which was hardly available to translators before the present stage of ICT development. Corpora and corpus analysis software have been around for quite a long time, but their use is only now beginning to extend beyond a restricted segment of language professionals, such as lexicographers, language engineers, as well as linguists in educational and training institutions.

I would like to suggest that corpora and concordancing software could find a larger place in the translator computerized workstation, and that more corpus resources could and should be made more accessible to professional translators. In order to do so, however, corpus builders and software producers should take into account the specific needs of this group of users. Learning to use corpora as translation resources should also be part of the curriculum of future translators and become part of their professional competence.

2　Corpora and Translation

According to the EAGLES text typology elaborated by John Sinclair (1996) we can make a general distinction between Monolingual and Multilingual (including Bilingual) corpora. As regards bilingual (and multilingual) corpora a further distinction can be made between Comparable corpora (corpora compiled using similar design criteria but which are not translations) and Parallel, or Translation Corpora, which are texts in one language aligned with their translation in another. This picture can be further complicated by involving variables such as direction and directness of translation, number of languages, number of translations per text, etc., producing bi-directional, reciprocal, control, star and diamond corpus models (cf. Johansson, forthcoming; Teubert, 1996; Zanettin, 2000; Malmkiaer, forthcoming). Still another type of translation related corpus is the Monolingual Comparable Corpus (Baker, 1993), or a corpus composed of two sub-sections, one of texts originally composed in one language and the other of texts translated into that same language (from a number of other languages). This type of corpus, however, while undoubtedly an extremely useful tool for translation theorists, researchers and students, is arguably of less immediate relevance for professional translators dealing with actual translation jobs.

Professional translators working in the technical sector are perhaps more familiar with the parallel concordancing feature of translator memory systems. A translation memory is data bank from which translators automatically retrieve fragments of past translations that match, totally or to a degree, a current segment to be translated, which must match, totally or to a degree—an already translated segment. But it can also be seen as a parallel corpus which translators manually query for parallel concordances of (already translated) specific terms or patterns. Aligned translation units are conveniently displayed on the screen, offering the translator a range of similar contexts from a corpus of past translations. A translation memory is, however, a very specific type of parallel corpus in that:

(a) it is "proprietory": TMs are created individually or collectively around specific translation projects. They are highly specialized and very useful when used for the translation or localization of program updates—indeed that is their origin—but are not much help when starting a new translation project on a different topic or text type.

(b) TMs tend to closure, to progressively standardize and restrict the range of linguistic options. This may be an advantage from the point of view of terminological consistency and of processing costs for clients or translation agency managers, but is often detrimental for readability (texts translated using a "Workbench" can become very repetitive) and the translators eyesight (translators using a well-known Workbench often testify to a "yellow-and-blue-eye-syndrome").

Translation workbenches and translation memories have indeed become the most successful technological product to be created for professional translators, but—as it often happens with MT products—their use is best limited to specific text types, such as online help files, manuals and all types of reference work which do not require sequential reading and for which the scope of translation can be limited to the sentence of phrase level (and thus left to a machine). When dealing with other types of texts translators are perhaps better off with a different kind of language resource, i. e. the type of corpora which are more familiar to lexicographers and linguists and which are only now beginning to enter the selection of tools available to professional and trainee translators.

3 Corpora as Translation Aids

The respective potential uses on the part of professional translators of monolingual target corpora, bilingual comparable corpora, and of parallel corpora can be illustrated drawing an analogy with other respected tools of the trade, i. e. dictionaries: Monolingual target corpora can be compared to monolingual target language dictionaries, and comparable source corpora to monolingual source language dictionaries. While dictionaries favor a synthetic approach to lexical meaning (via a definition), corpora offer an analytic approach (via multiple contexts). Translators can use target monolingual corpora alongside target monolingual dictionaries to check the meaning and usage of translation candidates in the target contexts. Like source language dictionaries, source language corpora can be consulted for source text analysis and understanding. Large reference corpora (BNC, CORIS/CODIS, etc.) can function as general dictionaries, while smaller, specialized and bilingual comparable corpora can be seen as analogous to specialized monolingual dictionaries (either or both in the source and in the target language).

Parallel corpora can instead be compared to bilingual dictionaries, with a few important differences: bilingual dictionaries are repertories of lexical equivalents (general dictionaries) or terms (specialized dictionaries and terminologies) established by dictionaries makers which are offered as translation candidates. Parallel corpora are repertoires of strategies deployed by past translators, as well as repertoires of translation equivalents. In selecting a translation equivalent from a general bilingual dictionary a translator has to assess the appropriateness of the candidate to the new context by starting from a definition and a few usage examples. A parallel corpus will offer a repertoire of translation strategies past translators have resorted to when confronted with similar problems to the ones that have prompted a search in a parallel corpus.

Parallel corpora can provide information that bilingual dictionaries do not usually contain. They can not only offer equivalence at the word level, but also non-equivalence, i. e. cases where there is no easy equivalent for words, terms or phrases across languages. A parallel corpus can provide evidence of how actual translators have dealt with this lack of direct equivalence at word level. For example, in the translations by two different Italian translators of a number of novels by Salman Rushdie (Zanettin, 2001b), the word "edges," which usually collocates with a preposition, as in the phrases "around the edges," or "at the edges," was never translated literally, but rather omitted:

1. ... biting the skin around the edges of a nail ... mordicchiandosi lapelle attorno all'unghia ...

2. ... around the edges of Gibreel Farishta's head ... intorno alla testa di Gibreel Farishta ...

3. ... around the edges of the circus-ring ... intorno alla pista da circo.

4. ... and there was a fluidity, an indistinctiness, at the edges of them ... vicinissime a loro c'erano una fluidita e un'indeterminatezza ...

5. ... the horses grew fuzzy at the edges ... i cavalli diventavano semprepiu sfocati ...

6. ... blurred at the edges, my father ... con la mente annebbiata, miopadre ...

7. ... looking somewhat ragged at the edges ... con l'aria di un uomo distrutto.

8. ... Mrs Qureishi, too, was beginning to fray at the edges ... anche Mrs Qureishi si stava consumando ...

In all these cases, the two professional translators have consistently chosen to resort to "zero-equivalence," which being a translation strategy rather than a case of comparative linguistic knowledge would be hardly reported in any bilingual dictionary.

4　Corpus Resources for Translators

Not all dictionaries are the same, nor are all corpora. Apart from translation memories, corpus resources which are of potential use for professional translators could be classified along a scale which goes from "robust" to "virtual. " A "corpus" is a collection of electronic texts assembled according to explicit design criteria which usually aim at representing a larger textual population. "Robust" corpora are ready-made corpora created and distributed by the research community and the language industry on CD-ROM or accessible through the Internet. Prototypical examples are large reference national corpora, such as the British National Corpus (BNC) for British English, and the Dynamic Corpus or Written Italian (CORIS/CODIS) for Italian. This type of resource, which requires a large building effort, is only now becoming available to the wider public outside the (corpus) linguistics community, and will probably require some "customization" effort in order to become more widespread among language services providers.

Parallel corpora are usually smaller and even less available to the general public than monolingual corpora. Their construction requires more work than that of monolingual corpora. Among other factors, text pairs (rather than single texts) have to be located and before they can be used they need to be aligned, at least at the sentence level (cf. Veronis, 2000).

There are of course varying degrees of robustness, according to the effort and care which has been put in achieving a balanced and representative selection of texts, in providing explicit linguistic and extralinguistic information (corpus annotation) and the means (the software) to query the corpus for that information (McEnery & Wilson, 1996). Corpus design criteria also vary according to the purpose for which a corpus is built, e. g. a comparable monolingual corpus for descriptive translation research. In this sense, the less "robust" (i. e. the more "virtual") corpora are the most truly professional type, with reference to translators, since they are "rough-and-ready" products created for a specific translation project. A distinction is usually made by corpus linguists between "corpora" and "archives" of electronic texts. An "archive" is simply a repository of electronic texts. In this sense the WWW is an immense (multimedia) text archive. Virtual or "disposable" corpora are created by a translator using the WWW as a source "archive." The WWW and HTML documents need not to be the only source for small, specialized DIY corpora, and textual archives of various types and targeted to various users (newspapers, collections of laws, encyclopedias, etc.) are available on cd-rom. The WWW is however certainly the most familiar and user friendly environment for translators: it is always available; it is the most comprehensive source of electronic texts, and corpus creation, management and analysis can be a relatively straightforward operation (Austermuhl, 2001; Zanettin, forthcoming). Building a corpus of web pages basically involves an information retrieval operation, conducted by browsing the Internet to locate relevant and reliable documents which can then be saved locally and made into a corpus to then be analysed with the help of concordancing software. The additional time required by creating and consulting a corpus is compensated for by saving in other translation-related tasks, such as dictionary consultation (both on paper and electronic), paper documentation (often in the form of "parallel texts," e. g. Williams, 1996), help from experts, and by the fact that the corpus contains information not available elsewhere. Moreover, the effort is rewarded by improving quality in terms of terminological and phraseological accuracy (Friedbichler & Friedbichler, 2000).

A number of studies have reported on experiments in translation and language teaching classes with DIY corpora, either made of "disposable" web pages (e. g. Varantola, 2000, forthcoming; Maia, 1997, 2000, forthcoming; Zanettin, forthcoming; Pearson, 2000) or of texts taken from other electronic sources such as newspapers (Zanettin, 2001a) or magazines (Bowker, 1998) on CD-ROM. Corpora created from sources other than web pages can require more time and effort to be built, and can be more or less "disposable" depending on the size of the translation project and on the resources available to create and manage them.

Reports on the use of corpora by professional translators are fewer: Friedichler & Friedbichler, drawing on their experience as translators of medical texts and trainers of technical translators, suggest that domain-specific target language corpora may usefully complement dictionaries and the Web as resources in the translation process, filling the gap between the two. Jaasklainen and Mauranen (2000) report on an experimental study involving a team of researchers from the University of Savonlinna and a team of professional translators translating for the timberwood industry. The researchers created a corpus from a variety of sources (web sites, PDF documents, etc.) following suggestions from the translators, and then trained them in using concordancing software (WS Tools, Scott, 1996) to analyze the corpus. In exchange, the translation team agreed to answer a questionnaire. One of the results of the study was learning that translators often complained that the user-friendliness of the concordancing software was very low. This complaint was seconded by translator trainees in other studies with "disposable" corpora where students, usually working in groups, collected a corpus of HTML documents and used them to help them translate a specific text.

These studies have underlined, nonetheless, the value of corpus building as a way of getting acquainted with the content and terminology of the translation. They have stressed the importance of type and topic of the text to be translated as well as of the target language (some text types, topics, and target languages are better helped with corpora than others) and also of adopting sound criteria in choosing suitable texts for inclusion in the corpus. Most of the corpora in these experiments were target monolingual corpora, though some use of bilingual comparable and even parallel corpora was reported.

The main benefits and shortcoming of DIY corpora may be summed up as follows:

Benefits:

- They are easy to make.
- They are a great resource for content information.
- They are a great resource for terminology and phraseology in restricted domains and topics.

Shortcomings:

- Not all topics, not all text types, not all languages are equally suitable or available.
- The relevance and reliability of documents to be included in the corpus needs to be

carefully assessed.

- Existing concordancing software is not well equipped to handle HTML or XML files, i. e. web pages. There are no or few parallel corpora, since while some parallel texts (i. e. source texts + translations) can be found on the Internet, hardly all of them could be included in a parallel corpus designed to provide instances of professional standards (Maia, forthcoming).

DIY web corpora stand midway the WWW itself, which can be used as if it were a corpus and robust, "proper" corpora. As for the Web, a "quasi-concordance" view of documents indexed and retrieved is provided by such as search engines Google (http://www.google.com) or Copernic (http://www.copernic.com). Corpus linguistics-oriented software currently being constructed for browsing the WWW as a corpus, such as KwicFinder (Fletcher, 2001) and WebConc (Kilgarriff, 2001), will certainly prove a useful tool for translators among other language professionals. However, while this "web as corpus" approach has certainly advantages in terms of time over DIY web corpora (the "corpus" is always already there), it necessarily looses in precision and reliability.

The advantages of "robust" corpora over "virtual" corpora can instead be summed up as follows:

- They are usually more reliable.
- They are usually larger.
- They may be enriched with linguistic and contextual information.
- If parallel, they are already aligned.
- They come with user-friendly, customized software (though, again, not necessarily targeted to the needs of professional translators).

5 Conclusions

Translators can tolerate the learning curve necessary to adopt corpora and concordancing software among their everyday working tools only if they derive benefits. These benefits are the fact that corpora provide information not available elsewhere at an affordable cost.

As a way of concluding, I would like to point out possible improvements for existing corpora and concordancing software:

(a) "Robust " reference corpora need to become more accessible: for instance, a BNC license is still relatively expensive and the interrogation software might do with some customization; the CORIS/CODIS corpora and others have limited access.

(b) In order for "virtual" corpora to become more widespread among translators, concordancing software for work with small monolingual corpora has to become capable of dealing with HTML and, increasingly, XML texts. For example, it may be useful to interface the concordancing software with the Internet browser to provide facilities for file downloading and management, and for allowing the user to switch between concordance lines and full text view, in order to take advantage of multimedia features of electronic texts.

(c) Bilingual and parallel corpora are scarcely available and usually of limited size. Bilingual concordancers require bilingual corpora, and given what it takes to locate and align text pairs, it is not very likely that individual translators will resort to consulting parallel concordances unless parallel (aligned) corpora are already available. The creation of more corpora of this kind is a matter of computational resources (especially parallel concordancers and efficient aligning utilities) as well as of more awareness of the usefulness of this resource among translators and language resources providers.

Notes:

1. (i. e. whether a translation is produced directly from the original text or via an intermediate translation in another language).

2. So-called "production dictionaries," which focus on usage information, can be thought of as standing somehow in between the two.

选文三　语料库翻译研究的代表性问题

蒋　林　金　兵

导　言

第一作者蒋林系浙江师范大学外国语学院教授。他在本文提出语料库翻译研究是翻译界的一个新兴领域,语料的代表性是需要关注的一个重要问题。目前翻译理论界在语料库的收录对象和内部结构方面都有比较大的分歧,而翻译理论难以指导语料库翻译研究。只有解决好了语料的代表性问题,语料库翻译研究才能更好地健康发展。

1　引　言

翻译研究是跨学科的,涉及到的学科不下 20 门。但是,在所有这些学科中,与它联系最紧密的莫过于语言学。翻译研究的语言学派兴盛于 20 世纪 50 到 70 年代,后来影响力逐渐被文化学派所超越。不过,到了 90 年代,由于语料库翻译研究的出现,语言学派又出现了新的发展,什么是语料库呢? 按照《语言学和语音学辞典》的定义,语料库是"语言资料的收集,资料来源既可以是书面语篇,也可以是话语的记录脚本,语料库可以被用作语言描述的起点或用作验证语言假设的方式"。将这一定义用于翻译研究中,翻译语料库就应当是收集起来的书面的和口头的翻译材料。既然构建语料库要收集材料,那么一个重要的问题是,如何保证收集到的语料具有代表性,从而使研究结论更具普遍性呢? 本文首先概括了语料库翻译研究的现状,然后重点讨论语料库翻译研究的语料代表性问题。

2 语料库翻译研究概述

语料库语言学是 20 世纪 50 年代发展起来的新兴研究方法,它通过对大量的语料进行描述性研究从而得出带普遍性的结论。目前,"语料库语言学已经成为语言研究的主流……它正在对语言研究的许多领域产生愈来愈大的影响。"但长期以来,语料库语言学家对翻译研究并没有产生多大兴趣,其原因主要有两点:第一,语言学家过分强调语言的形式因素而忽略语言发生的社会文化背景;第二,传统语料库语言学家认为翻译语言背离了规范,不同于标准语言,因此翻译文本一直被排除在语料库之外。20 世纪 90 年代中期以来,以 Mona Baker,Gideon Toury,Kirsten Malmkiaer 为首的一批翻译理论家开始将语料库和翻译研究结合起来,并取得了显著成果。Baker 认为,与翻译研究有关的语料库有三类:平行语料库、多语语料库和可比语料库。Baker 认为,可比语料库对翻译研究的意义最为深远。1995 年,英国曼彻斯特大学理工学院语言工程系的翻译研究中心(UM IST)创建了世界上第一个可比语料库———翻译英语语料库(Translational English Corpus,TEC)。该语料库收集的原著的语种众多,包括德语、法语、西班牙语、意大利语、阿拉伯语等等。2001 年的库容已经达到 2 000 万,最后的目标将是 5 000 万。目前,语料库翻译研究在诸多方面,特别是在发现翻译普遍性方面,已经取得了重要成果。

3 语料库翻译研究中的代表性问题

3.1 语料库翻译研究的对象

著名语料库语言学家 Douglas Biber 认为代表性实际上就是数据在多大程度上包括了群数(population)的全部变动范围。他指出,要保证代表性,先决条件是对目标群数进行定义。那么如何定义呢? 他认为,定义包括两个方面,一是确立群数的边界,即哪些文本应当包括在目标群数内,而哪些则应当排除在外;二是确立群数的内部结构,即哪些文本范畴应当包括在目标群数中以及对这些范畴的定义。任何一个学科都有自己特定的研究对象,否则,它就没有存在的必要。那么语料库翻译研究的对象又是什么呢? 从总体上来看,目前翻译研究界在确定研究对象上主要有两派。一派为翻译划出一系列的对等样式,而研究对象就是那些达到了对等要求的文本。显然,无论将对等划分为多少类,必然会有大量的文本因为不符合对等要求而被翻译研究排除在外。因此,这种做法有很大的局限性。另一派则采取更为宽容的态度,如 Toury 就认为,翻译是"无论出于什么原因而在目的语文化中被呈现或被视为是翻译的作品"。毫无疑问,这种观点极大地拓展了翻译研究的对象。任何作品,只要有理由被认为是翻译,就可以成为研究对象。总体来看,虽然以 Toury 为代表的这一派目前是主流,但是传统派仍然有相当的影响力。因此,翻译研究界在确定研究对象上还存在较大分歧,这就给语料库翻译研究提出了难题。

3.2　翻译语料库的内部结构

上面提到,保证语料库代表性的第二个要求是对语料进行分类。翻译语料库是一个大范畴,研究者必须把它进一步分成若干小范畴,才能更好地进行研究。那么,现有的翻译理论又是如何对研究对象进行分类的呢? 在翻译文本的分类方面,Katharina Reiss 可谓开先河者。她借鉴了语言学里有关语言功能的理论,将文本分为三类:信息型、表现型和施事型。信息型文本往往只叙述事实,传递知识,文本的重点在于话题或内容,参考书可谓这类文本的代表;表现型文本重在表达情感,用来传递信息的形式往往比较重要,最能代表这类文本的当属诗歌;施事型文本目的在于影响读者,使读者按照某种方式行事,广告是这类文本的代表。需要指出的是,Reiss 的分类针对的是原文,但翻译时,原文的功能经常并不是原封不动地被照搬到译文中。因此,她的分类标志实际上很难用于对翻译文本进行分类。即使在已经建成的英语翻译语料库里,我们也很难看到较为统一的分类标准。英语翻译语料库下设四个子库:小说、传记、报纸和杂志。这种分类标准到底是材料类型,还是刊登渠道? 只能说小说和传记是根据类型来分,而报纸和杂志则是根据渠道来分的。然而,这里必然有一些交叉的情况,如杂志里面可能也有小说或传记。因此,该分类标准事实上是很模糊的。

3.3　语料库语言学的代表性问题及其对语料库翻译研究的启示

综上所述,翻译理论未能解决语料库代表性的办法。那么,我们是否可以向语料库语言学借鉴呢? 毕竟,语料库语言学的历史相对较长,对它的研究也比较深入。一般来说,语料库语言学确定研究对象时两个最重要的原则是"自然发生"(naturally occurring)和"母语者"(native speaker)。因此,以某种语言为母语者在自然状况下发生的言语就成为其研究对象。这两个界定标准相对来说还是比较清楚的,语料库研究者对此已经达成了一定程度的共识。定义目标群数的第二个要求是将语料进行分类。通常有两个分类标准,即可以根据情境分类,也可以根据人口统计学的标准来分类。例如,根据前者我们可以将语料按照信道、格式、场景等标准来进行分类;根据后者我们可以将语料按照发话人的职业、性别、年龄等来进行分类。以上这两种分类方法都有实证基础,研究者在运用过程中也取得了一定的成绩。语料库翻译研究与语料库语言学有着紧密的联系,因此,后者如何确保语料代表性的做法对于前者具有重要的借鉴意义。但是,由于二者在研究对象和方法上的差异,语料库语言学的研究方法并不能直接运用于语料库翻译研究。语料库语言学在定义研究对象时使用的两个界定范畴是"自然发生"和"母语者"。语料库翻译研究能否借用这两个范畴呢? 先看"自然发生"。什么样的翻译是自然发生的呢? 很显然,翻译作品并不像原创文本那样"自然发生",如何界定"自然"还需要理论家做进一步的工作。"母语者"这个范畴移植到语料库翻译研究中就成了"土生土长的译者"(nativetranslator)。Toury 在批判 Harris 的"自然翻译"概念时,就提出了这个概念,但他同时指出,这个概念只是假设的,并不一定真实存在。土生土长的译者必须具备两种能力:双语能力和比较语言的能力。一般的双语者都具有语言能力,却不具备比较能力,从语言能力到比较能力绝不是一个"自然"过程,这一点同母语者习得母语的过程有很大不同。另外,考虑到翻译既可能是从母语到外语,也可能反过来,因此 native translator 这个概念也很难用于翻译研究。

再看研究对象的内部结构问题。Biber 为语料库分类设定了一系列参数,主要包括信道、格式、场景、说话者、受话者等等。可以看出,这些参数基本上都是根据情境来设置的。当然,我们还可以从其他方面对语料进行分类,比如语言功能、用途和内容等。显然,语料库语言学所运用的这些分类方法与翻译研究也有着密切关系。单语语料库采用的功能和情境参数也可用于对译作分类,事实上,这方面的工作已经开始。但是,单语语料库使用的参数主要是为了区分文本,而不是译作。因此,这些参数虽然有参考价值,但翻译研究者必须将它们加以改造才能运用于翻译研究。另外,翻译研究者可能还需要根据翻译的特点增加一些新参数,如翻译的方向性、译作同原作之间的功能关系等等。

3.4 原型理论与语料库翻译研究

上面提到,目前的翻译理论尚不能明确界定研究对象并将其合理分类。Halverson 认为,这主要是由于传统分类法的缺陷所致。传统分类法将研究对象分成界限分明的数个范畴,一个事物要么属于一个范畴,要么不属于该范畴。属于同一范畴的各事物之间有着相同的特点和相同的地位。将这一分类法运用到翻译研究上,人们就会认为某些作品要么是译作,要么不是,而属于译作的那些作品在研究中应当占据同等的地位。但是,哲学和心理学的新发展使人们认识到,范畴并不是那么界限明确的。Wittgenstein 以"游戏"这个范畴为例,说明了所谓有着固定边界的范畴不过是一个幻觉。各种游戏之间并没有共同的地方,不过是一些游戏同另一些游戏有相似点而已。而且,有些游戏更能代表游戏这个范畴,比如在美国,篮球就是游戏的代表。在心理学方面,Rosch 通过对颜色的研究,发现"红色"这个范畴并没有明确的界限。在此基础上,她提出了原型理论。该理论认为,一个范畴内的各个事物并不是平等的,有些事物比其他事物更能代表该范畴。Halverson 指出,将原型理论运用到翻译研究中就可以较好地解决研究对象问题。Toury 的理论认为所有的译作都具有同等的合法性,但现实中职业翻译却明显地具有优先性。Halverson 认为,原型理论可以很好地解决这一矛盾。根据该理论,职业翻译应被视为"翻译"这个范畴的原型,占据中心位置,而诸如"自然翻译"和非职业翻译都可视作原型的扩展。因此在语料库翻译研究中,研究者可以侧重于职业翻译,但是他也可以建构一个包括非中心成员在内的综合语料库。在这样一个综合语料库中,各类文本的地位是不平等的,因此在收集语料的过程中也可以相应地有所侧重。这样做的好处是研究得出的结论更具针对性,同时也便于比较研究。

4 结 语

语料库翻译研究的方法论是一个大问题,但为了学科的健康发展,这又是一个必须解决的问题。早在 1995 年,Toury 在研究翻译规范时就曾指出,当时还没有严格的统计学方法用于研究规范,"甚至还不能提供用于实际研究的取样规则(由于人的局限性,这些规则只能适用于那些样本)"。但 Toury 并没有放弃希望,他认为研究者需要将更多的精力用在提出系统的研究方法上。他的建议在今天仍然有很大的现实意义,语料库翻译研究要想超越"空洞的不必要的量化研究",就一定要有更好的方法论,更好地解决语料的代表性问题。

【延伸阅读】

[1] Blackwell, S. Syntax versus Orthography: Problems in the Automatic Parsing of

Idioms//R. Garside, G. Leech & G. Sampson (eds.), *The Computational Analysis of English: A Corpus-based Approach*. London: Longman, 1987.

[2] Brown, P., et al. A Statistical Approach to Machine Translation. *Computational Linguistics*, 1990, 16:2, 79-85.

[3] CEC. *LRE Programme Call for Proposals 1992: Technical Background Document*. Luxembourg: CEC, 1992.

[4] Garside, R. The CLAWS Tagging System//R. Garside, G. Leech & G. Sampson (eds.), *The Computational Analysis of English: A Corpus-based Approach*. London: Longman, 1987.

[5] Leech, G. Corpus Annotation Schemes. Paper presented at Pisa Workshop on European Corpus Resources, January 1992.

[6] Leech, G., & Garside, R. Running a Grammar Factory//S. Johansson & A.-B. Stenstrom(eds.), *English Computer Corpora: Selected Papers and Research Guide*. Berlin: Mouton de Gruyter, 1991.

[7] Marcus, M., & Santorini, B. Building Very Large Natural Language Corpora: The Penn Treebank. Unpublished manuscript, 1992.

[8] McEnery, A., & Daille, B. Database Design for Corpus Storage: The ET 10-63 Data Model. Unit for Computer Research on the English Language Technical Papers 1, 1993.

[9] Oakhill, J., & Garnham, A. Linguistic Prescriptions and Anaphoric Reality. *Text*, 1992, 12(2): 161-182.

[10] Oakhill, J., Garnham, A., Gernsbacher, M., & Cain, K. How Natural Are Conceptual Anaphors? *Language and Cognitive Processes*, 1992, 7(3/4): 257-280.

[11] Sadler, V. The *Bilingual Knowledge Bank—A New Conceptual Basis for MT*. Utrecht: BSO-Research, 1989.

[12] Tsujii, J., Ananiadou, S., Carroll, J., & Sekine, S. Methodologies for the Development of Sublanguage MT System II. *CCL, UMIST Report*, 1991, No. 91/11.

[13] Wilson, A., & Rayson, P. The Automatic Content Analysis of Spoken Discourse. Paper presented at 12th International Conference on English Language Research on Computerized Corpora, Ilkley, May 1991.

[14] Austermuhl, F. *Electronic Tools for Translators*. Manchester: St Jerome, 2001.

[15] Baker, M. Corpus Linguistics and Translation Studies. Implications and Applications//M. Baker, G. Francis & E. Tognini-Bonelli (eds.), *Text and Technology*(pp. 233-252). Philadelphia/Amsterdam: John Benjamins, 1993.

[16] Bowker, L. Using Specialized Monolingual Native-language Corpora as a Translation Resource: A Pilot Study. *META* 1998, 43(4): 631-651.

[16] 黄昌宁,李涓子. 语料库语言学. 北京:商务印书馆,2002.

[17] 廖七一. 当代英国翻译理论. 武汉:湖北教育出版社,2000.

[18] Baker, M. *Routledge Encyclopedia of Translation Studies*. Shanghai: Shanghai Foreign Language Education Press, 2004.

[19] 胡显耀. 语料库翻译研究与翻译普遍性. 上海科技翻译，2004，(4):47.

[20] Biber，D. Representativeness in Corpus Design. *Literary and Linguistic Computing*，1993，(4)：243-246.

[21] Toury，G. *Descriptive Translation Studies and Beyond*. Shanghai：Shanghai Foreign Language Education Press，2001.

[22] Halverson，S. Translation Studies and Representative Corpora：Establishing Links between Translation Corpora，Theoretical/Descriptive Categories and a Conception of the Object of Study. *Meta*，1998，(4)：502-512.

[23] Tymoczko，M. Computerized Corpora and the Future of Translation Studies. *Meta*，1998.

[24] 丁树德. 浅谈西方翻译语料库研究. 外国语，2001，(5).

【问题与思考】

1. 语料库有几种类型？它们各自有什么特点？
2. 语言的各类信息在语料库中是如何被标注的？
3. 平行语料库在机器翻译中是如何被运用的？
4. 语料库在翻译中如何发挥辅助性作用的？
5. 可供译者使用的语料库资源有哪些？它们之间有什么区别？
6. 平行语料库与单语语料库相比较有何特点？请举例说明。
7. 如何保证收集到的语料具有代表性，从而使研究结论更具普遍性呢？
8. 举例说明语料库分类的参数是如何设置的？
9. 原型理论与语料库翻译研究之间有何关系？

第七章　机器翻译的特点与运作

导　论

随着国际交流越来越频繁,互联网深入到人们的工作、生活中,社会的信息化程度越来越高。人们为使自己不被时代所淘汰,不得不紧跟时代的步伐,时刻关注并获取世界上的最新信息。而这些信息中的大部分是在互联网上以外文形式出现的。于是,语言成了阻碍人们信息获取的最大障碍。鉴于人工翻译在便捷和费用等方面的限制,人们对机器翻译或机器辅助翻译系统的需求越来越迫切,因而对机器翻译的研究成为热点。目前对机器翻译的研究很多,其中比较先进的机器翻译方法是基于大型语料库和统计学的机器翻译。要了解机器翻译,就必须了解它的历史和现状、各种类型的机器翻译系统和机器翻译的实现过程;就必须了解机器翻译的方法,如形态自动分析方法、基于规则和基于统计的句法分析方法、语义自动分析方法、词义排歧方法、目标语言生成方法、机器翻译词典的编制方法等;就必须了解因特网上的各种翻译工具。本章的选文对人工智能,机器翻译理论的起源、发展、国内外研究现状作了阐述,并就其存在的问题及发展方向作了分析。同时,部分选文提出了机器翻译系统的设计框架,这种框架包括电子词典的设计方法、电子词典的存储结构、语料库的建立、规则库的建立、语义的消歧系统及跨语本体映射与匹配技术等。机器翻译的确切定义是用计算机把一种语言全自动翻译为另一种语言。机器翻译研究的意义是不言而喻的,但又是一项艰巨的研究课题。自20世纪40年代美国为获取情报而首次开发出机器翻译技术以来,机器翻译已有六十余年的发展历史,其间经历了几起几落的曲折历程,人们对它的评价毁誉参半。尽管20世纪90年代以来,已有许多机器翻译系统进入了市场,但其翻译结果却不尽如人意。机器翻译系统面临的主要"瓶颈"之一就是语言歧义消解问题,这也成为研究的重点。近年来,机器翻译的研究主要集中在统计性机器翻译领域并取得了进展。本章的相关选文也介绍了机器翻译的原理和特点、机器翻译的发展历程和现状、基于词的机器统计翻译方法、基于句法的机器统计翻译方法等,并对机器翻译研究今后的发展进行了讨论和展望。尽管机器翻译的研究由来已久,但尚未完全达到人类期望的目标。随着计算机软硬件技术的高速发展,以及语料库建设的完善,利用统计性知识的机器翻译成为可能,翻译质量有望离人类的期望更近一步。

选 文

选文一　Machine Translation: A Concise History

W. John Hutchins

导　言

　　本文追溯了用于自然语言翻译的计算机程序(软件)的发展。从一般和传统意义上来说,这种程序被称为机器翻译(MT)。本文介绍了其发展简史,只能提到其最重要的研究体系和项目、最重要的操作和商务体系。研究人员从一开始就把研究集中在科学和技术文档的翻译上。在科学和技术领域,人们对翻译的需求几乎总是超过翻译职业人员的能力,而这些需求正在快速增长。此外,互联网的出现带来了即时在线翻译的需求,而这种需求是人工译员无法满足的。对翻译的需求有两种类型:译文质量达到出版的要求;以及让人理解主要意义式翻译。第一种类型主要运用于大公司的多语文档翻译。翻译系统输出的译文可节省时间和成本,它首先提供初步的译文,然后由译员审校、编辑、出版,这种模式被称为"人工辅助式机器翻译"(HAMT)。然而在很多情况下,译文并不一定需要完美、准确,机器翻译只要快速译出原文的主要意思就达到了要求,这通常被称为"理解式机器翻译"。最近,机器翻译又被用于社会交流中,这主要通过电子邮件、聊天室等。这种机器翻译被称为"交流沟通式机器翻译"。机器翻译这一领域还融合了基于计算机的翻译工具开发、电子词典和词汇表的发展、术语管理系统、翻译数据库和翻译工作站等相关知识。

1　Introduction

This paper traces the history of efforts to develop computer programs (software) for the translation of natural languages, commonly and traditionally called "machine translation" (MT), or, in non-English-speaking countries, "automatic translation" (*traduction automatique*, *avtomaticheskij perevod*). A brief history can of course mention only the most significant research systems and projects and only the most important operating and commercial systems (and none in any detail).

2　Precursors and Pioneers, 1933—1956

Although we may trace the origins of machine translation (MT) back to seventeenth century ideas of universal (and philosophical) languages and of "mechanical" dictionaries, it was not until the twentieth century that the first practical suggestions could be made—in 1933 with two patents issued in France and Russia to Georges Artsrouni and Petr Trojanskij respectively. Artsrouni's patent was for a general-purpose machine which could also function as a mechanical multilingual dictionary. Trojanskij's patent, also basically for a mechanical dictionary, went further with proposals for coding and interpreting grammatical functions using "universal" (Esperanto-based) symbols in a multilingual translation device. Neither of these precursors was known to Andrew Booth (a British crystallographer) and Warren Weaver when they met in 1946 and 1947 and put forward the first tentative ideas for using the newly invented computers for translating natural languages. In 1948 Booth worked with Richard H. Richens (Commonwealth Bureau of Plant Breeding and Genetics, Cambridge, UK) on morphological analysis for a mechanical dictionary. By this time, the idea of mechanical translation (as it was known almost invariably in the period up to the early 1960s) had occurred independently to a number of people, and in July 1949 Warren Weaver (a director at the Rockefeller Foundation) put forward specific proposals for tackling the obvious problems of ambiguity (or "multiple meanings"), based on his knowledge of cryptography, statistics, information theory, logic and language universals. This memorandum was the stimulus for MT research in the United States. Then, in May 1951 Yehoshua Bar-Hillel was appointed to do research at the Massachusetts Institute of Technology (MIT). After visiting all those interested in the subject he wrote a state-of-the-art report, in which he outlined some of the basic approaches to MT questions; and in June 1952, he convened the first MT conference (at MIT), which was attended by nearly everyone already active in the field. It was already clear that full automation of good quality translation was a virtual impossibility, and that human intervention either before or after computer processes (known from the beginning as pre-and post-editing respectively) would be essential; some hoped this would be only an interim measure, but most expected that it would always be needed. At the conference, various ideas were put forward for pre-editing and post-editing, for micro-glossaries as means of reducing ambiguity problems (selecting appropriate target lexical items), and for some kind of syntactic structure analysis. Various suggestions for future activity were proposed; in particular, Léon Dostert from Georgetown University, who had come as a sceptic, argued that what was required was a public demonstration of the feasibility of MT in order to attract research funding. Accordingly, he collaborated with IBM on a project which resulted in the first demonstration of a MT system on 7th January 1954. It was the joint effort of Peter Sheridan of IBM and Paul Garvin at Georgetown. A carefully selected sample of 49 Russian sentences was translated into English, using a very restricted vocabulary of 250 words and just six grammar rules. The demonstration attracted a great deal of media attention in the United States. Although the system had little scientific value, its output was sufficiently impressive to stimulate the large-scale funding of MT research in the USA and to inspire the initiation of MT projects elsewhere in the world, notably in the USSR. In the same year, the first journal was founded by William Locke and by Victor Yngve, who had succeeded Bar-Hillel at MIT in 1953—the journal *Mechanical Translation* was to carry some of the most significant papers until its eventual demise in 1970—and also in this year, the first doctoral thesis in MT, Anthony G. Oettinger's study for a Russian mechanical dictionary. The years 1954 and 1955 saw the foundation of a group in Cambridge, England, under Margaret Masterman, a group in Milan under Silvio Ceccato, the first Russian groups at the Institute of Precise Mechanics and Computer Technology, the Institute of Applied Mathematics, Leningrad University, etc. and the start of various Chinese and Japanese projects. And in 1955 the first MT book appeared, a collection edited by Locke and Booth (1955), including Weaver's 1949 memorandum, Booth and Richens' experiments, some papers given at the 1952 conference, and other contributions from Bar-Hillel, Dostert, Oettinger, Reifler, and Yngve.

3　High Expectations and Disillusion, 1956—1966

When MT research began, there was little help to be had from current linguistics. As a consequence, in the 1950s and 1960s, the research methods tended to polarize between, on the one hand, empirical trial-and-error approaches, which often adopted statistical methods for the "discovery" of grammatical and lexical regularities which could be applied computationally, and, on the other hand, theoretical approaches which involved the projects in fundamental linguistic research, indeed the beginnings of research in what was later to be called "computational linguistics." The contrastive methods were usually described at the time as "brute-force" and "perfectionist" respectively; the aim of the former being the development of systems producing useful if crude quality translations in the near future, and that of the latter being the eventual development of systems producing output requiring little or no human editing. This first decade saw the beginnings of the three basic approaches to MT (until the appearance of corpus-based approaches in the late 1980s, see section 9 below). The first was the "direct translation" model, where programming rules were developed for the translation specifically from one source language (SL) into one particular target language (TL) with a minimal amount of analysis and syntactic reorganization. Many researchers sought to reduce the problems of homonyms and ambiguity by simplifying bilingual dictionaries, i. e. by providing single TL equivalents for SL words which would hopefully "cover" most senses, and would therefore not demand the analysis of contexts (usually immediately adjacent words), and would permit the word order of the SL original to be maintained as much as possible. The second approach was the "interlingua" model, based on abstract language-neutral representations (codes or symbols independent of both SL and TL), where translation would then be in two stages, from SL to interlingua and from interlingua to TL. The third approach was less ambitious: the "transfer approach," where conversion was through a transfer stage from abstract (i. e. disambiguated) representations of SL texts to equivalent TL representations; in this case, translation comprised three stages: analysis, transfer, and generation (or synthesis). In most cases, the "empiricists" adopted the "direct translation" approach, often using statistical analyses of actual texts to derive dictionary rules—often of an ad hoc nature, with little or no theoretical foundation. The "perfectionists" were explicitly theory-driven, undertaking basic linguistic research, with particular attention given to methods of syntactic analysis. Some groups pursued the interlingua ideal, and believed that only fundamental research on human thought process (what would later be called artificial intelligence or cognitive science) would solve the problems of automatic translation. The more pragmatic among them concentrated on simpler syntax-based "transfer" models, leaving problems of semantics to some later stage. Any evaluation of the period must remember that computer facilities were frequently inadequate; much effort was devoted to improving basic hardware (paper tapes, magnetic media, access speeds, etc.) and to devising programming tools suitable for language processing—in particular, COMIT developed at MIT by the team under Victor Yngve. Some groups were inevitably forced to concentrate on theoretical issues, particularly in Europe and the Soviet Union. For political and military reasons, nearly all US research was for Russian-English translation, and most Soviet research focused on English-Russian systems, although the multilingual policy of the Soviet Union inspired research there on a much wider range of languages than elsewhere. The research under Erwin Reifler at the University of Washington (Seattle) epitomized the dictionary-based "direct" approach; it involved the construction of large bilingual dictionaries where lexicographic information was used not only for selecting lexical equivalents but also for solving grammatical problems without the use of syntactic analysis. Entries gave English translations with rules for local reordering of output. The huge lexicon made extensive use of English "cover terms" for Russian polysemes, the inclusion of phrases and clauses and the classification of vocabulary into sublanguages. After initial work on German and English, the group was engaged on the foundations of a Russian-English system for the "photoscopic store," a large memory device. From 1958 practical development was directed by Gilbert King at the IBM Corporation (Yorktown Heights, New York), and a system installed for the US Air Force produced "translations" until the early 1970s. By any standards the output was crude and sometimes barely intelligible, but no excessive claims were made for the system, which with all its deficiencies was able to satisfy basic information needs of its users.

Many researchers at the time distrusted linguistic theory—the formal linguistics of Zellig Harris and Noam Chomsky had scarcely begun—and preferred to develop methods based on the analysis of language corpora. For example, researchers at the RAND Corporation undertook statistical analyses of a large corpus of Russian physics texts, to extract bilingual glossaries and grammatical information. On this basis, a computer program was written for a rough translation; the result was studied by post-editors; the glossaries and the rules were revised; the corpus was translated again; and so it continued in cycles of translation and post-editing. The main method of analysis was initially statistical distribution, although it was at RAND that David Hays later developed the first syntactic parser based on dependency grammar. The research under Léon Dostert at Georgetown University had a more eclectic approach, undertaking empirical analyses of texts only when traditional grammatical information was inadequate. Initially there were several groups at Georgetown, for many years the largest in the USA. One group was led by Paul Garvin, who later left to found his own group at the Bunker-Ramo Corporation, and to develop his "fulcrum" method, essentially a dependency parser; another led by Ariadne Lukjanow worked on a code-matching method; a third one-man "group" (Antony Brown) experimented with a pure example of the cyclical method on a French-English system; and the fourth group under Michael Zarechnak developed the method eventually adopted. This, the Georgetown Automatic Translation (GAT) system, had three levels of analysis: morphological (including identification of idioms), syntagmatic (agreement of nouns and adjectives, government of verbs, modification of adjectives, etc.), and syntactic (subjects and predicates, clause relationships, etc.). GAT was initially implemented on the SERNA system, largely the work of Peter Toma, and then with the programming method developed by Brown. In this form it was successfully installed by Euratom in Ispra (Italy) in 1963 and by the US Atomic Energy Commission in 1964, both continuing in regular use until the late 1970s. Anthony Oettinger at Harvard University believed in a gradualist approach. From 1954 to 1960 his group concentrated on the compilation of a massive Russian-English dictionary, to serve as an aid for translators (a forerunner of the now common computer-based dictionary aids), to produce crude word-for-word translations for scientists familiar with the subject, and to be the basis for more advanced experimental work. From 1959 research focused on the "predictive syntactic analyzer"—originally developed at the National Bureau of Standards under Ida Rhodes—a system for the identification of permissible sequences of grammatical categories (nouns, verbs, adjectives, etc.) and the probabilistic prediction of following categories. However, the results were often unsatisfactory, caused primarily by the enforced selection at every stage of the "most probable" prediction. (Nevertheless, an improved version, the Multiple-path Predictive Analyzer, led later to William Woods' familiar Augmented Transition Network parser.) The research at MIT was directed by Victor Yngve from 1953 until its end in 1965. Here syntax was placed at the centre: a SL grammar analyzed input sentences as phrase structure representations, a "structure transfer routine" converted them into equivalent TL phrase structures, and the TL grammar rules produced output text. But in the end, Yngve recognized that a "semantic barrier" had been reached, and that further progress would be very difficult. It may be noted that despite Chomsky's association with the group for a short time, transformational grammar had little influence—indeed there is virtually no evidence of Chomskyan approaches in any MT research at this time. The Linguistic Research Center (LRC) at the University of Texas, founded by Winfried Lehmann in 1958, concentrated also on basic syntactic research.

Efforts were made to devise reversible grammars to achieve bi-directional translation within an essentially "syntactic transfer" approach, laying foundations for the later development of the METAL system. At the University of California, Berkeley, the project under the direction of Sydney Lamb stressed the importance of developing maximally efficient dictionary routines and a linguistic theory appropriate for MT. This was Lamb's stratificational grammar, with networks, nodes and relations paralleling the architecture of computers. Translation was seen as a series of decoding and encoding processes, via a series of strata (graphemic, morphemic, lexemic, sememic). There were no American groups taking the interlingua approach; US projects tended to adopt less speculative approaches despite Weaver's earlier advocacy. Interlinguas were the focus of projects elsewhere. At the Cambridge Language Research Unit, Margaret Masterman and her colleagues adopted two basic lines of research: the development of a prototype interlingua producing crude "pidgin" (essentially word-for-word) translations, and the development of tools for improving and refining MT output, primarily by means of the rich semantic networks of a thesaurus (utilizing mathematical lattice theory as a basis.) At Milan, Silvio Ceccato concentrated on the development of an interlingua based on "cognitive" processes, specifically on the conceptual analysis of words (species, genus, activity type, physical properties, etc.) and their possible correlations with other words in texts—a forerunner of the "neural networks" of later years. In the Soviet Union research was as vigorous as in the United States and showed a similar mix of empirical and basic theoretical approaches. At the Institute of Precision Mechanics the research under D. Y. Panov on English-Russian translation was on lines similar to that at Georgetown, but with less practical success—primarily from lack of adequate computer facilities. More basic research was undertaken at the Steklov Mathematical Institute by Aleksej A. Ljapunov, Olga S. Kulagina and Igor A. Mel'čuk (of the Institute of Linguistics)—the latter working on an interlingua approach that led to his "meaning-text" model. This combined a stratificational dependency approach (six strata: phonetic, phonemic, morphemic, surface syntactic, deep syntactic, semantic) with a strong emphasis on lexicographic aspects of an interlingua. Fifty universal "lexical functions" were identified at the deep syntactic stratum covering paradigmatic relations (e. g. synonyms, antonyms, verbs and their corresponding agentive nouns, etc.) and a great variety of syntagmatic relations (e. g. inceptive verbs associated with given nouns, *conference: open*, *war: break out*; idiomatic causatives, *compile: dictionary, lay: foundations*, etc.) Interlingua investigations were consonant with the multilingual needs of the Soviet Union and undertaken at a number of other centres (Archaimbault and Léon 1997). The principal one was at Leningrad State University, where a team under Nikolaj Andreev conceived an interlingua not as an abstract intermediary representation but as an artificial language complete in itself with its own morphology and syntax, and having only those features statistically most common to a large number of languages. By the mid-1960s MT research groups had been established in many countries throughout the world, including most

European countries（Hungary，Czechoslovakia，Bulgaria，Belgium，Germany，France，etc.），China，Mexico，and Japan. Many of these were short-lived; an exception was the project which begun in 1960 at Grenoble University（see Section 5 below）. Throughout this period, research on MT became an "umbrella" for much contemporary work in structural and formal linguistics（particularly in the Soviet Union）, semiotics, logical semantics, mathematical linguistics, quantitative linguistics, and nearly all of what would now be called computational linguistics and language engineering（terms already in use since early 1960s）. Initially, there were also close ties with cybernetics and information theory. In general, throughout the early period, work on MT（both theoretical and practical）was seen to be of wide relevance in many fields concerned with the application of computers to "intellectual" tasks; this was true in particular for the research on "interlingual" aspects of MT, regarded as significant for the development of "information languages" to be used in document retrieval systems.

4　The ALPAC Report and Its Consequences

In the 1950s optimism was high; developments in computing and in formal linguistics, particularly in the area of syntax, seemed to promise great improvements in quality. There were many predictions of imminent breakthroughs and of fully automatic systems operating within a few years. However, disillusion grew as the complexity of the linguistic problems became more and more apparent, and many agreed that research had reached an apparently insuperable "semantic barrier." In an influential survey, Bar-Hillel（1960）criticized the prevailing assumption that the goal of MT research should be the creation of fully automatic high quality translation（FAHQT）systems producing results indistinguishable from those of human translators. He argued that it was not merely unrealistic, given the current state of linguistic knowledge and computer systems, but impossible in principle. He demonstrated his argument with the word *pen*. It can have at least two meanings（a container for animals or children, and a writing implement）. In the sentence *The box was in the pen* we know that only the first meaning is plausible; the second meaning is excluded by our knowledge of the normal sizes of（writing）pens and boxes. Bar-Hillel contended that such problematic examples are common and that no computer program could conceivably deal with such "real world" knowledge without recourse to a vast encyclopaedic store. His argument carried much weight at the time, although later developments in artificial intelligence（and within MT on knowledge-based systems, see Section 7 below）have demonstrated that his pessimism was not completely justified. For some time MT research continued vigorously—indeed many new groups were set up, particularly outside the United States and Europe—with research now focused mainly on syntactic analysis and preliminary investigations of semantics. At the same time, the first working systems（from IBM and Georgetown）were being installed—prematurely in the view of many researchers—and the availability of poor-quality translations was being appreciated by users who wanted immediate results and did not need to have human-quality versions. Nevertheless, the imminent prospect of good-quality MT was receding, and in 1964 the government sponsors of MT in the United States (mainly military and intelligence agencies) asked the National Science Foundation to set up the Automatic Language Processing Advisory Committee (ALPAC) to examine the situation. In its famous 1966 report it concluded that MT was slower, less accurate and twice as expensive as human translation and that "there is no immediate or predictable prospect of useful machine translation" (ALPAC, 1966). It saw no need for further investment in MT research; instead it recommended the development of machine aids for translators, such as automatic dictionaries, and the continued support of basic research in computational linguistics. Paradoxically, ALPAC rejected MT because it required post-editing (despite the fact that human translations are also invariably revised before publication) and because it assumed the demand was for top-quality translations, even though the sponsoring bodies were primarily interested in information gathering and analysis, where lower quality would be acceptable. Although widely condemned at the time as biased and short-sighted, the influence of ALPAC was profound, bringing a virtual end to MT research in the USA for over a decade; and indirectly bringing to an end much MT research elsewhere—the funding bodies in the Soviet Union arguing that the chances of success were even smaller with their much poorer computer facilities. In addition, the ALPAC report ended the previous perception of MT as the leading area of research in the investigation of computers and natural language. Computational linguistics became an independent field of research.

5 The Quiet Decade, 1967—1976

Research did not stop completely, however. Even in the United States groups continued for a few more years, at the University of Texas and at Wayne State University. But there was a change of direction. Where "first generation" research of the pre-ALPAC period (1956—1966) had been dominated by mainly "direct translation" approaches, the "second generation" post-ALPAC was to be dominated by "indirect" models, both interlingua and transfer based. In the United States the main activity had concentrated on English translations of Russian scientific and technical materials. In Canada and Europe the needs were quite different. The Canadian government's bicultural policy created a demand for English-French (and to a less extent French-English) translation beyond the capacity of the translation profession. The problems of translation were equally acute within the European Community, with growing demands for translations of scientific, technical, administrative and legal documentation from and into all the Community languages. While in the United States MT was not revived for many years, in Canada and Europe (and later in Japan, and elsewhere) its need did not cease to be recognized, and development continued. At Montreal, research began in 1970 on a syntactic transfer system for English-French translation. The TAUM project (Traduction Automatique de l'Université de Montréal) had two major achievements: firstly, the Q-system formalism for manipulating linguistic strings and trees (later developed as the Prolog programming language), and secondly, the Météo system for translating weather forecasts. Designed specifically for the restricted vocabulary and limited syntax of meteorological reports, Météo has been successfully operating since 1976 (since 1984 in a new version). The TAUM group attempted to repeat this success with another sublanguage, that of aviation manuals, but failed to overcome the problems of complex noun compounds and phrases, and the project ended in 1981. The principal innovative experiments of the decade focused on essentially interlingua approaches. Between 1960 and 1971 the group established by Bernard Vauquois at Grenoble University developed a system for translating Russian mathematics and physics texts into French. Its "pivot language" (influenced to some extent by the research of Kulagina and Mel'čuk in Russia) represented only the logical properties of syntactic relationships; it was not a pure interlingua as it did not provide interlingual representations for lexical items—these were translated by a bilingual transfer mechanism. Analysis and generation involved three levels: phrase-structure (context-free) representation, a dependency structure, and a "pivot language" representation in terms of predicates and arguments. A similar model was adopted at the University of Texas during the 1970s in its METAL system for German and English: sentences were analyzed into "normal forms," i. e. semantic propositional dependency structures with no interlingual lexical elements. At the same time in the Soviet Union, Mel'čuk continued his research on a "meaning-text" model for application in MT (see above). However, by the mid-1970s, the future of the interlingua approach seemed to be in doubt. The main problems identified were attributed by the Grenoble and Texas groups to the rigidity of the levels of analysis (failure at any one stage meant failure to produce any output at all), the inefficiency of parsers (too many partial analyses which had to be "filtered" out), and in particular loss of information about surface forms of the SL input which might have been used to guide the selection of TL forms and the construction of acceptable TL sentence structures. As a consequence, it seemed to many at the time that the less ambitious "transfer" approach offered better prospects.

6 Operational and Commercial Systems, 1976—1989

In the decade after ALPAC, more systems were coming into operational use and attracting public attention. The Georgetown systems had been operating since the mid-1960s. As well as Météo, two other sublanguage systems appeared: in 1970 the Institut Textile de France introduced TITUS, a multilingual system for translating abstracts written in a controlled language, and in 1972 came CULT (Chinese University of Hong Kong) specifically designed for translating mathematics texts from Chinese into English. More significant, however, were the first Syst ran installations. Developed by Peter Toma, its oldest version is the Russian-English system at the USAF Foreign Technology Division (Dayton, Ohio) installed in 1970. The Commission of the European Communities purchased an English-French version in 1976 and followed it by systems for translation of most other languages of the European Communities (now European Union). Over the years, the original ("direct translation") design has been greatly modified, with increased modularity and greater compatibility of the analysis and synthesis components of different versions, permitting cost reductions when developing new language pairs. Syst ran has been installed at numerous intergovernmental institutions, e. g. NATO and the International Atomic Energy Authority, and at many major companies, e. g. General Motors, Dornier, and Aérospatiale. The application at the Xerox Corporation was particularly noteworthy: post-editing has been virtually eliminated by controlling the vocabulary and structures of technical manuals for translation from English into French, German, Italian, Spanish, Portuguese, and Scandinavian languages. From the early 1980s until recently, the main rival of Systran was the system from the Logos Corporation, developed initially by Bernard E. Scott as an English-Vietnamese system for translating aircraft manuals during the 1970s. Experience gained in this project was applied to the development of a German-English system which appeared on the market in 1982; during the 1980s other language pairs were developed. At the end of the 1980s appeared the commercial METAL German-English system, which had originated from the research at the University of Texas University. After its interlingua experiments in the mid 1970s this group adopted an essentially transfer approach, with research funded since 1978 by the Siemens company in Munich (Germany). Other language pairs were later marketed for Dutch, French and Spanish as well as English and German. Systems such as Systran, Logos and METAL were in principle designed for general application, although in practice their dictionaries have been adapted for particular subject domains. Special-purpose systems, designed for one particular environment, were also developed during the 1970s and 1980s. The Pan American Health Organization in Washington built two mainframe systems, one for Spanish into English (SPANAM) and the other for English into Spanish (ENGSPAN), both essentially by just two researchers, Muriel Vasconcellos and Marjorie León. Large tailor-made systems have been the speciality of the Smart Corporation (New York) since the early 1980s. Customers have included Citicorp, Ford, and largest of all, the Canadian Department of Employment and Immigration. The principal feature of the Smart systems is (as at Xerox) strict control of input (English) vocabulary and syntax so that minimal revision of output is needed. During the 1980s, the greatest commercial activity was in Japan, where most of the computer companies (Fujitsu, Hitachi, NEC, Sharp, Toshiba) developed software for computer-aided translation, mainly for the Japanese-English and English-Japanese markets, although they did not ignore the needs for translation to and from Korean, Chinese and other languages. Many of these systems were low-level direct or transfer systems with analysis limited to morphological and syntactic information and with little or no attempt to resolve lexical ambiguities. Often restricted to specific subject fields (computer science and information technology were popular choices), they relied on substantial human assistance at both the preparatory (pre-editing) and the revision (post-editing) stages. Some of the Japanese systems were designed for microcomputers. But they were not the first in this market. The earliest were the American Weidner and ALPS systems in 1981 and 1983 respectively. The ALPS system offered three levels of assistance: multilingual word-processing, automatic dictionary and terminology consultation, and interactive translation. In the latter case, translators could work with MT-produced rough drafts. The system also included an early form of "translation memory" (see Section 8 below.) However, the ALPS products were not profitable, and from the mid 1980s onwards the company diverted into providing a translation service rather than selling computer aids for translators. The Weidner systems offered packages for a large number of language pairs, with its Japanese-English systems being particularly popular. In the late 1980s Weidner was acquired by Bravice but shortly afterwards the company was wound up. By this time, however, other systems for personal computers had come onto the market (PC-Translator from Linguistic Products, GTS from Globalink and the Language Assistant series from MicroTac).

7 The Revival of Research, 1976—1989

The revival of MT research during the later half of the 1970s and early 1980s was characterized by the almost universal adoption of the three-stage transfer-based approach, predominantly syntax-oriented and founded on the formalization of lexical and grammatical rules influenced by linguistic theories of the time. After the disappointment of its interlingua system, the Grenoble group (GETA, Groupe d'Etudes pour la Traduction Automatique) began development of its influential Ariane system. Regarded as the paradigm of the "second generation" linguistics-based transfer systems, Ariane influenced projects throughout the world in the 1980s. Of particular note were its flexibility and modularity, its algorithms for manipulating tree representations, and its conception of static and dynamic grammars. Different levels and types of representation (dependency, phrase structure, logical) could be incorporated on single labelled tree structures and thus provide considerable flexibility in multilevel transfer representations. However, like many experimental MT systems, Ariane did not become an operational system (despite involvement in a French national MT project), and active research on the system ceased in the late 1980s. Similar in conception to the GETA-Ariane design was the Mu system developed at the University of Kyoto under Makoto Nagao. Prominent features of Mu were the use of case grammar analysis and dependency tree representations, and the development of a programming environment for grammar writing (GRADE). The Kyoto research has had great influence on many Japanese MT research projects and on many of the Japanese commercial systems. Since 1986, the research prototype has been converted to an operational system for use by the Japanese

Information Center for Science and Technology for the translation of abstracts. Experimental research at Saarbrücken (Germany) began in 1967, developing from the mid 1970s a multilingual transfer system SUSY (Saarbrücker Übersetzungssystem), displaying a heterogeneity of techniques: phrase structure rules, transformational rules, case grammar and valency frames, dependency grammar, the use of statistical data, etc. Its main focus was the in-depth treatment of inflected languages such as Russian and German, but other languages were also investigated, including English and French. The group also developed a generator (SEMSYN) to convert output from the Fujitsu ATLAS system in order to translate titles of Japanese scientific articles into German. One of the best known projects of the 1980s was the Eurotra project of the European Communities. Its aim was the construction of an advanced multilingual transfer system for translation among all the Community languages—on the assumption that the "direct translation" approach of the Communities' Syst ran system was inherently limited. Like GETA-Ariane and SUSY the design combined lexical, logico-syntactic and semantic information in multilevel interfaces at a high degree of abstractness. No direct use of extra-linguistic knowledge bases or of inference mechanisms was made, and no facilities for human assistance or intervention during translation processes were to be incorporated. A major defect, readily conceded by those involved, was the failure to tackle problems of the lexicon, both theoretically and practically. The project had involved many university research groups throughout the Community, but by the end of the 1980s no operational system was in prospect and the project ended, having however achieved its secondary aim of stimulating cross-national research in computational linguistics. During the latter half of the 1980s there was a general revival of interest in interlingua systems, motivated in part by contemporary research in artificial intelligence and cognitive linguistics. The DLT (Distributed Language Translation) system at the BSO software company in Utrecht (The Netherlands), under the direction of Toon Witkam, was intended as a multilingual interactive system operating over computer networks, where each terminal was to be a translating machine from and into one language only. Texts were to be transmitted between terminals in an intermediary language, a modified form of Esperanto. Analysis was restricted primarily to morphological and syntactic features (formalized in a dependency grammar). There was no semantic processing; disambiguation took place in the central interlingua component. The project made a significant effort in the construction of large lexical databases, and in its final years proposed the building of a Bilingual Knowledge Bank from a corpus of (human) translated texts (Sadler, 1989)—in this respect anticipating later example-based systems (see Section 9 below). A second interlingua project in the Netherlands, innovative in another respect, was the Rosetta project at Philips (Eindhoven) directed by Jan Landsbergen. The aim was to explore the use of Montague grammar in interlingual representations—semantic representations were derived from the syntactic structure of expressions, following the principle of compositionality; for each syntactic derivation tree there was to be a corresponding semantic derivation tree, and these semantic derivation trees were the interlingual representations. A second important feature was the exploration of the reversibility of grammars, i. e. the compilation of grammatical rules and transformations that would work in one direction for syntactic and semantic analysis of a language and in the other direction for the generation (production) of correct sentences in that language. Reversibility became a feature of many subsequent MT projects. It was in the latter half of the 1980s that Japan witnessed a substantial increase in its MT research activity. Most of the computer companies (Fujitsu, Toshiba, Hitachi, etc.) began to invest large sums into an areas which government and industry saw as fundamental to the coming "fifth generation" of the information society. The research, initially greatly influenced by the Mu project at Kyoto University, showed a wide variety of approaches. While transfer systems predominated there were also interlingua systems, e. g. the PIVOT system at NEC and the Japanese funded multilingual multinational project, launched in the mid 1980s (and continuing to the present day) with participants from China, Indonesia, Malaysia and Thailand and the involvement of major Japanese research institutes. During the 1980s many research projects were established outside North America, Western Europe, and Japan—in Korea (sometimes in collaborative projects with Japanese and American groups), in Taiwan (e. g. the ArchTran system), in mainland China at a number of institutions, and in Southeast Asia, particularly in Malaysia. And there was also an increase in activity in the Soviet Union. From 1976 most research was concentrated at the All-Union Centre for Translation in Moscow. Systems for English-Russian (AMPAR) and German-Russian translation (NERPA) were developed based on the direct approach, but there was also work under the direction of Yurij Apres'jan based on Mel'čuk's "meaning-text" model—Mel' čuk himself had been obliged to leave the Soviet Union in 1977. This led to the advanced transfer systems FRAP (for French-Russian), and ETAP (for English-Russian). Apart from this group, however, most activity in the Soviet Union focused on the production of relatively low-level operational systems, often involving the use of statistical analyses—where the influence of the "Speech Statistics" group under Raimund Piotrowski at Leningrad State University has been particularly significant for the development of many later commercial MT systems in Russia. During the 1980s, many researchers believed that the most likely means for improving MT quality would come from natural language processing research within the context of artificial intelligence (AI). Investigations of AI methods in MT began in the mid-1970s with Yorick Wilks' work on "preference semantics" and "semantic templates" (i. e. means for identifying the most common or most favoured collocations of entities, concepts, activities in particular structural relationships, such as subject-verb, verb-direct object, etc.). Further inspiration came from the research of Roger Schank at Yale University, and particularly from the development of expert systems and knowledge-based approaches to text "understanding. " A number of projects applied knowledge-based approaches—some in Japan (e. g. the LUTE project at NTT, and the ETL research for the Japanese multilingual project), others in Europe (e. g.

at Saarbrücken and Stuttgart), and many in North America. The most important group was at Carnegie-Mellon University in Pittsburgh under Jaime Carbonell and Sergei Nirenburg, which experimented with a number of knowledge-based MT systems (Goodman and Nirenburg, 1991). The basic system components were a small concept lexicon for the domain, an analysis and a generation lexicon for both languages, a syntactic parser with semantic constraints, a semantic mapper (for semantic interpretation), an interactive "augmentor," a semantic generator producing TL syntactic structures with lexical selection, and a syntactic generator for producing target sentences. The concept lexicon and the semantic information in the analysis and generation lexicons (i. e. defining semantic constraints) were language-independent but specific to the domain. The core of the system was the interlingual representation of texts, in the form of networks of propositions, derived from the processes of semantic analysis and of interactive disambiguation performed by the "augmentor" with reference to the domain knowledge of the "concept lexicon. " By the end of the 1980s, the Carnegie-Mellon team had fully elaborated its KANT prototype system and was ready to begin the development of an operational knowledge-based system for the Caterpillar Corporation—also involving a company-developed controlled language, in order to improve overall quality. Since the mid 1980s there has been a trend towards the adoption of "unification" and "constraintbased" formalisms (e. g. Lexical-Functional Grammar, Head-Driven Phrase Structure Grammar, Categorial Grammar, etc.) In place of complex multi-level representations and large sets of transformation and mapping rules there are mono-stratal representations and a restricted set of abstract rules, with conditions and constraints incorporated into specific lexical entries. It has led to a simplification of analysis, transformation and generation, and at the same time, the components of these grammars are in principle reversible. The syntactic orientation, which characterized transfer systems in the past, has been replaced by "lexicalist" approaches, with a consequential increase in the range of information attached to lexical units in the lexicon: not just morphological and grammatical data and translation equivalents, but also information on syntactic and semantic constraints and non-linguistic and conceptual information. The expansion of lexical data is seen most clearly in the lexicons of interlingua-based systems, which include large amounts of non-linguistic information. Many groups are investigating and collaborating on methods of extracting lexical information from readily available lexicographic sources, such as bilingual dictionaries intended for language learners, general monolingual dictionaries, specialized technical dictionaries, and the terminological databanks used by professional translators. A notable effort in this area was the Electronic Dictionary Research project in the late 1980s, supported by several Japanese computer manufacturing companies. This lexical activity continues to the present time. Large database and dictionary resources are available through the Linguistic Data Consortium (in the United States) and the European Language Resources Association (ELRA), an organization which has also inaugurated a major biennial series of conferences devoted to the topic—the Language Resources and Evaluation Conferences (LREC).

8   Translation Tools and the Translator's Workstation

During the 1980s, translators were becoming familiar with the benefits of computers for their work—word processing, creation of individual glossaries, facilities for on-line access and transmission of documents. They were not, however, satisfied with the quality of output of MT systems as such. It was clear already that translators wanted to have computer aids where they are in control of processes, and not to be "slaves" of automatic systems. Many tools were developed, notably for concordancing, dictionary creation, terminology management, and document transmission. In the early 1990s, however, came the most significant development, the marketing of integrated tools in the "translator's workstation" (or "workbench"). Translation workstations combine multilingual word processing, OCR facilities, terminology management software, facilities for concordancing, and in particular "translation memories." The latter facility enables translators to store original texts and their translated versions side by side, i. e. so that corresponding sentences of the source and target are aligned. The translator can thus search for phrases or even full sentences in one language in the translation memory and have displayed corresponding phrases in the other language, either exact matches or approximations. In addition, translation workstations often provide full MT programs (for translating segments, paragraphs or whole texts), to be used or adapted by translators as appropriate. The original ideas underlying these various computer-based facilities for translators go back to the early 1980s (see Hutchins, 1998). There are now many vendors of workstations. The earliest were Trados (Translator's Workbench), STAR AG (Transit), IBM (the TranslationManager, no longer marketed), the Eurolang Optimizer (also no longer available). During the 1990s and early 2000s many more appeared: Atril (Déjà Vu), SDL (the SDLX system), Xerox (XMS), Terminotix (LogiTerm), MultiCorpora (MultiTrans), Champollion (WordFast), MetaTexis, and ProMemoria. The translation workstation has revolutionised the use of computers by translators; they have now a tool where they are in full control, using any (or none) of the facilities as they choose.

9   Research Since 1989

The dominant framework of MT research until the end of the 1980s was based on essentially linguistic rules of various kinds: rules for syntactic analysis, rules for lexical transfer, rules for syntactic generation, rules for morphology, lexical rules, etc. The rule-based approach was most obvious in the transfer systems of Ariane, METAL, SUSY, Mu and Eurotra, but it was also at the basis of the various interlingua systems, both those which were essentially linguistics-oriented (DLT and Rosetta), and those which were knowledge-based (KANT). Since 1989, however, the dominance of the rule-based approach has been broken by the emergence of new methods and strategies which are now loosely called "corpus-based" methods.

9.1 Corpus-based Approaches

The most dramatic development has been the revival of the statistics-based approaches—seen as a return to the "empiricism" of the first decade (see Section 3 above) and a challenge to the previously dominant rule-based "rationalism" of the 1970s and 1980s. With the success of stochastic techniques in speech recognition, a group at IBM (Yorktown Heights, New York) began to look again at their application to MT. The distinctive feature of their Candide system was that statistical methods were used as virtually the sole means of analysis and generation; no linguistic rules were applied. The IBM research was based on the corpus of French and English texts contained in the reports of Canadian parliamentary debates (the Canadian Hansard). The essence of the method was first to align phrases, word groups and individual words of the parallel texts, and then to calculate the probabilities that any one word in a sentence of one language corresponds to a word or words in the translated sentence with which it is aligned in the other language (a "translation model"). The outputs were then checked and rearranged according to word-toward transition frequencies in the target language, derived from the corpus of bilingual texts (a "language model"). What surprised most researchers brought up in linguistics-based methods was that the results were so acceptable: almost half the phrases translated either matched exactly the translations in the corpus, or expressed the same sense in slightly different words, or offered other equally legitimate translations. Since this time statistical machine translation (SMT) has become the major focus of many research groups, based primarily on the IBM model, but with many subsequent refinements. The original emphasis on word correlations between source and target languages has been replaced by correlations between "phrases" (i. e. sequences of words, not necessarily "traditional" noun phrases, verb phrases or prepositional phrases), by the inclusion of morphological and syntactic information, and by the use of dictionary and thesaurus resources. There has been a vast increase in the sizes of aligned bilingual databases and of monolingual corpora used in "language models;" and the SMT approach is being applied to an ever widening range of language pairs. The main centres for SMT research are the universities of Aachen and Southern California, and they have been recently joined by the Google Corporation. The second major "corpus-based" approach—benefiting likewise from improved rapid access to large databanks of text corpora—was what is known as the "example-based" (or "memory-based") approach. Although first proposed in 1981 by Makoto Nagao, it was only towards the end of the 1980s that experiments began, initially in some Japanese groups and during the DLT project (see Section 7 above). The underlying hypothesis of example-based machine translation (EBMT) is that translation often involves the finding or recalling of analogous examples, i. e. how a particular expression or some similar phrase has been translated before. The approach is founded on processes of extracting and selecting equivalent phrases or word groups from a databank of parallel bilingual texts, which have been aligned either by statistical methods (similar perhaps to those used in SMT) or by more traditional rule-based methods. For calculating matches, some groups use semantic methods, e. g. a semantic network or a hierarchy (the saurus) of domain terms, other groups use statistical information about lexical frequencies in the target language. A major problem is the re-combination of selected target language examples (generally short phrases) in order to produce fluent and grammatical output. Nevertheless, the main advantage of the approach (in comparison with rule-based approaches) is that since the texts have been extracted from databanks of actual translations produced by professional translators there is an assurance that the results will be idiomatic. Unlike SMT, there is little agreement on what might be a "typical" EBMT model, and most research is devoted to example-based methods applicable in any MT system. Although SMT is now the dominant framework for MT research, it is recognised that the two corpus-based approaches are converging in many respects in so far as SMT is making more use of phrase-based alignments and of linguistic data, and EBMT is making wider use of statistical techniques. As a consequence it is becoming more difficult to isolate distinctive features of the two models. Since these corpus-based approaches to MT research rely to a great extent on the availability of bilingual and multilingual text corpora (and indeed also monolingual corpora), there has been a major focus in the last decade or more on the collection and evaluation of text databases. And since statistical corpus-based approaches have also become dominant in the wider field of computational linguistics and natural language processing, linguistic resources are now central to both MT and NLP, with the collateral consequence that the MT is now returning to the "mainstream" of computational linguistics—a position which it lost after ALPAC report (see Section 4 above), and which is reflected in the coverage of the already-mentioned Linguistic Data Consortium, the European Language Resources Association, the biennial Coling conferences, and the biennial Language Resources and Evaluation Conferences (LREC).

9.2 Rule-based Approaches

Although the main innovation since 1990 has been the growth of corpus-based approaches, rule-based research continued in both transfer and interlingua systems. A number of researchers involved in Eurotra worked within the theoretical approach developed, e. g. the CAT2 system at Saarbrücken; and one of the fruits of Eurotra research was the PaTrans transfer-based system developed in Denmark for Danish/English translation of patents. Another example of the linguistics-based transfer approach has been the LMT project, which had begun under Michael McCord in the mid-1980s, at a number of IBM research centres in Germany, Spain, Israel and the USA. Implemented in Prolog, LMT ("Logic-programming Machine Translation") has the traditional four stages: lexical analysis; syntactic analysis of source texts, producing representations of both surface and deep (logical) relations; transfer, involving both isomorphic structural transfer and restructuring transformations; and morphological generation of target texts. The interlingua approach continued at Carnegie-Mellon University (CMU). In 1992, it began a collaboration with the Caterpillar company on a large-scale knowledge-based and controlled-language system CATALYST for multilingual translation of technical manuals. Towards the end of the decade, the knowledge-based approach at CMU was combined with developments in statistical analysis of text corpora for the rapid prototyping and implementation of special-purpose systems (DIPLOMAT), e. g. for translation of Serbo-Croatian in military operations. In the mid 1990s other interlingua-based systems were started, e. g. the ULTRA system at the New Mexico State University developed by Sergei Nirenburg, the UNITRAN system based on the linguistic theory of Principles and Parameters, developed at the University of Maryland by Bonnie J. Dorr (1993), and the Pangloss project, a collaborative project involving the universities of Southern California, New Mexico State and Carnegie-Mellon. Pangloss itself was one of three MT projects supported by ARPA (Advanced Research Projects Agency), the others being the IBM statistics-based project mentioned above, and a system developed by Dragon Systems. The restitution of US government support for MT research signalled the end of the damaging impact of the ALPAC report (see Section 5 above). Finally, at the end of the 1990s, the Institute of Advanced Studies of the United Nations University (Tokyo) began its multinational interlingua based MT project—based on a "standardized" intermediary language, UNL (Universal Networking Language), for initially the six official languages of the United Nations and six other widely spoken languages (Arabic, Chinese, English, French, German, Hindi, Indonesian, Italian, Japanese, Portuguese, Russian, and Spanish)—involving groups in some 15 countries.

9.3 Speech Translation

One of the most significant developments since the late 1980s has been the growing interest in spoken language translation, presenting the formidable challenges of combining speech recognition and synthesis, interpretation of conversations and dialogues, semantic analysis, and sensitivity to social contexts and situations. British Telecom did some experiments in the late 1980s on a spoken language phrasebook type system. However, the first long-standing group was established in 1986 at ATR Interpreting Telecommunications Research Laboratories (based at Nara, near Osaka, Japan). ATR has been developing a system for telephone registrations at international conferences and for telephone booking of hotel accommodation. Slightly later came the JANUS project, under Alex Waibel at Carnegie-Mellon University, and subsequently collaborating with the University of Karlsruhe (Germany) and with ATR in a consortium C-STAR (Consortium for Speech Translation Advanced Research). The JANUS project has also focused on travel planning, but the system is designed to be readily expandable to other domains. Both the ATR and the C-STAR projects are still continuing. A third shorter-lived group was set up by SRI

(Cambridge, UK) as part of its Core Language project (Alshawi, 1992), and investigated Swedish-English translation via "quasi-logical forms." On a much larger scale has been the fourth spoken language project, Verbmobil, directed by Wolfgang Wahlster and funded from 1993 until 2000 by the German government at a number of universities. The aim of Verbmobil was the development of a transportable aid for face to face English-language commercial negotiations by Germans and Japanese who do not know English fluently. As with Eurotra (see Section 7 above), although the basic goal was not achieved the development of efficient methodologies for dialogue and speech translation and the establishment of top-class research groups in Germany in the field were considered notable successes. More recently, spoken language projects have been set up for doctor-patient communication between English, French and Japanese (MedSLT)—based on the above-mentioned SRI research in Cambridge and Sweden—and for commercial exchange and tourism between English, French, German and Italian (NESPOLE!), also involving Catalan and Spanish (in its FAME ancillary project). Simpler is conception is the "voice translator" developed for the US military (Phraselator), a kind of phrasebook with spoken output in a number of languages, Hindi, Thai, Indonesian, Pashto, Arabic, etc. Loosely related to this interest in spoken language translation are a number of systems developed for the translation of television captions (or subtitles)—from English into Spanish and Portuguese, from English into Korean, English into French and Greek, etc. The particular constraints of the task include not just dealing with spoken language (transcribed and then reduced) but also the space limitations on screens and the fact that comprehension of written texts can be slower than that of speech.

9.4 Hybrid Systems

The expansion of methodologies in the past decade and the introduction of new applications for automated translation processes have highlighted the limitations of adopting one single approach to the problems of translation. In the past, many MT projects were begun by researchers who saw MT as a testbed for a particular theory or particular method, with results that were either inconclusive or of limited application. It is now widely recognized that there can be no single method for achieving good-quality automatic translation, and that future models will be "hybrids," combining the best of rule-based, statisticsbased and example-based methods. One approach is the idea of running parallel MT systems and combining the outputs; the so-called "multi-engine" system—the group at Carnegie-Mellon University has investigated combinations of knowledge-based and example-based systems. More commonly, hybrids are currently envisaged as systems combining the statistical methods of SMT or EBMT with some linguistics-based methods (from rule-based approaches), particularly for morphological and syntactic analysis. An example is the research at Microsoft (Dolan et al., 2002). However, there are other ways to combine corpus-based and rule-based methods, as the research at the National Tsing-Hua University

(Taiwan) (Chang & Su, 1997) illustrates: lexical and syntactic rules can be statistically derived from corpus data and optimized by feedback from output.

9.5 Evaluation

MT evaluation has become a major and vigorous area of research activity. In the 1990s there were numerous workshops dedicated specifically to the problems of evaluating MT, e. g. Falkedal 1994, Vasconcellos 1994, and the workshops attached to many MT conferences. The methodologies developed by Japan Electronic Industry Development Association (JEIDA, 1992) and those designed for the evaluation of ARPA (later DARPA) supported projects were particularly influential (ARPA, 1994), and MT evaluation proved to have significant implications for evaluation in other areas of computational linguistics and other applications of natural language processing. Initially, most measures of MT quality were performed by human assessments of such factors as comprehensibility, intelligibility, fluency, accuracy and appropriateness. But such methods of evaluation are expensive in time and effort and so efforts have been made, particularly since 2000, to develop automatic (or semi-automatic) methods. One important consequence of the development of the statistics-based MT models (SMT, see Section 9.1 above) has in fact been the application of statistical analysis to the automatic evaluation of MT systems. The first metric was BLEU from the IBM group, followed later by the NIST (National Institute for Standards and Techniques). Both measures are based on the availability of human produced translations (called "reference texts"). The output from an MT system is compared with one of more "reference texts;" MT texts which are identical or very close to the "reference" in terms of word sequences score highly, MT texts which differ greatly either in individual word occurrences or in word sequences score poorly. The metrics tend to rank rule-based systems lower than SMT systems even though the former are often more acceptable to human readers. Consequently, there is no denying their value for monitoring whether a particular system (SMT or EBMT) has or has not improved over time, but there is much doubt about the general value of these metrics for comparative MT evaluations, and search for more suitable and sensitive metrics has intensified.

10 Operational and Commercial Systems Since 1990

The use of MT systems accelerated in the 1990s. The increase has been most marked in commercial agencies, government services and multinational companies, where translations are produced on a large scale, primarily of technical documentation. This was the major market for the mainframe systems: Syst ran, Logos, METAL, and ATLAS. All have installations where translations are being produced in huge volumes; already in 1995 it was estimated that over 300 million words a year were being translated by such companies. One of the fastest growing areas of use has been in the industry of software localization. Here the demand is for supporting documentation to be available in many languages at the time of the launch of new software. Translation has to be done quickly (as soon as software is to be marketed), but the documentation contains much repetition of information from one version to another. The obvious solution has been MT and, more recently, translation memories in translation workstations. A recent related development has been the localization of web pages on company sites—again, the demand is for immediate results and there is much repetition of information. Translation for website localization is growing perhaps even more rapidly than that for software products, and there are now a number of computer tools to support website developers, e. g. IBM's WebSphere. During the 1990s, the development of systems for specific subject domains and users has also expanded rapidly—often with controlled languages and based on specific sublanguages. Controlled languages involve restrictions on vocabulary (selection of authorized terms or use of unique senses) and grammar (style norms appropriate for particular document types or subject areas), in order to reduce problems of disambiguation during translation. Systems were produced by Volmac Lingware Services for a textile company, an insurance company, and for translating aircraft maintenance manuals; Cap Gemini Innovation developed a system to translate military telex messages; and in Japan, CSK developed its own system in the area of finance and economics, and NHK a system for translating Japanese news broadcasts into English. The LANT company (later Xplanation b. v.) has developed controlled language MT systems based on the old METAL system. The ESTeam company (based in Greece) concentrated initially on the "controlled language" of manufacturers' lists of equipment components, but then expanded to more text-like documents, developing customer systems for many companies (and recently including the European Union). Most successful of all controlled language systems continues to be the previously mentioned "Smart Translator" from the Smart Corporation. Since the beginning of the 1990s, many systems for personal computers have appeared. The increasing computational power and storage capacities of personal computers makes these commercial systems the equal of most mainframe systems of the 1980s and earlier—and in many cases, more powerful. However, there has not been an equivalent improvement in translation quality. Nearly all are based on older transfer-based (or even "direct translation") models; few have substantial and well-founded dictionaries; and most attempt to function as general-purpose systems, although most vendors do offer specialist dictionaries for a variety of scientific and technological subjects. In nearly all cases, the systems are sold in three basic versions: systems for large corporations ("enterprise" systems), usually running on client-server configurations, systems intended for independent translators ("professional" systems), and systems for non-translators ("home use"). Two of the earliest systems to be sold widely on personal computers were PC-Translator (from Linguistic Products, Texas) and Power Translator (from Globalink). Globalink merged first with MicroTac (producer of the Language Assistant series), and was later acquired by Lernout & Hauspie. The original mainframe systems of Syst ran are now marketed not only in versions for use by enterprises, but also on personal computers for professional translators and for home use. The two mainframe systems from the Pan American Health Organization (SPANAM and ENGSPAN) are likewise now also available as PC software for independent translators. The METAL system was adapted by GMS (now Sail Labs) as the T1 system sold by Langenscheidt (mainly as a "home" system), and as the Comprendium system sold by Sail Labs itself primarily for enterprises and professional users. IBM's LMT system was also downsized as the Personal Translator PT (sold initially by IBM and von Rheinbaben & Busch, and now by Linguatec GmbH). The Transcend system (Transparent Language) derived from the old Weidner system (via Intergraph) and is now sold by the SDL company (developers of a translator's workstation) together with Easy Translator (a "home" system) and Enterprise Translation Server (both also originally from Transparent language Inc.) From the former Soviet Union have come Stylus (later renamed ProMT) and PARS, marketing systems for Russian and English translation, and various other languages (French, German, Ukrainian, etc.) In Western Europe the ProMT systems were for a time marketed as the Reverso series by the Softissimo company. Other PC-based systems from Europe include: PeTra for translating between Italian and English; the Winger system for Danish-English, French-English and English-Spanish (now no longer available); and TranSmart, the commercial version of the Kielikone system (originally developed for Nokia), for Finnish-English translation. Numerous systems for Japanese and English have continued to appear from Japanese companies; in fact, there has been an almost bewildering history of systems appearing one year, selling successfully for a brief period and then disappearing. Among the longest lasting have been products from Fujitsu (ATLAS), Hitachi (HICATS), Toshiba (initially known as ASTRANSAC), NEC (Crossroad, previously Pivot), Cross Language (formerly Nova: the Transer series), and Sharp (Power E/J, now Honyaku Kore-Ippon). But there are also good-quality US products, the LogoVista system from the Language Engineering Corporation (later absorbed by LogoMedia), the Tsunami and Typhoon systems from Neocor Technologies (also bought by Lernout & Hauspie, and now no longer available), as well as systems from WebSphere and Syst ran. Systems for English to and from Korean came only late in the 1990s (e. g. Syst ran, LogoMedia, TranSphere, etc.). There are now a number of systems for Arabic (notably the Sakhr, Cimos and AppTek systems), and a growing number of systems for Chinese (e. g. Transtar, LogoMedia, Systran, TranSphere)—with the spotlight from US government agencies there is now much encouragement for the developers of other systems for these two languages based on more recent research. Systems for language pairs other than English as either source or target have been less prominent. However, most of the American and European companies mentioned above do offer systems for such pairs as French-German, Italian-Spanish, Portuguese-Spanish, and there are a number of system offering Japanese-Chinese, Japanese-Korean, etc. Despite all this commercial activity there are many other languages which have been poorly served. There is still a lack of commercial systems for most languages of Africa, India, and South East Asia—and those that do exist are not easily accessible. The most recent development has been the incorporation in a number of PC systems of means for speech input of sentences (or texts) for translation, and for spoken output of the results. (These are not, of course, true speech translation systems which, as indicated in 9.3 above, have yet to reach operational implementation.). Undoubtedly based on the improvement reliability and ease of use of speech recognition systems, these products began appearing during the last years of the 1990s. One of the most recent examples is ViaVoice Translator from IBM, combining its LMT automatic translation system and its successful ViaVoice dictation system. The examples above of company acquisitions, the demise of old systems and the regular appearance of new systems and new versions of old systems illustrate that commercial change is as much part of MT history as research developments, and that failure is now as much a feature of MT as of any other business. The first instance was the Weidner/Bravice collapse (see Section 6 above). Many small companies have come and gone during the last two decades. But there have also been examples of apparently thriving companies which have not been able to maintain their position in the market. The Logos Corporation rivalled Syst ran Inc. with its "enterprise" systems in the 1980s, but was sold in the late 1990s to another company (globalwords AG), and has now gone completely. The Comprendium system offered good quality systems for large corporations during the 1990s (based in part on the METAL system), but it too has gone. A well-publicised (even notorious) example is the story of Lernout & Hauspie. This firm made its reputation in speech recognition products. In early 1998 it decided to expand into the MT area and purchased a number of companies (Globalink, Neocor, AppTek, Sail Labs, AILogic), with the aim of integrating systems for a wide range of languages as one product (iTranslator). At the same time it acquired interests in translation services (Mendez SA) and received financial support from government sources in Belgium. But the company overstretched itself, got into financial difficulties (including some alleged irregularities) and went into liquidation in late 2001. Some of the companies it had acquired managed to re-establish themselves (e.g. AppTek and, briefly, Sail Labs) but in other cases the market has lost competent and previously well-received systems (e.g. those of Globalink and Neocor). This fragility in the MT market may explain why it has not been until after 2000 that commercial systems based on SMT methods have appeared. In contrast to the well-established rule-based methods, statistical approaches have perhaps been seen as too risky or perhaps to be premature, as SMT research has been active for little more than a decade. Nevertheless, there are now SMT systems on the market (from Language Weaver), significantly for language pairs which attract government support (Arabic-English, Chinese-English, Hindi-English, Somali-English) and which have represented particularly difficult challenges for rule-based approaches. Recently, Language Weaver has been joined by Google, whose vast text resources are particularly appropriate for SMT approaches—again, the language pairs currently on test are Arabic-English, Chinese-English, Japanese-English, etc.

11　MT on the Internet

Since the mid-1990s, the Internet has exerted a powerful influence on MT development. First, there has been the appearance MT software products specifically for translating Web pages and electronic mail messages offline (i. e. on receipt or before sending). Japanese companies led the way, but they were followed quickly elsewhere. Second, beginning in the mid 1990s, many MT vendors have been providing Internet-based online translation services for on-demand translation. The pioneer was the service offered in France by Syst ran on the Minitel network during the 1980s, but the idea was not taken up more widely until CompuServe introduced a trial service based on the Transcend system in 1995. Shortly afterwards, the now best known service Babelfish appeared on the AltaVista site offering versions of Syst ran to translate French, German and Spanish into and from English (and later many other language pairs). It was followed by numerous other online services (most of them free of charge), e. g. Softissimo with online versions of its Reverso systems, LogoMedia with online versions of LogoVista and PARS. Some services offer post-editing by human translators (revisers), at extra cost, but in most cases the results are presented untouched in any way. Many of them can be accessed through "MT portals," i. e. independent services offering a range of translation systems from one or more system vendors. The translation quality of online MT services is often poor, inevitably given the colloquial nature of many source texts, but these services are undoubtedly filling a significant (and apparently widely acceptable) demand for immediate rough translations into users' own languages for information purposes—the function offered by earlier mainframe systems in the 1960s, often ignored then and in later years. Despite their widespread use and the obvious impact they have on the public "image" of MT—often negative—online MT services have been largely neglected by most MT researchers (Gaspari, 2004). A particular challenge for MT is the use of online systems for translation into languages which users do not know well. Much of the language used on the Internet is colloquial, incoherent "ungrammatical," full of acronyms and abbreviations, allusions, puns, jokes, etc.—this is particularly true for electronic mail and the language of chatrooms and mobile telephones. These types of language use differ greatly from the language of scientific and technical texts for which MT systems have been developed. However, recently a UK company Translation has released a system for online translation of e-mails (as well as web pages) between English, French, German, Italian and Spanish. The demand must be substantial, and no doubt more systems will come in the near future. The Internet has also encouraged somewhat less scrupulous companies to offer online versions of electronic dictionaries (or phrase books) as "translation systems." Anyone using such products for translating full sentences (and text) is bound to get unsatisfactory results—although if users do not know anything of the target languages they will be unaware of the extent of the incomprehensibility of the results. Such systems are undoubtedly damaging for the perception of MT as a whole; as damaging as the failure of some vendors and some service providers to stress that their fully automatic systems (whether online or not) produce only rough versions that should always be used with caution.

12　Conclusion

It is now clear that different types of MT systems are required to meet widely differing translation needs. Those identified so far include the traditional MT systems for large organizations, usually within a restricted domain; the translation tools and workstations (with MT modules as options) designed for professional translators; the cheap PC systems for occasional translations; the use of systems to obtain rough gists for the purposes of surveillance or information gathering; the use of MT for translating electronic mail and Web pages; systems for monolinguals to translate standard messages into unknown languages; systems for speech translation in restricted domains. Some of these needs are being met or are the subject of active research, but there are many other possibilities, in particular combining MT with other applications of language technology (information retrieval, information extraction, summarization, etc.). As MT systems of many varieties become more widely known and used, the range of possible translation needs and of possible types of MT systems will become more apparent and will stimulate research and development in directions not yet envisioned.

选文二　计算机辅助翻译漫谈

章宜华

导　言

作者章宜华为广东外语外贸大学词典学研究中心主任、教授、国家重点文科基地"语言学及应用语言研究中心"重大课题的主持人,其研究方向为应用语言学、词典学和翻译学。

本文发表在《上海科技翻译》2002 年第 1 期。

本文提到目前市场上出现了各种各样的电子词典和翻译软件,据称能解决外语阅读、写作和翻译的各种问题。实际上,许多词典或软件并不像宣传的那样神奇,其质量参差不齐。若选择使用得当,对翻译等工作会有一些帮助,否则也会带来麻烦。本文指出:认识和了解各类电子词典以及翻译软件的结构、功能和用途,有利于使用者正确选择和有效利用这些工具。

随着计算机应用的普及,电子词典和翻译软件的增多,越来越多的人会借助计算机进行写作或翻译。人们在文字工作中遇到不明白的事和词慢慢习惯于求助电子词典或网络词典。那么,现在市场上众多的电子词典到底有什么样的功能? 它们对翻译或外语写作能提供什么样的帮助? 选择什么样的电子词典或翻译软件对自己的工作更有利呢? 本文拟从应用的角度来探讨电子词典和翻译软件的功能及其特征。

一、电子词典的类别

电子词典按其承载介质或功能的不同可分为芯片词典、单机光盘词典、计算机网络词典和翻译软件四种。

1. 目前,我国市场上的芯片词典主要有快译通、好易通、商务通、名人、锦囊、佳能等系列,近来又出现了学习型的"雷登智典"。"快译通"和"好易通"还有芯片插卡系列:一个芯片词典可配十多种单本词典或专业词典的插卡,如商务、机械、电子、经贸、建筑等。这种词典的特点是携带和查阅都十分方便,但提供的词汇信息有限。

2. 单机光盘词典的版本很多。欧美国家从 60 年代开始发展电子词典,80 年代末期到 90 年代初期开始出现电子词典出版的高峰。国内外常见的有《汉英机器词典》、《牛津英语词典》、《美国传统有声词典》、《朗文交互式英语词典》、《韦氏新世界词典 Power CD 版》、《译典灵人声语言英汉辞典》、《21 世纪多媒体英汉辞典》、《莱思康综合有声词典》、《超级莱思康》、《远东英汉百科大辞典》、《远东图解英汉词典》、《牛津高级双解英汉词典》等。这些词典大多是海外或我国港台出版的,技术比较成熟,界面设置比较复杂,查检入口多,词典知识信息丰富、编排合理。我国内地虽然在上世纪 70 年代就有人尝试开发电子词典,但直到 90 年代才面世。近几年来出版势头似乎很猛,市场上能见到的也不下几十种,具有代表性的大概有《即时通》、《译林在线英汉词典》、《朗道电脑词典》、《汉神电子词典》、《惠丰有声英汉双向词典》、《华建双向电子词典》、《新世纪汉英科技大词典》、《地球村》、《东方快车》、《金山词霸》、《着迷词王》等等。

3. 网络词典往往是依附在一个网站上,供人们随时调用查阅。典型的网络词典就是一个网站,它由几十、上百,甚至是上千个不同语种、不同专业的词典构成。网络词典的网站很多,有关词典的网页就更多。比如,进入 www. go. com 网站 InfoSeek 主页后,查询框内仅输入"dictionary"一词进行查询,所得到的匹配总数就有 268 120 个之多! (这是 2000 年 10 月中旬的查询结果。到 2001 年 1 月中旬再以同样方法查询,得到的匹配总数增加了一倍多,已达到 630 037 个。)(参见图 1)匹配数目显示在该网页左上角"WEB SEARCH RESULTS 的下方,然后又依次给出每个词典网页所包含的信息量和网址。如果你的网络出口够宽的话,只需用鼠标点击一下词典名称,即可进入该词典进行查询。

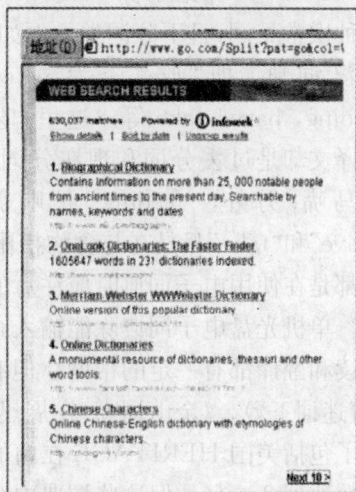

图 1 利用广域网查找网络词典的结果

目前,世界上有 4 亿多人上网,我国的上网人数由 1999 年的 400 万人猛增到今年的 2 000 多万;因此,在网上求助网络词典的人也越来越多。通过上网实践,我们认为以下几个网站对提供网络词典资源信息很有帮助:1) Onelook Dictionaries—The Faster Finder;2) yourDictionary. com;3) www. 1000Dictionaries. com;4) Linguist List。这些网站都是综合性的,你可以得到你想要的东西。

4. 翻译软件也分单机版和网络版两种,按翻译的方法有单词、句子和语篇翻译三种。单机版有《华建机器翻译系统》、《东方快车》、《东方网译》、《IBM 翻译家》、《即时通汉化专家》、《译王》、《超强英汉翻译词典》、《译林专家翻译》等。网络版翻译软件很多,比较好用的如:巴比伦语言翻译软件(www. babylon. com),金山词霸在线翻译(www. iciba. net),看世界(www. readworld. com),中国翻译网(www. chinatranslate. net),北京翻译网(www. transnetwork. com. cn)等。

二、电子词典的主要性能

1. 芯片词典 这种词典便于携带,词典功能齐全、查检方便。以快译通 EB8000 为例,除英汉/汉英双向词典外,还附有语音规则解析、万用词汇、复习测验、全能记事、旅游指南、健康指南等几十种功能。此外还配置十几种专业词典的插卡,译者可以根据需要随时更换。不足的是这类词典知识信息不全,释义单一,甚至谬误的地方也很多。为避免这些自编词典的问题,"好易通"与出版社合作推出了"牛津系列"芯片词典。

2. 单机光盘词典 国内版本的词典信息量大,往往都有十几万,乃至几十万词条,有些在一个版本中包含了十多部大型词典。但其界面单一、释义不详、体例呆板、检索入口少,没有充分发挥多媒体的效果。在《新世纪汉英大词典》(见图 2)中,"控制"词条的英文对等词没有常用的 dominant,govern,command 等,却给了像 curb 和 cybernation 这种次常见词,且不分词类。再如《译林在线英汉词典》把"吃"译为 eaten,eating,feeding,have,take 等。这里"吃"是动词,而译文却是过去分词和现在分词等,驴唇不对马嘴;另外,"feeding"是喂养的意思,

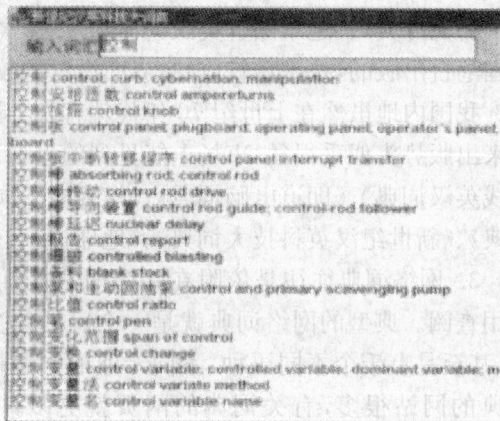

图 2 《新世纪汉英大词典》的释义实列

"have"和"take"只是在与食物搭配才有"吃"义,把这些词都列在"吃"的条目下实在不妥。这些都是在使用电子词典时应注意的问题。

单机光盘电子词典除能输入查询外,一般都有屏幕取词、即时翻译的功能,这对外文写作、阅读和翻译都有一定的帮助。但有些词典的解释很简单(如《金山词霸》),有些则较详尽(如《着迷词王》)。《金山词霸》发展迅速,总销量达 500 万套。《金山词霸. net2001》功能强大,集合了包括美国 HERITAGE 在内的 11 本权威词典、32 本专业词典,专业词条多达 60 多万,总字数达到 2.6 亿。但这些词典内容还是按文本的方式、流水账似地排列,内容也是机械重复;一个词目的释义若几十本词典加起来可多达 20～30 页,且检索入口单一,显示内容庞杂,查检十分不便;没有体现电子词典及多媒体的功能。下面从 ask 的释义可见一斑。

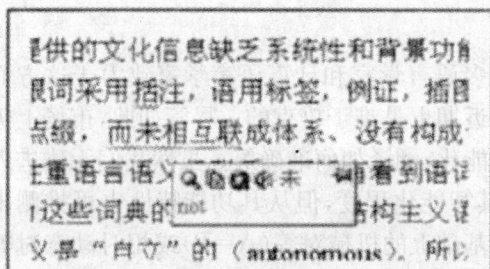

图 3 《金山词霸》屏幕取词实例

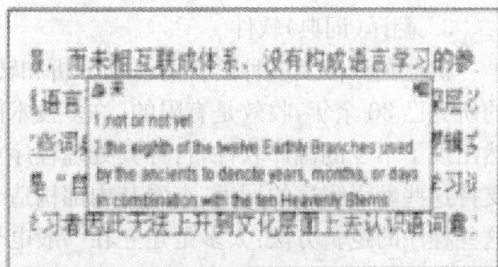

图 4 《着迷词王》屏幕取词实例

朗文英汉综合电脑词典：ask 问，询问
＝Amplitude Shift Keying，振幅移位键控法
＝Analog Select Keyboard，模拟选择键盘
＝Applications Software Kit（DEC），成套应用软件（数据设备公司）

《英汉心理学词典》：ask 询问[1]

《英汉化学大词典》：ask *vt.* 问，询问，要求

《英汉计算机大词典》：ask *vt.* 问（询问，要求[2]）

《新英汉法学大词典》：ask *v.* 请求，要求，问

《英汉能源大词典》：ask *n.* 自动定位

《英汉水利大词典》：ask *n.* 问，要求，请求

《英汉石油大词典》：ask *vt.* 问，询问，要求

《英汉中医大词典》：ask *n.* 要求，请求，问

《英汉地质大词典》：ask *n.* 自动定位

《英汉航空大词典》：ask *n.* 部，询问

在"朗文英汉综合电脑词典"中，把"ask"单词和"ask"的缩写形式混在一起，令人疑惑（缩写词一般应由大写字母组成）。此外，各词典对"ask"的词类的标注不一，解释也不尽相同，会给读者造成混乱。还有把"ask"解释为"部"、"自动定位"等，更是让人费解。相比之下，《着迷词王》的释义合理一些。它的检索入口比较多，便于读者取舍和查找。现仍以 ask 为例（见图5）。首先，在查询窗口下有一个浏览窗，显示出以 ask 为中心词的动词短语和与 ask 形态相近的词。在查询显示窗

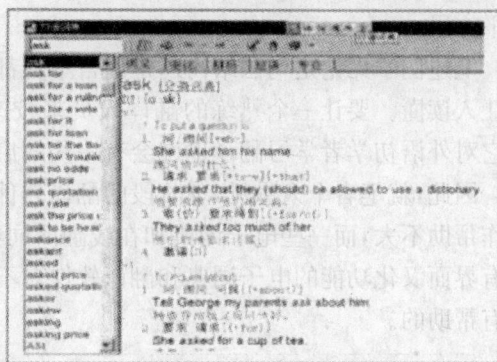

图 5 《着迷词王》的界面结构

内，设置了一排控制按钮，可以把词条的内容分类显示，如词义的解释、词的形态变化、同义词辨析、以词目词为中心的各种短语和专业词义等。这样，读者可根据自己的需要，快速选择查询显示内容。《译典通》电子词典也采用了分类显示的方式。

此外，《着迷词王》还有"写作助理"的功能。当你用英文写作时，会有一浮动窗口提供许多参考搭配短语，帮助你选词造句；当你不会写某一单词时，只需打出其中文义，词典就会显示出

英文对等词来。

3. 翻译(词典)软件

机器翻译涉及多种语言的自动分析和转换,许多语言学家和计算语言学家致力于这方面的研究已 30 余年,收效是有限的,许多技术问题在近期也是难于攻克的。尽管如此,市场上仍然出现了不少的翻译软件,自称其处理程序如何智能化、翻译如何准确等。虽然我们无法进入支持这些翻译程序的词库,查看其内部构造、鉴定其智能化程度,但从其功能特性也可推测出这些程序的逻辑方法:大多是建立在一般电子词典基础上的机械对等(A=B)或相对动态对等(A=或 B,或 C 或 D),这种对等不可能有多高的智能化程度;然而,翻译确实是一种智能化程度很高的思维过程,单靠机械的查询、找等值词的方法是难以解决问题的。从下面的翻译实例中可见一斑。

1) 通译 5.0

原文:War has escaped the battlefield and now can, with modern guidance systems on missiles, touch virtually every square yard of the earth's surface.

译文:既然战争已经逃脱战场和能,同在导弹上的现代人引导系统,触觉地球的表面的实际上每个的平方的码。

2) 朗道 5.0

原文:War has escaped the battlefield and now can, with modern guidance systems on missiles, touch virtually every square yard of the earth's surface.

译文:战争逃离了 battlefield,现在能,与在导弹上的现代化的指导系统,地球的表面几乎触每个方形的院子。

3) IBM 翻译家

原文:War has escaped the battlefield and now can, with modern guidance system s on m issiles, touch virtually every square yard of the earth's surface.

译文:战争已逃过战场和现在罐在导弹上现代制导系统地碰实际上每一个 earth's 表面的平方码。

上述例子无论是句法结构还是语言本身都不复杂,但中外三个翻译软件的翻译结果都难以让人读懂。要让一个熟练的翻译人员来校改或加工这种译文,还不如自己重新翻译省心;但它对外语初学者学习翻译也许会有一些的启发。

因此,就笔者个人愚见,现阶段的翻译软件(起码是涉及汉语的软件),对专业翻译人员的工作帮助不大,而一些电子词典和在线翻译词典对翻译或外语写作则是十分有益的。此外,一些有界面汉化功能的电子词典和翻译软件对不懂外语,或外语能力较差的读者上网漫游也是很有帮助的。

选文三 Cross-lingual Ontology Mapping—An Investigation of the Impact of Machine Translation

Bo Fu Rob Brennan Declan O'sullivan

导 言

本文提出本体是知识管理的核心,它不仅是利用英语记录的信息,还是利用许多其他自然语言记录的信息。为了发现知识、共享和反复使用这些语言本体,我们有必要支持机器翻译中的本体映射,尽管这面临许多自然语言障碍。本文涉及机器翻译工具和单语本体匹配技术在跨语言本体映射场景中的使用,并检测了通用使用方法的稳受性。文中特别讨论了从案例研究中收集的实验结果以及它们独立的本体映射现象。本文基于上述研究的结果,讨论了通用使用方法的局限性。有证据表明,在跨语本体映射中使用单语匹配技术时,对本体的概念标签进行妥当翻译是至关重要的。文章最后建议建立跨语性语义取向本体映射框架并进行了讨论。

1 Introduction

The evolution of the World Wide Web in recent years has brought innovation in technology that encourages information sharing and user collaboration as seen in popular applications during the Web 2.0 era. The future of the Web—the Semantic Web will "allow for integration of data-oriented applications as well as document-oriented applications." In the process of achieving this goal ontologies have become a core technology for representing structured knowledge as well as an instrument to enhance the quality of information retrieval and machine translation. Benjamins et al. identify multi-linguality as one of the six challenges for the Semantic Web, and propose solutions at the ontology level, annotation level and the interface level. At the ontology level, support should be provided for ontology engineers to create knowledge representations in diverse native natural languages. At the annotation level, tools should be developed to aid the users in the annotation of ontologies regardless of the natural languages used in the given ontologies. Finally, at the interface level, users should be able to access information in natural languages of their choice. This paper aims to tackle challenges at the annotation level, in particular, it investigates issues involved in cross-lingual ontology mapping and aims to provide the necessary support for ontology mapping in cross-lingual environments. Cross-lingual ontology mapping (CLOM) refers to the process of establishing relationships among ontological resources from two or more independent ontologies where each ontology is labeled in a different natural language. The term "multilingual ontologies" in this paper refers to independent ontologies o and o' where the labels in o are written in a natural language which is different from that of the labels in o. It must not be confused with representing concepts in one ontology using multilingual labels. In addition, this paper focuses on multilingual ontologies that have not been linguistically enriched, and are specified according to the Resource Description Framework (RDF) schema. Furthermore, this paper presents a first step towards achieving CLOM in generic knowledge domains, which can be improved upon to accommodate more sophisticated CLOM mapping strategies among ontologies in more refined, particular knowledge domains.

A generic approach is investigated in this paper, CLOM is achieved by first translating the labels of a source ontology into the target natural language using freely available machine translation (MT) tools, then applying monolingual ontology matching techniques to the translated source ontology and the target ontology in order to establish matching relationships. In particular, the impact of MT tools is investigated and it is shown with evidence that when using the generic approach in CLOM, the quality of matching results is dependent upon the quality of ontology label translations. Based on this conclusion, a semantic-oriented cross-lingual ontology mapping (SOCOM) framework is proposed which is specifically designed to map multilingual ontologies and to reduce noise introduced by MT tools. The remainder of this paper is organised as follows, Section 2 discusses related work. Section 3 details the application of the aforementioned generic approach in CLOM experiments which involve mappings of ontologies labeled in Chinese and English. Findings and conclusions from these experiments are presented and discussed in Section 4. The proposed SOCOM framework and its current development are discussed in Section 5.

2 Related Work

Considered as light weight ontologies, thesauri often contain large collections of associated words. According to the Global Word Net Association2, (at the time of this publication) there are over forty WordNet3-like thesauri in the world covering nearly 50 different natural languages, and counting. Natural languages used include Arabic (used in ArabicWordNet4); Bulgarian (used in BulNet5); Chinese (used in HowNet6); Dutch, French, German, Italian, Spanish (used in EuroWordNet7); Irish (used in LSG8) and many others. To make use of such enormous knowledge bases, research has been conducted in the field of thesaurus merging. This is explored when Carpuat et al merged thesauri that were written in English and Chinese into one bilingual thesaurus in order to minimize repetitive work while building ontologies containing multilingual resources. A language-independent, corpus based approach was employed to merge Word Net and HowNet by aligning synsets from the former and definitions of the latter. Similar research was conducted in to match

Dutch thesauri to Word Net by using a bilingual dictionary, and concluded a methodology for vocabulary alignment of thesauri written in different natural languages. Automatic bilingual thesaurus construction with an English-Japanese dictionary is presented in, where hierarchies of words can be generated based on related words' co-occurrence frequencies. Multi-linguality is not only found in thesauri but also evident in RDF/OWL ontologies. For instance, the Onto Select Ontology Library reports that more than 25% (at the time of this publication) of its indexed 1,530 ontologies are labeled in natural languages other than English. To enable knowledge discovery, sharing and reuse, ontology matching must be able to operate across natural language barriers. Although there is already a well-established field of research in monolingual ontology matching tools and techniques, as ontology mapping can no longer be limited to monolingual environments, tools and techniques must be developed to assist mappings in cross-lingual scenarios.

One approach of facilitating knowledge sharing among diverse natural languages builds on the notion of enriching ontologies with linguistic resources. A framework is proposed in which aims to support the linguistic enrichment process of ontological concepts during ontology development. A tool, Onto Ling is developed as a plug-in for the ontology editor Protege to realize such a process as discussed in. Similar research aiming to provide multilingual information to ontologies is discussed in, where a linguistic information repository is proposed to link ontological concepts with lexical resources. Such enrichment of ontologies provide knowledge engineers with rich linguistic data and can be used in CLOM, however, in order for computer-based applications to make use of these data, standardization of the enrichment is required. As such requirement is currently not included in the OWL 2 specification, it would be difficult to make use of the vast number of monolingual ontology matching techniques that already exist.

Similar to linguistically enriching ontologies, translating the natural language content in ontologies is another approach to enable knowledge sharing and reuse. The translation of the multilingual AGROVOC thesaurus is discussed in, which involves a large amount of manual work and proves to be time and human resource consuming. An ontology label translation tool, Label Translator is demonstrated in. It is designed to provide end-users with ranked translation suggestions for ontology labels. The motivation of its design is to ensure that information represented in an ontology using one particular natural language could still achieve the same level of knowledge expressivity if translated into another natural language. Users must select labels to be translated one at a time, Label Translator then returns the selected label's suggested translations in one of the three target natural languages, English, Spanish and German. It can be used to provide assistance in the linguistic enrichment process of ontologies as discussed in. Label Translator is designed to assist the human to perform semi-automatic ontology label translations and linguistic enrichments, it is not concerned with generations of machine-readable ontologies in the target natural language so that matching tools can manipulate. In contrast to Label Translator, the ontology rendering process presented in this paper differs in its input, output and aim. Firstly, the input of our ontology rendering process is ontologies and not ontology labels. Secondly, the output of this rendering process is machine-readable formally defined ontologies that can be manipulated by computer-based systems such as monolingual matching tools. Lastly, such an ontology rendering design aims to facilitate CLOM, it is designed to assist further machine processing whereas the Label Translator tool aims to assist humans.

An example of CLOM scenario is illustrated by the Ontology Alignment Evaluation Initiative(OAEI) contest in 2008, where a test case requiring the mapping of web directories written in English and Japanese was defined. Among thirteen participants, only four took part in this test scenario with results submitted from just one contestant. Zhang et al. used a dictionary to translate Japanese words into English (it is unclear whether this translation process is manual or automated) before carrying out the matching process using RiMOM. The generic approach presented in this paper is based on Zhang et al. 's method, instead of using a dictionary, freely available MT tools are used. Montiel-Ponsoda & Peters classify three levels to localizing multilingual ontologies, at the terminological layer, at the conceptual layer and at the pragmatic layer. The translation process presented in the generic CLOM approach concerns translations at the terminological layer, i. e. the terms used to define classes and properties are translated into the target natural language. Pazienza & Stellato propose a linguistically motivated approach to ontology mapping in. The approach urges the usage of linguistically enriched expressions when building ontologies, and envisions systems that can automatically discover the embedded linguistic evidence and establish alignments that support users to generate sound ontology mapping relationships. However, as mentioned previously, the multilingual linguistically enriched ontologies demanded by this approach are hard to come by when such specifications are not currently included in the OWL 2 standardization effort. Trojahn et al. propose a multilingual ontology mapping framework in, which consists of smart agents that are responsible for ontology translation and capable of negotiating mapping results. For each ontology label, the translation agent looks up a dictionary and returns a collection of results in the target natural language. The ontology labels are then represented with a group of the returned translation results. Once source and target ontologies are in the same natural language, they are passed to the mapping process which consists of three types of mapping agents, lexical, semantic and structural. These agents each conclude a set of mapping results with an extended value-based argumentation algorithm. Finally, globally accepted results are generated as the final set of mappings. Such an approach is based on the assumption that correct mapping results are and always will be generated by various matching techniques regardless of the algorithms used. However, as stated by Shvaiko & Euzenat, "despite the many component matching solutions that have been developed so far, there is no integrated solution that is a clear success," therefore, looking for globally accepted results may limit the scope of correct mapping relationship discovery. In contrast, the proposed SOCOM framework in this paper aims to maximize the performance of individual monolingual ontology matching algorithms in CLOM by providing them with ontology renditions that contain appropriate label translations.

3　A Generic Approach to Cross-lingual Ontology Mapping

A generic approach to achieve CLOM is presented in this section, as shown in Figure 1. Given two ontologies representing knowledge in different natural languages, the ontology rendering process first creates a translated source ontology which is an equivalent of the original source ontology, only labeled in the target natural language. Then monolingual matching tools are applied to generate matching results between the translated source ontology and the target ontology. An integration of the generic approach is discussed in Section 3.1. To evaluate the soundness of this approach, two experiments involving the Semantic Web for Research Communities (SWRC) ontology and the ISWC ontology were designed to examine the impact of MT tools in the process of ontology rendering (discussed in Section 3.2), also the quality of matching results generated using such an approach (discussed in Section 3.3).

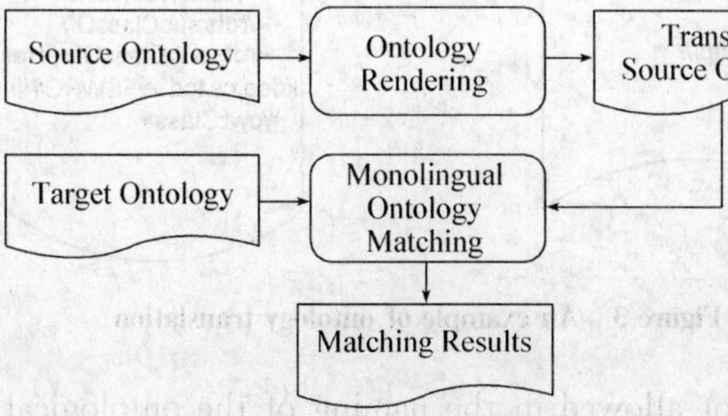

Figure 1　A generic cross-lingual ontology mapping approach

3.1　Integration of the Generic Approach

The ontology rendering process shown in Figure 1 is achieved with a Java application—OntLocalizer, which generates machine-readable, formally defined ontologies in the target natural language by translating labels of the given ontology's concepts using MT tools, assigning them with new namespaces and structuring these resources—now labeled in the target natural language—using the Jena Framework in the exact same way as the original ontology. Figure 2 shows the components of the OntLocalizer tool. Labels of ontology resources are extracted first by the Jena Framework, which are then passed onto the MT tools to generate translations in the target natural language. Given the original ontology's structure, these translated labels can be structured accordingly to create the translated source ontology. The integrated MT tools include the Google Translate API and the SDL FreeTranslation online translator.

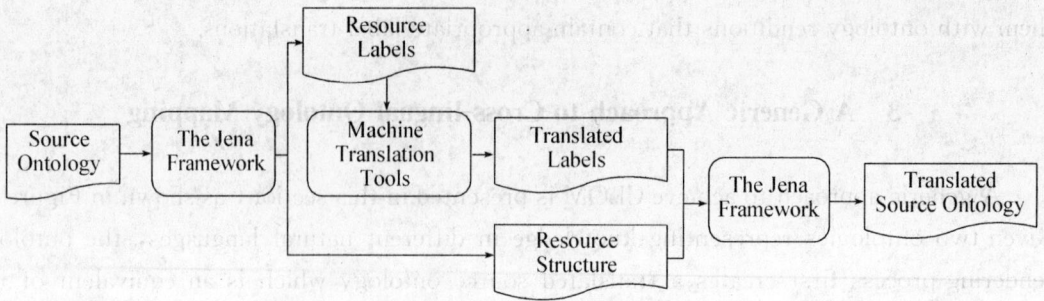

Figure 2　OntLocalizer component overview

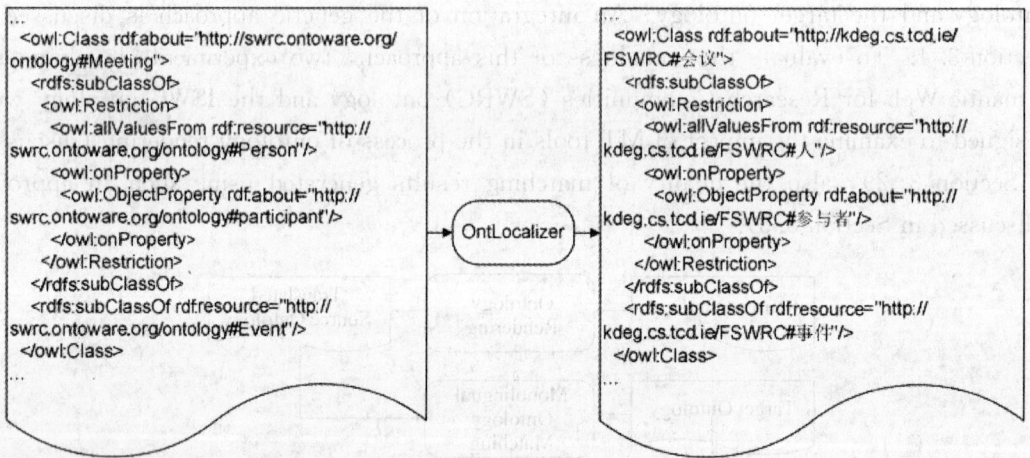

Figure 3　An example of ontology translation

As white spaces are not allowed in the naming of the ontological resources, ontology labels often contain phrases that are made up by two or more words. An example of such labels can be a class named "AssistantProfessor", where the white space between two words has been removed and capital letters are used to indicate the beginning of another word. Another example can be an object property labeled as "is_about," where the white space between two words has been replaced by an underscore. As these labels cannot be translated by the integrated MT tools, the OntLocalizer tool thus breaks up such labels to sequences of constituent words based on the composing pattern, before sending them to the MT tools. In the aforementioned examples, "AssistantProfessor" is transformed to "Assistant Professor," and "is_about" is transformed to "is about." Now both in their natural language forms, phrases "Assistant Professor" and "is about" are passed to the MT tools to generate results in the target natural language. Such a procedure is not required when translating labels written in languages such as Chinese, Japanese etc. , as phrases written in these languages naturally do not contain white spaces between words and can be processed by the integrated MT tools. Finally, when structuring the translated labels, white spaces are removed to create well-formed resource URIs. Translation collisions can happen when a translator returns the same result for several resources in an ontology. For instance, in the SWRC ontology, using the GoogleTranslate API (version 0. 4), the class "Conference" and the class "Meeting" are both translated into "zjIX" (meaning "meeting" in Chinese). To differentiate the two, the OntLocalizer tool checks whether such a resource already exists in the translated source ontology. If so, a number is assigned to the resource label which is under consideration. In the aforementioned example, "Conference" becomes and "Meeting" becomes "z? 0" in the translated ontology. As the integrated MT tools only return one translation result for each intake phrase, it is therefore unnecessary to disambiguate the returned translations in the experiment. A part of the SWRC ontology and its translation in Chinese using the OntLocalizer tool is shown in Figure 3.

Once the source ontology is labeled in the target natural language, monolingual ontology matching techniques can be used to generate matching results. Currently, this is achieved by the Alignment API (version 2. 5).

3. 2 Experiment One Design and Integration

Experiment one is designed to examine the impact of MT tools in the process of ontology rendition, specifically, the quality of machine translated resource labels. In this experiment, labels in the SWRC ontology are translated from English to Chinese through two media, the OntLocalizer tool and a human domain expert—being the lead author. Three translated versions of the SWRC ontology are then created, the GSWRC ontology when using the GoogleTranslate API, the FSWRC ontology when using the FreeTranslation online translator, and the HSWRC ontology which is created manually using the Protege ontology editor. Each translated version has the original structure of the SWRC ontology with new namespaces assigned to labels in the target natural language. The SWRC ontology is mapped to itself to generate a gold standard of the matching results as M(1), which consists of pairs of matched ontology resources in English. M(A) which contains results of matched resources in Chinese, is then created when the HSWRC ontology is mapped to itself. If exactly the same pairs of resources are matched in M(A) as those found in M(1), then M(A) can be considered as the gold standard in Chinese. The GSWRC ontology and the FSWRC ontology are then each mapped to the HSWRC ontology to create the mappings M(B) and M(C), both containing matched resources in Chinese. Finally, M(B) and M(C) are compared against M(A). This process is shown in Figure 4. Eight matching

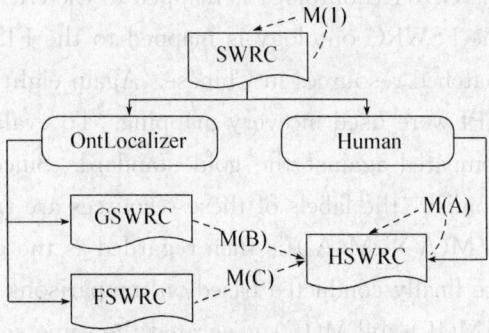

Figure 4　Experiment One overview

algorithms supported by the Alignment API are used in this experiment.

The hypothesis of this experimental setup is to verify whether the label translation procedure using MT tools would impact on the quality of translated ontologies. If M(B) and M(C) show the same set of results as suggested by M(A), it would mean that MT tools are able to perform like humans and a generic approach using them in CLOM is ideal. If M(B) and M(C) proves to be poorly generated, it would mean that the ontology rendition process is flawed.

3. 3　Experiment Two Design and Integration

The second experiment is designed to further investigate the impact of MT tools in CLOM by evaluating the quality of matching results generated using the generic approach. An overview of the experimental steps is shown in Figure 5. The English SWRC ontology and the English ISWC ontology are both translated by OntLocalizer to create ontologies labeled in Chinese. The GSWRC ontology and the GISWC ontology are created when using the GoogleTranslate API, and the FSWRC ontology and the FISWC ontology are generated when using the SDL FreeTranslation online translator integrated in OntLocalizer.

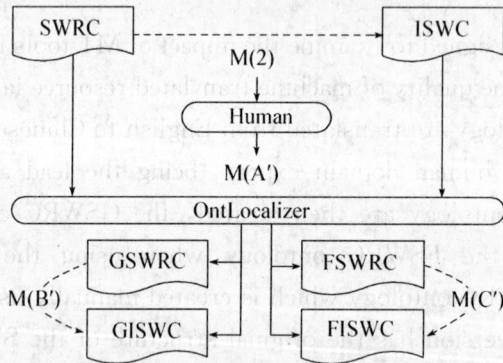

Figure 5　Experiment Two overview

The original SWRC ontology is mapped to the original ISWC ontology to generate M(2) as the gold standard which contains matched resources in English. M(B') is generated when the GSWRC ontology is mapped to the GISWC ontology, similarly M(C') is generated when the FSWRC ontology is mapped to the FISWC ontology. Both M(B') and M(C') contain matched resources in Chinese. Again eight matching algorithms provided by the Alignment API were used in every mapping. To evaluate the quality of M(B') and M(C'), they are compared against the gold standard. Since M(2) contains matched resources written in English, the labels of these resources are translated manually to Chinese by the lead author as M(A'). M(A') is then regarded as the gold standard. Evaluations of M(B') and M(C') are finally conducted based on comparisons to M(A'). The hypothesis of this experiment is, if M(B') and M(C') generated the same sets of matching results as M(A'), it would mean that the generic approach is satisfactory to achieve CLOM. If M(B'), M(C') fail to conclude the same results as found in the gold standard, it would mean that the generic approach would be error-prone when applied to CLOM scenarios.

Precision, recall, fallout and f-measure scores were calculated in both experiments for all the matching algorithms used. Precision measures the correctness of a set of results. Recall measures the completeness of the number of correct results. Fallout measures the number of incorrect matching results based on the gold standard. Finally, f-measure can be considered as a determination for the overall quality of a set of results. If the established gold standard has R number of results and a matching algorithm finds X number of results, among which N number of them are correct according to the gold standard, then precision = N/X; recall = N/R; fallout = (X-N)/X; and f-measure = 2/(1/precision + 1/recall). All scores range between 0 and 1, with 1 being very good and 0 being very poor. An example can be that low fallout score accompanied by high precision and recall scores denote superior matching results.

4　Findings and Conclusions

Findings and conclusions from the two experiments are presented in this section. The results of experiment one is presented and discussed in Section 4.1. Section 4.2 shows the results from the second experiment. Finally, data analysis is given in Section 4.3.

4.1　Experiment One Findings

Regardless of the matching algorithms used from the Alignment API, the exact same sets of matching results generated in M(1) were found in M(A). Thus, it is with confidence that M(A) can be considered as the gold standard in Chinese. Figure 6 shows an overview of the evaluation results of experiment one. As M(A) equals M(1), its precision, recall and f-measure scores are 1.00 and with 0.00 fallout. The results generated by the eight matching algorithms from the Alignment API are evaluated based on comparisons made to M(A). In M(B) and M(C), a pair of matched resources is considered correct when it is found in the gold standard regardless of its confidence level. Such an evaluation approach aims to measure the maximum precision, recall and f-measure scores that can be achieved in the generated results.

As Figure 6 shows, in experiment one, NameEqAlignment and StringDistAlignment algorithm had the highest precision score, however, their low recall scores resulted just above the average f-measure scores. Structure-based matching algorithms had lower recall scores and higher fallout scores comparing to lexicon-based matching algorithms. For each set of results evaluated, the precision score is always higher than its other scores, which suggests that a considerable number of correct matching results is found, however, they are always incomplete. On average, regardless of the matching algorithms used, f-measure scores are almost always less than 0.50, showing that none of the matching algorithms could meet the standard which is set by the gold standard. Moreover, M(B)'s average f-measure is 0.4272, whereas M(C)'s average f-measure is 0.3992, which suggests that GoogleTranslate

API performed slightly better than SDL FreeTranslation online translator in this experiment. Nevertheless, it must be noted that neither of the MT tools was able to generate a translated ontology which, when mapped to itself, could produce a same set of results that are determined by the gold standard. This finding suggests that MT tools had a negative impact on the quality of ontology rendition output.

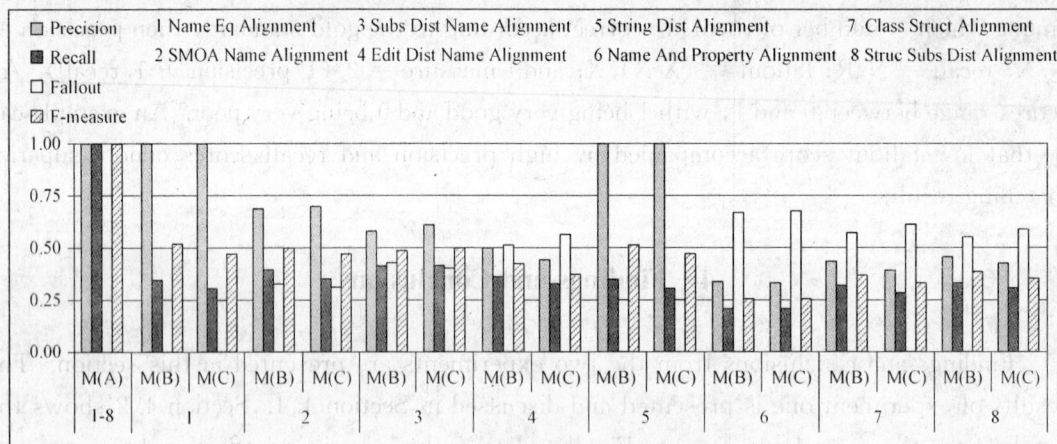

Figure 6   Experiment One results

4.2   Experiment Two Findings

To further validate this finding, the same evaluation approach is used in the second experiment, where a pair of matched result is considered correct as long as it is found in the gold standard, regardless of its confidence level. A series of gold standards were generated for each of the eight matching algorithms in M(2)—written in English, and later manually translated as M(A')—written in Chinese. The evaluation of the results found in M(B') and M(C') is shown in Figure 7.

The String Dist Alignment matching algorithm had the highest precision and recall scores in this experiment, thus yielding the highest f-measure score in M(B') and M(C'). Similar to the results found in experiment one, structure-based matching algorithms had lower recall scores comparing to lexicon-based matching algorithms. In experiment two, fallout scores for all the matching algorithms are higher than that of experiment one's, which suggests that the matching procedure was further complicated by the translated ontologies. Also, f-measure scores indicate that structure-based matching algorithms were unable to perform as well as lexicon-based matching algorithms. The average f-measure in M(B') was 0.2927 and 0.3054 in M(C'), which suggests that the Free Translation online translator had a slightly better performance than the Google Translate API in this experiment. Nevertheless, from an ontology matching point of view, such low f-measure scores would mean that when used in CLOM, the generic approach would only yield less than fifty percent of the correct matching results. The findings from experiment two show that it is difficult for matching algorithms to maintain high-quality performance when labels have been translated in isolation using MT tools, and the generic approach in CLOM can only yield poor matching results.

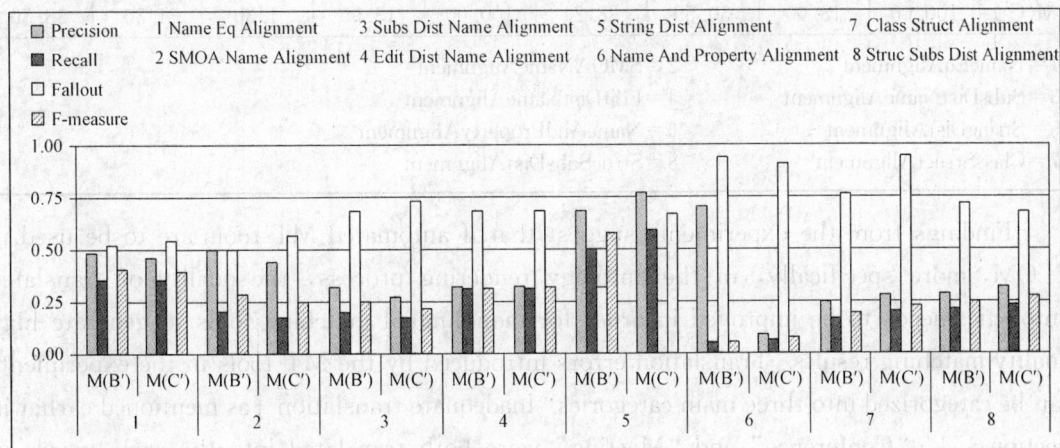

Figure 7　Experiment Two results

4.3　Result Analysis

So far, the evaluation results that are shown in the previous sections disregard confidence levels. When these confidence levels are taken into account, it is shown that there is a drop in the number of matching results generated with absolute confidence. Table 1 gives an overview of the percentages of matching results with 1.00 confidence levels. In both experiments, all pairs of matched resources generated by the Name Eq Alignment algorithm and the Name And Property Alignment algorithm have 1.00 confidence levels. This is not the case for other algorithms however, where more than half of the results with absolute confidence was not found. For example, every matched pairs of resources by the Edit Dist Name Alignment algorithm from the gold standard in experiment one had 1.00 confidence levels. This was not achieved in M(B) or M(C), where the former contained 47.31% of confident results and only 41.94% for the latter. Averagely, the gold standard in experiment one established a 96.25% of confident results, whereas only 49.53% were found in M(B) and 49.37% in M(C). A similar finding can be concluded for experiment two based on the statistics shown in Table 1.

Table 1　Matched pairs of results with 1.00 confidence levels (%)

	1	2	3	4	5	6	7	8	Avg.
M(A)	100.00	77.34	100.00	100.00	100.00	92.68	100.00	100.00	96.25
M(B)	100.00	33.78	47.83	47.31	100.00	37.25	15.05	15.05	49.53
M(C)	100.00	35.38	44.32	41.94	100.00	34.62	19.35	19.35	49.37

(Continued)

	1	2	3	4	5	6	7	8	Avg.
M(A′)	100.00	30.89	26.56	48.57	100.00	30.36	0.00	10.94	43.42
M(B′)	100.00	16.00	30.86	36.23	100.00	11.63	3.23	3.23	37.65
M(C′)	100.00	18.00	30.59	38.24	100.00	13.95	1.30	4.30	38.30

1=NameEqAlignment	2=SMOANameAlignment
3=SubsDistNameAlignment	4=EditDistNameAlignment
5=StringDistAlignment	6=NameAndPropertyAlignment
7=ClassStructAlignment	8=StrucSubsDistAlignment

Findings from the experiments suggest that if automated MT tools are to be used in CLOM, more specifically, in the ontology rendering process, the quality of translated ontologies needs to be improved in order for monolingual matching tools to generate high quality matching results. Translation errors introduced by the MT tools in the experiments can be categorized into three main categories. Inadequate translation—as mentioned earlier in Section 3. 1, "Conference" and "Meeting" were both translated into the same words in Chinese. However, since conference is a specified type of meeting, the translated term was not precise enough to capture the intended concept presented in the original ontology. This can be improved if given the context of a resource label to be translated, i. e. the context of a resource can be indicated by a collection of associated property labels, super/sub-class labels. Synonymic translation—where the translation result of a label is correct, however it is different with the one that was used by the target ontology. This can be accounted by algorithms that take structural approaches when establishing matching results, however, it can be very difficult for lexicon-based algorithms to associate them. This can be improved if several candidates are provided in the translation process, and the selection of these candidates gives priority to labels which are used by the target ontology. Incorrect translation—where the translation of a term is simply wrong, yielding poor matching results. Similar to inadequate translations, this can be improved if the context of an ontology resource is known to the translation process.

To overcome these challenges and maximize the performance of monolingual matching tools in CLOM, appropriate translations of ontology labels must be achieved. A Semantic-Oriented Cross-lingual Ontology Mapping (SOCOM) framework designed to achieve this is proposed and discussed in the next section.

5　The SOCOM Framework and On-going Research

The semantic-oriented cross-lingual ontology mapping (SOCOM) framework is presented and discussed in this section. The SOCOM framework illustrates a process that is designed specifically to achieve CLOM, it has an extensible architecture that aims to accommodate easy integrations of off-the-shelf software components. To address challenges identified in the experiments and reduce noise introduced by the MT tools, the selection of appropriate translated labels is under the influence of labels used in the target ontology. The SOCOM framework divides the mapping task into three phases—an ontology rendering phase, an ontology matching phase and a matching audit phase. The first phase of the SOCOM framework is concerned with the rendition of an ontology labeled in the target natural language, particularly, appropriate translations of its labels. The second phase concerns the generation of matching results in a monolingual environment. Finally, the third phase of the framework aids ontology engineers in the process of establishing accurate and confident mapping results. Ontology matching is the identification of candidate matches between ontologies, whereas ontology mapping is the establishment of the actual correspondence between ontology resources based on candidate matches, this distinction is reflected in the SOCOM framework. Figure 8 shows a process diagram of the proposed framework.

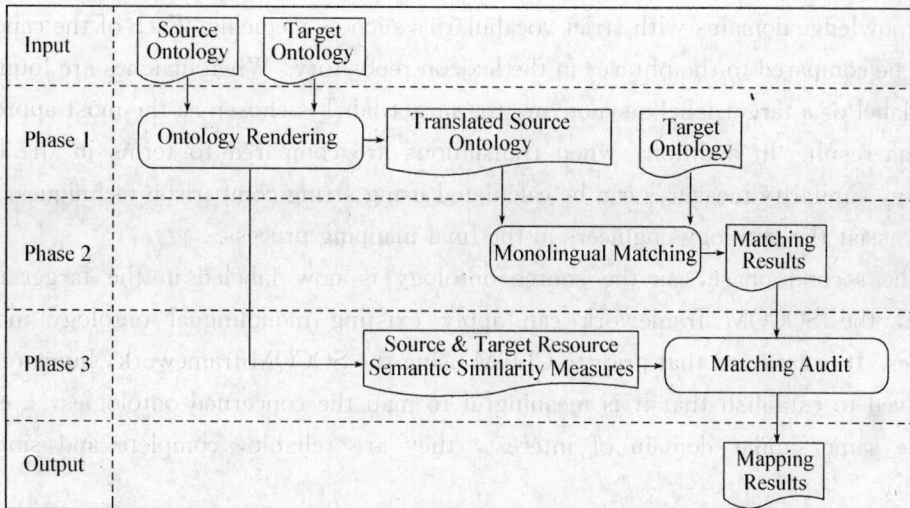

Figure 8　The SOCOM framework process diagram

In phase one, the SOCOM framework searches for the most appropriate translation results for ontology labels in the target natural language. To achieve this, the selection of translation candidates is defined by the context a resource that is used in, and influenced by the labels that appear in the target ontology. As experimental results show that translating ontology labels in isolation leads to poorly translated ontologies which then yields low-quality matching results, thus, label translations should be conducted within context. As the meaning of a word vary depending on the context it is used in, it is therefore important to capture what a word/phrase signifies as accurately as possible in the target natural language. For instance, the sentence "there is a shift in the tone of today's news broadcasts" and the sentence "research shows that an inevitable side effect of night shifts is weight gain" both use the word "shift." However, in the first sentence, it is used to express a change, whereas in the second sentence, it refers to a period of work. In the SOCOM framework, to capture the meaning of a word/phrase in the ontology rendering phase, the context is characterized by the surrounding ontology concepts. As the purpose of translating the source ontology is that it can be mapped to the target ontology for generations of high quality mapping results (i. e. the translation of the source ontology concepts is within a specific context), the identification of the most appropriate translation results is aided by the labels that appear in the target ontology. Instead of blindly accepting translation results that are returned from a MT tool, for each resource label, a group of translation results are collected and treated as translation candidates. A translation repository containing source labels and their translation candidates can be created given a source ontology. On the other hand, a lexicon repository can be constructed based on the labels presented in a given target ontology. For each target label, a collection of synonyms can be assembled to maximize knowledge representation with various words and phrases other than those that originally appeared in the target ontology. This can be achieved by querying dictionaries, WordNet, etc. , or accessing refined lexicon bases for precise knowledge domains with strict vocabularies such as medicine. Each of the candidates can then be compared to the phrases in the lexicon repository. When matches are found with a target label or a target label's synonym, the target label is chosen as the most appropriate translation result. In addition, when translations are compared to terms in the lexicon repository, similarity measures can be calculated using string comparison techniques, which can then assist the ontology engineers in the final mapping process.

In the second phase, as the source ontology is now labeled in the target natural language, the SOCOM framework can apply existing monolingual ontology matching techniques. It is assumed that prior to CLOM using the SOCOM framework, human experts are involved to establish that it is meaningful to map the concerned ontologies, i. e. they cover the same/similar domain of interest, they are reliable, complete and similar in granularity.

Lastly, in phase three, the matching audit procedure aids ontology engineers in the process of generating the final mapping results. This procedure makes use of the semantic similarity measures that have been concluded in phase one, and displays these findings to the mapping expert providing background information to assist the final mapping. Phase one and two of the SOCOM framework have been integrated, phase three of the proposed framework is currently under development. In the near future, evaluation results of the SOCOM framework and suitability of matching algorithms will become available.

The SOCOM framework is semantic-oriented for two reasons. Firstly, during the ontology rendition phase, the context of an ontological resource is studied in order to determine the most appropriate translation result for its label. This context is defined by the semantics an ontology resource represents, which can be obtained by studying its surrounding concepts, i. e. super/sub-classes and property restrictions. Secondly, the mapping process makes uses of the similarity measures established in the ontology rendition phase in order to generate mapping results. The similarity measures are determined based on the semantics from each pair of ontology resources. An experimental version of the SOCOM framework has been integrated and is currently being evaluated.

Acknowledgement This research is partially supported by the Science FoundationIreland (Grant 07/CE/I1142) as part of the Centre for Next Generation Localization at Trinity College Dublin.

选文四　Ambiguity Reduction for Machine Translation： Human-Computer Collaboration

Marcus Sammer　Kobi Reiter　Stephen Soderland
Katrin Kirchhoff　Oren Etzioni

导　言

本文的五位作者分别来自于美国华盛顿大学的图林研究中心和电子工程系。

当统计性机器翻译(SMT)被操作的数量有限时或被操作的目标应用程序来自不同的域或类型文本时,它的精确性就会降低。然而,机器翻译的跨域应用是来自现实世界的真实任务。文章显示:通过使用一个被控制的语言界面,统计性机器翻译可减少译文词汇的歧义,在跨域应用中提高译文的质量。本文涉及的 CL-MT 系统为单语翻译使用者在处理输入性文本时提供了文本实词的词义选择,该系统调整了其统计性机器翻译(SMT)系统的底层短语界面,极大促进了翻译的质量。

1　Introduction

Statistical Machine Translation (SMT) is sensitive to the genre and domain of the training data that is used to train the translation model. The best performance is typically achieved when the texts to be translated are drawn from the same population of texts as the training data. Unfortunately, many real world applications are for target domains or genres for which readily available parallel training corpora do not exist. Mismatches between training and test data result in deteriorated performance.

One source of translation errors is lexical ambiguity in the input text, which may result in lexical errors in the translation. State-of-the-art SMT systems use a phrase-based approach to translation (Och et al., 1999; Koehn et al., 2003; Tillmann, 2003; Zens and

Ney, 2004), where translations are obtained by concatenating translations of chunks of words (as opposed to single words) in the input sentence. When training and test data are matched, a phrase-based SMT system can implicitly perform word-sense disambiguation (WSD) and choose the correct translation because the local context of the input word is taken into consideration. In fact, additional explicit WSD has not been shown to be helpful (e. g. Carpuat and Wu, 2005). Under mismatched conditions, however, lexical ambiguity may become a much more significant source of errors because word senses occurring in the test data may never have occurred in similar context in the training data.

In this paper we present CL-MT, a hybrid controlled language-statistical MT system where cross-domain SMT is improved by human guided WSD. This study is part of a larger research effort on utilizing machine translation technology to enhance human-human communication. A typical application scenario is on-the-fly automatic e-mail translation, where two users that do not share the same language are engaged in an e-mail exchange, and an automatic MT system is used to translate typed input while the e-mail message is being composed. Such applications need to handle data from a wide range of domains, and we cannot assume that in-domain data will be available in all cases. Thus, cross-domain application of MT components will be the norm. On the other hand, we can assume that a monolingual human user will not only be available but will also be motivated to assist in improving the automatic translation.

Our proposed CL-MT system generates a controlled language (CL) lexicon where each entry is for a distinct word sense of a term in the source language, and entries are associated with one or more possible translations of that word sense into the target language. CL-MT has a graphical user interface that presents a monolingual speaker with alternate senses for words in an input sentence. Scores in an SMT phrase table are then boosted for translations associated with the selected word senses and scores are decreased for those word senses that were not selected.

One key feature of CL-MT is that it is both domain-independent and genre-independent. This distinguishes it from other controlled language systems that operate in a narrow domain, typically on technical specifications (Nyberg and Mitamura, 1996; Fuchs et al., 1998; Schwitter, 2002). In a narrow domain, a CL lexicon can assume that nearly all words have a single word sense—open domain CL must handle ambiguity in nearly all words.

In this paper we demonstrate that:

(a) Human lexical disambiguation can improve translation accuracy in an SMT system.

(b) A CL lexicon can be created automatically that gives useful, intuitive word sense choices to a monolingual user.

(c) This can be done in a domain-independent, genre-independent manner.

Our empirical evaluation of cross-domain translation from Spanish to English shows that using the CL-MT system yielded a statistically significant improvement in translation adequacy. Adequacy improved for 33.8% of the sentences over a baseline SMT system, while it was reduced for 12. 1% of the sentences. Section 2 describes creating the CL lexicon. This is followed by an explanation of how the user's preferences are incorporated into the underlying SMT system in Section 3. Empirical results are presented in Section 4. The paper finishes with Sections 5 and 6 discussing related research and future work respectively.

2　Creating a CL Lexicon

The first step in adapting CL-MT to a new language pair is to create a CL lexicon. This serves as the basis for the alternate word senses that CL-MT's interface presents to the user. The desired characteristics of a CL lexicon are the following:

- Each entry is a distinct word sense for a word in the source language (L1).

- Each entry is associated with one or more translations of that word into the target language (L2).

- Each entry has a short, intuitive gloss or set of cue words that enables a user to select the entry with the intended word sense.

We experimented with various methods of creating such a CL lexicon. The method that gave best results requires a bilingual dictionary and a machine readable dictionary (MRD) for L2 that provides glosses that are then translated into L1. We continue to work on methods that do not require an MRD, and thus scale to a larger set of languages.

2. 1　Lexicon with MRD Glosses

CL-MT begins by looking up each source word in a bilingual dictionary. We used a dictionary from UltraLingua for our Spanish-English experiments (http://www. ultralingua. net). The system then looks up each translation t in an MRD for language L2. This gives one or more distinct word senses for t, each with a gloss written by a lexicographer. The system translates these glosses from L2 into L1.

Each entry in the CL lexicon is for a distinct word sense, where each entry has a meaningful gloss in L1 (which, of course, may be poorly translated). The algorithm for creating a CL lexicon with MRD glosses is shown in Figure 1. We used WordNet 2. 0 (wordnet. princeton. edu/w3wn. html) as our MRD for experiments in which the target language was English. WordNet has good coverage, although only for nouns, verbs, adjectives, and adverbs. It has a separate entry for each word sense, with the more common senses listed first, and rare usages towards the end of the list. We created CL lexicon entries for the first k WordNet entries for each part of speech for each translation t, with k set to 3 if there were more than 5 word senses and k set to 2 otherwise. WordNet glosses are often extremely long, so we truncated the gloss at the first semicolon.

```
For each term s in the source language {
  Look up s in a bilingual dictionary
  For each translation t of s {
    Look up t in a target language MRD
    For each of the first k glosses g of t {
      Translate g into the source language
      Create a CL lexicon entry with s, g, t
      Merge entries with matching s, g
    }
  }
}
```

Figure 1　Algorithm to create a CL lexicon using a bilingual dictionary and a machine readable dictionary for the target language

An example entry for a CL lexicon for Spanish to English is shown in Figure 10. This is for the Spanish word "dia," which has three translations according to the bilingual dictionary: "day," "daylight," and "daytime."

The first two entries ("time for Earth to make a complete rotation on its axis" and "some point or period in time") have the English translation "day." The next entry ("light during the daytime") is for the English "daylight." The last entry ("the time after sunrise and before sunset … ") has three translations, "day," "daylight" and "daytime."

We used Google Translator to translate glosses into L1 (http://www.google.com/language_tools). This could also have been done with the SMT system that was trained for our CL-MT system.

Since the L2 MRD gives all senses for a word in L2, some of the senses may be inappropriate for their corresponding L1 translations. The CL lexicon will contain these inappropriate word senses, but because of the clear glosses provided by the MRD, a monolingual source language speaker is easily able to disregard the incorrect senses.

Día	Categoría Léxica	Sentido
☑	N	hora para la tierra de hacer una rotación completa en su eje
☑	N	cierto punto o período en tiempo
☐	N	luz durante el día
☐	N	el tiempo después de la salida del sol y antes de la puesta del sol mientras que es exterior ligero
◯	PN	Nombre Propio [sin traducción]
◯	???	Ninguna de estos / No sé

Figure 2　CL lexicon entry for the Spanish word "dia"

The first two entries correspond to the English translation "day," the third entry corresponds to "daylight," and the fourth entry corresponds to "day," "daylight" or "daytime."

Because Word Net only contains entries for nouns, verbs, adjectives, and adverbs, we also provided hand written entries for a few dozen pronouns that specify gender and number. The CL interface also gives the user two additional options for each word: to leave it untranslated as a proper noun, or to leave the word unannotated.

The current implementation of CL-MT includes only single words in its lexicon. This is problematic for phrases whose meanings are not compositional. In such cases, none of the word senses of the individual words in a phrase are appropriate. Future work is needed to extend the CL lexicon to handle multi-word phrases.

2.2 Lexicon with Back Translation Cues

We also experimented with a lexicon building method that does not assume an MRD for the target language. CL-MT begins by looking up each source words in a bilingual dictionary, and creating a separate entry for each translation t of s. In place of a gloss, each entry has two sets of cue words: (a) back translations of t into the source language and (b) context words of s that are translations of context words of t.

Figure 3 shows the Spanish source word "dia," where the first entry corresponds to the

Día		
	Categoría Léxica	Sentido
☑	N	día; fecha hora; próximo; siguiente; después
☐	N	día; luz del día hora; durante; luz; lámpara; encender
☐	N	día platicar
○	PN	Nombre Propio [sin traducción]
○	???	Ninguna de estos / No sé

Figure 3   An entry for the Spanish word "dia" using back translations and context words as cues

English translation "day" which has back translations into Spanish of "dia" and "fecha" (date). The second entry corresponds to "daylight," and has back translations of "dia" and "luz del dia" (light of day). The third entry corresponds to "daytime," which has no back translations other than the original word "dia."

We had mixed results with this method for many of the entries in the CL lexicon. For some words and some lexicon entries, either the back translations or the context cues provided clear information to the user. For other entries, this was not the case.

Another difficulty with the back translation method is that the L2 translations themselves are often ambiguous. This leads to lists of back translations that include extraneous meanings along with the intended word sense. As opposed to the MRD method, we have no simple method for separating out the inappropriate senses so they can be disregarded without also throwing out the correct sense. For example, the Spanish word "enlace" has the intended meaning of "link" to a Web page. Unfortunately, the back translations of link include "campo de golf" (golf course), which may lead a user to reject this as the wrong sense of the word "enlace."

3 Influencing the SMT Decoding

The final step is to use the output of the CL interface to bias the SMT system to favor translations that reflect the word sense intended by the user.

3. 1 Baseline SMT System

For our experiments we used a phrase-based SMT system (Kirchhoff and Yang, 2005) based on the public-domain decoder, Pharaoh (Koehn, 2004), that utilizes a log-linear combination of feature scores. The translation model was trained on 15M words of parallel Spanish-English European Parliament proceedings. The model combines two lexical and two phrasal translation scores (one for each translation direction), a phrase length penalty, a word transition penalty, a distortion score and a language model score. Score combination weights were optimized on a development set from the parliamentary proceedings domain. The language model was trained on the English side of the training corpus. Thus, none of the system components were tuned to the new domain (news text). The system has a state-of-the-art performance (around 31% BLEU score) on a standard benchmark task for the Europarl corpus (Koehn and Monz, 2005). For the present experiments, single-pass monotone decoding was used. This disallows word reordering and ignores potential benefits from more advances models (i. e. higher-order language models) but results in faster decoding, which may be crucial for real-world applications. On the out-of-domain test set used in the experiments described below, the system obtained a BLEU score of 21. 7%, with a 95% confidence interval from 18. 7% to 24. 7% on a test set of 198 sentences.

3. 2 Using Output of the CL Interface

CL-MT uses the output of the CL interface to modify the feature scores of entries in a temporary copy of the SMT phrase table. For these experiments we use the baseline system and rerun decoding with the modified phrase table. Additional parameter settings determine the degree to which the baseline feature scores are altered, depending on whether a phrase table entry includes translations from a CL lexicon that are preferred or disfavored.

If the user has annotated a word with one or more preferred senses, the preferred translations are those translations associated with at least one of the selected word senses. The disfavored translations are those where none of the word senses associated with the translation were selected by the user. The translations associated with each word sense in the lexicons are in root form，so CL-MT adds morphological variants to the lists of preferred and disfavored translations.

CL-MT creates a temporary copy of the SMT phrase table for each message. Since multiple occurrences of the same word in a message may be annotated by the user with different word senses，a unique identifier is appended to each token in the message. Thus a word that is repeated in a message has distinct entries in the temporary phrase table for each appearance of the word in the message. For each source language phrase sp in the message，CL-MT looks up the target language translations of sp in the original phrase table. For each of these translations tp，CL-MT copies the sp-tp translation pair along with its corresponding feature scores into the temporary phrase table.

CL-MT modifies the temporary phrase table to ensure that words annotated as proper nouns are not translated. For each source language phrase sp in the temporary phrase table that contains a token w annotated by the user as a proper noun，if a translation tp of sp in the temporary phrase table does not contain w，then this sp-tp translation pair is removed from the temporary phrase table. This blocks CL-MT from translating a proper noun as something other than the source language word itself. Annotating proper nouns is necessary because our system uses an all lowercase word representation and does not contain a named entity recognition component and many components of proper names in our input language （Spanish） may be common nouns or adjectives as well.

Next，the counts shown in Figure 12 are used to modify scores in the temporary phrase table for each translation pair sp-tp. CL-MT counts the number of words in sp that have preferred translations，disfavored translations，or neither preferred nor disfavored translations in tp. This is done for for each lexicon L：the pronoun lexicon and the MRD generated lexicon.

---

pw_L = the number of tokens w in sp for which w is in L and a preferred translation of w appears in tp.

dw_L = the number of tokens w in sp for which w is in L and no preferred translation of w appears in tp，but a disfavored translation of w does appera in tp.

nw_L = the number of tokens w in sp for which w is in L and w is annotated with one or more preferred word senses，but none of the preferred and none of the disfavored translations of w appear in tp.

Figure 4　Counts of preferred and disfavored translations used in modifying phrase table entries

For each lexicon L，the lexical and phrasal translation scores in the temporary phrase table are then multiplied by the parameter αL for each word of sp in lexicon L that has a preferred translation in tp，by βL for each word that has a disfavored translation in tp，and by γL for each word that has neither a preferred nor a disfavored translation in tp. More precisely，CL-MT multiplies the translation scores by

$$\prod_L \alpha_L^{pw_L} \beta_L^{dw_L} \gamma_L^{nw_L}$$

where L varies over the two lexicons，αL，βL，and γL are parameters，and pwL，dwL，and

nwL are the counts described in Figure 4.

CL-MT also handles the cases where a translation from the CL lexicon is missing from the SMT phrase table. If no preferred translation of a token w is found in the phrase table, CL-MT presents the preferred translations of w to the decoder using the XML markup facility provided by the decoder for introducing external knowledge. The decoder is allowed to bypass these suggested translations which are weighted with another parameter δ.

We tuned these parameters using a separate development set of 50 sentences. During tuning, performance was measured using the BLEU score. In addition to δ, and αL, βL, and γL for the two lexicons, CL-MT has on/off parameters for processing the proper noun annotations, for presenting translation options to the decoder using the XML markup, and for allowing the decoder to bypass these translations. Our baseline system is equivalent to setting αL, βL, and γL to 1.0, turning off the processing of proper noun annotations and turning off the presentation of translation options to the decoder using the XML markup.

4 Experimental Results

We conducted experiments to test CL-MT on Spanish sentences that were found on Web pages where there was an English translation suitable for a reference translation. These were primarily news stories, but also included press releases.

This gave us only a single reference translation, which means that in order to improve standard metrics for translation accuracy such as BLEU and position-independent word error rate (PER), precisely the same words as in the reference translations would need to be hypothesized. In order to better assess the effect of acceptable but non-matching translation hypotheses we supplemented the automatic scores with human evaluations of the adequacy and fluency of CL-MT translations compared to translations by the baseline SMT system.

We presented human evaluators with the reference translation and two output translations: from the baseline SMT system without disambiguation, and from CL-MT. Pairs of outputs were presented in random order without indication of the system identity. The evaluators judged which output had better adequacy or if they were equal; and also judged which output had better fluency or if they were equal.

We had three fluent speakers of Spanish use CL-MT's interface to annotate a test set of 198 sentences randomly selected from our collection of Spanish news stories and press releases. Our most prolific annotator did the entire test set and the other annotators each did a portion of the same test set to help us assess inter-annotator agreement.

4.1 Parameter Tuning

We set parameters empirically for our CL-MT system as described in Section 3.2, and found values shown in Figure 5 to optimize for BLEU score. The system is not sensitive to small changes in these parameter settings: even doubling a setting or reducing a setting by half makes only a small difference in performance.

From WordNet lexicon	multiply by
α_{WN} (preferred translations)	5.0
β_{WN} (disfavored translations)	0.8
γ_{WN} (neither)	1.0
From Pronoun lexicon	multiply by
α_{PR} (*preferred translations*)	12.0
β_{PR} (*disfavored translations*)	0.5
γ_{PR} (*neither*)	1.0
Enforce exact translation of proper nouns	
Add missing translations to phrase table with weight	0.2

Figure 5   Parameter settings for CL-MT with MRD gloss

Note: These settings strongly increase scores for preferred translations, and decrease scores for disfavored translations.

The results of these parameter settings confirm that the output of our CL interface is indeed giving useful information to an SMT system. The optimal settings are to give a strong preference to translations preferred by the user, and to avoid disfavored translations. There is also a boost in performance by knowing when not to translate a proper name. It also helps to add translations that are missing from the phrase table with a small score, although too high a score hurts performance.

4.2   Automatic Evaluation

Figure 6 compares CL-MT with the baseline system. We found that CL-MT raises BLEU score and lowers PER, both indicating better translation accuracy. However, our sample was not large enough for this improvement to be statistically significant. Our CL interface is inherently labor intensive and precludes generating the large test sets common for fully automated methods.

Figure 6 also shows performance of an "oracle" system. One of the authors of this paper used a version of CL-MT that displayed the English translation for each entry, and selected only entries with translations that matched words in the reference translation. If no entry matched the reference translation, the source word was left unannotated. This gives an upper bound for automatic scoring for CL-MT. We found that 3% of the content words had no CL lexicon entry due to gaps in the dictionary and that 6.6% of the entries had no word sense that was synonymous with the target translation. This was often because the meaning of words changed when used in a phrase.

Method	BLEU	PER
CL-MT	22.6	44.3
Baseline	21.7	45.0
Oracle CL-Mt	27.6	39.6

Figure 6   CL-MT with MRD glosses improves both BLEU score and PER

Note: An Oracle CL-MT with perfect annotation shows the ceiling on performance gain.

4.3   Human Evaluation

We also evaluated CL-MT with human judgments, particularly since we had only one reference translation. Human evaluation takes into account synonyms and can distinguish adequacy (correct content) from fluency (correct grammar and style). Figure 7 shows two examples from the interface used for manual evaluation. At the top is the reference translation, followed by the output of CL-MT and the baseline system in random order. The evaluator does not know which method was used or who did the annotation. We used two evaluators, who had 76% agreement, and then reconciled the differences.

| \multicolumn{3}{l|}{Grace period voters may not cancel their votes and then vote on election day at the polling stations.} |

Fluency	Adequacy	Sentence Text
✓	✓	Voters of the grace period cannot cancel their vote and vote on the day of choice in the casillas.
✓	☐	Voters of the grace period cannot cancel their vote and vote on the agenda choice in the casillas.

When his father, lorenzo rubio, upset that his son had been suspended from school for two days, asked watts what his son had done wrong, he said she told him, I don't want to hear it [spanish] in my building.

Fluency	Adequacy	Sentence Text
✓	✓	when his father, lorenzo rubio-irritating because his son had been suspended of school for two days-asked watts what was done badly his son, the citing she replied, 'i do not want to hear it (spanish) in my building.
✓	☐	when his father, lawrence hair-annoying because his son had been suspended of school for two days-asked watts what was done wrong his son, the citing she replied. 'i do not want to hear it (spain) in my building.

Figure 7   Two examples from an evaluation tool to compare fluency and adequacy between CL-MT and a baseline SMT translation

Note: The top line in each example is the reference translation, followed by baseline and CL-MT output in random order. Here the two outputs have equal fluency, but the first output has a more adequate translation of one or two phrases (e. g. "day" instead of "agenda").

These examples are fairly typical of the system output. Fluency is generally comparable—the baseline is not fluent English, and CL-MT does little to improve this.

When CL-MT improves adequacy, it typically improves translation of one or two words in the sentence. The translation "day of choice" is better than "agenda choice," even though both systems should have "election" rather than "choice." The second example has better adequacy from not translating the proper name, Lorenzo Rubio, and from "Spanish" rather than "Spain." Near synonyms such as "done badly" for "done wrong" do not affect adequacy.

We saw a significant improvement in adequacy from CL-MT over the baseline system, as shown in Figure 8. CL-MT increased adequacy in 33.8% of the sentences, lowering adequacy in 12.1%. This means that CL-MT improved adequacy 2.8 times more often than hurting it. Some cases where human annotation hurt adequacy were from words whose meaning in a phrase was not the same as the word in isolation; some were from confusion about the meaning of a gloss; some were where annotating a word caused suboptimal translation of an adjacent word. There was no significant difference in fluency between CL-MT and the baseline system.

Method	% better fluency	% better adequacy
CL-MT	10.6	33.8
Baseline	10.6	12.1
Both systems equal	78.8	54.0
Oracle CL-MT	13.1	39.9
Baseline	5.6	2.5
Both systems equal	81.3	57.6

Figure 8　CL-MT gives a statistically significant boost to adequacy over the baseline SMT system

Note: With perfect annotations (oracle), CL-MT rarely makes choices that hurt adequacy.

Figure 8 also compares the "oracle" system with optimal annotation to the baseline. Our real CL-MT system improves adequacy over the baseline only a little less often than a perfect annotator would have. However, a perfect annotator increases adequacy 15.8 times more often than decreasing it.

4.4　Results from Content Words Only

CL-MT can improve lexical translation in several ways: annotation of the preferred word senses of content words (nouns, verbs, adjectives, and adverbs); annotation of the preferred word senses of pronouns; enforcing non-translation of proper nouns; and supplying translations that are missing from the SMT phrase table.

Of these, the largest boost in BLEU score comes from annotation of pronouns and of proper nouns. The former is a peculiarity of our Spanish-English language pair. Pronouns in Spanish do not mark gender or number, while English pronouns do; some are ambiguously a pronoun or a determiner; and some pronouns are omitted in the English translation. Without the CL interface, a pronoun such as "su" is indiscriminately translated as "his," "her," "their," "your," "one's," or "its."

The most interesting part of CL-MT, however, is the annotation of content words. We ran CL-MT with all parameters set to neutral values except those for the MRD lexicon. This shows the contribution of our WordNet lexicon to translation accuracy without the other functionality of CL-MT. There was only a modest gain of 0.2% in BLEU score. The effect was more pronounced with human evaluation that takes into account synonymous translations.

Figure 9 shows the percent of sentences where CL-MT with only the MRD lexicon improved fluency or adequacy with respect to the baseline SMT system. Disambiguation of content words accounts for 69% of the gain in adequacy from the full CL-MT and for 54% of the cases where CL-MT hurts adequacy. Annotating only content words helps adequacy 3.5 times more often than hurting it, an even better ratio than for the full CL-MT system. As before, there is no significant net effect on fluency.

Method	% better fluency	% better adequacy
CL-MT(content words)	6.6	23.2
Baseline	7.1	6.6
Both systems equal	86.4	70.2

Figure 9   This shows the contribution of CL-MT where only nouns, verbs, adjectives, and adverbs are annotated.

5   Related Research

There have been several research papers recently on incorporating WSD into SMT. Carpuat and Wu conducted experiments using a WSD classifier for Chinese based on an ensemble of naive Bayes, maximum entropy, AdaBoost, and Kernel PCA-based classifiers (Carpuat and Wu, 2005). These classifiers had a much richer feature set of contextual information than was available to the phrasal SMT system that Carpuat and Wu used. They found that BLEU scores declined when the WSD system was used to override the translation chosen by the SMT system.

A research group at Stanford (Vickrey et al., 2005) applied automatic WSD where the word senses of an English word were taken to be its possible French translations. Their system succeeded in finding the correct translation in a "fill in the blank" experiment, but did not find significant improvements in translation accuracy of full sentences.

The use of human-verified WSD has been explored by Translution.com (Orasan et al., 2005). Their method applies only to language pairs where both languages have EuroWordNet thesauri (www.illc.uva.nl/EuroWordNet). They use Word-Net's interlingual index to link word senses in the source language with corresponding senses in the target language. They reported on techniques to prune out irrelevant word senses to avoid overburdening a user, but did not report on how the WSD affected translation accuracy.

A promising approach to building a CL lexicon without an MRD available is corpus-based clustering (Kikui, 1999). Kikui uses distributional clustering to identify the word sense of a source language word, and then tests each translation from a bilingual dictionary to find a translation whose context in the target language corpus best matches the context for that sense in the source language corpus.

The controlled language of CL-MT is qualitatively different than that of other research in controlled language. Our CL lexicon is designed to be domain independent and must deal directly with ambiguity of nearly all terms. Other CL systems have been developed for narrow domains, or at best, with a domain-independent architecture that relies on domain-specific knowledge.

The Kant system (Nyberg and Mitamura, 1996; Mitamura et al., 2003) was developed primarily for one-way translation of Caterpillar Tractor manuals from English. Nearly all of the content words are restricted to a single word sense, and multi-word noun phrases are only allowed if explicitly in the lexicon. Kant would reject "oil filter change" even though "oil filter" and "change" are both in the lexicon ("change of oil filter" is permitted). Attempto Controlled English (ACE) (Fuchs et al., 1998) and Processable English (PENG) (Schwitter, 2002) are similarly designed for technical specifications in narrow domains.

6　Conclusions and Future Work

We have tested the hypothesis that human assistance in lexical ambiguity resolution by a monolingual source language speaker can improve translation accuracy of an SMT system. Adequacy improved for 33.8% of the sentences over a baseline SMT system, while it was reduced for 12.1% of the sentences. There was no significant difference in fluency. A small improvement in BLEU score, from 21.7% to 22.6% and a small reduction of position independent word error rate (PER) from 45.0% to 44.3% were not statistically significant. An oracle version of CL-MT shows the potential gain from optimal annotations: it improved adequacy on 39.9% of the sentences while only lowering adequacy for 2.5% of them, raising BLEU score to 27.6% and lowering PER to 39.6%.

Our experiments with CL-MT were designed as a proof of concept, so we did not formally measure the burden placed by our system on the user. In real world applications this aspect of the system becomes very important. We have a system under development that indicates to the user the word senses that the underlying SMT would choose absent any user disambiguation, easing some of the user's work.

Our CL-MT system demonstrates that human input can give a significant improvement to the adequacy of SMT translation. This performance boost can be realized if the CL lexicon provides entries for each word that distinguish separate word senses, are associated with one or more translations for each entry, and have an intuitive gloss for each entry. These criteria are met by a CL lexicon that we created using a bilingual dictionary and an MRD for the target language. The third criterion, intuitive glosses, was not met by a CL lexicon we built without using an MRD. Neither back translation cues nor context word cues allowed a user to select the correct word sense reliably.

Results from an oracle system show that there is room for greater improvement by CL-MT with better coverage by its bilingual dictionary, better morphological analysis, and a better way to handle phrases where the meaning is not compositional. For the latter problem, corpus-based techniques to find collocations may prove useful, as well as mining the SMT phrase table for phrasal translations to be included in the CL lexicon.

We are interested in pursuing methods that scale to language pairs without an MRD for either language. We are optimistic that CL-MT can be extended to any language pair where there is a simple bilingual dictionary and a corpus is available for each language. In the absence of an MRD, the main challenges are to identify distinct word senses automatically and to provide meaningful cues to the user to distinguish the word senses.

One key direction for the problem of mixed word senses is to use clustering algorithms on local context words to distinguish separate word senses (Yarowsky, 1995; Schutze, 1998), so that entries are not a mixture of partly correct and partly incorrect word senses. Using example sentences or phrases containing the word to be disambiguated may prove to be more useful descriptors than context words for aiding the user in disambiguation.

【延伸阅读】

[1] AAMT. MT Summit IX: The Tenth Machine Translation Summit: Proceedings, September 12—16, 2005, Phuket, Thailand.

[2] Alshawi, H. *The Core Language Engine*. Cambridge, Mass.: The MIT Press, 1992.

[3] AMTA. Expanding MT Horizons. Proceedings of the Second Conference of the Association for Machine Translation in the Americas, 2—5 October 1996, Montreal, Quebec, Canada.

[4] AMTA. Envisioning Machine Translation in the Information Future. 4th Conference of the Association for Machine Translation in the Americas, 2000.

[5] Powell, S. Guru Interview: Sir Timothy Berners-Lee. *KBE*, 2006.

[6] Soergel, D. Multilingual Thesauri and Ontologies in Cross-Language Retrieval. Presentation at the AAAI Spring Symposium on Cross-Language Text and Speech Retrieval, 1997.

[7] Simonet, M., & Diallo, G. Multilingual Ontology Enrichment for Semantic Annotation and Retrival of Medical Information. *MedNET*, 2006.

[8] Benjamins, R. V., Contreras, J., Corcho, O., & Gomez-Perez A. Six Challenges for the Semantic Web. *SIGSEMIS Bulletin*, 2004(April).

［9］Fuchs，N.，Schwertel，E.，& Schwitter，R. Attempto Controlled English（ACE），Language Manual，Version 2.0，Institut fr Informatik，University of Zurich，1998.

［10］Kikui，G. Resolving Translation Ambiguity Using Non-parallel Bilingual Corpora. Proceedings of ACL99 Workshop on Unsupervised Learning in Natural Language Processing，1999.

［11］Kirchhoff，K.，& Yang，M. Improved Language Modeling for Statistical Machine Translation. Proceedings of the 2005 ACL Workshop on Building and Using Parallel Texts，2005.

［12］Koehn，P. & Monz，C. Shared Task：Statistical Machine Translation Between European Languages. Proceedings of the ACL Workshop on Building and Using Parallel Texts，2005.

［13］Koehn，P. Och，F. J. & Marcu，D. Statistical Phrase-based Translation. Proceedings of HLT/NAACL，2003.

［14］Koehn，P. Pharaoh：A Beam Search Decoder for Phrase-based Statistical Machine Translation Models. Proceedings of AMTA，2004.

【问题与思考】

1. 机器翻译起源于何时？这一阶段有何特点？
2. 为什么称 20 世纪 80 年代为机器翻译研究的复兴期？其主要标志是什么？
3. 举例说明网络在线机器翻译研究的发展。
4. 目前市场上的电子词典有哪些类型？它们之间有何区别？
5. 请举例说明电子词典的主要性能？
6. 翻译(词典)软件程序的逻辑方法是什么？目前它们有何不足？
7. 机器翻译中一般性的跨语本体映射是如何进行的？
8. 举例说明跨语语义映射框架是如何进行运作的？
9. 如何检测机器翻译工具在跨语本体映射过程中的作用？
10. 选文四中的 CL-MT 语言系统与其他可控语言系统的最大区别是什么？这种区别有何特点？
11. 如何对 CL-MT 语言系统进行机器自动评价和人工评价？
12. CL-MT 语言系统的试验展示了怎样的结论？它对机器翻译的发展有何启示？

第八章　翻译与资源环境的建构

在过去百年间,翻译研究蓬勃发展。这一研究致力于在相关的领域中确立翻译原则和研究方法,现已成为一门独立的学科。翻译是一种跨文化、跨学科的创新活动,具有国际性。翻译作为沟通中外的纽带和桥梁,在国际间政治、经济、科学和文化等各个领域的频繁交流中发挥了重要作用。翻译研究也随着翻译事业的日益繁荣而不断发展,并已取得一定的成果。目前翻译研究也采用了语言学、认知学、心理学、文体学和跨文化交际学等西方理论轨迹,在很大程度上拓展了翻译研究的学术视野和体系。翻译的过程不仅是译员本人翻译能力的体现,也是他们调动一切其他可用资源重塑译语的过程。传统意义上的翻译能力指的是内化了的潜能、策略、技巧或者各种语言能力的集合体。而在信息时代的网络技术辅助下,翻译能力得到了很大程度上的拓展,其内涵得到极大的丰富。信息时代的网络技术辅助工具有:机器翻译系统、因特网上的语言翻译资源、CD - ROM 上的语言翻译资源、计算机辅助术语管理系统、双语对应语料库、翻译记忆软件和本土化软件工具、机助翻译系统等。译者掌握了信息时代的这些翻译工具,运用一般的网络在线工具和更专业的网络术语资源,就可以大大地提高翻译的效率,满足信息时代对翻译的迫切需要。作为译者,他们在翻译中需要具备扎实的元翻译能力,更重要的是懂得如何利用各种网络技术辅助工具,构建翻译能力和各种辅助资源的和谐统一体。本章主要针对翻译与各种辅助资源的统一建构进行选题。

选文一　机器翻译系统及翻译工具的开发和使用

John Hutchins

导　言

John Hutchins 是英国东英吉利大学教授。本文综述了当前计算机翻译软件的需求和应用情况,着重讨论了如何设计翻译系统使其翻译质量能达到可出版水平,其中包括开发受限语言翻译系统、翻译工作站,及软件本地化。同时本文还涉及到如何开发非传统概念的翻译软件,特别是针对 Web 页面和其他应用在 Internet 上各类信息的翻译软件。本文还讨论了机器翻译未来的需要以及正在开发的一些系统。文中最后一部分比较了人译、机译以及机助人译方式的相对优缺点及适用领域。

一、机器翻译的几种需求

当我们纵观机器翻译系统和翻译工具的发展和使用时,很重要的一点就是要区分四种基本的翻译需求:第一是传统型的,它要求翻译结果和人(翻译家)翻译的一样好,即翻译结果达到出版水平,不管是真正印成铅字并当成商品卖出,或者仅仅在公司或单位内部使用。第二种需求对翻译质量要求稍微低一些(尤其是对各类文体的处理要求较低),此时用户最感兴趣的是想了解某篇文章的基本内容,并且通常是越快越好。第三种需求主要是对话双方一对一的交谈(如电话,Internet 聊天室)或无需写在纸上的发言(如外交场合的谈话)。第四种需求是在多语系统中信息检索,信息抽取,数据库访问等领域里所用的翻译。

第一种需求使用机器翻译是为了传播思想(dissemination)。从 60 年代开始开发机器翻译系统发展至今,这种需求可以说在某种程度上得到了满足。然而,要想达到用户需要的质量,机译输出结果常常需要由人工修改或"后编辑"。有时这些修改是必须的(并不是可改可不改的),因为机译系统实际上只是产生了一个"草稿型"译文。要么,输入文件必须做规整(即对词语和句子结构做"限制"),这样机译系统才不至于产生那么多必须修改的错误。有些机译系统只能处理受限的文本,其中文本的内容和语言风格都限制在一个非常狭窄领域内,此时这些系统才需要很少或不需要文本的前处理。最近几年,作为传播思想目的之用的机译系统由于机译工具的开发,如术语数据库和翻译记忆器(translation memories),已经大大改进了。机译系统被集成到写作和出版过程中。"翻译工作站"比人工翻译者更有吸引力。使用机译系统的翻译人员把他们自己看成机器的附属品,他们仅能对计算机得到的输出进行编辑、修改、重译。而在翻译工作站中,翻译者是计算机设备的主动控制者,他们可以随意选择接受或拒绝翻译结果。第二种需求,即为获得信息而使用机译系统,事实上已经作为第一种需求的副产品得到了实现。虽然机译系统还没有也尚不能产生出高质量的译文,有些用户觉得他们能从未经编辑的译文中获得他们需要的信息。毕竟翻译出一部分总比一点没有翻译要好,尽管译文结果很糟糕。随着市场上 PC 机译系统越来越廉价,这种需求大大增长了。第三种需求,即以交流信息为目的的机译,目前变化很快。对 Internet 上的电子文本进行翻译发展迅速,如翻译 WEB页面、EMAIL 或在线聊天信息等。在这种情况下,由人来翻译就很困难了。此时要求马上得出翻译结果以便传达信息的基本内容,不管输入多么糟糕。MT 系统正在探索如何"自然"地扮演自己的角色,因为它的特点是能够事实上实时在线地运行,虽然不可避免地输出质量较差。另一种机译用于人际交流的情况是口语翻译系统的开发,它吸引了很多人研究。可以应用于电话交谈,商务会谈等领域。这里话语语音合成和自动翻译的难点显然是很难对付的,但仍然正在取得一定进展。将来———尽管还遥远———我们可以指望在非常受限领域里有在线的口语机器翻译系统。第四种机译应用,是信息访问系统的组成部分,是把翻译软件集成到(1)数据库查询系统和库内文档的全文检索(一般是电子版的科学,医学和技术期刊杂志),以及文献信息检索系统;(2)从文本,特别是新闻报道中提取信息(亦即产生细节知识);(3)对文本进行自动文摘;(4)查询非文本数据库系统。目前,有几个这方面的项目正在欧洲进行,目的是使所有欧盟成员国都能访问公有的数据和信息源,无论其采用何种源语言。

二、机器翻译的历史背景

自动翻译系统的研究开发已进行了50年了———事实上自从20世纪40年代电子计算机诞生之日起就开始了计算机应用于语言翻译的探索。之后,这种系统主要是以一个双语字典为基础进行直接翻译,几乎没有什么细致的句法结构分析。直到80年代,随着计算语言学的发展,人们探讨了许多较深层的方法,一些系统采用了间接的方法进行翻译。在这些系统中,源语言文本被分析转换成某种"意义"上的抽象表达形式,相继有一系列程序识别词结构(词法分析)和句子结构(句法分析)以此解决歧义问题(语义上的)。后者包含识别多义词的模块,如,英语中,light既是名词(光),又是形容词(轻);solution既是数学术语(解)又是化学术语(溶剂)。还包含识别正确语义关系的模块,如,The driver of the bus with a yellow coat。人们希望抽象表达是无歧义的,并为生成一个或多个目标语言提供根据。这种"间接"的翻译主要包括两种。其一,抽象表达设计为一种与具体语种无关的"中间语言",它可以作为许多自然语言的中介。这样,翻译就分成两个阶段:从源语言到中间语言,从中间语言到目标语言。其二,通常用得更普遍,抽象表达首先要转化成为目标语言的等价表达形式。翻译即分成三个阶段:输入文本分析成为抽象的源语言表达;转换成为抽象的目标语言表达;最后生成目标语言。直到80年代末,以上提到的方法都被很多系统采用。确实目前正在商业运作的翻译系统都可以分为三个基本类型:直接型、中间语言型和"转换"型。运行在大型机上的一些最有名的机译系统本质上都是"直接翻译"型的,如Syst ran,Logos和富士通的Atlas。然而,它们属"改进"了的直接翻译型。这些系统和他们的前辈不同,是高度模块化的,易修改,易扩展。例如Syst ran系统,开始设计时只为了翻译俄文到英文,现在可以进行很多语种之间的翻译。Logos开始只开拓德语到英语的翻译市场,现在可以翻译英语到法语、德语、意大利语,以及德语到法语、意大利语。而富士通的Atlas系统,至今仍把自己局限于英日、日英的翻译。一个重要的大型"转换"型机译系统是METAL,80年代德国的西门子公司提供了大部分资金支持。直到80年代末METAL才面市,但销售状况很不好。90年代,METAL的开发权转给两个单位(GMS和LANT),其组成机构变得比较复杂。最知名的采用"转换"型方法的两个研究项目,一个是(Grenoble的GETA的Ariane),该机译研究项目启动可以回溯到60年代,另一个是欧洲共同体委员会提供基金的Eurotra项目。Ariane曾有希望成为法国国家机译系统,人们曾计划把它集成进Eurolang翻译者工作站中,但最终无一实现。至于Eurotra,无疑是最复杂的机译系统之一,但经过西欧许多国家几百个研究人员近十年的努力,仍未能够开发成功投资者希望的实用系统。本来,欧委会希望由自己内部开发的Eurotra能够替换他们使用的syst ran系统。80年代末,日本政府机构出资支持开发用于亚洲语言之间的中间语言系统,有中国、泰国、马来西亚和印度尼西亚等研究人员参加。同样,这一计划历经十年也未能开发成功。

三、政府和非商业目的使用

早期的机译系统安装于国家和国际的政府机构和军队中,主要是只有他们才付得起昂贵的计算机硬件设备费用。美国空军于 1970 年研制 Syst ran,目的在于将俄国军事方面的科学技术文献翻译成英语。虽然有些文献经过编辑,但大部分译文输出都直接交给用户未做修改;据称技术报告翻译准确率达 90% 以上。现在美国国家空军智能中心接管了美国空军的翻译服务,可以为美国政府提供广泛的翻译服务(许多不做译后编辑)。除俄英翻译,Syst ran 还有从日语、汉语、韩语到英语的翻译,目前正在开发从塞尔维亚—克罗地亚语到英语的翻译。

在欧洲,最大的翻译服务是属于欧洲共同体的,他们是最早安装机译系统的单位之一。从 1976 年开始,它一直在用 Syst ran 将英语翻译成法语。后来,Syst ran 又开发了很多对语种之间的翻译版本,覆盖了欧盟各语种之间的翻译需要。目前,虽然很多法律文件仍需要人工翻译,Syst ran 系统越来越多地得到使用,不仅用来翻译内部文件(可以有译后编辑也可以没有),而且在辅助官员们编写非母语文章时发挥作用。

四、技术文档的生成

直到 90 年代,一般认为机器翻译系统要生成达到出版水平的文档,主要是(但不仅仅是)科学和技术性的文档。换句话说,机译系统可以用于代替需要雇佣专家才能做的翻译工作。显然,实际的机译输出还不适于直接使用,还需要做大量修改才能达到出版水平。因此翻译家被雇来做"后编辑",在这种情况下,机译系统的使用变成了一个经济问题。只有人机结合的总体质量和速度优于只雇佣人做翻译,并且成本低廉时,机器翻译才能生存。

尽管今天机译系统还有如上所述的其他用处,但直接用来进行翻译文档仍然是最重要的应用,特别对大型系统的供应商和开发商来说(例如 Syst ran 和 Logos)。他们的主要客户和用户是面向全球市场出口仪器设备的跨国公司。此时主要需求就是翻译产品的市场宣传材料和技术资料。技术资料通常需要翻译的量非常大。一件设备的操作手册可能多达上千页。而且新机型出来还常常要做手册的修改。除此之外,必须保证翻译中的一致性,同样的部件每次翻译说法必须一样。技术资料的翻译量之大通常使人望而却步,无能为力。为了取得最大程度的高效率低成本,应该将机译系统和公司技术资料总体编纂工作集成起来,而且应该贯彻到从一开始的编写到最终的出版发行的全过程。专门为技术资料的编纂人员开发的系统已经将翻译和出版过程无缝连接起来,这种连接不仅为了保证术语翻译的准确,而且保证在线手册的风格和语法正确性。

有许多长期使用机译系统翻译多语种技术文档的成功例子。最有名的例子是加拿大的 Lexi-Tech 公司利用 Logos 系统进行资料翻译。一开始是为了将海军护卫舰维修手册翻译成法语。为此,该公司曾建立一个服务中心专门负责承接各种其他翻译项目。Ericsson, Osram, Oce Technologies,SAP 以及 Corel 也使用了 Logos 翻译系统。Syst ran 有许多大客户,如,福特公司,通用汽车公司,Anospatiale, Berlitz, Xerox 等。METAL 德英翻译系统曾成功应用于一些欧洲公司,如:Boehringer Ingelheim, SAP,飞利浦,以及瑞士联合银行等。

大公司成功安装机译系统有一个前提条件:即用户希望在一个确定领域内(主题,产品等确定)翻译相当大量的资料。同时必须保证有一定量的术语数据库和字典维护方面的合理资金投入。不论一个公司的资料是否是自动整理出来的,人们都希望术语的使用能够保持一致。甚至许多公司坚持使用他们自己的说法,不接受其他公司的说法。如果不使用自动翻译系统是不太可能维持这种一致性的。然而,在使用机译系统前,确实需要先建立一个术语数据库,其中必须包括用户要求有关术语对应什么译法,或至少必须承诺开发一个词汇数据库。基于同样原因,人们希望机译系统能够同时输出多种目标语言的翻译结果。大多数大型机译系统都多多少少面向特定用户对文件中发现的特殊语言进行专门处理(定制),比如对常见句子或子句结构加些专门的语法规则,除去特定公司需要的特定词汇外,还针对一般的词汇项添加一些特定规则等。这样的定制的工作在一般情况下可能是不合情理的,除非输出的目标同时包括好多种不同语种。

五、受限语言和特殊领域系统

某些情况下,对被翻译的源语言做一些限制通常是可行的。一个早期比较有名的例子是Xerox公司使用的Syst ran系统。在Xerox公司,技术文献的作者必须用所谓的多国特定规格的英语(Multinational Customized English)来编写文件,这时不仅某个术语的说法确定下来,而且怎样造句也确定下来了。这种做法的好处是,排除了许多机译系统难以处理的输入歧义,其输出质量越好,同步生成多个其他语种的速度就越快,而且可以产生更多容易理解的英文资料。这些优点已经被其他跨国公司认同。"受限语言"用得越来越多,例如Caterpillar公司设计了他们自己独特的英文格式,以便使用卡奈基梅龙大学开发的基于知识的机器翻译系统。还有一些公司提供为某些特定用户建立"受限"语言的机器翻译系统。最早的采用这种办法的是纽约Smart公司,其开发的系统主要客户有:Citicorp, Chase, Ford, General Elec tric等。其中,每个客户都与Smart合作提供一个所谓对英文文档进行"正规化"的系统。这部分非常重要,以至于真正的翻译过程被看作它的"副产品"。Smart系统可以翻译从英语到法语、德语、希腊语、意大利语、日语和西班牙语等多种目标语言。Smart为加拿大就业部设计的系统,可能是其最大的一个应用。该系统多年来一直用于翻译就业广告等相关信息。

在欧洲,荷兰的Cap Volmac公司和比利时的Lant公司也同样提供类似服务,用他们的基于受限语言的翻译软件为各种客户建立专业翻译系统。Cap Volmac位于Lingware的翻译中心是Cap Gemini Sogeti集团的荷兰附属机构。多年来,这家软件公司一直在为纺织业和保险业公司建立受限语言翻译系统,翻译方向主要是从荷兰语翻译到英语。然而最成功的面向客户定制的机译系统可能是为LingTech A/S开发的PaTrans系统,它将英文专利翻译成丹麦语。这一系统建立在参加欧洲委员会的Eurot ra项目时所获得的方法和经验基础之上。

从较早的时候开始,越来越多的公司和单位开始开发他们自己的机译系统,而不是去购买商用系统。加拿大的Météo是一个成功的面向英法天气预报翻译的机译系统(后来又提供了法英方向的翻译),它是一个面向特定客户的系统,为加拿大环境服务中心提供服务。值得指出的是该系统的一个版本在亚特兰大奥运会上应用很成功。Météo是一个子语言系统的例子,它只处理气象语言。另一种用户定制的系统是TITUS。它处理一种高度限制的"子语言",专门将纺织工业文摘在英语、法语、德语和西班牙语之间互译,从70年代开始一直到现在还在使用。还有两个用户特制的系统是华盛顿的泛美卫生组织(PAHO)开发的,进行英语和西班牙语之间的翻译,设计开发的都是该组织内部的工作人员。该系统开发的相当成功(现在在 PAHO 外部也可以使用该系统),属于通用型的,并不限制所使用的词汇和文本种类,尽管其使用的字典在翻译公共卫生方面的材料时性能最好。

90 年代还有一些其他类似的例子。在芬兰,Kielikone 系统开发成功,开始作为诺基亚的翻译工作站。后来在芬兰其他公司也装上了各种版本,现在该系统正在开拓更加广泛的应用市场。GSI2Erli 也是这样,这家大型语言工程公司开发了一个集成的内部翻译系统,它在一个公共平台上集成了机译系统和各种翻译辅助工具。近来已经开始为客户提供对外服务。Hook 和 Hatton 是一个小型对外翻译服务公司,其系统同样很成功,他们将化学文本从荷兰语翻译成英语(Lewis,1997)。设计者从简单的短语匹配开始,逐渐建成了有更多句法分析的系统,然后开始考虑输出结果的合情合理和降低成本的一些优化工作。

卡耐基梅隆大学的机译小组成员,多年来一直在开发基于知识的机译系统并试验言语翻译和基于语料库翻译的各种方法。在此基础上,开发了一个快速为特定用户生成可用机译系统的体系结构,这种结构仅限于几种不太常用的语言,如塞尔维亚-克罗地亚语和海地人讲的法语。他们并没有自吹能达到高质量,只是强调语言的"可用性",否则就"不可接受"。还有一个客户定制的机译系统是 Simon Fraser 大学的 TCC 通讯公司开发的专门翻译电视节目解说词的系统。这种翻译系统不仅有时间上的约束(即翻译必须是实时的),而且需要面对口语、对话、鲁棒性和上下文语境等各方面的挑战。该系统目前可以进行英语到西班牙语的电视解说词的翻译,此处的技术要求与 Internet 中的应用技术相似。

在日本有更多的为用户定制的系统。日本科学技术信息中心可以将日本科学技术文献的摘要翻译成英语。该中心从 80 年代末开始,采用了 Kyoto 大学开发的 Mu 日英机器翻译系统,现在该系统是日本最大的机译系统。其他重要的日本机译系统有 IBM 日本开发的 SHALT 系统,主要为公司内部所用;东京的 CSK 公司开发的 ARGO 系统,可以将日本股票市场报告翻译成英语,及将英语新闻文章译成日语的 NHK 系统。

六、翻译工作站

到了 90 年代,由于翻译工作站(或翻译家工作台)的出现拓宽了大规模翻译的可能性。将各种计工具软件集成在一起让翻译者使用,这种想法首创于 80 年代,特别是随着 ALPS 的出现。翻译工作站集成了多语种字处理软件,接收和发送电子文档工具,OCR 设备,术语管理软件,索引工具软件,特别是"翻译记忆器"(Tanslation Memories)。"翻译记忆器"让翻译者可以方便地将原始文本和对应的翻译文本并列地保存起来,也就是将源句子与目标句子对齐。这样翻译者可以从翻译记忆器中的一种语言中查出短语或整句,然后在另一语言中显示它的翻译结果。匹配可以是精确的,也可以按照贴近程度进行模糊匹配。

在一个大公司内,技术文献、技术手册经常经过很多次修改,其中大部分未经变动。有了翻译记忆器,就可以把曾经翻译过的部分直接取出来再利用。即使无法精确匹配,显示出的部分经过小小修改也是可以利用的。对那些在翻译记忆器中找不到的词汇或短语,还可以访问术语数据库,尤其是公司对术语的译法有特殊要求的。另外,许多翻译工作站提供使用象 Syst ran, Logos, Transcend 这样的全自动机译系统接口。翻译者可以任意使用它翻译全文或片段,可以接受或拒绝其翻译结果。

翻译工作站现在主要有四家销售商：Trados（这也许是最成功的），德国（Transit）的STARAG，IBM 的 Translation Manager，以及比利时的 LANT（Eurolang 的改进版，原来由法国的 SITE 公司销售）。翻译工作站给翻译工作者使用计算机带来了革命性的变化。翻译工作者有了可以自己完全控制的工具。他们可以自由地选择使用其中任一个工具，或一个都不用。每个资源的价值决定于它的数据处理质量。在机译系统中，字典和术语数据库的建立需要很多精力、时间和资源。翻译记忆器好坏取决于是否有合宜的、容量大的、有权威译文的语料库，如果公司或客户不接受翻译结果，就没有理由使用这种翻译工具。

尽管欧洲委员会行政官员广泛使用 Systran，该委员会的职业翻译家还是相对较少使用这种机器翻译系统。翻译服务中心正专门为他们开发自己使用的工作站，例如 EURAMIS，（欧洲高级多语信息系统，European Advanced Multilingual Information System）。该系统提供的服务很多，包括访问委员会自己所有的巨大的多语数据库（Eurodicautom），Systran 的词典库，方便个人或团体创立及维护术语数据库的工具（用 Trados'MultiTerm 软件）、翻译记忆器，访问 CELEX（欧盟法律和法令全文数据库），文件比较软件（探测哪里发生了变化），以及访问 Systran 翻译系统本身。其中的翻译系统可以翻译从英语到荷兰语、法语、德语、希腊语、意大利语、葡萄牙语和西班牙语；从法语翻译到荷兰语，英语，德语，意大利语，西班牙语；从西班牙语翻译到英语和法语；从德语翻译到英语和法语等。整个 Euramis 系统与其他工具相连（如，拼写检查，语法检查，语言风格检查，多语写作辅助），系统与欧洲委员会行政管理内部网相连，可以访问因特网上的外部资源。

七、软件本地化

使用计算机翻译发展最快的领域是软件本地化行业。这时要求在软件发布的同时各种语言版本的文档也同时能够发布。翻译必须迅速，但从一个版本到另一个版本有很大部分的重复，显然使用机译或最近的翻译记忆器是一个解决办法。这一领域最早的公司是德国的 SAP 公司。他们目前使用了两个机译系统，用 METAL 做德语到英语的翻译，用 Logos 做英语到法语的翻译，他们还计划对其他语种之间的翻译启用其他系统。

大部分本地化工作使用的还是翻译记忆器和工作站的方法。典型的是 Corel，Lotus 及 Canon 公司。有趣的是许多本地化的活动是在爱尔兰做的———这要感谢当地政府和欧盟对计算机工业的支持。然而本地化是一个跨国的、全球性的行业，它本身有自己的组织，总部是设在日内瓦的本地化行业标准委员会。该组织定期在各洲组织讨论会和报告会。本地化公司在欧洲最积极推行确定标准化词典及文本处理格式，以及推广架构共同的网络基础结构。这就是 Lotus 在荷兰组织协调的 OTELO 项目。其他参与成员有 SAP，Logos 和 GMS。主要是要建立一个一般性的翻译环境，使之能充分利用翻译记忆器、机器翻译和其他工具，人们普遍认为这是将来软件本地化产业成功的基础。

八、PC 机译系统

在 80 年代早期，微机上的机器翻译软件开始出现（其中 Weidner MicroCAT 系统取得了巨大的成功）。几乎所有日本主要的计算机公司都开发出了翻译从日文到英语或从英语翻译到日文的系统,例如 NEC 公司的 PIVOT 系统,东芝的 ASTRANSAC 系统,日立公司的 HI2CATS 系统,Oki 公司的 PENSEE 系统以及夏普公司的 DUET 系统。

在其他国家,微机上的机器翻译系统出现得更早一些,但是只有相对较少的一些公司在做。美国的第一个机器翻译系统是由 ALPS 和 Weidner 在 80 年代早期完成的。ALPS 的产品主要用来做翻译的辅助工具,它提供了存取和创建术语资源的工具,并包含交互式翻译的功能。尽管初期的销售很成功,生产商在十年后总结到:那时市场还不成熟,并且产品实际上在退步。后来 ALPS 转换成一家翻译服务商,在内部使用它自己的翻译工具。与此相反的是,Weidner 销售了一套完整的翻译系统,其中包含越来越多的语言互译系统(英语、法语、德语、西班牙语)。这一市场繁荣了起来。Weidner 设计了两个版本的系统:为微机设计的 MicroCat,为小型机或工作站设计的 MacroCat。后来,它被一家日本公司 Bravis 收购了,随后生产了一个日语版本。不久,这家日本公司认为微机的机器翻译市场还不成熟,就把这一项目卖了出去。MicroCat 完全消失了,但是 MacroCat 被 Intergraph 购买了。Intergraph 在其上作了修改,使其适用于它的一系列出版软件。后来,该公司把它以 Transcend 的名称卖了———最近,Transparent Language 公司获得了这一软件版权。

80 年代末,大多数目前市场上的商业系统出现了。首先出现的是由 Linquistic Products 生产的基于 Texas 面向低端个人机的 PCTranslator 系统。接下来的几年,许多语言互译系统被生产出来并被推到市场上。从销售来看,它们是很成功的。Globalink 开发出了法语、德语、西班牙语和英语之间的互译系统。还有一套俄语—英语系统,它得益于 Globaling 在 60 年代从 Georgettown 项目得到的经验。过了没几年,Globalink 和 MicroTac 合并了。MicroTac 曾经在销售个人机上的廉价的语言助手软件上获得很大成功———尤其是能够翻译短语的自动词典。90 年代初,Globalink 生产出了它的很著名的"Power Translator"系列。它可以实现法语、德语、西班牙语和英语之间的互译。最近,Globalink 推出了更加强大的"Telegraph"系列。后来,一家在语言技术上领先的公司 Lernout & hauspie 收购了 Globalink。

从 90 年代初开始,出现了许多其他个人机上的翻译系统。Language Engineering 公司生产出了日语和英语互译的 LogoVista 系统,还有 Neocor Technologies 公司的 Tsunami 和 Typhoon 系统(现在归 Lernout & Hauspie 所有)。前苏联在 60 年代和 70 年代对机器翻译进行了积极的研究,并开发了 Stylus(最近更名为 ProMT)系统和 PARS 系统。它们都是用于俄语和英语互译的商业系统。其中 Stylus 还可用于法语,PARS 可用于乌克兰语。在欧洲的其他基于个人机的机器翻译系统包括:用于意大利语和英语互译的 Hypert rans;用于丹麦语—英语、法语—英语、西班牙语—英语的 Winger 系统,该系统现在也出现在北美的市场上;还有用于芬兰—英语的 Kielikone 系统的商业版本 TranSmart。

传统的大型系统厂商(如 Syst ran, Fujit su, Metal, Logos)现在被迫精简他们的系统来参与竞争。许多厂商取得了成功,在基于个人机的版本中保留了原来的许多特色。例如,Syst ran Pro 和 Syst ran Classic 是从 60 年代就开始开发的基于 Windows 的十分成功的系统,它可以在多种语言之间互译。Syst ran 提供的巨大的字典数据库使这种产品相比其他基于 PC 的产品来说具有明显的优越性。Syst ran Classic(家庭用)和 Syst ran Pro(职业翻译者用)现在都以低于 500 美元的价格出售,其中有多种语言版本:英语—法语,英语—德语,英语—西班牙语,还有从英语到意大利语和从日语到英语的版本。一家出版公司 Langencheidt 取得了销售 MET2AL 的一种版本,将它与 GMS 集成在一起(GMS 是 Gesellschaft 多语言系统,现在归

Lernout & Hauspie 所有）——这个联合在一起的系统被称为"Langenscheidt T1"，它提供了德语和英语互译的各种各样的版本。另一来自德国的机器翻译系统 Personal Translator 是 IBM 和 von Rheinbaben & Busch 的合作产物，系统基于 LMT（即基于逻辑编程的机器翻译），从 1985 年就开始开发。LMT 本身是 IBM 的系统 Tanslation Manager 有效的组件。Langenscheidt T1 和 Personal Translator 都主要用来供非职业的翻译者使用，因此和 Globalink 以及其他类似的产品产生了竞争。

商业 PC 机翻译软件的销售现在有了巨大的增长。据估计，目前市场上有 1 000 多种不同的机器翻译软件在销售。仅 Globalink 的产品就在北美的至少 6 000 家商店中销售。在日本，据说由 Catena 生产的用于英语和日语互译的 Korya Eiwa 在推到市场的第一年就销售出超过 100 000 份的数量。尽管统计卖出的软件有多少被正常使用是困难的（有些批评家宣称只有很少的一部分被多次使用），但实时翻译这一市场具有巨大的容量是不容怀疑的。例如，各种背景的人们需要用他们自己的语言润色外语，或者需要用别的语言和他人进行交流。这种低质量的翻译的潜在市场是最近才被开发出来的，它十分有利地促进了翻译软件的巨大的增长。

九、Internet 上的机译系统

与此同时，许多机译系统销售商一直在提供应客户要求的网络翻译服务，包括附加人工修正。一类情形是固定关系客户以客户/服务器方式进行的；另一类情形是试用，允许公司看看机译对他们特定的情况是否值得使用。这些服务 Syst ran, Logos, Globalink, Fujit su, J ICST 和 NEC 等公司都提供。

有些公司现在主要是以提供这种服务而建立的，如比利时的 LANT，以开发 METAL 系统和 Eurolang Optimizer 为依托，提供网络翻译服务。它的专长是面向用户定制受控语言系统以便利用它的机译系统和翻译记忆器设备。1997 年下半年这个公司启动了多语种电子邮件、网页及各种附件翻译服务。新加坡有 MTSU（由新加坡国立大学系统科学研究所开发），使用由其自己本地开发的系统将英语译成汉语、马来西亚语、日语和朝鲜语（主要是英汉），并有职业翻译家进行译后编辑。这类服务是面对因特网上全世界客户（主要是跨国组织）提供大规模的翻译服务。包括在汉英市场上的许多软件公司的软件本地化的需求。

因特网影响增大的一个迹象是越来越多的要求机译软件翻译 web 页面的请求。以日本公司为主，几乎上面提到的所有公司都在这一有利可图的市场上有其相应的产品。其他公司也紧随其后（如：Syst ran, Globalink, Transparent Language, Logo Vista）。随着 PC 翻译软件翻译 web 网页，可以看出 Internet 服务使翻译更加便利：近期的一个例子是 Syst ran 应用于 Al2taVista 上，可以在英语和法语、德语、西班牙语之间实现翻译。但现在评论这一举动是否成功及用户是否满意还为时尚早。用于电子邮件和"聊天室"的机译同样很重要。两年前 CompuServe 开始了一个试用性服务，以 Transcend 系统为基础，让 MacCIM Support Forum 的用户使用。六个月之后，WorldCommunity Forum 开始使用机译软件翻译对话性的电子邮件。机器翻译的使用直线上升，最近，CompuServe 推出它自己的翻译服务，可以翻译更长一点的文件，翻译结果可以无须编辑也可以选择人工后期编辑。不久，CompuServe 将会推出电子邮件翻译标准的机器翻译。同时，Globalink 加入了 Uni2Verse 以提供多语种的 Internet 聊天室服务。

机器翻译的使用并不只是出自好奇心,尽管一开始往往是这样的。CompuServe 创下了大量客户重复使用其服务器的记录,其无须编辑的机器翻译需求高达 85%,比预料的比例要高得多。大多数人用机器翻译只是想粗略了解信息,翻译得差一点也能接受。问题的关键是客户已经打算付钱买机器翻译产品,如果机译服务质量下降,CompuServe 就会疲于应付一大堆抱怨。

显然,Internet 的机译潜力正在全速增长,所有公司都不甘落后,否则就会遭受到巨大的经济损失。大家都有雄心勃勃的计划,如,Lernout & Hauspie,它现在从 Globalink, Neocor 和 App Tek 及老的 METAL 系统得到机译系统。

十、未来需要和发展

尽管近来对微机和因特网上的机译需求有上升的趋势,实事求是地说,还没有一个机译系统特别适合于独立职业翻译工作者,也就是那些既不隶属于一个大公司也不在一个翻译组织里工作的人。据知有些翻译者曾试图使用商用 PC 软件,但需适应的东西太多,输出结果太差,他们感到不满意,经济上也不划算。其实更适合于独立翻译工作者的应该是价格适中的翻译工作站,但当前还是太贵了。尽管人们希望在这一潜在大市场有低成本的计算机工具,比如术语和主题索引词典、翻译对齐软件等,然而这些工具当前覆盖的领域还是太少。

当用户不是一个专职的双语翻译家时,要将文档翻译成一种用户不熟悉的外国语就需要成本低廉并且输出质量相对可靠的系统。目前该领域做得还很糟糕。将别种语言翻译成"接受者"方的语言没问题,PC 系统可以给出大致"粗略"的译文,此时至少可以告诉用户大致说的是什么。但如果输出的是用户不知道的目标语言,目前还没有什么好的解决办法。最近日本研制出来了一些廉价的产品可以对特定的"用外国语言写作"提供服务,比如写一封商务信函(基于标准短语和文件模板),但对其他领域或较长的文件,由于缺少标准模板,目前还不能提供服务。如果让用户翻译成另一种未知语言(或了解很少的语言),真正需要的是能够提供好的质量输出的软件,目前大部分 PC 上的产品输出都不够好。一些研究小组正在研究交互式系统,用户可以按照模板要求与计算机合作编写他们的文件。如果输入文件足够"标准化",机译系统就能保证结果按照正确的语法和语言风格输出。然而,这项工作仍然处在实验室研制阶段,例如法国的 GETA 项目就是如此。

同样,人们在尝试着将机译技术结合到信息访问、信息提取和自动文摘中。目前市场上还没有相应的商用产品,相关的工作仍处在研究阶段。但人们已经意识到这种潜在的需要。例如,与 80 年代不同,最近大多数欧盟提供基金支持的研究都不是着重开发纯机器翻译或"纯"自然语言处理的,除非已有直接应用的多语工具项目。大多数一定程度的翻译,通常是领域受限的或翻译状态受控的。举例说,AVENTINUS 项目是专门为警察部队在缉毒和执法方面开发的。用欧盟任一语言都可以查询到数据库中关于毒品、犯罪和嫌疑犯的信息。这类跨语言应用在全球范围内越来越引起人们的兴趣。而最吸引人的应用是"跨语言信息检索",即允许用户用自己的语言搜索外语数据库的软件。当前,大多数工作主要集中于如何建立和运行合适的翻译字典,以便将查询词串与数据库文档中的词和词组匹配——尽管翻译软件已经有希望迅速地将源语言翻译成查询者自己的语言。无疑商用软件用于此种目的已经不会是太遥远的事情了。未来还有一个应用是公众迫切需要的,就是口语的翻译。但无论从商业角度还是从研究角度来看,全自动话语翻译还是一件十分遥远的事。仅到 80 年代之后,语音识别和语音合成取得的进展使得人们感到口语翻译是可行的目标。日本的政府和工业界于 1986 年在 Osaka 附近联合组建了 ATR 机构,现在已经是主要的自动话语翻译中心了。其目标是开发一个不依赖于讲话者的实时的日英、英日电话翻译系统,开始是面向旅馆预定房间和办理会议注册手续提供服务的。后来又有一些其他的话语系统相继开发。JANUS 系统是卡耐基梅隆大学和德国 Karlsruhe 的一个联合研究项目。其研究者和 ATR 合作形成一个合作体(C2STAR),各方开发他们自己语言的识别和生成模块(英语、德语、日语)。卡耐基梅隆大学在这一研究得出的一个副产品我们在前面曾提到。话语翻译方面第四种努力是开始于 1993 年 5 月的德国科学技术部出资支持的一个长期项目 VERBMOBIL。其目标是开发一个便携式商业谈判辅助工具,作为用户自己语言(德语、日语、英语)知识的补充。好几家德国大学参与了这项包括对话语言学、言语识别和机器翻译设计等方面的基础性研究工作,目前原型系统已经接近完成,希望 21 世纪初能够拿出演示产品。

话语翻译可能是目前基于计算机翻译研究的最富有创新意义的领域,吸引了大量的资金投入和公众的注意。但观察家们并不认为这一领域在近期会取得迅速进展。书面语机器翻译花了许多年才达到现在的阶段,即广泛应用在跨国公司中,有大量基于 PC 机的不同质量和应用层面的产品,同时在网络和电子邮件方面的应用也日益增加。尽管基于书面语的机器翻译目前已有很强能力,研究人员知道要提高翻译质量还有许多工作要做。而口语机器翻译目前甚至还没有达到非实验室设备上的实时测试阶段。

十一、人和机器翻译之比较

综上所述可看出,使用计算机进行自然语言翻译并没有也不可能对职业翻译家的饭碗有什么威胁。翻译家的翻译技巧将继续有需求。例如,机器翻译从没有也不敢试图翻译文学或法律文件。同时,在 Internet 粗略翻译电子邮件文本方面还没有什么方法能与机器翻译相比——人在速度方面比不过机器,即使人愿意承担这类结果生存期很短的、质量很差的翻译。我们可以根据本文开头提到的几种翻译需求来比较一下人和机器翻译的相对优缺点。对于"传播思想"这种需求而言(即产生可出版的翻译),凡是需要翻译某个特定领域(科学、技术、医学、法律或文学)的特殊文字,由人(翻译工作者)来翻译质量比较可靠而且总的来讲成本较低。此时机器翻译字典的维护与更新以及译后编辑工作需要的成本比较高。只有当需要翻译某个领域的很大量文件时才是划算的。如果要翻译成多种目标语言并且源文件有大量重复那就更划算(如果可以对源文本做译前编辑和/或词汇语法限制的话)。对这种翻译任务,由于太大的工作量、令人厌烦的重复以及保持前后术语使用的一致性等方面会让人工翻译者望而却步。反之,计算机可不怕翻译量大和自动保持一致性的麻烦。简而言之,机器翻译适合于处理大量的,和/或需要快速处理的一些资料,例如令人生厌的技术文档,大量重复性的软件本地化手册,以及实时的天气预报信息等。人类翻译家在语言非重复性的复杂文本(例如文学、法律等方面的文本)方面起着无可竞争的作用,在将来同样是如此。

对于为了获得信息而需要翻译情形,这时对翻译质量要求不高,显然使用机器翻译比较理想。翻译家不打算而且很反感被要求去"粗略"地翻译科学技术资料。当只有一个人只是想大致了解一下某篇文章的内容,并不想知道该文的一切细节,而且他并不讨厌看到译文文体拙劣、语法错误百出时,用人进行翻译是很不合适的。当然,如果机器翻译给出的译文输出比目前要强些的话情况会更好,毕竟有一点翻译总比一点都没有翻译要好得多。

对于信息交流,在未来的一段时间里,人类翻译家在翻译商务信函方面继续起着主要作用(尤其是在内容比较敏感或与法律有关时)。但对于个人信件,机器翻译可能会用得越来越多;而对于翻译电子邮件、网络页面的信息提取及基于计算机的信息服务来说,机器翻译是唯一可行的解决方案。

而对于口语翻译,人类翻译家将继续有市场。没有迹象表明自动翻译会代替外交和商贸领域的口译家。尽管在高度受限领域有电话翻译方面的研究,未来也有希望实现,但对大量电话交谈来说,不可能出现什么能代替口译家的机器翻译。最后,机器翻译系统正开拓人类翻译从未涉及的领域:为需要用外语写作的作家提供生成文章草稿的帮助,在线翻译电视字幕,翻译数据库信息等。无疑未来还会出现更多这类新应用。这些领域不会对人类翻译家构成威胁,因为这些内容从来是职业翻译家未曾涉猎的。无疑机器翻译和人类翻译将来也一定会各司其职、和谐共存的。

选文二　The New Information and Communication Technologies (ICTs) and Translation Competence

Alain Esc arra Jimenez

导　言

本文是论述翻译能力的一篇论文,它把论述重点放在一个翻译子能力上。这种子能力包括专业译员所需获得的知识,比如对文档资料和翻译信息技术的使用。本文将对能力,尤其是更具体的翻译能力展开探讨,接着将重点讨论通用和特定的信息与通讯技术对专业译员的用处。同时,本文举出实例来说明如何在医学翻译实践中使用信息与通讯技术。

A translator is a person who expresses in a language (generally in his mother tongue and in writing) what is written in another language. The function of translators is far more important of what it is believed. Some wars have broken due to an error of the interpreter. More recently, people have died due to bad translations of medications. It is obvious then that translation is much more than just knowing two languages. There is something that distinguishes a bilingual person from a professional translator: translation competence. Starting by Saint Jerome and his translation of the Bible to the Latin of the people (the Vulgate) in the 4th century, there have been very competent translators throughout history.

The competence needed to translate has also evolved due to different factors, mainly technological factors.

Translators have always been associated with the image of a man writing or typing behind a heap of dictionaries and with a bunch of books behind him. However, in recent years this image has changed. Now when we think of a translator we can imagine a man behind a computer with Internet connection and maybe a couple of books on his desk. Yes, with the arrival of the information era many things changed. The translation profession has also changed. Now, in order to be a competent translator it is necessary to be computer literate and to keep one's information technologies skills updated. First of all the term competence and then more specifically the term translation competence will be defined. Competence is the combination of skills, attitudes and behaviour that leads to an individual being able to perform a certain task to a given level.

Different authors have developed the term communicative competence: Chomsky 1957, Hymes 1967, Oliva 1998, Forgas 2003. Thus, the term competence has been applied to different areas of life: the labor market, business, education and translation.

Translation competence is a complex concept that has been addressed by a number of researchers in the field of Translation Studies. Yet, as stated by Ezpeleta (2005: 136): Reflection on the matter is a relatively recent development and results from empirical studies are still scarce. Some authors talk of translation abilities or skills (Lowe, 1987; Pym, 1992; Hatim and Mason, 1997) while others refer to translation performance (Wilss, 1989). The term competence—translational competence—was first used by Toury (1980, 1995), because of its similarity to Chomsky's (1965) famous distinction between linguistic competence and performance, to explore certain aspects of translation practice. Nord (1991) employs transfer competence and Chesterman (1997) called it translational competence.

Several authors have mentioned translation competence but have not defined it; for instance, Nord (1991: 150, 152, 155; 1996: 101), Riedemann (1996: 117), Lorscher (1991: 41; 1992a: 426), Toury (1991: 62; 1995: 250 - 51), Krings (1986: 501, 522 in Fraser 1996a: 72), Fraser (1996b: 87), Lowe (1986: 53, 61), Hansen (1997: 205) and Kiraly (1995: 13 - 19). It is obvious that these authors have a definition of translation competence in mind, but they do not make it explicit.

We have found only four explicit definitions of translation competence, which are the following: Bell (1991: 43) defines translation competence as "the knowledge and skills the translator must possess in order to carry out a translation;" Hurtado Albir defines it as "the ability of knowing how to translate" (1996: 48); Wilss says translation competence calls for "an interlingual supercompetence [...] based on a comprehensive knowledge of the respective SL and TL, including the text-pragmatic dimension, and consists of the ability to integrate the two monolingual competencies on a higher level" (1982: 58).

Finally, the fourth definition, and the one we adopt in this investigation, is that of PACTE research group (Process of the Acquisition of Translation Competence and

Evaluation）（2000，2003，2005）as we think it is the more complete and coherent as it includes all the aptitudes and skills needed to translate. Their definition is the following:

Translation competence is the ability to carry out the transfer process from the comprehension of the source text to the re-expression of the target text, taking into account the purpose of the translation and the characteristics of the target-text readers.

More specifically, they propose a model of translation competence that they consider to be the underlying system of knowledge that is required to be able to translate（2000：100；2001：39；2003：126）and which has, they claim（2005：610），four distinguishing features:

（a）It is expert knowledge and is not possessed by all bilinguals;（b）it is basically procedural（and not declarative）knowledge;（c）it is made up of various interrelated sub-competencies;（d）the strategic component is very important, as it is in all procedural knowledge.

In fact, the Translation Competence Model proposed by this research team（2003）is made up of five sub-competencies and psycho-physiological components（2005：610，611）that overlap each other as they operate.

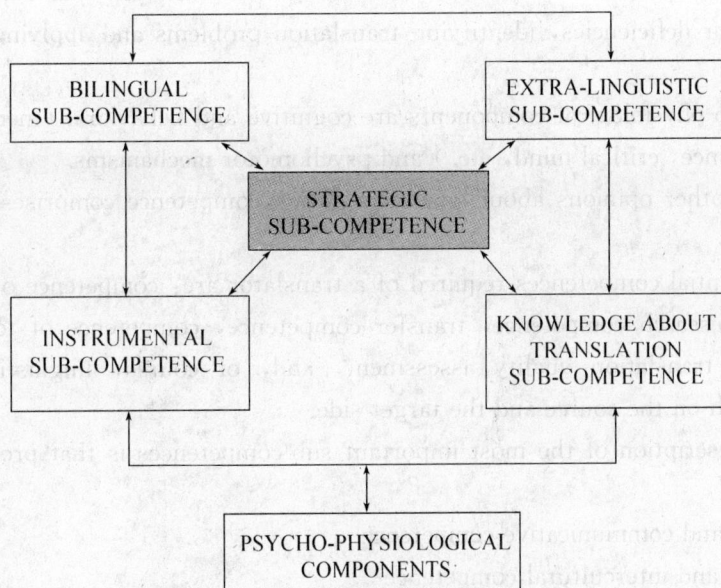

Figure 1　PACTE Translation Competence Model（2003）

The bilingual sub-competence consists of the underlying systems of knowledge and skills that are needed for linguistic communication to take place in two languages. It is made up of comprehension and production competencies, and includes the following knowledge and skills: grammatical competence; textual competence（which consists in being proficient in combining linguistic forms to produce a written or oral text in different genres or text types）; illocutionary competence（related to the functions of language）; and socio-linguistic competence（concerned with appropriate production and comprehension in a range of socio-linguistic contexts that depend on factors such as the status of the participants, the purpose of the interaction, the norms or conventions at play in the interaction, and so forth).

The extra-linguistic sub-competence is made up of encyclopedic, thematic and bicultural knowledge.

The translation knowledge sub-competence is knowledge of the principles guiding translation, such as processes, methods, procedures, and so forth.

The instrumental sub-competence comprises the knowledge required to work as a professional translator, such as the use of sources of documentation and information technologies applied to translation.

The strategic sub-competence integrates all the others and is the most important, since it allows problems to be solved and ensures the efficiency of the process. It consists in the capacity to follow the transfer process from the source text to the production of the final target text, according to the purpose of the translation and the characteristics of the target audience (Hurtado, 2001: 395 - 397; PACTE, 2005: 611).

It intervenes by planning the process in relation to the translation project, evaluating the process and partial results obtained, activating the different sub-competencies and compensating for deficiencies, identifying translation problems and applying procedures to solve them.

The psycho-physiological components are cognitive and behavioral (memory, attention span, perseverance, critical mind, etc.) and psychomotor mechanisms.

There are other opinions about what translation competence comprises. Nord (1991) states:

... the essential competences required of a translator are: competence of text reception and analysis, research competence, transfer competence, competence of text production, competence of translation quality assessment, and, of course, linguistic and cultural competence both on the source and the target side.

Another description of the most important sub-competences is that proposed by Kelly (2005)

—Textual and communicative competence

—Cultural and intercultural competence

—Competence about the knowledge of the theme of the translation

—Professional and instrumental competence

—Interpersonal competence

—Competence related with the aptitudes necessary for a good composition and production of texts.

It is interesting that although the sub-competences mentioned by Kelly and PACTE differ in some ways, one is common: Instrumental competence.

In this investigation, we would like to deepen in the instrumental sub-competence.

As it has already been defined, the instrumental sub-competence is the knowledge required to work as a professional translator, such as the use of sources of documentation and information technologies applied to translation.

There is a wide range of information and communications technologies (ICT) available to translators today, including both general tools and specific tools. For the effects of this investigation ICT is defined as a group of information and communication technological applications, both general and specific, traditional or advanced that are especially useful for the professional translator. Among the general applications or tools, we have the Internet, the use of corpus linguistics and concordance generator programs as the most important ones. Among the specific ICT for the translator we have automatic translation (AT), and computer assisted translation (CAT) including translation memories.

1　General ICTs for Translators

1.1　The Internet

The services offered by the Internet provide the professional translator with considerable advantages in the documentation task as it allows him/her to access to a huge quantity of data and publications, as well as to communicate with experts and translators in other parts of the world with the purpose of exchanging ideas and experiences. In our opinion one of the most important tools offered by the Internet are the search and location information engines. At the current time, the three leading search engines are Google; Yahoo!, operated by Yahoo! Inc. of Sunnyvale, Calif.; and Microsoft's Bing (formerly Live Search), operated by Microsoft Corporation of Redmond, Wash. They allow to access in a few seconds to an enormous quantity of interrelated information. Further, the usefulness of these tools in our work as medical translator will be explained.

1.2　The Use of Corpus Linguistics

This is another tool that can be of great help for the professional translator. Corpora are classified in two types. On the one hand, the monolingual corpora, for example CREA (Corpus de Referencia del Espanol Actual) of the Royal Spanish Academy. On the other hand, we have the bilingual corpora that can, in turn, be divided in parallel corpus and comparable corpus. The former is made up of a group of source texts and their respective translations. The best example of this is the Canadian Hansards. The latter are texts originally written in two or more languages.

1.3　Concordance generator programs

A third example of general ICT is the concordance generator programs, which can find all the times that a certain term appears in a text or in several texts written in electronic format. It can also show a list of the context in which the term appears.

Regarding specific ICT tools for the work of the professional translator, we have: machine translation and computer assisted translation.

2 Specific ICTs for Translators

2.1 Machine Translation (MT)

Machine Translation is a procedure whereby a computer program analyzes a source text and produces a target text without further human intervention. In reality, however, machine translation typically does involve human intervention, in the form of pre-editing and post-editing.

2.2 Computer-assisted Translation (CAT)

Computer-assisted translation (CAT), also called "computer-aided translation," "machine-aided human translation (MAHT)" and "interactive translation," is a form of translation wherein a human translator creates a target text with the assistance of a computer program. The machine supports a human translator.

Computer-assisted translation can include standard dictionary and grammar software. The term, however, normally refers to a range of specialized programs available to the translator, including translation-memory, terminology-management, concordance, and alignment programs.

Effective use of translation technology starts from the translator's point of view. The translator has to determine what types of translation technology are needed at what stages of the translation process in order to optimize his or her professional performance.

Within each of the three main phases of the translation process—reception, transfer, and formulation—different sub-competencies are demanded by translators, and the tools used to support them have to offer specific features and contents.

During the reception phase, a translator can use electronic encyclopedias, digital knowledge databases or information retrieval systems or can contact domain experts through online newsgroups or mailing lists in order to retrieve missing background knowledge, allowing him or her to combine text, domain, and world knowledge to fully understand the content of the source text.

The transfer phase, i.e. the adaptation of the source text information to the context of the target text culture is uniquely translational. Neither readers nor writers share this phase with the translator. It requires deep cross-cultural understanding and strong intercultural communication skills. The tools needed during this stage of the translation process need to offer a high degree of intercultural knowledge, while at the same time providing the translator with a comparative analysis of the cultures affected by the translation project. Resources in this field are still rare, and special kinds of translator dictionaries or culturally-sensitive terminology databases providing a thorough combination and networking of linguistic, encyclopedic and intercultural knowledge have to be designed to assist translators during the transfer phase.

Finally, the formulation phase confronts the translator with challenges regarding the production of the target language text. Here again, the use of dictionaries and terminology databases can assist the translator quite efficiently. The information contained in those resources needs to offer support especially with regard to the syntagmatic relations of terms, as can be found in many style guides or in collocation dictionaries. Dictionaries providing such information become valuable production dictionaries (see Kornelius, 1995). In addition, the translator can turn to text archives available on CD-ROM or over the Internet for the verification of tentative translation solutions in the target language.

Now, we will provide some examples on how the use of ICTs has been of great importance for our translation work. Corsalud is the name of the journal of Ernesto Che Guevara Cardiology hospital, located inSanta Clara, Villa Clara. We work in the translation of summaries of articles from Spanish into English.

In this kind of translation, the formulation phase poses a greater challenge than the other two phases do. As the translator is translating into a foreign language, he/she should devote more time to the verification of terms and the sintagmatic relations of those terms. In our experience, we have found that the search engine Goggle offers a great help in this sense.

Bellow two examples will be given. In one of the summaries to be translated into English, we find the following fragments:

(a) La coartacion de la aorta abdominal es una afeccion vascular no hereditaria poco frecuente, que afecta a hombres y mujeres por igual. Recientemente ha sido nombradacomo "Sindrome aortico medio," y los hallazgos clinicos son similares a los de la CoAo tipica.

Tentative translation: Coarctation of the abdominal aorta is an uncommon, non-inherited vascular condition that affects men and women alike. It has been recently called "middle aortic syndrome," and the clinical findings are similar to those of typical Aortic Coarctation.

In this first example, we find a neologism "sindrome aortico medio." After some attempts based on medical dictionaries and other translation techniques and procedures, we have come to the tentative translation "middle aortic syndrome." Now it is time to prove if it is correct and if it is used in the specialized medical literature. A medical translator should know which the leading journals of each medical specialty are. In our case, we have a list of some of the leading cardiology journals in the world that are written in English. Then by using Google advanced search we type the tentative translation in quotation marks in the "with all the words" blank, followed by the name of the journal. Then in the results, we find many articles in which this term has been used in the specified cardiology journal. So, the tentative translation has been verified.

The second example is the following:

(b) El estudio gammagrafico con 99Tc-MIBI fue util para demostrar la recanalizacion de la arteria relacionada con el infarto, tras la utilizacion de tratamiento trombolitico con Estreptoquinasa Recombinante Cubana.

Tentative translation: The 99Tc-MIBI gamma scan study was useful to demonstrate the recanalization of the infarct-related artery, after the administration of Cuban Recombinant Streptokinase therapy.

In this case, "recanalizacion de la arteria relacionada con el infarto" has been translated as "recanalization of the infarct-related artery." Now after following the same procedures as explained above, the results showed that the sintagmatic relation of terms is correct because in the specialized medical literature in English it is used just like this.

3 Conclusions

With the arrival of the information era, the translation profession has changed. The new Information and Communication Technologies are very useful for the professional translator. There are general and specific ICTs for the translator. In our specific case, it has been found that the use of the search engine Google offers a great advantage in the verification of terms in their context and in the syntagmatic relation of terms. To sum up, in order to be a competent translator in our days it is necessary to make use of the new ICTs, mainly the general ICT tools.

选文三 Translation Technology Skills Acquisition

Amparo Alcina   Victoria Soler   Joaquin Granell

导 言

三位作者来自于西班牙海梅一世大学翻译与传播系。在 21 世纪,译者有望使用更高效的翻译技术,因此施教者应教会学习翻译的学员如何利用现存的翻译技术,而这造成在认知和程序性方面的许多困难。在本文中,这些问题被放置在一个创新教育项目的背景中加以研究,以提供给学习者正确的学习之路,提高他们所需的技能水平,培养他们如何使用翻译技术,使他们为专业的翻译环境做准备。

These subjects consist of theoretical and practical sessions to understand the foundations and methods to use the translation technology available to translators and to get acquainted with the usage of computer-based tools and resources for translation and terminology management purposes.

In the practical sessions students are taught how to use and practise using the software applications that help a translator work more efficiently. The training provides student translators with the abilities, knowledge and know-how to become professional translators, including the acquisition of general computing skills and specialized computer software for translators, such as computer-aided translation tools, terminology management tools or localization tools. This type of knowledge demands regular and repetitive practice to be assimilated and develops the skills to automatically use the technology. Thus, even if a large part of the lecture time is devoted to demonstrating how to use these computer-based tools and undertaking practical assignments, the level of practice required cannot only be achieved through the real-time instruction sessions. However, on many occasions students find no reason to practise further with these tools outside teaching hours.

Another problem arises from the diverse level of general computing skills that the students may have acquired previously. Some students might need closer interaction with their instructor, further repetitive practice or simply more time to experiment with the software to gain confidence in their usage of new pieces of software and develop the skills to use translation technology confidently. In addition, student attitudes towards new technologies vary considerably. Some students may develop a negative attitude towards the use of computers if the training is concentrated in a limited number of hours taught intensively or if they do not have an in-depth knowledge of the subject which allows them to follow the lectures. In such cases, it is important to help students to overcome the psychological barrier towards technology that might hinder their progress in learning to use new translation technology. In addition to these problems, and due to the practical nature of these sessions, most of the problems that the students experience when using translation technology happen during these taught sessions. In addition, the large number of students in each group (occasionally, this number varies from 20 to 40 students) and the shortage of time (usually two hours per session) make the lecturer's job more difficult, as the lecturer cannot give personal attention to every student in the classroom.

3　Encouraging Student Translators to Develop Their Technology Skills

Once these difficulties were observed, we realized that it was necessary to try: (a) to motivate the autonomous acquisition of knowledge and skills; (b) to encourage these translator trainees to further practice with the translation technology they will need as professional translators; (c) to acquaint students with the needs of the real professional environment; and (d) to encourage students and familiarize them with creating and working with resources useful for purposes beyond class assignments. A number of initiatives were taken to foster the practice with available technologies among student translators and encourage them to work autonomously. More specifically, the creation and use of the mailing list INFOTRAD and of the virtual environment for collaborative work Basic Support for Cooperative Work (BSCW), and the CREC project. Here these initiatives are explained more in detail: The INFOTRAD mailing list was created with the aim of encouraging the use of e-mail applications and mailing lists among students of translation and to interpreting to help them to become familiar with the translation market they will face. The subject matter of the list had to respond to the interests of these particular students so that they would feel motivated to use e-mail on a regular basis. Since one of the main concerns students have when they finish their degree is finding a job, it seemed that the idea of creating a mailing list where they could find work would be of interest to them. The technical aspects of its creation, how it was started up and how it works are described in detail in Alcina (2003a). The virtual environment for collaborative work BSCW is a web-based shared workspace system which allows authenticated access upon invitation, and that holds folders and documents uploaded by its users, thereby facilitating access to shared resources and management of group tasks. Furthermore, details on the technical features of this virtual environment, the resources available within it, and how it was structured are described in detail in Alcina (2002b). This environment has also been used in other universities with similar purposes (Aula. Int, 2005).

In line with these initiatives, the CREC project was designed as a complementary pedagogical methodology to further motivate students to use translation technology by involving them in the process of creating electronic language resources to be used in the future as real teaching materials and as resources for research activities. As a further incentive for the students to participate, apart from gaining confidence with and a deeper knowledge of the software tools used, an extra score for their final grade of the related subjects was granted for each piece of work undertaken. The main aim of CREC project is therefore threefold: (a) to increase the time that student translators are exposed to translation technology; (b) to simulate the conditions of real work environments; and (c) to generate language resources in electronic format. These aims are explained more in detail.

3.1 Increasing Students' Exposition Time

Undertaking additional intensive practice with translation technology is a very important issue for the students, as it helps to develop their skills at the procedural level of learning and develop automatisms to use this technology. Undertaking assignments is a rewarding task for students as it helps them to acquire new knowledge, do research, think, and share their views with their fellows. To encourage students to further access and manipulate the computer tools outside the classroom, the CREC project offers an opportunity to work with real materials and create useful resources which do not just go into a file, but which are

4.2 Stages of a CREC Project

The assignments undertaken so far include tasks such as the digitalization of documents, search and evaluation of specialized documents, the alignment of source and translated texts, the creation of lemmatization files, the creation of "stop-lists" for automatic term extraction, and the validation of domain-specific terminology. The lifecycle of each assignment goes through three stages: (a) preliminary planning work; (b) students' autonomous work; and (c) evaluation and quality control.

4.2.1 Preliminary planning work

In this first stage, a step by step protocol including the guidelines to be followed by the students is designed and written. Then the lecturers coordinate meetings with the mentoring team members to organize the materials to be used for each task and establish the guidelines to be followed throughout the process. The individual assignment kits prepared for each student include the source materials for the autonomous piece of work that each student is required to undertake. For instance, photocopies of articles to be scanned are provided for digitalization assignments, lists of verbs are given for lemmatization tasks, and files containing texts in English and Spanish are made available for alignment purposes. Finally, the lecturer informs the students during the taught sessions of the subjects "Computing for Translation" and "terminology Management" about the opportunity of undertaking the practical assignments outside the classroom. In addition, the lecturer tells the students about the benefits that they can reap from participating in the project, such as gaining confidence with the computer tools they have to use or gaining an extra score for their final grade in the related subjects.

In order to support students' participation a number of instruments have been prepared, namely, detailed protocols for each type of assignment, computer labs with all the technological facilities to accomplish the assignments, a shared-workspace online tool for collaborative work, a dedicated network drive, and a shared e-mail address. These instruments are explained more in detail: A detailed protocol with step-by-step guidelines has been developed for each type of assignment. This document includes an introduction explaining the work to be done and the objective of each task, an explanation of the materials in the assignment kit, and detailed instructions to undertake the assignment and to submit the output obtained from it. Explanatory notes and screenshots are used where necessary to explain how to configure each piece of software, how it works, and how to save the results obtained so that the document presents clear guide-lines and facilitates the autonomous work of the student in each type of assignment. For instance, how to use OCR software to digitalize documents, alignment tools to create bilingual documents, or terminology management tools to store terminology databases.

The translation laboratory consists of two computer labs that are used for teaching purposes and are also available for general access when not booked for teaching purposes.

These computer labs are used to teach subjects of the degree which require translation technology support. Facilities available include 60 networked PCs in two different rooms, installed with Windows XP and general-purpose and translation specialised software. These labs also provide scanning and printing facilities, and reference works for translators. Some of these facilities and resources were acquired through part of the funding available for the research projects TXTCeram and ONTODIC. A more detailed description of how this translation laboratory has previously been used for educational purposes can be found in Borja et al. (1998).

BSCW is a shared-workspace tool for collaborative work which can be accessed online. This virtual collaborative workspace is made available to the students upon invitation from the lecturer, and consists of a set of folders where output files are stored along with the names of the students who provide them, and where corrected files can be placed if necessary. It is used for hosting the electronic format materials for the assignments and exchanging the output files for revision for each piece of work between students and mentors. In addition, BSCW is used to host the folder, only available to the mentoring team, where management files supporting the project are stored. More information about how this tool is used as a collaborative work virtual environment to mentor students' work can be found in Alcina (2002b). A dedicated network drive is made available to the students to save the temporary versions of their work, as well as to make backup copies of it. This drive is in the departmental intranet and can be accessed from any of the computers in the translation laboratory. A specific folder is also created for each of the assignments of the CREC project.

A shared e-mail address (crec@uji. es) is given to the students as a permanent support channel and to inform about completed assignments. This address is an inbox shared by all the mentoring team members, who regularly check for new messages and reply to them.

4.2.2 Students' autonomous work

Once the preliminary work stage is over, those students willing to participate attend informative sessions held in the translation laboratory in small groups of up to six people to learn what needs to be done in the assignment. In these sessions, an overall explanation of the whole process and the purpose of the assignment is given, followed by a demonstration of how to do it using the appropriate software. For instance, showing how to configure and use OCR software for digitalization or how to use aligning tools for bilingual documents alignment.

At the end of these sessions, those students who decide to participate are allocated an assignment kit, including a protocol and the materials that enable them to start working by themselves. From that moment on, students are expected to employ 10 hours of work to accomplish the assignment, and a period of around two weeks is given to them to deliver the resulting resources from their work. This output varies for each type of assignment, but as a rule of thumb they have to electronically deliver the resulting files and inform the mentoring team by e-mail about the completion of their work. All this time, a mentor of the CREC project is also available in the translation lab at set hours to provide face-to-face guidance and support.

4.2.3 Evaluation and quality control

When the students complete their assignment, they are expected to submit the results to the mentoring team through the channels indicated in the protocol (i. e. uploading the resource files generated to the right shared folder in the BSCW virtual environment, and sending a message to the shared e-mail address of the mentoring team). At this point, the resources generated by each student are examined by a mentor to make sure they have followed the instructions of the protocol and that the resulting files meet the requisite quality. In case of mistakes, or if the student has not followed the right steps of the protocol, the mentor informs the student about the issues that need to be addressed. In this communication, the mentor tries to make the students aware of the relevance of the revision process, to motivate them to deliver a correct piece of work, and to stress the importance of following the work guidelines accurately for their future working environment. Finally, once the participating students have submitted the correct resource files, another quality check is performed before the files are stored in a server for their future use in lectures or research.

4.3 Example of a CREC Project: Digitalization of Documents

In order to provide an example of how this methodology was implemented within CREC, a brief explanation of what was done for an assignment to digitalize documents is provided here for the three stages of the project.

4.3.1 Preliminary planning work of a digitalization project

The first step included the design of a protocol which included the guidelines to be followed by the students for digitalizing documents. In order to help students throughout their autonomous work, screenshots and step by step instructions were also given about how to configure the optical character recognition software Omnipage, how to use it to transfer the information from hardcopy articles to the computer, and how to perform a revision of the digitalized documents before saving them in different formats (such as RTF and TXT). In the initial coordination meeting, the documents to be digitalized were selected from a variety of scientific and technical reference works, preferably those which had a bilingual version available. As our research group is working on the creation of a domain-specific dictionary of industrial ceramics, this was the subject area from which works were used. In particular, papers belonging to multilingual proceedings of an international conference available in hardcopy only were selected. The volumes containing the papers were divided into sets of around 80 pages (which were called "digitalization kits"), and each set of papers was allocated a record sheet with the bibliographic reference of the source document and a unique code to identify it throughout the process. This code included a number for each group of pages, an identifier of the subject area and of the language of the contents. For instance, the code "CEp01-1e" would stand for the document labelled "01 -1," which belongs to the industrial ceramics subject field ("CE"), is written in Spanish (ending "e") and has a parallel kit in another language ("p").

4.3.2 Students' autonomous work in a digitalization project

After the respective informative session and a practical demonstration of the process to be followed with a computer, a scanner, and a sample digitalization kit, students who were interested in participating were registered, allocated a digitalization kit and a protocol. This registration process involved adding the student's details to a table (name, e-mail address and telephone), along with the information of the digitalization kit (a unique code for identifying each kit, its bibliographic reference and the pickup date), and granting access to the shared folder of the digitalization assignment in the BSCW environment.

From this moment, the students started to work on their assignments. The specific tasks to be accomplished by the students for the digitalization assignment involved: (a) scanning the source document using OCR software Omnipage in the translation lab; (b) selecting the suitable language and settings for processing the digitalized image of the document; (c) performing the optical recognition of the characters in this image; (d) editing types of area (text, table or graphic) in the scanned document to include all relevant information; (e) exporting the resulting document to RTF format; (f) revising the results of the OCR and cleaning the format of the output document in Word; and (g) saving a TXT copy of the revised document to feed the linguistic corpus. More details of this process can be found in Soler et al. (2006).

4.3.3 Evaluation and quality control in a digitalization project

Once the students completed their digitalization assignment, they had to follow these steps: (a) creating a subfolder under the digitalization folder in the BSCW environment with the code of the digitalization kit and the student's name; (b) uploading the resulting TXT and RTF files to this folder; (c) communicating the assignment delivery to the mentoring team's shared e-mail address; and (d) when necessary, performing any corrections on the assignment to obtain output files of the TXT and RTF files. This final step involved exchanges of e-mail messages with project mentors to clarify corrections and uploading the final (amended) files to the BSCW. The digitalized sets of documents were then revised and fed into an industrial ceramics corpus. During this final stage the delivery dates of the assignments, the dates in which they were uploaded to the BSCW, the dates when the revised files were returned to the students, and the delivery dates of the final files, were also added to the registration table mentioned before, so that the information of the whole process was logged into a document. In this document, the additional points achieved by the students to be added to their grade were also logged.

5　Results

This project has been running for three academic years to date. From the results of the project it can be seen that this initiative has contributed positively to the didactic objectives presented and the creation of authentic language resources. With regard to the student participation in the project, it has turned to be higher than initially expected, as a total of 92 students have participated, undertaking one or more assignments over the first two years of the project. This figure represents around 40% of the students enrolled in these subjects each year. In addition, a larger proportion of students have sat exams in comparison with the year before the start of the project: there were increases in the number of students who took exams for "Computing for Translation" (19% for the year 2005, and 14% for the year 2006) and "terminology Management" (5% for the year 2005 and 10% for the year 2006). In the current year, the third year of implementation of the project, 27 students have already participated during the first academic semester.

Table 1   Results for computing in translation (first semester)

	2004	%	2005	%	2006	%
Number of registered students	112	100	115	100	118	100
Number of exams taken	37	33.04	16	13.91	23	19.49
Failed	11	9.82	11	9.57	13	11.02
Passed	64	57.14	88	76.52	82	69.49

Another sign of the success of the project can be observed in the increase of the number of students passing the exams of both subjects. More specifically, there were increases of 19% and 12% in the number of students successfully passing their exams of the subject "Computing for Translation," for the years 2005 and 2006, respectively. As for the case of the subject "terminology Management," there were increases of 5% (for 2005) and 25% (for 2006) in the number of students successfully passing their exams. Data from the year 2004, in which the project had not been implemented yet, is used as a benchmark for all the data provided. Tables 1 and 2 summarize these results. With regard to the resources generated as a result of the project, a number of language resources have been obtained. For instance, a corpus of the ceramics subject field was compiled in Spanish, consisting of almost 2.5 million words (2,340,161 words), stored in 114 files (in both, plain text and MS Word formats); a corpus of the ceramics subject field was also compiled in English, including 263,195 words stored in 14 files, and Catalan, including 12,426 words stored in one file (also in plain text and MS Word formats); a "stoplist" file including 488 words in Spanish; a "stoplist" file including 683 words in Catalan; a file with around 5,500 lemmatized verbs in Spanish; and a file with around 9,700 lemmatized verbs in Catalan. In addition, a bilingual corpus of Spanish and English texts is still being compiled by aligning the files which are present in both the Spanish and the English corpus. Thus, students have been involved, in collaboration with the members of the mentoring team, in the generation of electronic resources which have followed a quality control process to be ready for teaching and research purposes. This process of development imitated part of the tasks that are found in the professional environment of translators. Another important outcome has been that the teamwork of most of (if not all) the students in the classroom helped to greatly improve the communication and interaction between them, the lecturers and mentors involved in the project. This synergy resulted in a very favorable learning environment and provided final-year and postgraduate students with training and experience of mentoring which will enable them to use their experiences gained at university for the benefit of others and to enhance their CV. These were only the impressions of lecturers and mentors. Strangely enough, these results did not have any effect (positive or negative) on the teachers' annual assessment conducted by the university, which consists of a brief survey undertaken by students about each subject and its teacher. Finally, it is worth mentioning that the experience with the eight students who have acted as mentors during the project has been very satisfactory. This experience has helped them to develop their teamwork, managerial and training skills. Apart from sound and up-to-date computer skills, companies in the translation and localization industry demand professionals who are able to join a team and work collaboratively, manage projects, specify problems and do queries when it makes sense, make decisions, etc. From the perspective of the students participating in the project, the mentoring scheme has proved to be a means of gaining study assistance and vital one-to-one help from a more experienced student, a way of increasing academic confidence, an introduction to professional expectations, a way to extend access to translation technology resources available, and overall, a learning opportunity for both students and mentors. In fact, it has been observed that the face-to-face support from the mentors frequently asked for by the students at the beginning of their individual tasks, gradually decreased as students gained more independence. In addition, some students also reported that they had successfully applied the (transferable) skills acquired during this project to other subjects.

Table 2 Results for terminology management (yearly)

	2004	%	2005	%	2006	%
Number of registered students	128	100	126	100	147	100
Number of exams taken	52	40.63	45	35.71	45	30.61
Passed	50	39.06	56	44.44	94	63.95

6 Conclusions

Given the results presented, it could be concluded that the overall objectives of the CREC project have been accomplished, thus showing that the proposed methodology has managed to increase the exposition time of student translators to translation technology, improving students' grade prospects, increasing student's self-confidence when using translation technology, and involving students into the process of creating authentic language resources that are subject to quality control and that can be useful for the teaching and research community. All these achievements have contributed to developing students' competences as future professional translators and helped them to be able to use a variety of computer applications and face problems, in order to make decisions to find solutions. Moreover, the work undertaken by participating students has been personally supervised by more experienced mentors (as in a real working environment), resulting in a positive interaction between them and the students and helping some students to overcome the technology barrier they may face when learning to use translation technology as part of a large group of students. Another positive conclusion can be drawn from the improvement observed in the students' teamwork capability (e. g. collaborating with/ helping fellow students, or interacting with the mentors), as well as in the mentoring team, where advanced students had the opportunity of teaching and supervising the work undertaken by the students in the role of a project manager.

All in all, the benefits obtained from the project helped to increase the relevance of translation technology, not only within the classroom, but also outside it and towards the future of the students as professional translators. This educational experience has proved to support the pedagogical process of translation technology programmes at three levels: delivering and assimilating theoretical contents at the cognitive level, developing and improving practical skills and abilities at the procedural level, and helping to overcome the psychological barrier towards the use of technology at the attitudinal level.

【延伸阅读】

[1] AMTA. Expanding MT Horizons: Proceedings of the Second Conference of the Association for Machine Translation in the Americas, 2 - 5 October 1996, Montreal, Canada.

[2] Arnola, H. Kielikone Machine Translation Technology and Its Perspective on the Economics of Machine Translation. *EAMT Workshop*, 1996: 73 - 88.

[3] Bian, G. W., & Chen, H. H. Integrating Query Translation and Document Translation in a Cross-language Information Retrieval System. *AMTA*, 1998: 250 - 265.

[4] Boitet, C., & Blanchon, H. Multilingual Dialogue-based MT for Monolingual Authors: the LIDIA Project and a First Mockup. *Machine Translation*, 1994, 9 (2): 99 - 132.

[5] Brace, C., Vasconcellos, M., & Miller, L. C. MT Users and Usage: Europe and the Americas. *MT News International 12*, October 1995: 14 - 19.

[6] EAMT Workshop. EAMT Machine Translation Workshop. Vienna, Austria, 29 - 30 August 1996. Proceedings. [Geneva: EAMT].

[7] EAMT Workshop. Language Technology in Your Organization ? 1997 EAMT Workshop, Copenhagen, 21 - 22 May 1997. Proceedings. [Geneva: EAMT].

[8] Heyn, M. Integrating Machine Translation into Translation Memory Systems. *EAMT Workshop*, 1996: 111 - 124.

[9] Humphreys, L. Use of Linguistic Resources Like Translation Memories in Machine Translation Systems. *EAMT Workshop*, 1996: 101-110.

[10] Hutchins, W. J. *Machine Translation: Past, Present, Future*. Chichester: Ellis Horwood, 1986.

[11] Alcina, A. Translation Technologies Scope, Tools and Resources. *Target*, 2008, 20 (1): 80-103.

[12] Aula, Int. Translator Training and Modern Market Demands. *Perspectives: Studies in Translatology*, 2005, 13 (2): 132-142.

[13] Austermuhl, F. *Electronic Tools for Translators*. Manchester: St. Jerome, 2001.

[14] Kelly, D. *A Handbook for Translator Trainers*. Manchester: St. Jerome, 2005.

[15] Nord, C. *Text Analysis in Translation. Theory, Methodology, and Didactic Application of a Model for Translation-Oriented Text Analysis*. Amsterdam/New York: Rodopi, 1991.

[16] O'Hagan, M. & Ashworth, D. *Translation-Mediated Communication in a Digital World Facing the Challenges of Globalization and Localization*. Clevedon: Multilingual Matters, 2002.

【问题与思考】

1. 对机器翻译的几种需求之间有何联系与区别？
2. 人工翻译与机器翻译相比较而言有何特点？
3. 举例说明机器翻译的未来需求和发展趋势是什么？
4. 根据选文二，译员可采用哪些一般性的信息与通信技术？
5. 计算机辅助翻译的双语转换过程有何特点？
6. 翻译能力模式具有哪些特点？它们在实践中是如何体现的？
7. 译者在学习翻译技术的过程中会面临哪些困难？该如何解决？
8. 选文三中提到的数字化项目中，针对学员的翻译技术培训重点采用哪种方法？它是如何被实施的？
9. 该数字化项目如何对学员的任务完成情况进行质量监控和结果评价？